W9-BNE-870

data about adult learners and potential learners from some thirty state and national surveys; examine the needs, developments, problems, and crucial role of programs and services at the local level; report what administrators and program directors can expect from state and national governments in terms of financial support, development and continuation of programs, coordination of activities, and leadership; identify over 300 sources of information and expertise on lifelong learning, ranging from organizations to ongoing research projects; and offer, on the basis of this factual analysis, important recommendations for program directors and educational leaders.

THE AUTHOR

RICHARD E. PETERSON is Senior Research Scientist at the Educational Testing Service, Berkeley, California.

The other authors are identified in the front of the book.

Richard E. Peterson

and Associates

Lifelong Learning in America

BRIAR CLIFF COLLEGE
LIBRARY
SIOUX CITY, IOWA

Jossey-Bass Publishers

San Francisco • Washington • London • 1980

LIFELONG LEARNING IN AMERICA
An Overview of Current Practices, Available Resources, and Future Prospects
        by Richard E. Peterson and Associates

Copyright © 1979 by: Jossey-Bass Inc., Publishers
                    433 California Street
                    San Francisco, California 94104
                            &
                    Jossey-Bass Limited
                    28 Banner Street
                    London EC1Y 8QE

Copyright under International, Pan American, and
Universal Copyright Conventions. All rights
reserved. No part of this book may be reproduced
in any form—except for brief quotation (not to
exceed 1,000 words) in a review or professional
work—without permission in writing from the publishers.

Library of Congress Catalogue Card Number LC 79-83576

International Standard Book Number ISBN 0-87589-414-3

Manufactured in the United States of America

LC
5251
.P44

JACKET DESIGN BY WILLI BAUM
FIRST EDITION
        First printing: May 1979
        Second printing: February 1980

Code 7913

7196679

*The Jossey-Bass
Series in Higher Education*

Preface

The concept of lifelong learning and strategies for its implementation are topics of widespread and lively discussion among educators both in this country and abroad. This active interest reflects a seemingly new understanding that participation in education and learning throughout life can benefit both the individual and the society. Generally speaking, European countries are ahead of the United States in providing, via government policy, major avenues for continued learning by adults. In America, the pattern has been more one of local, institutional initiatives. There are, as a consequence, many gaps in available services, and also some unnecessary duplication. Low-income and poorly educated people are severely underrepresented in the "learning force," and there are still numerous pockets of illiteracy in American society. Much is underway to facilitate lifelong learning, to be sure, but there is also much that still needs to be done.

The purpose of *Lifelong Learning in America* is to provide in one document substantial information about the wide range of policies and practices in America for enabling lifelong learning. The book offers: (1) a policy-oriented conception of lifelong learning—as an integrating, "master" concept for a host of diverse programs; (2) a description of the many existing sources of education and learning in the United States; (3) an array of facts about the learning interests of adult learners, as well as perceived barriers to further learning; (4) an overview of policies and programs, implemented and under consideration, at the local, state, and federal levels; (5) a comprehensive guide to sources of further information; and (6) suggestions about what the myriad organizations—both school and nonschool—that are interested in human growth can do to further lifelong learning.

My coauthors and I take the position that lifelong learning policy should facilitate learning for people of all ages; involve all manner of organizations—libraries, museums, churches, corporations, and so on—as well as schools and colleges; and seek to reduce the fragmentation now characterizing American education in order that lifelong learners can be better served. Although this concept of lifelong learning holds promise for reforms at all levels of education, readers should understand that the contents of the book—its scores of illustrative policies, practices, and implications for changes—deal in the main with education and learning at the postcompulsory or postsecondary level, that is, with learning opportunities during adulthood.

During 1976, Frederick deW. Bolman, then the executive director of the Exxon Education Foundation, foresaw the need for a project that would assist concerned individuals and agencies to better understand the broad and expanding domain of adult and continuing education—to, in a sense, "map" the field through a review of the key programs and organizations. As the project took shape, it was agreed that its guiding concept, nebulous as it was at the outset, should be *lifelong learning,* rather than some narrower term, and that all the information gathered during the project should be assembled into this single, convenient document chiefly for use by planners and directors of lifelong learning programs.

Our intended audiences for the book are not only program planners and directors but also educational policy makers and analysts working in a variety of settings, including schools and colleges, community organizations (such as libraries, museums, Y's, churches, and senior centers), businesses and industries, labor unions, professional associations, the military, state-level bodies concerned with adult education and postsecondary coordination, and federal agencies and congressional staffs. For these readers, we have sought to furnish a comprehensive and up-to-date account of activities germane to planning improved services for lifelong learners. Rather than tracing the long and significant history of adult and continuing education, we emphasize recent and current programs, projects, and proposals. And rather than describing a few activities in detail, we have tried to alert readers to as many as possible—citing numerous documents. The volume may be regarded as a guide to materials for further study, a stimulus for more intensive analysis of questions of special interest. While some of the facts it reports—enrollment figures and names of agencies, for example—will have changed by the time the book is published, its basic conclusions about innovations and trends should remain valid into the 1980s.

Many people have contributed either to the content of the volume or to its production, and we wish to acknowledge their aid. First are the members of the project's advisory group. They met with the staff in March 1977 to help determine the general outlines of the study as well as procedures to be followed, and then, later in the year, provided reactions to sections of the volume in draft form. The group included:

Solomon Arbeiter, program planning officer, The College Board, New York

Robert Calvert, chief, Adult and Vocational Surveys Branch, National Center for Education Statistics, Washington, D.C.

James M. Furman, executive director, Illinois Board of Higher Education

Richard W. Jonsen, project director, Western Interstate Commission on Higher Education, Boulder, Colorado

Norman Kurland, chairman, Committee on Adult Learning
  Services, University of the State of New York
Francis U. Macy, director, National Center for Educational
  Brokering, Washington, D.C.
Constance McQueen, dean of students, Manhattan Com-
  munity College (past-president, Coalition of Adult Ed-
  ucation Organizations)
George Nolfi, president, University Consultants, Inc., Cam-
  bridge, Massachusetts
Milton Stern, dean, University Extension, University of Cal-
  ifornia, Berkeley

Special assistance in arranging interviews and for otherwise
gathering information in the four "case study" states discussed in
Chapter Four was provided by James M. Furman in Illinois,
Joseph Bard, director, and Elizabeth Garber, program associate,
of the Office of Special Programs, Department of Education in
Pennsylvania, George Nolfi in Massachusetts, and Paul C. Parker,
associate vice-chancellor and director of outreach and research services, State University System of Florida.

Several individuals in the Berkeley office of Educational
Testing Service provided indispensable assistance. Major editorial
work was performed by Alice Setteducati. Susan Eason drafted a
number of the abstracts of projects in Chapter Six. Adrienne
Ryken and JoAnn Wright did the typing. Proofreading and minor
editing was done by Mary Corder, Arthur Neumann, and Carolyn
Lieber. Margaret Williams did most of the library reference work.
At the Educational Policy Research Institute, typing was done by
Gloria Graham and Joan Baquis. Joan Westcott edited the entire
manuscript with extraordinary skill. To all these good people, our
sincerest thanks.

We dedicate this book to the memory of I. Bruce Hamilton,
colleague and friend.

Berkeley, California   RICHARD E. PETERSON
March 1979

Contents

The Authors

RICHARD E. PETERSON is Senior Research Scientist at the Educational Testing Service (ETS), Berkeley, California. He was awarded B.A. degrees in political science (1953) and psychology (1957) and the M.A. and Ph.D. degrees in education (1959, 1962) from the University of California, Berkeley. For four years, while a graduate student, he was a psychology instructor and counselor at Contra Costa (community) College, north of Berkeley.

Between 1962 and 1969, when he worked at the main office of ETS in Princeton, New Jersey, Peterson directed development of several instruments used for college self-study. In the late 1960s he became interested in, and conducted several surveys of, the student protest movement nationally, and his book, *May 1970* (with J. Bilorusky, 1971) for the Carnegie Commission on Higher Education, dealt with campus reactions to the Kent State shooting and the Cambodia invasion.

Peterson's interest in lifelong learning as public policy began in 1972, when he worked on a national survey of adult learning for the Commission on Non-Traditional Study, funded by the Carnegie Foundation. This interest was furthered when he directed a feasibility study for the California legislature, the results of which were reported in *Postsecondary Alternatives to Meet the Needs of California's Adults* (with J. L. Hefferlin, 1975). Very recently, Peterson participated in a three-week study tour in the People's Republic of China, which afforded him the opportunity to learn something about the nature and scope of adult and "spare-time" education in that country. His professional concerns for the immediate future focus on policies for advancing lifelong learning at the federal, state, and—in particular—the local community level.

K. PATRICIA CROSS is Distinguished Research Scientist at the Educational Testing Service, Berkeley, California, and also teaches graduate courses in higher education at the University of California, Berkeley. She was awarded the B.S. degree in mathematics (1948) from Illinois State University and the A.M. degree in psychology (1951) and the Ph.D. degree in social psychology (1958) from the University of Illinois. She was assistant dean of women at the University of Illinois (1953–1959) and dean of women and then dean of students at Cornell University (1959–1963). She joined ETS in Princeton, New Jersey, in 1963 and moved to the Berkeley office in 1967, where she held a joint appointment with ETS and the Center for Research and Development of the University of California (1969–1977).

Cross was selected as a leader in American Higher Education in the *Change* magazine poll of 1974 and was elected a member of the National Academy of Education in 1975. She has long been active in professional organizations, serving as president of the American Association of Higher Education in 1974–1975, vice-chair of the American Council on Education's Commission on Women in Higher Education, and as a member of numerous national advisory boards.

Cross' publications include *Beyond the Open Door* (1971), *Accent on Learning* (1976), *Planning Non-Traditional Programs* (with John R. Valley and Associates, 1974), and *The Missing Link* (1978).

She is currently working on a book on the implications of research and theory for lifelong learning.

TERRY W. HARTLE is Associate Research Scientist with the Education Policy Research Institute (EPRI) of the Educational Testing Service, Washington, D.C., and a doctoral candidate in public administration at George Washington University. Hartle was awarded the B.A. degree in history *summa cum laude* (1973) from Hiram College and the M.P.A. (master's of public administration) degree (1974) from the Maxwell School of Citizenship and Public Affairs at Syracuse University, after which he joined the Policy Institute of the Syracuse University Research Corporation (SURC). In 1975, when the Washington office of the SURC Policy Institute merged with ETS, Hartle joined the newly established EPRI.

Hartle has served as consultant for a number of organizations, including the National Institute of Education, the American Council on Education, and the International Council for Educational Development. He has published articles on education policy in a variety of periodicals, including *Change, Public Administration Review, The New Republic,* and *The Progressive.* He is currently directing a study of the effects of imposing tuition at the City University of New York.

JUDITH BONNETT HIRABAYASHI is Senior Research Assistant at the Educational Testing Service, Berkeley, California. She was awarded the B.A. degree in history and sociology (1968) from the University of California, Berkeley.

At ETS she has been involved with a number of studies on higher education, ranging from a project developing measures of competence in general education, sponsored by the Fund for the Improvement of Postsecondary Education, to a study of attrition-retention patterns of SAT-takers, funded by The College Board. Hirabayashi is currently participating in a study of the Office of Education's accreditation procedures and working on the Carnegie Council's project on institutional change in the 1970s.

MARK A. KUTNER is Senior Research Assistant at the Education Policy Research Institute (EPRI) of the Educational Testing Ser-

vice, Washington, D.C., and a doctoral candidate in education policy at George Washington University. He previously was a research
analyst for the Japan Trade Center. Kutner was awarded the B.A.
degree in political science (1973) from Brooklyn College and the
M.P.A. degree (1974) from the Maxwell School of Citizenship and
Public Affairs at Syracuse University.

     Kutner has served as consultant to the Education Staff Sem-
inar of the Institute for Educational Leadership, worked on a number of EPRI projects, and coauthored a guide to Pennsylvania
school finance. He is currently studying state minimal competency
standards in postsecondary education and examining the issues
surrounding tuition tax credits.

SUSAN A. POWELL is Director of Program Planning and Coordination for the Minnesota Higher Education Coordinating Board.
She was awarded the B.A. degree in political science (1971) from
the University of California, Santa Barbara, and the Ph.D. degree
in higher education (1979) from the University of California,
Berkeley.

     Powell served as a full-time consultant to the California leg-
islature's Joint Committee on the Master Plan for Higher Education (1971–1973) and was a postgraduate researcher at the Carnegie Council on Policy Studies in Higher Education (1974–1975).
She has also had consulting assignments for the Department of
Health, Education, and Welfare (Office of the Assistant Secretary
of Education); California State Department of Education; Washington Council on Postsecondary Education; California Postsecondary Education Commission; and the Montana Commission on
Postsecondary Education.

JOHN R. VALLEY is Director of Nontraditional Learner Support
Services, College Board Division, at the Educational Testing Service, Princeton, New Jersey. He was awarded the B.A. degree in
sociology (1941) and the M.A. degree in psychology (1947) from
Western Reserve University. Prior to joining ETS in 1954, he
taught psychology at the Case Institute of Technology (now Case
Western Reserve University) and was also assistant dean of students.

Valley directed the two major national programs of credit by examination that ETS administered in behalf of the College Board—the Advanced Placement Program and the College-Level Examination Program. In 1970, with Jack N. Arbolino, Valley worked on plans to expand external degree programs—plans instrumental in the creation of the ETS–College Board Commission on Non-Traditional Study and the Office of New Degree Programs, of which he was director. With K. Patricia Cross, he directed the research program undertaken by the commission, which was reported in *Planning Non-Traditional Programs* (1974). He was also associated with the Cooperative Assessment of Experimental Learning (CAEL) project, where he directed membership, forum, and information dissemination functions.

Valley is now serving as a consulting editor for the *Journal of Higher Education* and on the academic council of Thomas A. Edison College. Two areas of current interest are noncredit continuing education and the articulation of experiential education opportunities at the secondary and postsecondary levels.

Lifelong Learning in America

AN OVERVIEW
OF CURRENT PRACTICES,
AVAILABLE RESOURCES,
AND FUTURE PROSPECTS

Introduction:
On the Meaning
of Lifelong Learning

Richard E. Peterson

> During recent years we have been witnessing the develop-
> ment of an exciting new concept in education. We have seen its
> beginning in many educational institutions and organizations
> throughout the country, and we have heard it identified in a va-
> riety of different ways. . . . But whatever we call it, this is a move-
> ment based on the growing recognition of education as a means
> of meeting diverse and changing needs of Americans throughout
> all stages of their lives.—Walter F. Mondale, in hearings before the
> Subcommittee on Education of the Committee on Labor and Public
> Welfare, U.S. Senate, 94th Congress, First Session on S.2497 (the
> Lifetime Learning Act), December 18, 1975.

American society is indeed undergoing changes. The population is growing older, bringing an increase in the attendant

stresses of middle and older age. Traditional patterns of family life and work are changing. Women, notably mothers, many divorced, are joining the work force in unprecedented numbers. The notion of a single career line no longer holds: Job changing in mid career has reached an all-time high. The customary five-day, forty-hour workweek is beginning to give way to more flexible arrangements—with more time, possibly, for engaging in learning. Technology advances; specialized information expands; new products are urged on us; advice for living better abounds. Sensible day-to-day existence—making decisions in one's best interest—becomes increasingly difficult. That there is evidence of widespread bewilderment and dissatisfaction—with work lives, with personal lives, with political institutions, with so-called human services, with the schools and colleges—is hardly surprising. Nor is it surprising that people are looking for new sources of satisfaction and meaning in their lives, especially as they grow older.

Although it is probably fruitless to try to predict the shape of the future society, it does make some sense to recognize our own time as a time of transition and to undertake to cope with this reality. The fact of change itself, it has been argued, requires people capable of adapting to change. Such adaptation might involve learning *how* to learn early in life, and later in fact learning new things at various points in one's life.

In response to many of the societal changes just mentioned, a vast array of educational organizations and programs has been created at all governmental and institutional levels. Typically, there has been little connection among them. Ordinarily springing from special legislation and sets of regulations, they are likely to operate independently with separate funding sources. Not infrequently, the programs are in competition with each other. Thus, even though the nation's education complex has been comparatively successful at least by access standards, it has come to resemble a hundred-headed hydra.

As a result of these social and educational changes, our views of education—particularly, whether it should all be packed into the early years—are shifting. For example, while twelve or so years of schooling are still compulsory, there are clear trends toward options for early graduation from high school. College is now less often believed to be the automatic best next step. Once in college, students do not necessarily feel they must press through to a bachelor's degree in four years.

These new realities—the aging population, the changes individuals are experiencing in their lives, the disjointed educational system—have kindled a widespread feeling that some new concept, some new lens, is needed for viewing the totality of education and learning in the United States. The idea of *lifelong learning*, we observe, has emerged as that potentially integrating concept—the new lens.

Interestingly enough, a number of European countries and several African nations, with UNESCO in a supporting role, have led the way with concepts such as *universal adult education, education permanente, recurrent education,* and *lifelong education.* In this country, in addition to compulsory education up to about age sixteen and college for all who are willing and able, there have also long been programs for older adults—university evening and extension divisions, for example. Most of the types of programs described in Chapter One have existed for decades. However, an integrating idea has been lacking. The concept of lifelong learning opens the prospect for totally fresh thinking about new ways to better serve continuing learners of all ages.

The Mondale Act

In 1976, the Lifelong Learning Act, or Mondale Act—Part B of the amended Title I of the Higher Education Act of 1965—was passed into law (see Chapter Five). Its "Findings" constituted a kind of manifesto on the need for new lifelong learning services. The act's "scope of lifelong learning" includes some nineteen types of programs (from "adult basic education" to "activities designed to . . . serve family needs and personal development"). It calls for numerous initiatives, including the following: establishing an educational clearinghouse, studying methods for financing lifelong learning; reviewing nonschool learning opportunities; analyzing barriers to lifelong learning; analyzing appropriate federal, state, and local roles; assessing the educational needs of adults; and reviewing use of educational benefits by trade union members. And it called for the Assistant Secretary of the Department of Health, Education, and Welfare (HEW) to submit a report to the President and Congress in January 1978.

Preparation of the bill and its journey through Congress created a focus of concern and activity for a good many Washington-based organizations and programs, as Hartle and Kutner point out in Chapter Five. A precise meaning for the term *lifelong learning,* however, has not been forthcoming—which may be a reason why so many diverse organizations have appropriated it. At any rate, the past half decade has seen the rise of a sizable movement made up of a wide range of different, often competing, institutions and programs (mainly for older and other nontraditional populations) marching under the provocative, but as yet undefined, banner of "lifelong learning."

Defining Lifelong Learning

Many definitions or conceptions of lifelong learning have been put forth in this country and abroad in the past decade (see Merriam, 1977). They generally are focused on adults only. (Two important exceptions are Faure and others, 1972, and the Lifelong Learning Project, 1978, the latter defining *lifelong learning* [p. 1] as "the process by which individuals continue to develop their knowledge, skills, and attitudes over their lifetimes"—a psychologically oriented definition.) They agree generally that adults do or should continue learning throughout their lives and that there should be arrangements for them to do so (see Dave, 1976). But as to the arrangements—the types of programs or models—there is no consensus, at least not in this country. In short, there is substantial agreement among theorists concerning broad goals for lifelong learning but not about the means for achieving those goals. Our own policy-oriented definition of lifelong learning does not advocate a particular organizational model or operating strategy, such as alternated periods of full-time work and full-time education, proposed by the Organization for Economic Cooperation and Development (OECD) in its concept of "recurrent education." Instead, it takes the form of a brief general proposition followed by seven statements of goals for early action. (Of course, new goals should be established as substantial progress is made toward achieving the first priority goals.) *Lifelong learning is a conceptual framework for conceiving, planning, implementing, and coordinating activities designed to facilitate learning by all Americans throughout their lifetimes.* We believe this framework should consist for the present of the following seven priority goals:

1. To invent and test entirely new kinds of learning programs, involving new combinations of services and new organizational arrangements, in order to better meet identified needs of populations of learners.
2. To assist all adults—particularly those with young children—to become literate and otherwise competent to function in American society.
3. To assist all individuals—particularly school age children and youths—to become resourceful, autonomous, continuous learners in their various future roles.
4. To develop learning programs that will attract and serve people having poor educational backgrounds.
5. To involve nonschool organizations providing educational services—museums, for example—in planning learning programs.
6. To include other human services organizations—social welfare, housing, and transportation, for example—in planning and implementing learning programs.
7. To maintain high standards of educational practice in all programs; to guard against fraudulent practice.

Three key lifelong learning concepts are implicit in the above statements: (1) there should be coordinated learning opportunities for people of all ages; (2) all manner of organizations—school and nonschool—concerned with the well-being of people should take part in facilitating learning; and (3) the community (or city or metropolitan region) should be the locus for planning and conducting learning activities (this last strategy is not often emphasized in the foreign literature).

Several more things can be said about our definition. First, we take the word *lifelong* seriously, to mean education and learning literally from cradle to grave (though not compulsory education).

Second, the definition is meant to embrace all forms of learning, both in and outside of school; it sets no limits on what may be learned, by whom, and for what reasons. Third, it calls for new configurations of services, designed at the outset mainly for heretofore poorly served populations. And, last, it suggests using the concept of lifelong learning as a philosophical basis for bringing together into cooperative networks a broad range of educational and other organizations, governmental and private, that are concerned for the continuing development of individuals. No specific organizational models or instructional methods, however, are proposed.[1] Nor do we think they should be. Instead, programs should spring from and be shaped according to *local* learning needs and resources.

Lifelong Learning as a "Master Concept"

By now it should be clear that this conception of lifelong learning, embracing as it does learning by people of all ages through all manner of organizations in the community, may serve as a very basic integrating or organizing principle. Lifelong learning may be viewed as a *master concept*.

That lifelong learning should become the master concept for education was the conclusion reached by the UNESCO International Commission on the Development of Education in its widely esteemed book *Learning to Be* (Faure and others, 1972). In its language:

> Every person must be in a position to keep learning throughout his life. Education must be carried on at all ages . . . according to each individual's needs and convenience [p. 181].

> We propose lifelong learning as the master concept for educational policies in the years to come. . . . The lifelong concept covers all aspects of education . . . with the whole being more than

---

[1]The notion of a Community Lifelong Learning Council (CLLC), discussed in the concluding chapter, is merely illustrative of a very general organizational strategy. Elsewhere (Bunting, Moon, and Peterson, 1978), for example, I have suggested a unit called METRO, short for Metropolitan Learning Council.

the sum of its parts. Lifelong education is not an educational system but the principle on which the overall organization of the system is founded [p. 182].

Institutional systems must abandon their rigid interior divisions. Artificial or outmoded barriers between different educational disciplines, courses, and levels, and between formal and nonformal education should be abolished [p. 189].

Education should be dispensed and acquired through a
multiplicity of means. All kinds of existing institutions, whether
designed for teaching or not, and many forms of social and economic activity, must be used for educational purposes. The important thing is not the path an individual has followed, but what
he has learned or acquired [p. 185].

The recent UNESCO Recommendation on the Development of
Adult Education (1976) carried on the theme of lifelong learning
as the master concept:

The term "lifelong education and learning," for its part,
denotes an overall scheme aimed at both restructuring the existing
educational system and at developing the entire educational potential outside the education system [p. 2].

What, we may ask, might be some of the broad consequences
were lifelong learning, by a definition similar to the one suggested
here (and in the UNESCO reports), to become the master concept
for education and learning in America?

For education scholars, lifelong learning principles could,
arguably should, become the basis for a thorough intellectual reformulation of education in America. Lifelong learning concepts
would be the fundamental theoretical principles for understanding
and evaluating the totality of this country's educational efforts.
Such a reconceptualization has been proposed by Lawrence Cremin.
In his 1976 book *Public Education*, Cremin posits "a new formulation" in which the central assertion is that "the theory of education
is the theory of the relation of various educative interactions and
institutions to one another and to the society at large" (p. 24). In
a chapter entitled "Toward an Ecology of Education," he urges us
to recognize "the multiplicity of individuals and institutions that

educate—parents, peers, siblings, and friends, as well as families, churches, synagogues, libraries, museums, summer camps, benevolent societies, agricultural fairs, settlement houses, factories, radio stations, and television networks" (p. 29). While Cremin's main thesis is that we need to think comprehensively, in the sense of embracing a diversity of educative agents, he is concerned also with the lifelong nature of learning: "education must be looked at whole, across the entire life-span, and in all the situations and institutions in which it occurs" (p. 59).[2]

For education officials in government, lifelong learning principles could be used as the conceptual basis for organizing, or reorganizing, federal and state education bureaucracies—including the projected federal Department of Education. Lifelong learning might in time become the basis for a coherent national policy for education and learning. And this national policy might be expected to inform the organizational structure of government education bureaucracies. A federal Department of Education, for example, ideally should be more than simply the sum of a number of existing units and programs from various departments.

For public school staff, lifelong learning as public policy would mean radical changes indeed. Some changes that might be anticipated are these: generally less fragmentation of education, fewer "categorical" programs; increased attention to early childhood learning (also called for in the Faure report); instructional emphasis, throughout school, on learning how to learn; permission to leave school once essential skills are acquired; close relations between schools and employers of youth; and options to begin "higher" education at any age, with additional options to leave and return at *any* time—making colleges truly multigenerational. (Eventually, such distinctions as preprimary, elementary, junior high, senior high, and college might no longer be useful.) Schools, including colleges, would need to cooperate closely and share resources with all community organizations interested in education. The schools or colleges would become just one—albeit probably

---

[2]Fantini (1977) and Ziegler (1977) have also recently suggested fundamental changes somewhat along the lines proposed here.

the most significant—instrumentality for learning in the community, subject to the general plans of a cooperative body created to ensure needed, efficient, effective learning opportunities for people of all ages in the community.

For individuals, lifelong learning concepts of the sort advocated here would mean a host of new life options. Initial schooling could be shortened (or lengthened), and all "graduates" would have learned skills and attitudes requisite for pursuing further learning, as well as a sense of the advantages and disadvantages to them of various career or life options. Full-time work could begin early or late. Work could be combined or alternated with learning—either school-based or self-directed—throughout the middle years. In later years, full-time work and formal learning could give way to independent learning and increased recreational activities.

For the society, lifelong learning as public policy could in time lead to new social norms and cultural values. Continuous, serious learning would be valued and socially rewarded; all institutions in the society would facilitate it. Mindless activity, such as watching commercial TV, would be devalued. Families in all their forms would increasingly become agents for continuous learning. The media would be able to assume more responsibility for educating the public. Business and industry, in part spurred by tax incentives, would move to better integrate working and learning for their employees. And thus, in time, perhaps by the portentous year 2000, a genuine learning society would begin to emerge.

Overview of the Book

The general purpose of this source book is to aid planners and other officials and staff to realize the promise of lifelong learning locally and throughout the country. To this end, it has assembled a substantial amount of up-to-date information about activities and issues germane to facilitating continuous learning. It reports on a great many programs, projects, studies, and proposals, without analyzing any in very great detail. The book may be used as a reference: a starting point for further study, a source of leads to more detailed examination of particular topics of concern. While our perspective is *lifelong*, there is a clear concentration throughout the book on adult learning, for it is at this level that educational opportunities have been most lacking.

In the interest of coordination with other related projects, this book does not emphasize several facets of lifelong learning addressed in other recent or forthcoming volumes. For example, it does not seek to provide precise definitions for the plethora of terms relating to adult education, since this is the task of a major project recently completed at the National Center for Higher Education Management Systems (described in Chapter Six). Similarly, it does not provide an overview of the relation of education and work, which is discussed in reports for the Lifelong Learning Project of the Department of Health, Education, and Welfare (also summarized in Chapter Six). Nor does it analyze in detail proposed mechanisms for financing lifelong learning, since these proposals are considered in a recent set of papers assembled by Windham, Kurland, and Levinsohn (1978).

Following this introduction, which advances the concept of lifelong learning as a philosophical framework rather than as a concrete program, Chapter One describes most of the major programs and other sources through which people of all ages in this country can presently learn. The chapter considers sources for both *deliberate* education and learning (schools, nonschool organizations, and individually used sources) and *unintentional* learning (family, work, friends, and the mass media).

In Chapter Two, Patricia Cross focuses on adult learners and potential learners and what is known about them from some thirty national and state statistical surveys. A number of conclusions are drawn on the basis of consistent findings across several studies. Cross points to numerous policy-relevant questions that remain unanswered, and she suggests that new survey and analytic procedures will be needed to obtain clear answers.

In Chapter Three, John Valley discusses the operation of lifelong learning programs in local settings, where policy, in Valley's words, is "translated into learning opportunities." The chapter describes a number of locally conducted needs studies; it reviews a broad range of actual programs and services, organized under nine "strategy" themes; and it analyzes several unresolved issues related to needs studies, adoption of innovation, coordination of programs, and the setting of goals and priorities.

Chapter Four, by Susan Powell, provides a review of the major types of recent activities and plans in the states, based on documents especially assembled for this project. The focus is on initiatives from state agencies and systems of (mostly postsecondary) institutions rather than from individual schools or colleges. The overview, which includes case studies of four states, indicates considerable activity but as yet not much implementation of substantive innovations.

In Chapter Five, Terry Hartle and Mark Kutner summarize federal programs related to lifelong learning; they provide an account of the origins and development of the Mondale Act; and they speculate about the future federal role in lifelong learning. Hartle and Kutner conclude that there will be wide acceptance in Washington of the concept as a philosophy but little acceptance of lifelong learning as a program that requires new money.

Chapter Six, by Judith Bonnett Hirabayashi, is a guide to additional resources related to lifelong learning. It consists of directories of concerned organizations, relevant statutory advisory councils, clearinghouses, journals and newsletters, abstracts of recent and ongoing research projects and services, and the text of relevant 1976 federal legislation. The chapter's general purpose is to provide a ready guide to information sources on topics of interest to program and policy planners.

The brief final chapter, by Richard Peterson, summarizes the case for lifelong learning and then sets forth fifteen general implications for planners and administrators based on key findings and conclusions from earlier chapters. It outlines, in short, the probable benefits to individuals and the society from lifelong learning and then suggests what could be done to achieve them.

To sum up, after first suggesting "lifelong learning" as a conceptual framework for fashioning new sets of services to better aid continuing learners, we attempt to provide planners and policy makers with: (1) a view of many of the potential partners in broadly conceived cooperative lifelong learning enterprises; (2) an array of facts about the motivations of adult learners, their perceptions about barriers to further learning, and related matters; (3) a sense

of the kinds of programs and problems existing in local settings;
(4) an overview of the types of policies and programs being actively
considered, if not yet implemented, by the federal and various state
governments; (5) a range of leads to further information; and
(6) several ideas for changes in institutions that could advance lifelong learning. This book is not a policy study; it contains no detailed recommendations, although the concluding chapter raises
numerous implications for policy. Instead, it provides a base that
can *inform* planning toward the ends of intelligent and effective
programs.

Adult education, lifelong learning, and even education in
general, are not high-priority matters in most legislative halls in
the late 1970s, particularly if new funding is required, as Powell
concludes in Chapter Four. Lifelong learning *ought* to have high
priority; nothing could more benefit the culture. Its public policy
importance somehow must be raised. Educational statesmen are
desperately needed, and we are hopeful that the information and
ideas in this volume can give them new support.

Lifelong learning, as we have tried to conceive it, offers a
vision—a prospect of a future education and learning order in
which all people, in many ways and using a great variety of resources, can with ease engage in learning throughout their lives.
The promise is that through lifelong learning lives can become
more meaningful and, in consequence, the society more perfect.

CHAPTER ONE

Present Sources of Education and Learning

Richard E. Peterson

This chapter seeks to convey a sense of the total range of sources of education and learning presently available to Americans. Its organizing typology of learning sources is meant to be comprehensive: it includes the places where people learn; the sponsors of more or less formal, intentional education; and also the major agents in the society from which people learn unintentionally. Thus this chapter introduces the principle types of educational programs in both school and nonschool settings, and it also calls attention to the ways people learn without consciously seeking to do so.

The field of adult education has evolved a vocabulary possibly unparalleled in its confusion. Most of the conceptual disorder arises from multiple meanings for single words or phrases, such as *continuing education* or *career education*. This chapter tries to clarify terms by indicating their most common meanings, but it offers no lengthy definition for any term. Recent monographs by Broschart (1977) and Hiemstra (1976) cover the definitional terrain quite well, and the terminology project of the National Center for Higher Education Management Systems (NCHEMS), described in Chapter Six, has sought definitive meanings that should warrant wide adoption.

The key terms chosen for the fundamental divisions of the Sources of Education and Learning (SEL) typology are, as shown in Table 1, *deliberate* education and learning and *unintentional* learning. These terms attest to the fact that much learning occurs through deliberate effort, but probably more occurs incidentally. Both general types need to be recognized by education planners.

The domain of deliberate education and learning is divided into three broad categories of learning sources: (1) the schools, (2) nonschool organizations, and (3) individually used sources. (The distinction between school-based and nonschool learning corresponds roughly to Moses' [1971] dichotomy between the school-based "core" and the nonschool "periphery," although Moses considers proprietary schools to be part of the "periphery.") In the context of the life span, school-based education occurs—is compulsory—during the years of childhood and youth. For many people, therefore, deliberate education ceases at about age eighteen—a fact that leads some observers to refer to the American educational system (and those of most other countries) as "front-loaded." Most learning through nonschool organizations—for example, in the workplace—involves people in their adult years. Learning by means of individually used sources may be engaged in at any age.

The domain of unintentional learning has not been the subject of extensive conceptual analysis by adult education theorists. Our categorization of sources—home, work, friends, the mass media—is merely suggestive; it has no systematic empirical basis, nor basis even in theoretical literature. Unintentional learning may occur throughout life, although one's openness to such learning undoubtedly decreases with age.

Two more sets of terms deserve comment before we move

on to the more factual information about learning sources. Numerous adult education theorists draw distinctions between *formal, informal,* and *nonformal learning. Formal* generally refers to institution-based, structured learning relying on teachers' instruction; *in-*

Table 1. Sources of Education and Learning in the United States

	Deliberate Education and Learning	*Usual Age of Students*	*Approximate Number of Participants (in millions)*
I.	Schools		
	A. Preprimary education	1–4	10.0
	B. Elementary and secondary education	5–17	42.0
	C. College and university undergraduate education	18–21	9.5
	D. Graduate and professional education	21–27	1.5
	E. Public school adult education	16 and older	1.8
	F. Proprietary schools	18 and older	1.2
	G. University extension and continuing education	28 and older	3.3
	H. Community education	All ages	.5
II.	Nonschool Organizations		
	A. Private industry		5.8
	B. Professional associations		5.5
	C. Trade unions		.6
	D. Government service		3.0
	E. Federal manpower programs		1.7
	F. Military services		1.5
	G. Agriculture extension		12.0
	H. City recreation departments		5.0
	I. Community organizations		7.4
	J. Churches and synagogues		3.3
	K. Free universities		.2
	L. Parks and forests		No meaningful estimate
III.	Individually Used Sources		
	A. Personal—at hand		Virtually everyone
	B. Personal—at a distance		"
	C. Travel		"
	D. Print media		"
	E. Electronic media		"

Table 1. Sources of Education and Learning in the United States
(Continued)

Unintentional Learning

	Usual Age of Students	*Approximate Number of Participants (in millions)*
I. In the Home		Virtually everyone
II. Work		"
III. From Friends		"
IV. Mass Media		"
V. Other sources (for example, travel, community activities, recreation, and entertainment)		"

formal usually refers to nonschool-based, less structured learning not pursued for credit, including what we call unintentional learning. *Nonformal* refers to organized educational activities offered by nonschool organizations; this concept has evolved chiefly among adult education leaders in developing nations. Nonformal education is usually characterized by flexibility, relevance to contemporary problems, and voluntary participation (Harmon, 1976).

Although the terms *formal* and *informal* are in wide use, we could not make these terms work in our typology. School-based education is mostly formal, to be sure, but what about when the class goes on a field trip? Learning in nonschool organizations is often informal, but just as often it is formal, as in company-run training classes. Individually conducted learning activities would almost always be considered informal. In short, the boundaries between the three terms seem unclear, and consequently the terms will not be used in the remainder of this chapter.

Finally, the distinction between *education* and *learning* is increasingly stressed in the conceptual literature (for example, Ziegler, 1977). We consider the distinction to be sufficiently useful to include both words in the title of Table 1. *Education* may be thought of as taking place in "instructional" settings; in large degree the instructor sets the terms of the process, and the student is relatively passive. *Learning,* by contrast, often occurs outside of such settings and is more determined by the individual's own purposes. These definitions are admittedly arbitrary; it is by no means simple to classify any particular activity as either *education* or *learning;* and the conceptual overlap, and potential for confusion, with the terms *formal* and *informal* learning is apparent.

Within the SEL framework, the schools clearly emphasize "education," as do some nonschool organizations. Other nonschool organizations primarily facilitate "learning." In Table 1, the listing of nonschool organizations begins with those in which people are "educated" or "trained" (as in a specialized occupational skill area) and ranges roughly down through those in which learning (as self-determined) is more the pattern. "Learning" may also be said to characterize the activities that draw on individually used sources as well as all the cognitive, affective, or motor changes that happen unintentionally.

Few typologies are entirely satisfying. Forcing diverse activities into categories oversimplifies and occasionally misleads. Table 1, however, does serve to give the reader a sense of the full range of general sources of education and learning in the United States. As such it may serve as a broad context for policy making and program planning.

The estimated numbers of participants for each source come from various surveys, mostly governmental, conducted in the past seven years. Some of the estimates are from recent surveys; others are older and hence less accurately describe the current situation. All should be regarded as rough estimates, subject to all the shortcomings inherent in surveys, including those conducted by the most respected organizations. Many individuals, pursuing learning through multiple sources, are counted in more than one estimate.

Nevertheless, the figures provide a general picture of the overall deployment of learners, of what Moses (1971) has called the "learning force," in the United States. Mindful that there is double and even multiple counting, we estimate a total of some 116 million deliberate learners in organizational settings. Some 70 million, or 60 percent, are estimated to be in the school and college sector (42 million, 36 percent of the total, are in compulsory education); some 46 million, 40 percent, are involved in education and learning through nonschool organizations. At the postsecondary level only, there are an estimated 64 million participants. Roughly 18 million (28 percent) are enrolled in schools and colleges, compared with the 46 million (72 percent) learning through nonschool organizations. All of these figures are "head count" estimates. Comparisons between the school and nonschool sectors are not simple. There are clearly many more people participating in the nonschool sector; typically, however, they are employed adults who are studying on a part-time basis. In terms of total "learning hours" or "learning effort" on the part of participants, the two sectors appear to be fairly similar.

Regarding individually used sources of learning—the third domain in the SEL framework—studies based on the work of Tough (1971), including most recently a survey by Penland (1977), suggest that in a given year about four fifths of all adults engage in self-directed or "do it yourself" learning that relies on these sources. The methods and general findings of the Tough and Penland surveys are described later in this chapter and also in Chapter Two.

Finally, of course, unintentional learning is a fact of life for everyone; it is a concomitant of living. However, one can conceive of environments, particularly interpersonal environments, that are more stimulating than others and thus make for more frequent unintended learning. The implications for policy of this line of reasoning are extensive.

In the next three sections of the chapter, we discuss sources of deliberate education and learning and then in the fourth section examine unintentional learning.

Schools

Preprimary Education

Children begin learning from infancy, ordinarily with much help from parents. The first organized educational experience for many, besides Sunday school, is some form of public or private preschool, nursery school, or day- or childcare center. Roughly ten million children ages three and four were enrolled in preprimary programs during 1975, about half of all children of that age (National Center for Education Statistics, 1977). Preschool programs run by public school districts have expanded markedly in the past decade. Many are funded by the federal Head Start program. Some nineteen states have established child development offices. A good source of information about the nature and scope of preprimary schools is the Early Childhood Project, funded by HEW's Office of Child Development (OCD) and located at the Education Commission of the States.

Elementary and Secondary Education

It is then compulsory for the young to attend school until age sixteen or seventeen—usually from kindergarten through the twelfth grade. Nationally, almost 90 percent are in public schools, with the balance in private schools (independent or church-related) and academies (such as the all-white schools throughout the southern states). On the order of 85 percent of secondary school students graduate after the prescribed thirteen years. Many participate in one of two federally funded programs that are often confused—vocational education and career education.

Vocational and commercial programs enroll about a third of high school students. Tending to come from lower socioeconomic backgrounds and to be relatively less gifted academically, students in vocational programs ordinarily aspire to jobs rather than college after graduation. Although federal support goes back to the Smith-Hughes Act of 1914, since 1958 vocational education has been very heavily funded by the federal government. In the fiscal year (FY) 1976, $800 million was distributed to the states pursuant to the Vocational Education Act of 1963. Roughly 80 percent has been spent in secondary schools, with the balance, through various "set asides," going to community colleges, proprietary schools, and other technical schools. Altogether some $4 billion from federal, state, and local sources was reportedly (Carlson, 1976) spent in FY 1975 for vocational education, which has basically meant training for specific entry-level semiskilled and skilled jobs. Data on the national scope of vocational education are provided annually by the Division of Vocational and Technical Education of the U.S. Office of Education (Carlson, 1976), and a recent analytical overview of the role and significance of vocational education has been prepared for the National Academy of Education (Task Force on Education and Employment, 1979).

Career education, as a concept, is strictly a federal invention— introduced in 1974 by then Commissioner of Education Sidney Marland. Passage of the Career Education Act in 1974 launched a variety of demonstration projects and other activities in a third of all the nation's school districts (Hoyt, 1976). Funding under the act for FY 1979 was in the amount of $32.5 million. A useful guide to many of these activities has been prepared by the National Institute of Education (Tiedeman and others, 1976). The 1976 Career Education amendments generally call for moving from "demonstration to implementation." Implementation of what? one may ask. Career education can be said to differ from vocational education in that the latter means actual training, while the former, career education, has included such objectives as "career aware-ness," "career exploration," "values clarification," and learning about the "world of work" and other aspects of a "career," broadly defined. While the bulk of funds has gone into programs for high school age youths, the 1977 Career Education Incentive Act calls for career education programs at the elementary and postsecond-ary levels as well. Under the 1977 act, states will increase their con-tribution over the next five years, after which the programs are to be fully state supported.

Vocational education, as implemented pursuant to the fed-eral legislation, is a "front-loaded" program; to the extent that it is limited to high school age youths, it is inconsistent with lifelong learning concepts. Career education, however, depending on how it is implemented in the years ahead, could be an important spring-board in a lifelong learning approach to public education.

College Undergraduate Education

Approximately 50 percent of all high school graduates go on to college or university—a figure that has remained remarkably stable over the past decade. The figure, however, varies substan-tially from state to state (and region to region), depending in large part on the easy accessibility of colleges, for example, community colleges (Willingham, 1970). Some 75 percent of college students are in public institutions, where the tuition is much lower than at independent colleges. In many community colleges (in California, for example), there has been no tuition. The upshot is a national higher education system that is substantially stratified by social class (despite expanding financial aid programs nationally and in many states). Interestingly, there is an inverse relation between institutional prestige (and affluence of the student body) and the extent to which institutions embrace lifelong learning concepts. Thus, at the community colleges, the average age of students is on the order of twenty-six.[1] At many public four-year colleges, a number of which were formerly teachers' colleges, the average age of undergraduates is around twenty-two. At the more prestigious universities and independent colleges, the average age has not changed appreciably; here older (usually part-time) students have tended to be viewed as something of an inconvenience (see Peterson and Hefferlin, 1975).

Attrition and retention rates accordingly vary by type of institution, with higher retention associated with institutional selectivity and prestige. Nationally, across all institutions, the retention rate is about 50 percent—about half of all students graduate within four years—a figure that has also changed very little over the years. (On the order of 70 percent of all four-year college students *eventually* receive the bachelor's degree.) Apparently, heightened college efforts to retain students, in part to maintain fiscal viability, have been roughly balanced by student desires to drop out or stop out. The latter decision—to alternate education with work or leisure—is one strategy of lifelong learning with which college retention efforts seem to be at cross-purposes.

Graduate and Professional Education

Graduate or professional school is the next step in the normal educational progression for people aspiring to professional or scholarly careers. Graduate enrollments have dropped off slightly

---

[1]Of all the organization-based sources of education, the public community colleges, by all accounts, have the best track record of serving older and other nontraditional populations in both on- and off-campus settings. Community college enrollment increases have far outstripped those of all other types of schools in the past decade. Valley, in Chapter Three, comments further on the success of community colleges in accommodating older adults.

in the 1970s, in part in response to the economy's inability to suitably employ all the country's highly educated manpower. Certain subject fields, such as the humanities and education, have been much harder hit than others. The result is an expanding force of the underemployed, many pessimistic predictions (for example, Freeman, 1976), and a host of very difficult problems for educational and social policy—including the problem of justifying lifelong learning as a central social goal.

So much for the normal sequence of education in the United States. Next we consider several sources that operate either as alternatives to the normal pattern or as sources for additional education. All are designed mainly for adults.

Public School Adult Education

The great majority of school districts in the country operate adult education programs, or "adult schools," as they are commonly called. Taken together, the public school adult programs have several important functions. They enable people who dropped out of elementary or secondary school to come back and earn the equivalent of a high school diploma, often by preparing for and passing the General Education Development (GED) tests (see Chapter Six). They are the chief operating arm of the federal government's campaign against illiteracy; under the Adult Education Act of 1966 and subsequent amendments, funds (totaling $72 million in FY 1976) are distributed to the states for adult basic education (ABE).[2] Roughly one third of adult school enrollees are in ABE courses (Boaz, 1978). A related socialization function applies to non-English-speaking immigrants; great numbers of English-as-a-Second-Language (ESL) courses are conducted by school districts on the eastern, southern, and western coasts of the

_____

[2]The Right to Read Effort, which is directed at adults as well as children, is the other major federal literacy program. During FY 1976, $25 million was distributed for a variety of mostly demonstration projects (for example, reading academies) under the National Reading Improvement Program, established in 1974 (Shipman, 1976). ACTION, the principle federal volunteer program, is currently using some 33,000 older adults throughout the country as reading tutors for adults.

country. Adult school programs also typically provide an assortment of occupational skills courses, though not usually complete credential programs. And, finally, they offer a broad range of academic and avocational courses in response to local community interests.

As noted in Chapter Four, substitution of performance- or competency-based concepts for grade level is an important innovation taking hold in public school adult education (see Roth, 1976). The competency criterion stems largely from the national Adult Performance Level (APL) study, commissioned by the U.S. Office of Education's Division of Adult Education and completed in 1975 (Northcutt, 1975). Its finding that 20 percent of adult Americans are functionally illiterate drew wide editorial comment during the spring of 1976. A recent inventory of adult competency education resources is available from the Division of Adult Education (Parker, 1977a).

Adult school programs are funded from a combination of local district and state sources, which totaled $43 million in 1976, augmented by the federal ABE money. Fees are ordinarily nonexistent or very minimal. Courses, which seldom carry degree credit, are almost always held at night in local elementary and secondary schools. The age range of students is typically very large. From a lifelong learning perspective, public school adult education, in both content and spirit, seems exemplary indeed as a school-based source of education.

Proprietary Schools

An important alternative to conventional post high school education is offered by the for-profit (or sometimes nonprofit) proprietary schools. Some are owned by large corporations, for example, Bell and Howell; most are owned by individual entrepreneurs. Altogether there are about 9,000 (Kay, 1976), more than three times the number of conventional colleges and universities. They provide "no nonsense" (read, no general education) training for specific occupations; they seldom have entrance requirements; and they usually promise job placement. As a type of postsecondary education, they are controversial. Even-handed analyses (for example, Wilms, 1975; Nolfi and Nelson, 1976) are rare. Numerous critics have accused proprietaries of fraudulent practices (for example, the Federal Trade Commission, 1976; Cowen, 1977). Others have been highly supportive (for example, Hebert and Coyne, 1976). Although some questionable practices persist— promising job placement on completion of the programs, for example—the majority of the proprietaries are undoubtedly responsible—particularly those accredited by the National Association of Trade and Technical Schools, the Association of Independent Colleges and Schools (mostly business schools), or the National Home Study Council, which together accredit about 20 percent of the industry.

University Extension and Continuing Education

Yet another important school-based source for lifelong learning is extension and continuing education (not to be confused with agriculture extension, which is described later). According to a recently published survey by the National Center for Education Statistics (NCES), an estimated 1,233 four-year colleges and universities operate extension, continuing education, correspondence, and various noncredit programs (Kemp, 1978). Historically, while such programs have often concentrated on the professional upgrading of elementary and secondary teachers, they have been the route to college degrees and job mobility for hundreds of thousands of Americans in all walks of life. In 1975 there were some 3.3 million participants (Boaz, 1978), with more than four fifths enrolled at public institutions. While some courses may be taken for credit, typically they are noncredit. The range of course offerings by university extension units can be astonishingly diverse. The courses are conducted in a variety of formats, usually in the evening, at many different sites.

It is difficult to distinguish between "continuing" and "extension" education. Some institutions have "extension" divisions; many more have "continuing education" divisions. Their activities, however, are much the same. If anything, *extension* may imply a broader range of courses. *Continuing education* often (and usefully) is taken to mean continuing education in the professions, and many continuing education or extension divisions administer courses and programs for doctors, pharmacists, teachers, and other groups of professionals. Increasingly, such course work is being made mandatory by states for purposes of relicensure.

Participants in extension or continuing education are typically well educated and relatively affluent. Programs are commonly self-supporting; that is, they operate almost entirely from student fees. Fees can be high—around $75 for a course at a public university that meets three hours a week for a semester. The range in fees is tremendous, with fees for particular courses depending on whether the courses are for credit or not and whether the institutions are public or private. Nonetheless, the number of four-year institutions with continuing education programs has more than doubled since 1967–68.

Community Education

Community education, the last of the school-based sources of education and learning to be considered, is also difficult to define precisely, because of both the expansive rhetoric used to describe its purposes and the diverse, sometimes competing, activities sponsored by different organizations in its name. The basic operating idea, however, is that school buildings (and other community facilities) are made available during nonschool hours to all members of the community for a wide assortment of educational and learning activities.

Community education goals extend beyond instruction. They have been variously said to include using the school as "a focus of community life"; mobilizing all available resources toward resolving community problems; viewing the school as a "total opportunity center"; and developing a "sense of community" among residents in a neighborhood or other locality (see also Valley's discussion in Chapter Three).

The general idea has long received strong advocacy by the Charles Stewart Mott Foundation of Flint, Michigan, which has supported community education in Flint and elsewhere for close to four decades. In 1974 the federal Community Schools Act was passed. However, funding under this act has been small: $3.5 million for FY 1979. Grants have been made to thirty-two states (nine have added their own funds) and to a somewhat larger number of local districts. The community education idea is clearly relevant to

the work of most community colleges, which are also eligible for
funds under the 1974 act. The concept has been embraced by the
American Association of Community and Junior Colleges, which,
aided by a grant from the Mott Foundation, launched a major project in 1977 to promote community education (Fletcher, Rue, and
Young, 1977).[3]

To its participants, who frequently are parents of school
children, community education costs little or nothing. Learning
activities, which tend to be loosely organized, may cover a very
broad range of topics—from effective parenting, to health matters,
to community issues and problems—in response to community
needs. Adults of all ages participate. Recently, community education leaders in the U.S. Office of Education have been speaking of
the community school as a focus for a wide range of human services—"as a one-stop shopping center for community services"
(Paul Tremper in 1977 testimony before the House Committee on
Education and Labor).

This completes our overview of the major parts of the
school-based education complex in the United States. It was brief
compared with the sections that follow largely because we suspect
that a good many readers will be academic professionals who are
reasonably familiar with the general outlines of the nation's education system. It is hardly a *system*, however, if that word implies
order and coherence. Not only is there little communication, coordination, or cooperation among the school-based sources of education, there is often aggressive competition and, not infrequently, open hostility between them.

[3]The semantic/programmatic confusion surrounding community
education is further compounded by the term *community service*. Many two-
year colleges, especially, have community service divisions (Kemp, 1978),
which typically arrange lectures, forums, workshops, and other short-du-
ration, noncredit activities. "Community service" is also a major focus for
Title I (Part A) of the Higher Education Act of 1965, under which grants
are made to numerous states and individuals for action research and other
activities in a variety of public policy domains (for example, energy conservation, or citizen alienation from government) "designed to assist in the
solution of community problems." A number of these projects are described in Chapter Six. A useful overview and assessment of many Title
I projects has been prepared by Farmer and Knox (1977).

Increasingly the competition is centering on adult students. They are strenuously sought by four of the eight types of institutions or programs described (C, E, F, and G in Table 1), as the size of the traditional college-age population declines and as state funding of institutions continues to be based on numbers of students enrolled. The competition, while it mainly involves schools and colleges, also increasingly involves nonschool organizations, to which we now turn.

Nonschool Organizations

The twelve types of nonschool sources of education and learning discussed in this chapter (see Table 1) are ordered roughly according to the degree of organization or structure characteristic of each. The first six are ordinarily classroom based (the military excepted); the last six are much more varied and flexible in their settings and modes of instruction. The first six types of organizations are typically quite large; the last six tend to be much smaller. The first six generally provide education and training oriented toward the objectives of the organization itself or toward occupational advancement; the last six enable learning motivated by personal, usually nonoccupational, interests (agriculture extension, in part, excepted). In general, the first set of nonschool sources are used for "occupational advancement" and the second set for "personal development."

From the perspective of lifelong learning, it is noteworthy that the occupational advancement-oriented sources are used almost entirely by people in the period between compulsory schooling and retirement—that is to say, by adults in the work stage of the life cycle (see Stern and Best, 1977). The personal-development-oriented sources are used, in different ways to be sure, by individuals of all ages.

Private Industry

Many analysts, perhaps in part because of the high estimates made by the Carnegie Commission on Higher Education (1973), regard private industry as the largest provider of adult education in the country. They cite the huge training programs of such corporate giants as IBM, AT&T, and Xerox, some of which are now granting bachelors' degrees and in at least one instance—Arthur D. Little—masters' degrees. Fortunately, a study has been recently published by the Conference Board (Lusterman, 1977) that describes in detail the current nature and scope of education in U.S. industry. Most of what follows in this section, including the figures (except where noted), will be from this report.[4]

The Conference Board report divides industry-sponsored education and training activities into four categories:

- *In house-during hours:* This category is by far the largest of the four; 20 percent of all companies surveyed give at least one training course, with 30 percent giving at least one course of thirty-hours or more duration. In the last year, 3.7 million participated in such courses—11 percent of the total employee force.
- *In house-after hours:* After-hours training is provided by 39 percent of the firms surveyed, with an estimated total participation of .7 million.
- *Outside the company-during hours:* Paid education leaves are provided by 9 percent of the firms surveyed; no estimate of participation rate is given (we will estimate .1 million).
- *Outside the company-after hours:* Tuition-aid programs are in effect at 89 percent of the companies surveyed; an estimated 1.3 million—4 percent of the total employee force—participate.

The total level of participation, about 5.8 million during the year prior to the receipt of the survey, agrees closely with the 1972 survey finding of 5.9 million by the Commission on Nontraditional Study (Carp, Peterson, and Roelfs, 1974); but it is much higher than the 1975 NCES figure of 2.6 million (Boaz, 1978) and much lower than the Carnegie Commission (1973) estimate of 16 million.

---

[4]The Conference Board is an independent, nonprofit business research organization. Funding for the Education in Industry survey came from the Carnegie Corporation and the Rockefeller Brothers Fund. The report is based on a 1975 survey of a sample of 610 companies having at least 500 employees. This segment accounts for about half of private employment in the United States but virtually all of industry formal training programs.

Lusterman divides the subject matter of education and training provided by industry into four categories: (1) management development-supervisory (involving 37 percent of all employees who took in-house courses); (2) functional-technical (61 percent); (3) basic-remedial (1 percent); and (4) other (1 percent).

Prevalence of training programs varies by type of company: 90 percent of the financial and insurance firms reported courses; 79 percent of the transportation, communications, and utility companies; 64 percent of the manufacturing companies; and 57 percent of the wholesale and retail businesses. Size of firm is also an important factor, with provision of courses ranging from 96 percent of firms with 10,000 or more employees down to 55 percent of companies having 500 to 999 employees.

Altogether, the Conference Board estimates that private industry spent $2 billion for education and training in 1975—$1.6 billion for in-house training and $.4 billion for education outside the company. This represents a sizable investment by the private sector in the development—certainly of job competencies—of a good many people. Granted that such education reflects the "corporate mission," it can be assumed to serve the interests of the individuals, as well, in a nation where success and personal well-being are widely defined by occupation and income level.

Professional Associations

Nearly all occupational groups have associations of member practitioners to advance the interests of the occupation as a whole and, often, the occupational or professional competence of individual members as well. They may be organized nationally, statewide or regionally, or locally (as in chapters). *Professional association* is not an ideal term for this category of organizations, in that many occupations with member organizations are not generally regarded as "professions" (for example, real estate brokers, secretaries, and bartenders). The term *trade association*, however, usually means an organization of companies or firms of a given kind (for example, trucking companies) rather than individuals practicing a given trade or profession.

The nature and scope of education and training sponsored by professional associations have not been surveyed in any systematic way. Certainly there is wide variation in programs. Some professional associations, for example, the California Bar Association, design and conduct extremely well-conceived courses for their members. Others, such as associations of health professionals, may rely on cooperation with colleges and universities. Still others, often groups of academic professionals, rely mainly on national meetings. Probably most active are associations for middle-level business managers, which conduct countless seminars in accounting, data processing, supervisory skills, and so forth in conference centers all around the country. Undoubtedly the association with the largest single educational program is the combined American Management Associations, boasting 792 staff, 7,500 lecturers and discussion leaders, 2,000 formal educational programs, and a budget of $31.8 million (*PER* Editors, 1977a).

The numerous engineering and technical societies are also heavily involved in continuing education, according to a recent report by Greenwald (1977). Of fifty-seven societies responding in a survey, thirty-nine indicated a continuing education program either in operation or under development; six more reported programs in the planning stage. They reported currently offering 1,100 courses (many of them short courses, lasting from one to three days) to close to 30,000 enrollees. A significant finding was that 55 percent of the enrollees were nonmembers. About half of the organizations reported cooperative programs with local universities; one third indicated cooperating with proprietary schools. Finally, the survey found that "the goals of most organizations include the expansion of continuing education in order to meet the current and future challenges of technical change" (p. 2).

For the lifelong learning planner, especially at the state level, the activities of professional associations are of particular consequence in view of the expanding legislation calling for mandatory relicensure. Professional associations are keenly interested in this issue, and they are a logical partner in any apparatus for ensuring continuing professional competence.

Trade Unions

Unions are usually listed with business among the major sponsors of learning. Yet educational activities in most trade unions are not extensive, certainly not in comparison with the educational activities sponsored by industry and government. There are some twenty million organized workers in the United States, with a little over two thirds in AFL/CIO-affiliated unions. On the order of .6 million, about 3 percent, are estimated to be involved in education and training through some four general types of programs.

Roughly 500,000 workers are in apprenticeship programs operated jointly, under contract, by management and labor. Close to 300,000 of these workers are in apprenticeship programs registered with the Bureau of Apprenticeship and Training in the Department of Labor, according to a recent U.S. Department of Labor (1977) report. (Courses for registered apprentices are federally funded.) Apprentice training typically involves both on-the-job practice and classroom work (144 hours), which, in many localities, is conducted in cooperation with community colleges (Abbott, 1977). Some trainees receive an AA degree and journeyman union card at the same time. Apprentices are guaranteed jobs before they begin their 2,000 hours of training.

A second type of program, involving as many as 75,000 trade unionists a year, is the labor education sponsored by the education departments of individual unions. The emphasis here tends to be on "tool" courses—shop steward training and grievance handling, for example.

A third type of program is what is now commonly called "labor studies," a special curriculum offered through colleges and universities. Forty-one universities (Turner, 1977) currently have labor studies curriculums, either through extension divisions or regular degree programs. Numerous community colleges, many at the urging of the United Auto Workers, offer the AA degree in labor studies. Some thirty-one institutions reportedly have labor studies majors (Dwyer, 1977). In contrast to the earlier "labor education," which consisted mainly of "tool" courses, "labor studies" is more broadly conceived to include topics from all the social sciences that may be relevant to modern collective bargaining.

Two other degree-granting institutions for trade unionists are particularly noteworthy. One is the AFL/CIO's George Meany Center for Labor Studies, which offers an external B.A. through Antioch College. The other is part of the College of New Rochelle,

New York, which is operated by District Council 37 of the American Federation of State, County, and Municipal Employees.

A fourth type of educational opportunity for trade union members consists of partial or total tuition payment for college courses, an arrangement negotiated by a good number of unions as a fringe benefit. Currently there are 200 such contracts, up from only 29 in 1967 (Charner, 1978). Many of these plans stipulate that courses be job related, although increasingly there are no such strings attached. Somewhat surprisingly, only about 1 percent of the 2.5 million eligible workers take advantage of this opportunity; the reasons for this low level of participation are being analyzed in a major study underway at the National Manpower Institute (summarized in Chapter Six).

While apprenticeship training is clearly "front-loaded," the other types could in principle be utilized at any time in the worker's career. Participation rates, however, generally are not high, and education is often narrowly focused on the conduct of union affairs. Union-sponsored retraining or upgrading programs seem not to be common. As a source for lifelong learning, trade unions have yet to fulfill their potential.

Government Service

As of early 1978—before Proposition 13—about one sixth of the national work force was in the employ of government at some level. Altogether there are some 15 million civilian government workers (U.S. Bureau of the Census, 1976); 60 percent are employed by local government, 22 percent by state government, and 18 percent by the federal government. Extensive training opportunities in a variety of formats are made available to government employees at all three levels.

Currently there are on the order of 2.8 million federal employees. According to a recent training effort report from the U.S. Civil Service Commission (1977), close to 600,000 individual employees (21 percent of the total) accounted for 958,297 "instances" of training during the 1976 fiscal year. ("Instances" are planned units of formal classroom instruction of at least eight hours duration, the average "instance" covering about forty-three hours.) Two thirds of the training was provided "internally" by the employee's own agency or department; the balance was provided by interagency training groups, other departments, or nongovernment organizations (such as colleges, commercial firms, and professional associations). With regard to subject matter, development of the employee's technical specialty accounted for over a fourth (29 percent) of the training instances, followed by administration and analysis (19 percent), legal and scientific topics (13 percent), supervisory principles (11 percent), orientation to government service (9 percent), clerical skills (8 percent), trades or crafts (5 percent), and basic literacy skills (1 percent).

Few data are available on the nature and scope of employee education and training conducted by state governments. No doubt they vary according to the population and wealth of the state. In California during FY 1975, for example, just over 191,000 state employees reportedly were involved in in-house training, and the state contributed slightly over $1 million for outside (career-related) education (Seaton, 1977).

By contrast, there is reasonably good information about training of local government employees. A 1975 national survey of cities of over 10,000 population, conducted by the International City Management Association (Brown, 1976), ascertained the following. Two thirds of all the cities surveyed operate training programs. Ninety percent have on-the-job and specific skill development programs; 79 percent have supervisory training; 40 percent and 31 percent have interpersonal relations and team-building programs, respectively. A variety of outside agencies is also used in training municipal employees. A college or university was the most frequent choice (73 percent of the cities). Other major outside trainers include state agencies (60 percent of the cities), private consultants (35 percent), the International City Management Association (30 percent), American Managment Associations (11 percent), and the National Training and Development Service (10 percent).

Government service at all levels, it is clear, affords continuing training and retraining opportunities for great numbers of its employees. The proportion of government employees involved in education and training is roughly twice the proportion in private industry. Most of the training is specific to performance on a given task in a given agency. Yet much, such as that in supervision and interpersonal relations, is transferable to a variety of settings and is potentially applicable throughout one's career span.

Federal Manpower Programs

Work and training programs administered by the Department of Labor are an important and often overlooked source of education for both adults and youths. Altogether involving $5.2 billion and 3.3 million first-time enrollees in FY 1976, they are in general designed to increase the employability of people who are out of work or underemployed.[5] There are three separate programs that have education components: the Comprehensive Employment and Training Act (CETA) program, the Job Corps, and the Work Incentive (WIN) Program.

CETA, enacted in 1973, consolidated a range of previously existing programs aimed chiefly at youths. Its basic policy premise is that every youth and adult should have an opportunity to work. Program planning and implementation are decentralized, their direction entrusted to some 500 local "prime sponsors" (for example, city or county governments). Most of the education and training—referral to training programs, sponsorship of class-size projects, on-the-job training—take place under Title I of CETA, in which there were 1.6 million new enrollments in FY 1976.

The Job Corps, a separate program (through Title IV of CETA), is a residential program for severely disadvantaged youths. It had some 44,000 new members in 1976. Education consists mainly of basic remedial work and skills training.

The recently enacted Youth Employment and Demonstration Projects Act (YEDPA), Title VII of CETA, will provide $250 million during FY 1978 for work experiences for unemployed youths age sixteen to twenty-three to aid in their "transition from

[5]There are also federal vocational training programs other than those administered by the Department of Labor. For example, in the Department of HEW, the Rehabilitation Services Administration conducts a relatively large program, with matching state funds, designed to rehabilitate disabled and handicapped people. During FY 1976, 2.3 million clients were served, and by the end of the year 1.25 thousand were reportedly prepared for gainful employment (U.S. Office of Human Development, 1977).

school to work." CETA prime sponsors, the administering agents, will enter into "cooperative agreements" with school districts. High schools will award academic credit for work experiences. The act also calls for occupational information, counseling, and placement services for unemployed youths.

The WIN program—now, as modified, WIN-II—is operated in cooperation with local welfare agencies. Some 20,000 AFDC (Aid to Families with Dependent Children) recipients lacking marketable skills received job experience and limited amounts of classroom and on-the-job training during FY 1976.

CETA is a major federal initiative in human resource development. The statistic of 1.7 million participants is more significant than it appears since most of the participants—marginally employable youths and adults—are receiving nearly full-time training. Local CETA prime sponsors would typically welcome proposals from education planners for ways to coordinate their programs with others.

Military Service

Currently about two million people—most of them relatively young, most of them men—serve in America's armed forces. Military requirements are said to call for recruiting one of every four qualified eighteen-year-old males. With the declining numbers of young people, it is estimated that by 1980 that figure will be one in three (Carr, 1976). In the all-volunteer military service, education is used as a prime incentive in recruitment; all branches of the service have acted to expand educational opportunities for their members.

In general, education and training fall into two categories: (1) training directly related to performance as a member of the armed forces, and (2) voluntary education, which allows individuals to pursue personally determined educational goals. The first, military training, in which 1.25 million servicemen are involved, is divided by the Department of Defense into five categories: (1) recruit training; (2) officer acquisition (service academies, ROTC, officer candidate schools); (3) flight training; (4) specialized skill training; and (5) professional development education (military science, engineering, management). Much of this training focuses on essential military skills. But most of the training now has broader applicability; since the end of the Vietnam War, according to Carr (1976), about 90 percent of all military occupations are transferable to civilian jobs.

Some 575,000 service personnel, about one fourth of the total complement, are participating in what is called the Voluntary Education Program. They are part-time students during off-duty hours at some 1,000 colleges operating on or near military bases. Seventy-five percent of tuition costs are ordinarily reimbursed. Each service operates its own program.

The Army's General Education Development program involves some 600 cooperating colleges and provides study opportunities ranging from basic or remedial to graduate work together with regular counseling and aid in enrolling. Project AHEAD (Army Help for Education and Development) enables individuals to enroll in one of 1,300 cooperating colleges prior to enlistment. The "hometown" college advises the soldier throughout active duty, grants credit for courses taken anywhere in the world, and then enrolls the student upon discharge for the remaining credit hours.

The Air Force Education Services Program involves 300 civilian colleges and universities. An important component is the Community College of the Air Force (CCAF), which includes seven major technical schools, all regionally accredited, and ninety-four programs, of sixty-four semester units each, leading to Career Education Certificates (for which half the work must be done at civilian institutions). CCAF has plans—legislation has been enacted—for awarding associate degrees.

The Navy Campus for Achievement (NCFA) includes 400 civilian colleges and universities, a number of which have waived residency requirements. An interesting component is the Program Afloat for College Education (PACE); professors from five universities and one college sail with the fleet and teach courses.

The Marine Corps' Voluntary Education Program involves 272 cooperating colleges, which provide programs ranging from high school completion work through graduate studies.

There are three major programs for voluntary learners in the military that apply across all the branches. The first is the Defense Activity for Non-Traditional Education Support (DANTES). It has two principal missions: (1) to administer several nationally recognized credit-by-examination programs, namely CLEP, DSST (DANTES Subject Standardized Test, covering seventy-five technical and academic subjects), GED (overseas only), ACT, SAT, and ACT/PEP, and (2) to facilitate use of independent study (correspondence) courses from regionally accredited civilian institutions. DANTES publishes *The DANTES Examination Program Handbook* and *The DANTES Independent Study Catalog*. An activity of the Department of Defense, DANTES is based at the Ellyson Center (Navy) at Pensacola, Florida.

The Servicemen's Opportunity College (SOC) is a network of over 360 colleges and universities—half, two year; half, four year—that have agreed to support education of service personnel chiefly through flexible residency and transfer policies. During the fall of 1977, an associate degree program was launched that involves thirty-one colleges and all major army bases. SOC is jointly funded by the Department of Defense and the Carnegie Corporation and is co-sponsored by twelve organizations, mostly associations of postsecondary institutions. Its headquarters is at the offices of the American Association of State Colleges and Universities (AASCU) in Washington, D.C.

Finally, the American Council on Education's Office on Educational Credit (OEC) evaluates military courses and periodically publishes a *Guide to the Evaluation of Educational Experiences in the Military*. The current *Guide*, which contains degree credit recommendations for over 5,000 formal military courses, has been forwarded to approximately 3,000 postsecondary institutions to assist in assigning credit to veterans for their education in the military. (More information about OEC is in Chapter Six.)

Education in the military, needless to say, is a significant part of the nation's panoply of education. For a great many youths it is an opportunity for basic education and skill training that would not otherwise have been available. Thirteen percent of enlisted men have not graduated from high school, and many more than that are deficient in basic skills. Each of the services has high school equivalency programs, and in 1975 diplomas were granted to 80,000 active-duty servicemen.

Providing good education for service personnel, because of their geographic mobility, presents numerous problems. Continuity in, say, a degree program is problematic; the advantages of residency can seldom be realized. The quality of the many courses and programs offered by numerous, far-flung colleges is difficult to ensure. Issues of program integrity and related matters—evaluation, local and state cooperation, uniform national policies—are considered by a recent task force sponsored by the Education Commission of the States (1977).

Agriculture Extension

The Cooperative Extension Service is indeed a cooperative, certainly a multiconstituency, enterprise. Overall guidance and approval of state plans come from the Science and Education Administration—Extension, U.S. Department of Agriculture. States, in consultation with county governments and other public and private interests, propose programs, which are then administered by the land-grant universities in the respective states. What is done each year in each state is an amalgam of all the interests and requirements of the parties involved. (The State Extension Director acts as the key administrator and mediator). Certain of the federal funds, for example, are earmarked for 4-H urban programs, assistance to small and part-time farmers, nutrition education, and safety education. The total financial outlay for Cooperative Extension in FY 1976 was $527 million; federal, state, and county contributions were 43 percent, 39 percent, and 17 percent, respectively.[6]

Cooperative extension work nationally is divided into four categories: Agriculture and Natural Resources; Home Economics; 4-H Youth; and Community Resource Development. The percentage of resources (in terms of staff years) expended on each in 1975 was 39 percent, 21 percent, 32 percent, and 8 percent, respectively.

[6]Most of the material in this section is from the Extension Service, USDA publication *Cooperative Extension Programs: A Unique Partnership between Public and Private Interests* (1976). Harrington's volume (1977) is particularly instructive on the history and operation of the Cooperative Extension.

The Agriculture and Natural Resources program includes crop production, livestock production, business management, marketing, and environment improvement and pest management. Agriculture agents spend 70 percent of their time with commercial farmers, 25 percent with small and low-income farmers, and 5 percent with home gardeners. Nationwide, 3,000 agricultural extension agents are involved, along with over 3,000 specialists. In rural areas, they meet with farmers and ranchers individually and in small groups. In urban areas, extension education occurs mainly through the electronic media.

The Home Economics program seeks to help family members "identify their needs, make decisions, and utilize resources to improve their quality of home and family living." Some 4,000 Extension home economists, 7,000 paraprofessionals, and 700,000 volunteers ("extension homemakers") bring home and family living education to approximately ten million families annually. General topics include food and nutrition (38 percent of staff years, twice the outlay of the nearest other category), family resource management, family life education, family health and safety, textiles and clothing, and aid to the elderly and handicapped.

The 4-H Youth programs reportedly enlist 38 percent of the total farm youth population. (The four "H's" stand for head, heart, hands, and health.) Broad goals are to develop employable skills, explore careers, and develop leadership ability. Twenty percent of the membership live in suburbs and central cities; 25 percent are minorities. There is a special Food and Nutrition Program for low-income city youth, and over 400,000 youths go to 4-H sponsored camps each year. 4-H is run chiefly by volunteers—some 560,000 of them in 1975. Educational content includes the topics covered by the Agriculture and Natural Resources program, community development, economics and career planning, personal development (including health), and family living.

The Community Resource Development program is the smallest and newest Extension component. It is designed to render assistance—toward "sound community decisions that will increase economic opportunities and the quality of life in rural areas"—in towns with populations of 50,000 or less. Extension staff, many in this program from land-grant universities, work mainly with local government officials on matters of unemployment, housing, health, education, community leadership, citizen participation, and governmental effectiveness.

All this adds up to an impressive array of educational services, centering on farm operations and rural family living, for "farmers and ranchers, agricultural industries, rural families and youth, and rural communities." The great number of volunteers is especially impressive. It is difficult to estimate the total number of people who learn through the Cooperative Extension in a given year. Perhaps the figure is close to twelve million.

City Recreation Departments

City recreation (or parks and recreation) departments are an integral part of municipal government in the great majority of American cities, including all the large ones. The types of services and facilities sponsored, many of which enable deliberate learning, span a great range. An A to Z sampling would include the following: aquariums, arboretums, archery ranges, arts and crafts centers, bandstands, beaches, bicycle trails, botanical gardens, camps, childcare centers, community centers, environmental education centers, golf courses, music shells, museums, nature centers, parks, planetariums, swimming pools, tennis courts, theaters, and zoos. Such a list scarcely indicates the variety of activities available, especially in arts, crafts, athletics, and other avocational areas. Programs, courses, and other events are developed as the need arises. Recreation theorists (for example, Gray and Greben, 1974) see recreation less as a leisure-time pursuit than as another form of learning. City recreation activities are often designed for special groups—especially senior citizens, preschool children, and the physically handicapped and mentally retarded. Frequently, city recreation departments cooperate with local schools to provide after-school activities on school grounds.

According to a 1970 survey conducted by the National Recreation and Park Association (1971), roughly three quarters of the funding for city recreation departments comes from local public appropriations. (Local funds for city recreation programs are likely to be reduced markedly in states that have passed legislation similar to California's Proposition 13.) Fifteen percent comes from state sources, with the rest from federal (for example, the Federal Community Services Administration) and private sources, and from fees (for example, for certain classes) and concessions. Volunteers are indispensable; serving both as recreation leaders and board members, they outnumber paid personnel by almost two to one.

Community Organizations

A great deal of education and learning takes place in so-called community organizations, as a 1972 survey by NCES (Kay, 1974) made clear. One perhaps thinks first of the YMCA and Red Cross, with their well-organized programs in swimming and first aid. But there are also the local historical society, the Jewish Community Center, the Senior Citizens, the Chess Club, the Junior League, the Lions, and, in more recent years, the myriad small self-help groups. Some are highly organized; others are hardly organized at all. Membership in many is tightly controlled; others are open to all. Many are affiliated with national organizations; others are strictly local. They are nongovernmental, possibly excepting libraries, and nonprofit. The learning that takes place is seldom "certified" in any sense (except for, say, lifesaving certificates), and much of the teaching is done by volunteers.

Motivations for associating with community organizations are, of course, highly varied. Some organizations are used sporadically and impersonally by some people—for example, to obtain a book or to perfect a skill. More commonly, however, community organizations serve as vehicles for association with people of similar interests and values. A common consequence of such association, one may assume, is some kind of learning—which could be either deliberate or unintentional. Assuming, as we are, that learning takes place in most any social setting, we think it useful to conceive of community organizations in as broad and inclusive a manner as reasonably possible. The typology in Table 2 should suggest the scope of these organizations, exclusive of churches; it is ordered roughly according to the presumed importance of education as an organizational goal.

As a typology, this one is by no means perfect. The Red Cross could go in several categories, for example, or in the first one. The table merely outlines the major types of community or-

Table 2. Typology of Community Organizations

1. Multipurpose Organizations
   a. Libraries
   b. Y's
   c. Ethnic organizations
2. Cultural or Intellectual Groups
   a. Museums and historical societies
   b. Literary groups
   c. Public affairs forums
   d. Performing arts: theater, musical groups
   e. College and university groups: American Association of University
      Women, alumni chapters
3. Personal Improvement Groups
   a. Cognitive skills classes: speed reading, languages
   b. Personal development groups: life-style seminars, sex-role-oriented
      groups
   c. Effective parenting groups
   d. Physical fitness and health classes
4. Church-sponsored Organizations
   a. Traditional adult education programs
   b. Community issues or action groups
   c. Personal or family living classes
   d. Services for specific groups: daycare centers, senior centers
5. Senior Adult Groups
   a. Chapters of national organizations: American Association of
      Retired Persons, Grey Panthers
   b. Local groups
6. Youth Programs
   a. Scouts
   b. Y groups
   c. Athletic teams
7. Recreation Groups
   a. Dance groups
   b. Sports: hiking, skin diving
   c. Games: bridge, scrabble
   d. Garden clubs
   e. Other hobbies: miniature railroading, bird watching
8. Political Organizations
   a. Units of major political parties
   b. Units of national issue groups: National Organization for Women
      (NOW), John Birch Society
   c. Local issue groups: neighborhood association, taxpayer
      organization

Table 2. Typology of Community Organizations (Continued)

9. Social Service Organizations
   a. Red Cross
   b. Health-related organizations: American Cancer Society, alcoholism council
   c. Charitable organizations
   d. Humane societies
10. Civic or Service Clubs
   a. Chapters of national organizations: Rotary, ZONTA
   b. Local clubs
11. Fraternal and Social Clubs
   a. Chapters of national fraternal societies: Elks, Red Men
   b. Local social clubs

ganizations, and it includes only two or three examples from the scores of groups that would fall into each subcategory.

It is difficult to estimate the numbers of people who learn through community agencies. The NCES study (Kay, 1974) surveyed a somewhat more limited range of community organizations than is outlined here, and it dealt only with participation in "adult education courses." For five different types of community organizations, the registration statistics were as follows: (1) religious organizations other than churches, 474,000; (2) Y's and Red Cross chapters, 3,050,000; (3) civic organizations, 1,175,000; (4) social service organizations, 2,285,000; and (5) cultural and other organizations, 370,000. The total is 7.4 million registrations, as reported by organization leaders. This contrasts somewhat with the NCES 1972 survey of participants (Okes, 1975), which found only 2.0 million individuals in organized education activities in community agencies, including churches. The Commission on Non-Traditional Study (Carp, Peterson, and Roelfs, 1974) found 4.2 million learning through "community organizations such as YMCA; museums, galleries, and performing arts studies; and recreation and sports groups." The Carnegie Commission on Higher Education (1973) estimated ten million in "other organized programs—for example, TV, churches and synagogues, community organizations, libraries and museums."

By content area, across all the community organizations, including churches, the NCES survey (Kay, 1974) found the following percentages of registrants: general (including adult basic) education, 3.3 percent; occupational training, 5.5 percent; religion, 29.3 percent, 90 percent of these enrolled in churches; community issues, 30.9 percent; personal and family living, 20.4 percent; sports and recreation, 7.7 percent; and miscellaneous and unclassified, 2.9 percent.

According to the NCES triennial surveys, participation (course taking) went from 1.5 million in 1969 to 2.0 million in 1972, then down to 1.8 in 1975—for a 20 percent increase over the six years. Over the same period, participation in courses on "civic and public affairs" at any and all locations increased 84 percent; "personal and family living," over the same time span, by 59 percent; "hobbies and handicrafts," 72 percent; and "sports and recreation," 93 percent.

We know that the image and role of public libraries in learning is changing markedly. Formerly seen as sources of books for the bookish, many libraries, especially metropolitan ones, are actively involved in a wide range of adult learning services—information and referral (I & R) concerning all locally available human services, GED preparation, television and video tape learning, and assistance with all sorts of independent or self-directed learning projects. (For a good overview of library independent study activities, see Mavor, Toro, and DeProspo, 1976.) The libraries are an obvious natural resource for lifelong learning. The museums, as Valley points out in Chapter Three, are still another institution that, shedding an old image, have begun to offer—and market—educational programs with wide appeal.

The rise of the psychological self-help groups—"personal improvement groups" in Table 2—is something of a social phenomenon in itself, so new as not to be recognized in any of the national surveys. Many of these groups are sponsored by churches and Y's; others are activities of various counter-culture and "personal development" organizations. Especially in metropolitan areas, there are special groups for just about everyone (the physically handicapped, single fathers, gay couples, and so on).

For purposes of lifelong learning policy, it should be emphasized that the members of most community organizations joined spontaneously; they do not have to be recruited. Different organizations tend to draw their members from different social classes. Many of these same clubs, furthermore, are exclusive in some way. By contrast, organizations like the libraries and the YMCA are open to anyone, of any age, making them particularly apt partners in a comprehensive lifelong learning enterprise.

A final note on policy implications of community organization-based learning concerns the substantial role of volunteers. The NCES survey (Kay, 1974) found that of the 654,000 persons "involved in teaching adult education in community organizations" in 1972, 78 percent were volunteers. A 1974 Bureau of the Census survey, cited in Manser and Cass (1976), found that one in four Americans over age thirteen does some form of volunteer work; 50 percent volunteered through religious organizations; health and education organizations each drew 15 percent; slightly smaller percentages fell into other types of community groups. A 1977 Gallup Poll stated that 27 percent of American adults engage in some kind of volunteer work, and a national survey reported by Penland (1977) found 38 percent of the respondents to have volunteered during the year prior to the survey.

Churches

There are several reasons for considering churches separately. For one thing, they far outnumber all the other types of community organizations; in fact they number more (172,000) than all the other types of organizations in the 1972 NCES survey combined (61,800). Second, in many small towns and rural areas, the church is the only site for community social life; churches are, indeed must be, multipurpose organizations. Finally, the constitutional separation of church and state could create problems for church involvement in a multi-institution, publicly funded learning endeavor.

Roughly 132 million Americans, 62 percent of the total population, are church members (Jacquet, 1976). The percentage has changed little in the past two decades, despite the increasing numbers of older people in the population. A little over half of all church members—40 percent of the adult population, according to the Gallup Poll—attend regularly. Perhaps one quarter, about

33 million, are "quite involved in" or regular participants in church activities other than the Sunday service. Enrollment of children and youth, as in Sunday or Sabbath school, has declined somewhat in the past decade, largely because of the declining birth rate; 35 million were reportedly enrolled in 1976 (Jacquet, 1976). Variation by denomination and region of the country would be substantial.

Let us quickly review the extent to which churches provide adult education courses, as determined by the 1972 NCES survey (Kay, 1974). First, of all the community organizations with adult education programs (66,770), three quarters of them (50,480) were churches. Twenty-nine percent of all churches reportedly conducted adult education courses. Total registrations numbered over 5.2 million, with 73.5 percent of these falling into the content area of religion; 17.2 percent, personal and family living; and the rest, community issues, occupational training, recreation, and general education.

Sixty-two percent of the participants were women; median age was 44.2 years. Both figures are somewhat higher than in the other community organizations. Volunteers outnumbered paid teachers nearly four to one. The most commonly reported source of income for conducting adult education programs was the church's general budget, reported by 85 percent of the churches; 18 percent reported contributions; 12 percent, student fees; 3.6 percent, special contracts or grants.

Adult education programs (in the NCES sense) are only a small part of the education and learning offered by the church. The modern church is a multifaceted social institution. The following list gives an idea of the types of church activities through which members (and nonmembers) can learn.

1. Sunday school or religious education.
2. Church youth activities or youth missions.
3. The Sunday sermon and other aspects of the worship service.
4. Discussion groups on religious topics (for example, Bible study).
5. Work with committees on particular aspects of church life.
6. Pastoral counseling.
7. Groups concerned with personal or family problems.
8. Discussion groups for specific people (for example, for singles, single parents, gays).

9. Discussion groups on almost any topic imaginable.
10. Special events, such as lectures and workshops.
11. Musical activities, such as choir and instrumental groups.
12. Other cultural or arts activities such as drama and graphic arts.
13. Child- or daycare and summer school programs.
14. Programs for older or retired persons.
15. Charitable projects of all kinds.
16. Community social action.

Many of the same policy-relevant themes touched on in the previous section are applicable to the churches: the reliance on volunteers; the nonvocational emphasis; the fact that people at all socioeconomic levels are church members; the fact that people do not have to be recruited. Granted, much of the learning is sectarian or otherwise circumscribed; yet much is not, as the list above suggests and the NCES survey makes clear. To be sure, there are negative attitudes toward certain or all churches held by some people, as well as the legal questions involved in churches receiving public funds for educational work. Yet the overwhelming fact remains: for hundreds of thousands of people, particularly those in their later years, the church is the single most preferred, most comfortable setting outside the home for almost any organized activity.

Free Universities

Free universities appear to be a genuine educational innovation—at least in the United States. They allow people to learn without the trappings and rigidities of conventional schools. Their basic premise is that people want to learn something for its own sake; no grades, credits, diplomas, or other credentials are ordinarily involved. They invite citizens to be teachers as well as students, in accordance with their philosophy that "anyone can teach and anyone can learn."

The first "Free U," called "The Experimental College," was established at Berkeley in 1964 in the wake of the Free Speech Movement. There now are about 200, with several in every major metropolitan area. This number has been fairly constant for the past five years. Free U's are somewhat ephemeral; several new ones are formed each year, while several close down. The largest is said to be the Experimental College at the University of Washington in

Seattle, with 18,000 people a year enrolled (Semas, 1976). About one half of the Free U's are based at conventional colleges or universities; often they are given funds and space by the respective student governments, and many of their enrollees are local students attending both institutions. About 40 percent have their own offices somewhere in the community. The rest are located at community agencies such as libraries or churches. A provocative rural Free U-community education model, described in Chapter Six, is spreading in Kansas. A directory of Free U's around the country is in Gross' widely available book, *The Lifelong Learner* (1977a).

Free U's operate by recruiting teachers, publishing a bulletin containing course descriptions and meeting times and places, registering students, sometimes collecting fees, and evaluating each of the courses. Classes are held in homes, community facilities, or college buildings. A wide range of courses is typically available; while unlimited in principle, topics tend to focus on crafts, performing arts, practical skills needed in everyday living, personal psychology, environment and energy issues, and political and social thought. Some are skills oriented by design, such as New York's Apple Skills Exchange and The Skills Exchange in Toronto.

Learning networks, the suggested name for what have heretofore been called learning exchanges, are often discussed along with free universities. They are quite different. Free U's arrange for classes; learning networks are telephone referral services for connecting people who want to study a subject with someone interested in teaching that subject, after which all further arrangements are made by the two parties. The content of the teaching and learning can be virtually any topic imaginable. Learning networks or exchanges, which seem to have been first suggested by Ivan Illich in *Deschooling Society* (1971), now number about twenty around the country. The first and probably the largest is The Learning Exchange, located in Evanston and serving greater Chicago. Instructors in more than 3,000 subjects are registered, and more than 20,000 Chicagoans are currently being served (Gross, 1977). A learning network would not be a "source" for education or learning, in the sense of the SEL framework. The cadre of teachers registered with the network would be the "source."

The free universities and learning networks are both extremely important models for serving the vast numbers of learners who are not motivated by the desire for credits and credentials. There are problems for the Free U's, of course, such as how to shed the traditional "university" connotation and university student constituency—to become learning sources for everyone, of all social classes, in the community. These and other issues are being actively deliberated by the Manhattan, Kansas based Free University Network (FUN), which was created in 1974 to help advance free universities and learning exchanges in the United States. FUN estimates that Free U's offered about 20,000 courses to a quarter million enrollees during 1976. A systematic survey of free universities and learning exchanges is presently being conducted by FUN, with sponsorship from the National Center for Education Statistics.

Parks and Forests

As any occasional domestic traveler knows, the federal government, the states, and other jurisdictions own and maintain vast park and forest preserves. There are also national and state monuments, memorials, historical sites, archeological sites, parkways, seashores, riverways, grasslands, and battlefields.[7] The statistics of acreage and use are staggering, and need not be recited in detail here. Usage trends are even more remarkable; as one example, visits to all areas of the National Park System numbered 33.3 million in 1950 and 238.8 million in 1975 (*1976 Statistical Abstract*)— a 700 percent increase.

A great deal can be learned while visiting the various parks and other sites, be it botany, geology, natural history, or cultural change. To varying extents, most of the parks and other sites conduct educational activities. The nature of these activities can obviously influence the extent to which people seek to learn during their visits, and how much they in fact do learn. This learning can include not only facts about nature but also attitudes toward conservation and related issues that are, arguably, in the national interest.

[7]A good overview of park and other recreational resources in the country is available in a volume by Jensen (1973).

Thus we conclude the review of types of nonschool organizations in the United States that are sources for education and learning. It is not easy, of course, to know where to draw the line. The nation's prisons, for example, reportedly provide educational services to .2 to .3 million inmates. Projects of the National Endowments of the Arts and Humanities provide learning opportunities for a good many people. Nonetheless, the section should give readers a sense of the most important nonschool organizations that also have education functions. At least twice as many adults are learning through this nonschool "periphery" as through the school-based "core," though usually not in as intensive a way. (Many children are also learning in the nonschool sector—through cooperative extension activities, city recreation programs, and churches and other community organizations, for example). The realities of education and learning in nonschool settings are indicative of the extent to which "lifelong learning" and "learning society" concepts have already taken hold in the country; they can hardly be ignored by planners of new lifelong learning opportunities.

Individually Used Sources

Up until now we have been discussing education and learning opportunities provided by organizations. The organization, school or nonschool, designs the course or programs; the individual learner ordinarily accepts most of the terms of the "provider." (It is possible to design one's own learning program through a school or other organization, as, for example, in the degree programs at Empire State College or Metropolitan State University.) In this section we will consider independent learning and the sources on which it draws. Wherever available, statistics on use of the various sources will be cited. Because of their overall incompleteness, however, such data were not included in Table 1.

Present interest in self-directed learning can be traced in good part to the seminal research of Allen Tough of The Ontario Institute for Studies in Education. In his major work, Tough (1971) described what he called *learning projects*—deliberate efforts, lasting over a minimum of seven hours, to gain some kind of knowledge or skill. He concluded that virtually all adults (as well as adolescents) engage in learning projects during a year's time (only one of sixty-six Canadian adults interviewed for the study failed to report a learning project). Less than 1 percent of the learning projects were undertaken for credit. Seventy-three percent of the projects, Tough concluded, were planned by the learner rather than an institutionally based professional. The elaborate interview schedule and general analytical approach developed by Tough and his colleagues have been used in some twenty subsequent studies on different types of people using similarly small samples; results similar to Tough's original findings have generally been reported (Tough, 1978). (For a critical analysis of the research generated by Tough, see *PER* Editors, 1977b.).

What has been needed is a national study using a sufficiently large sample to verify Tough's initial findings. Fortunately, such a study was conducted in the United States in November 1976. Directed by Patrick Penland with a grant from the U.S. Office of Education's Office of Libraries and Learning Resources, the survey involved a modified version of Tough's questionnaire administered by a reputable polling organization to a carefully selected sample of 1501 people age eighteen or older.

Penland (1977) found that 79 percent of American adults could be called "continuing learners"; 60 percent engaged only in self-initiated learning projects; 19 percent had been involved in course or school-like activities; 16 percent engaged in both self-planned and course work; 3 percent took courses only; and 21 percent were "nonlearners." In sum, a great many people—perhaps three times as many as those who take a course at a school or college—engage in "do-it-yourself" learning from time to time during a given year. Our general question at this point is, What sources do self-directed learners use to secure information?

Penland's survey included nineteen "main sources" for learners "when they want to know something or get information on a subject." These are listed in Table 3 in the order according to which each was judged to be "extremely important" by the sample of continuing learners. To the right, for another list of sources, are components of what Gross (1977a) calls the *Invisible University*.

Elsewhere (Gross, Hebert, and Tough, 1977), Gross has noted some additional parts of the Invisible University, most of which fall into our nonschool organizations category.

Do-it-yourself learning by people wishing to set the terms

Table 3. Individually Used Sources of Learning

Main Sources of Informative Data (Penland, 1977)	Judged "Extremely Important" (percentages)	The "Invisible University" (Gross, 1977)
Expert who was also a friend or relative	75.2	
Books	71.2	Reference books
Close friend or relative	58.7	
Travel	52.5	
Newspaper	48.1	
Paid expert	48.8	
Television	44.2	Television
Self-formed group of equals	41.8	Learning groups
Individual instruction or tutoring	49.2	
Group, class, or lecture series with an instructor	43.1	
Magazines	39.0	
Exhibits, museums, field trips	32.3	Arts centers
Browsing in libraries	32.3	Libraries
Radio	27.3	
Films	27.6	
Human relations training, role playing	26.8	Growth centers
Brochures, newsletters, mailings	20.0	
Records and tape recordings	16.3	Tape cassettes ("the cassette curriculum")
Correspondence study	19.3	Correspondence study ("tutor in your mailbox")
		Learning exchanges
		Networks (via correspondence or newsletters)
		Churches
		Do-it-yourself college (free universities)
		The campus connection

Table 3. Individually Used Sources of Learning (Continued)

Main Sources of Informative Data (Penland, 1977)	Judged "Extremely Important" (percentages)	The "Invisible University" (Gross, 1977)
		New "open" programs at colleges
		Education brokers
		Games
		Activist groups

of their learning—content details, pacing, and the like—can, of course, make use of the kinds of organization-based resources already outlined. Noncredit public school adult courses often allow students much flexibility. A few colleges allow students to individually tailor their own degree programs. Learning programs run by community agencies often are relatively unstructured. And the self-formed groups of colearners, noted by Tough (1978), Penland (1977), and Gross (1977), which cooperatively set the terms of their own learning activities, are undeniably important. Yet some learners, pursuing some subjects, find it appropriate to study in a wholly individualized manner, with little or no recourse to group activities.

Our outline of individually used sources in Table 1 can be divided into two general types of sources—personal and impersonal—with the distinction depending on whether or not there is human feedback. The personal sources can be further divided between "at-hand" and "at a distance," the former including advice from experts and private tutoring, and the latter, correspondence study and networks of correspondents. Most of the sources in the "impersonal" category are either print media or electronic media. Almost all are essentially home-based sources for education and learning (see Macken and others, 1976).

Personal—At Hand

Paid experts (Penland's term) are generally professionals, for whose services fees are charged. Examples are doctors, nurses, lawyers, psychotherapists, architects, engineers, builders, financial advisors, and specialized consultants. One suspects that paid experts are not extensively used in adults' learning projects; rather, their expensive information is used chiefly to target other more accessible sources of learning.

Experts who are also friends constitute the single most important source in Penland's list. Some of these are professionals in the sense used just above. More are simply experts in various vocations, trades, crafts, and hobbies. An individual's circle of friends could include many experts: an automobile mechanic, a librarian, a rock climber, a nursery owner, a print shop owner, a leather worker, a real estate broker, a newspaper reporter, a plumber, a gourmet cook, a seamstress, a chess player, a fly fisherman, and a college professor. From such expert-friends, information and advice would ordinarily be free.

A *tutor* is defined by Webster as "one employed to instruct another in some branch . . . of learning, especially a private instructor." Tutors and private instructors are generally paid; their association with the learner commonly extends over numerous lessons. While the tutor usually dictates the terms of each lesson, he or she serves at the pleasure of the learner. In one national study (Carp, Peterson, and Roelfs, 1974), "individual lessons from a private teacher" was the method used by 6 percent of the "learners" in the sample and the preferred method of 8 percent of "would-be learners." Only three other learning methods were more preferred.

Close friends or relatives constitute the third most highly regarded source in Penland's study. Clearly, people wishing to learn something rely most readily on friends or relatives. And, conversely, knowledgeable or talented people are most inclined to share their knowledge with friends and relatives. So much the better if the friend or relative is an expert. (There are some interesting implications of this phenomenon for the planning of lifelong learning. Accessible, and friendly, experts are apparently highly conducive to learning.)

Personal—At a Distance

Correspondence study has been a familiar feature on the American educational landscape for over seventy years. It is the learning method of choice for all those solitary learners—solitary by preference or by circumstance (for example, military assignment). Currently there are said to be about five million correspondence students in the United States.[8] A 1970 survey found 24 percent enrolled at private schools, 57 percent at federal and military schools, 7 percent at colleges and universities (usually their extension divisions), and 10 percent at religious schools.

A correspondence course has the advantage of allowing the student to set his own pace; this lack of structure, however, leads many to fail to complete the course. And completion rates, as is well known, are indeed low: about 61 percent in university extension divisions and about 20 percent in private schools. Low completion rates together with no or nonprorated refund policies for noncompleters at many private home study schools are major reasons why these schools have been strongly criticized.

The most popular subjects are business, high school equivalent courses, electronics, engineering, other technical and trade subjects, and art. Reasons for correspondence study vary by type of program: College or university correspondence students are usually working toward degrees; enrollees in private correspondence (home study) schools are overwhelmingly interested in job advancement. In the Carp, Peterson, Roelfs study (1974), 5 percent of the "learners" reported involvement in correspondence study during the previous year; 3 percent of the "would-be learners" cite it as their preferred method. The NCES 1975 survey of adult education participants (Boaz, 1978) found 4 percent enrolled in correspondence schools (606,000 individuals, rather than five million.) In the Penland survey, as was seen, correspondence study was ranked last in importance as a source in the respondents' "efforts to know or find out something."

Networks, cited by Gross (1977) as one strategy for learning, are mostly correspondence networks of people interested in sharing ideas and learning from each other. One might join such a network by writing to, say, an author of a particular magazine article and asking to be added to the author's correspondence net-

---

[8]The information in this section is from Macken and others (1976), which contains a thorough review of the literature on correspondence education.

work. Often the ideas shared are in the nature of "frontier thinking" in the field. Participants in correspondence networks are generally literary and other intellectuals. It is difficult to say to what extent specialized networks are opened to rank-and-file magazine readers.

Travel

That traveling is educational is a truism, and we will say a bit more about this under "Unintentional Learning." Here our purpose is to recognize the potential of travel as a means for deliberate learning. One thinks of at least two general approaches: (1) to learn as much as possible from a trip taken for any reason, such as business, and (2) to plan a trip, or join a group making a trip, with the express purpose of learning something. Regarding the first, probably all that is needed when one travels outside familiar environs is to consciously adopt a looking, listening, and questioning stance. Spare time can be spent finding out about the new locale.

As for the second, when one travels for the purpose of learning, preparation is necessary. A language may be learned; books on the history, economics, and geography of the area may be read; and recently returned travelers may be extensively queried—all to make the relatively brief time on the trip itself maximally productive of learning. It is also possible to join groups for trips that have fairly explicit educational goals—to study Tuscan art or the mating behavior of whales in the San Ignacio Lagoon. Trips of this kind are quite commonly available through university extension divisions, alumni organizations, and many noncollegiate organizations as well—environmental organizations, senior citizen groups, and scout troups, for example, as well as private agencies. Any extensive traveling, however, whether alone or with a group, is expensive. Consequently, travel as a source of learning tends to be class bound.

Print Media

The types of print media commonly available include books, newspapers, and magazines. As sources of learning, they are not of much use, however, to people who cannot read, or cannot read very well. Poor readers are likely to have negative attitudes toward books, libraries, and even their own learning potential.

Books are no doubt the independent learning source that first comes to mind for academic professionals and the relatively literate stratum of the population in general. If you want to learn something about a subject, you go out and get a book about it (that is, if you can read). And the range of types of available books—in libraries, bookstores, drug stores, supermarkets—is truly remarkable. A well-stocked drugstore bookshelf typically has reference, how-to-do-it, self-help, and travel books in addition to the usual fare of best-sellers, westerns, and mysteries. All these books, save perhaps the worst pulp fiction, can probably aid in some kind of learning—whether of knowledge, skills, attitudes, or feelings.

A number of companies are now publishing books as "courses" for independent learners. Some are in the format of programmed texts, which tend to be relatively inexpensive and widely available. Even in airports, for example, travelers can buy pocket-size books on such topics as introductory accounting and principles of personnel management.

In Penland's study, books were cited as the second most important source for learning. What is required, one may wonder, for books to become even more important, in an absolute as well as relative sense? Commercial book publishers, from both technical and marketing standpoints, have been extremely innovative, and the expansion of paperback publishing has held prices down. Public libraries, despite their limited funds, have made great strides in providing services for the reading public. The financially strapped can borrow from friends as well as from the library. According to a 1978 poll by the Yankelovich organization, 55 percent of the adult population are book readers. One concludes that for books to be even more widely used than they are it is mainly up to schools and families to teach the young to read and to value reading books.

Newspapers are read, according to surveys,[9] by practically all adults capable of reading. The photographs they contain are pre-

[9]Findings from surveys of the readership of newspapers, magazines, and books are reviewed by Knox (1977). The national Courses by Newspaper project is discussed in Chapter Three.

sumably viewed by an even larger number. As such, newspapers are probably the chief source of information about current events. Additionally, big city newspapers now have sections on such topics as business and finance, travel, weekend entertainment, home improvements, books, cooking, hobbies, and the arts. Sunday editions often compete in comprehensiveness with national news magazines. There are large differences, of course, in the quality of various newspapers as vehicles for learning. Some serve more to divert and titillate. Interestingly, the potential for learning from the local newspaper depends in large measure on what city one lives in rather than on one's income level, since almost everyone can afford a newspaper.

Magazines, like newspapers, are also widely read—by almost four fifths of adults in the country, according to a 1966 survey. Many, like some newspapers, consist heavily of pictures, and the amount of reading may be minimal; there is likely to be a modicum of learning, nonetheless, as from skimming a national news magazine. One may surmise that those magazines that seek to inform their readers are generally successful in doing so. Moreover, many people are highly loyal to and carefully read their favorite magazines.

Extremely important as a learning source is the vast assortment of hobby magazines, including such titles as *Outdoor Life, Camera, Popular Mechanics, Tennis, Sail,* and *Guitar Player*.

All this said, magazines fell below the midpoint in the importance ranking of the various information sources in Penland's study; they were the lowest ranked of the major print media.

Electronic Media

Electronic media seem so far to have played a relatively minor role in deliberate learning. For the continuing learners in Penland's study, only television, ranked seventh, is above the midpoint in importance among the nineteen sources considered; radio, films, and tapes or records are all in the bottom third. Interestingly, television, radio, and films are rated higher by the "nonlearners" (the 21 percent of the sample not engaged in any learning project); TV is ranked third (above books); radio is ranked seventh (above magazines). The chief function of the mass electronic media, certainly of commercial TV and radio, is to entertain. People seldom, we think, view them as sources of learning. Use of more personal electronic devices—tape cassettes, for example— may be another matter.

Television, commercial TV, is largely a wasteland from the perspective of deliberate learning. The scramble for ratings and sponsors militates against extensive serious programming. There is, of course, the occasional documentary, public affairs program, or television play, as well as the regular news. These programs can be tremendously effective and can attract great numbers of viewers (for example, "Roots" and "Holocaust"). The potential of commercial TV as a learning source is staggering. The major networks' production capabilities are consummate. Almost every home has a TV set. Yet commercial television, because of its capacity for distracting, may on balance be more harmful than helpful to potential learners—and the general quality of the culture.

Public television, by contrast, has, despite many difficulties, expanded to become a significant source of learning for people of all ages. Its future seems even brighter in view of current Carter Administration plans for greatly expanded federal funding (Leubsdorf, 1977). As of late 1977, there are 271 public television stations—connected into the Public Broadcasting Service (PBS)— located in all the major population centers. Sixty-five percent of the population is reached.[10] Public television is said to be watched by more than 50 percent of the population at least once a month. Stations are licensed to state agencies (35 percent), universities (30 percent), community nonprofit corporations (27 percent), and school boards and libraries (8 percent). There is a variety of interstation arrangements—regional associations, state networks, consortia, and "affinity groups." Some of the state networks, heavily funded from state revenues, provide various kinds of programs to specialized audiences, such as schools and medical personnel, as well as to the general public.

Programs for public television come from a number of

---

[10]Most of the material in this section and in the paragraphs about public radio are from the *Summary Report* of the Carnegie Task Force on Public Broadcasting (1977).

sources. About a fifth of all the program hours are produced by the Children's Television Workshop ("Sesame Street," "Electric Company," "The Best of Families"); over a quarter come from individual PBS stations ("The Adams Chronicles," from New York's WNET; "Mr. Rogers' Neighborhood," from Pittsburgh); 27 percent come from major production studios (operated, for example, by regional or state systems); 10 percent are locally produced; and many of the rest—including some of the best—for example, "The Ascent of Man," "Upstairs, Downstairs," "The Shakespeare Plays"— have come from the British Broadcasting Corporation (BBC).

Sources of funding for public television are also diverse. Only one quarter of total revenues comes from federal sources. In 1977, $103 million came from Congress through the Corporation for Public Broadcasting. Other funds come from other federal agencies—NASA, NSF, National Endowment for the Arts, and USOE (which provides $5.5 million annually to the Children's Television Workshop). One third of all the funding comes from state and local taxes, especially the former source, which is expanding. Foundations contribute about 7 percent; corporations (for example, Exxon and Mobil Oil), 6 percent. Most of the rest comes from viewer subscriptions, stimulated largely by the current regulations that require stations to raise $2.50 for every federal dollar received. In 1976, 1.5 million people contributed over $32 million.

Finally, the advent in 1979 of the public broadcasting satellite needs to be noted. Its chief significance will lie in allowing local stations to broadcast simultaneously over three channels (rather than one), which will substantially increase the variety of programming and the viewer's choice of programs.

As a vehicle for deliberate learning, then, television, as it exists in America, seems a mixed bag. Commercial network TV has the wherewithal for magnificent productions, but it lacks the incentives for applying these resources to educational and cultural programming. PBS, because it lacks the necessary resources and because many stations are on the hard-to-receive UHF band, cannot compete. Cable TV, where it exists, often affords its subscribers more variety—potentially up to eighty channels. In general, however, its potentials for diversity and for serving interest groups of limited size have not been realized. Cable TV programming seems all too often to be "a pale imitation of commercial television" (Huffman and Trauth, 1977).

Generally speaking, people learn from television in bits and pieces, as, for example, from the nightly news. Children may learn a good deal from programs like "Sesame Street." But by and large people view TV for entertainment and escape, not for learning. In one national survey (Carp, Peterson, and Roelfs, 1974), for example, only 1 percent indicated TV as their preferred method of learning, and less than 1 percent reported actually using it as a learning method. Yet television is one of the few feasible sources of learning for many people—the poor readers, the geographically isolated, and the many shut-ins.

Radio ranks relatively low as a source for deliberate learning, much lower even than television, as Penland's study indicated. Commercial radio, with its alternating current of music and commercials, is more narcotic than stimulating. The news stations, of course, attempt to inform, but their format of staccato news items punctuated by commercials limits their effectiveness.

Public radio, like public television, is making progress, and promises even better performance with the proposed Carter appropriations and the use of the satellite, which, beginning in 1979, will provide four new frequencies per station. Presently (December 1977) there are 203 public radio stations; they are licensed to universities (65 percent), communites (20 percent), and public school systems, libraries, and states (15 percent).

National Public Radio (NRP) was set up in 1971 by the Corporation for Public Broadcasting (CPB) to produce programs and to serve as an interconnection facility for public radio licensees. NPR produces and distributes approximately forty hours per week of programming (which may or may not be used by local stations). Perhaps NPR's best-known program is "All Things Considered," a very intelligent ninety-minute news magazine aired six days a week. Another well-conceived program from NPR is the weekly one-hour "Options in Education." The Carnegie Task Force reports that "the recognition factor for National Public Radio has jumped from 13 percent to 23 percent just over the past year." (There apparently are no available estimates of the number of listeners). In fact, public radio is essentially a local service, with all but 15 percent of the programming, mostly recorded music, originating locally.

Thirty percent of the funding for public radio (totaling $32 million) comes from federal sources; 50 percent is from state and local tax revenue; 1 percent is from foundations; and a similar small amount comes from foundation grants. Like public television, public radio stations must raise $2.50 from listeners and other nonfederal sources for every federal dollar received.

An advantage of radio is that it can be used while one is doing something else. Thus, "All Things Considered" can be listened to while preparing supper or commuting home from work. (In fact, some argue that because of the great amount of time spent commuting in automobiles, radio has extraordinary potential as a learning source.) However, it is severely limited by its format—audio only, the one-way communication, inability of the listener to control content and pace, and the essentially "bits and pieces" type of learning that inevitably results. Possibly, if the Carter Administration proposals are enacted, NPR will be able to expand production of in-depth programs. Potential listener-learners, however, will need to have advance notice of such programs (TV as well as radio programs) for them to be used, perhaps along with supplementary reading and special discussion groups, in something akin to a "learning project."

Tapes and records, while rated low in Penland's survey, are additional means for learning having considerable potential. Their great advantage over mass electronic media is that they can be controlled by the individual; they can be repeated in part or in total according to the learner's interests and needs. They may be a boon to the nonreader as well as to the blind. The major disadvantage is that the learner cannot talk back, ask questions, and so forth. Another disadvantage is the cost—the initial outlay for the tape player and then the costs for each tape. A reasonably good audio tape recorder may cost $50. Audio tape cassettes cost around $6 for a forty-five-minute tape; they can be borrowed from libraries and elsewhere.

Tape cassettes are already available on a great many topics, and more are being produced all the time. Some 750 titles, mostly in literature, are available from the Cassette Curriculum (Deland, Florida), at an average cost of $12 each. Gross (1977a) mentions that the Center for Cassette Studies publishes a catalogue listing thousands of tapes, arranged in twenty-three subject areas. Most libraries have a large stock of tapes to lend. Many publishing houses, especially publishers of specialized magazines, are now in the cassette business. Many professional associations supply tapes to their members, for example, to provide updatings on current developments in the field.

Video tapes (combined with audio) are also becoming increasingly available. Equipment for playing video tapes on one's home television set is on the market, but for most people it is prohibitively expensive—beginning at about $1,000. (Available video cassette recorders also enable television programs to be taped for playback at later times, but blank tapes are expensive—about $15.) High prices have accounted for the low consumer demand and hence rather slow production of quality video tapes. However, the prices are expected to come down. In the meantime, many libraries and other community organizations have video tape recorders. The cost of the tapes themselves—around $25 for a lecture or lesson—are such that most people will want to rent rather than purchase them. Video disks will be less expensive—about $10, as will video disk players ($300 to $500). In some quarters video disks are seen as the electronic innovation that will finally make a wide contribution to serious learning.

Home computers are the last type of electronic media reviewed here. Computers are obviously not for everyone, even those able to afford them. The cost, however, is not as great as one would expect, and it is expected to come down. More than 50,000 home computers—personal mini- or microcomputers, as they are called— have reportedly been sold in the past two years. About a third are kits, bought and assembled by computer hobbyists. The cheapest cost about $250. The average hobbyist is said to begin with about a $1,000 investment, which is then augmented by another $1,000 worth of attachments—additional memory capacity, a typewriter-like keyboard, a television monitor, a tape deck, a printer.

A wide variety of programs (software) is becoming available on either tape cassettes or plastic (floppy) disks. Home computers have already been found useful in teaching math and spelling. Programs in elementary logic, algebra, Russian, and computer programming were used in a project described in Macken and others (1976). Numerous other subjects are likely to be amenable to home computer learning—advanced logic and math, English grammar, most foreign languages, and various elements of the natural sciences, for example. Computerized games are played by people of all ages, and the intellectual processes involved are likely to be applicable in a good many other settings. For many potential learners, particularly reluctant ones, the fascination of the fancy gadget may alone be enough to get them plugged into some new kind of knowledge or skill.

We have discussed independent learning at some length because this is a domain that is probably not sufficiently appreciated by many educators and planners. Additional mechanisms for self-directed learning, beyond those described, could be cited— such as films and the telephone (teacher-student phone networks). To extend the analysis in this way, however, would worsen a conceptual problem for the SEL framework—that of distinguishing *sources* from *delivery systems*. (For Webster, a *source* can be either a "point of origin" or "one that supplies information.")

Unintentional Learning

The second major division of the Sources of Education and Learning framework is unintentional learning. From the standpoint of theoretical study, it is unfamiliar terrain. People learn without intending to; that much is clear. (Academic psychologists call it *incidental learning*.) Learning, as acquisition of new cognitive, affective, or motor response, is virtually synonymous with living. What is not clear is the most useful way—for the purpose of facilitating lifelong learning—to categorize the various sources of unintentional learning. The four types of sources included here —home, work, friends, the mass media—are largely intuitive.

In the Home

Few people live entirely solitary existences. Almost everyone has a "home" of some kind where one or more others live. Children for the most part are raised in homes, with a mother present much of the time, and father and siblings part of the time. About the only period away from relatives is between the time of leaving home around age eighteen (as to go to college) and the time of getting married or entering into some sort of relationship with one or more others. Marriage frequently leads to children. Later, often, grandparents or other relatives are added to the home. The so-called "nuclear family"—two parents and their children—is still the most common pattern, although increasingly there are variations. Most individuals live most of their lives in families of some sort.

Without necessarily trying to, family members learn from each other. Each one, with his or her unique set of interests, is a unique source of learning. Parents and older siblings become models for behavior. Children get help from parents in doing homework and in learning skills, for example, playing musical instruments; they learn recent history from grandparents. Parents learn from their children—about the schools, the community, and the directions of cultural change. All learn something, unintentionally, from each other's "learning projects" as well as from everyday conversation.

Could the nature and functioning of the family be influenced by public policy? Can incentives for fathers to spend more time with their kids, for example, be contrived? Would government incentives to establish and maintain "good" families be desirable? The family is usually the crucible in which attitudes and values of a lifetime are forged. The family is probably the key agent in developing autonomous lifetime learners. It certainly has the potential for being such an agent. One suspects that without a proliferation of "learning families," the "learning society" is far away.

What are the prospects for the American family as a vehicle for continuing learning? Seemingly not good, at least as indicated by most trends. The American divorce rate is at an all-time high; fathers spend little time with their children; an average of 6.5 hours per day is spent watching television; and the litany goes on. Yet there is an emerging concern for the renewal of the family prompted by President Carter and others. There is to be a White

House Conference on the Family in late 1979 (with talk of pref-
atory state conferences). Foundations and government agencies
are increasingly giving grants to universities for studies of the family and of public policy alternatives for strengthening families.

Work

On the order of three quarters of the nation's adult population have regular, paid jobs. Many youths work part time. For
most adults, nearly half of all waking hours are spent at a workplace. Employed youths may spend ten to twenty hours per week
at a job. Added up over a span of years, the impact of one's work
experience on one's intellect and personality can conceivably be
very substantial.

This is not the place for a commentary on education and
work. Possible policy options, such as combining working and
learning, or alternating them (in the manner of the European
"recurrent education"), have been very widely analyzed in books
and conferences in the past three to four years. Education and
work are treated extensively in reports from the HEW Lifelong
Learning Project (for example, Comstock, 1978; Levine and Fried,
1978; and MacKenzie, 1978).

We wish to make only one rather simple point: Because individuals spend so much of their lives on a job, the workplace is
inescapably a critically important source for unintentional learning. Two major subsources for unintentional learning at work
come to mind:

• Unintentional learning *from work assignments*. Without trying to,
  one may acquire new knowledge, skills, and feelings about oneself simply through undertaking different activities on the job:
  The secretary does editorial work; the engineer, cost accounting;
  the teacher, some administration; and so forth.
• Unintentional learning *from work associates*. People typically work
  closely with a rather small number of associates. Some people
  may spend more time with such coworkers in a lifetime than with
  anyone else, including a spouse. Workers also may spend one to
  two hours a day commuting with others. All of these work-

related people become important learning sources, mainly because of the great amount of time spent together. From each other, coworkers take on interests and beliefs, acquire ways of thinking about things, and come to share values about what is important and right.

Our interest here is whether work settings—involving the interrelated factors of (1) the nature and variety of the substantive work and (2) the character of relations among coworkers—can be arranged so that constructive learning, albeit unintentional, is increased. Can employers, unions and employee groups, and government agencies devise ways to make work more interesting, more stimulating? Surely the learning society will not be realized so long as there are masses of people whose workdays are characterized by a mindless sameness.

From Friends

Friends are a third important source of unintentional learning for people of all ages. As with the family and work, the more time one spends with friends, the more important they become as a learning source. Children begin forming close friendships at a young age—perhaps around five or six. Friends remain significant up until the time of marriage or entry into some other "family" relationship, when their importance may decline somewhat. Later in life friends seem to take on a renewed importance. Especially as people are divorced, the significance of, the reliance on, friends increases. With the death of a spouse, friends become even more important.

People generally (not always, certainly) prefer to do things with one or more others rather than by themselves. Experiences tend to take on more meaning when they are shared and then reflected upon. From shared experiences with respected friends, one can sharpen skills, gain insights, and improve understandings. What is the significance of all this for lifelong learning policy? Possibly none at all. One would need to think of the kinds of things friends can do together that, through mutual interaction, can lead to intellectual or personal growth for all involved. Many such activities would occur under the egis of community organizations. Thus, community organizations—Y's, museums, churches, and so on—need to have resources for programs designed to encourage friendships and shared experience.

From the Mass Media

When one thinks of the mass media, one generally thinks of television, radio, newspapers, and the mass circulation magazines. We have already remarked about the role of the various media as (individually used) sources for deliberate learning. Some—public TV and radio and the specialized magazines—were held to be valuable. Others, commercial TV and radio in particular, were viewed as only rarely contributing to serious learning and more often constituting a major distraction from learning activities. The major goal of commercial television and radio, other than maximizing earnings, of course, is to entertain (not to instruct). Nonetheless, these media do have a powerful impact on the personality and behavior of a great many people.

What, then, can be said about the role of the media—especially commercial TV and radio, since they are the most pervasive—as sources for unintentional learning? Our judgment, to no reader's surprise, is largely negative. What we suspect is unwittingly learned from commercial TV and radio, particularly by the young, is by and large counterproductive from the perspective of lifelong learning. Commercial TV and radio, it has been argued, engender neglect of necessary communication skills, counter-intellectual values (consumption, thrills), psychological passivity, and insensitivity to violence and other antihuman actions. The list could be extended.

Commercial television is one of the most broadly influential cultural agents we have. For teenagers, radio runs closely behind. These two media are immensely powerful, which is why it is so disheartening that they are not in the service of more estimable goals. Is it conceivable that this great cultural force could ever be redirected? Can concerned people work with the networks to gradually bring about greater programming responsibility, as some establishment reformers have counseled? (At least three organizations are making headway with TV programming for young people: PTA Television Action Center in Chicago, Action for Children's Television in Newtonville, Mass., and Prime Time School Television in Chicago.) Could congressional action be expected to have any impact? Can the viewing public be expected to ever demand different programming? While these eventualities appear unlikely, any efforts along such lines seem worthwhile. The stakes—no less than the quality of the culture—are high. The great networks, instead of so effectively serving an acquisitive society, have the potential for contributing just as effectively to building and supporting a learning society.

Trends Toward Lifelong Learning

There is a rich diversity of resources for learning in this country. The purpose of this chapter has been to afford planners and policy makers a glimpse of the whole—a view of the broad gamut of organizations and instruments through which Americans can study and learn. The chapter should give high-level planners better familiarity with the nature and scope of all the existing "pieces" that could conceivably be enlisted in cooperative learning enterprises, and it should give program administrators a better understanding, perhaps appreciation, of educational ventures other than their own. It can also furnish leads to further information about particular programs of interest to planners at all levels.

The SEL framework itself may have certain analytic uses. It could be used, for example, as a framework for surveying learning resources in a given locality. The general question would be: What is the nature and extent in X city or Y region of opportunities in each of the SEL categories? Somewhat more sophisticated needs analyses could be performed by combining the SEL typology with other factors of interest in two-way matrices. With subject-matter content, for example, as the factor on the second axis in such a matrix, the general question would be: Which subjects can be studied through which sources in X city? Type of delivery system, clientele types served, admission (access) policy, teaching or learning methods, and cost are examples of additional factors that could similarly be combined with the SEL typology for particular analytic purposes.

It is interesting to speculate about trends in future use of the various sources. We will suggest only a few possible directions; the topic could be the subject for an entire volume.

The population of children and youth will be diminishing during at least the next ten years or so. The familiar instruments for youth education, from the preschools through undergraduate colleges, will perforce be contracting. (The preschools will probably be an exception, as more and more new mothers join the work force.) Many of these schools, however, are also able to serve adults, and they will be doing so with vigor—as if their lives depended on it. A minor countervailing factor may lie in the basic skills and competency movements in the schools, which could reduce future enrollments somewhat in public adult schools (their Adult Basic Education programs).

The military, to maintain its present strength, will find it necessary to recruit one third of (the reduced pool of) eighteen-year-old men by 1984 rather than the current one fourth. This will somewhat affect enrollments at community colleges, proprietary schools, and some state colleges, although many of these institutions, especially those located near military bases, will themselves be drawn into the education-military complex (described earlier in this chapter.)

For the "middle" generation, one trend that seems clear is that many kinds of professionals will be required, commonly by state law, to continuously upgrade their professional competence. A number of both school and nonschool sources can be expected to compete for this clientele—including university professional schools, college and university (public and private) continuing education divisions, proprietary schools, employers, and professional associations.

As the occupational structure continues to change, in good part the result of technological innovation, new kinds of jobs and skill specialities will continue to be required. As women prepare to join or rejoin the work force, many will desire job training or upgrading. Most providers of occupational training seem likely to prosper—the occupational programs of community colleges and state colleges, technical institutes, proprietary schools, industry-based training activities, and the federal manpower development programs. And agencies that assist individuals in making career changes should have no shortage of clients.

Other possible currents are harder to be certain about. For the past several years now, particularly among the educated, affluent, and leisure classes, there has been an expanding concern with "personal development" and realization of one's "full human potential." This concern could be acted on by taking adult education and extension courses in the arts, humanities, and personal psychology. Related, though prevailing more widely throughout the society, is a growing desire to actively pursue recreational and avocational interests. To the extent leisure time increases (the workweek shortens) and more people have more disposable income, it seems likely that various recreation-related learning activities, including travel, will expand. A great many sources are prepared to serve—to offer courses, for example—to people seeking either personal improvement or new ways to spend leisure time. Even in a post Proposition 13 environment, there will be a range of schools and nonschool organizations—for example, community agencies, the churches, city recreation departments, the free universities—ready to accommodate the possible expansion of these learning interests.

To this writer's knowledge, there are no data on trends in the extent of independent learning. It is difficult to predict future use of the individually used sources. Greater leisure time would provide a positive incentive. Wider availability of organized learning programs might be a disincentive. It does seem evident that the various sources or means for independent learning are increasingly available. A host of new library services for independent learners are being implemented. Books and magazines for self-learners are improving in quantity and quality. Electronic matériel could be critical: audio tapes are increasingly available on a variety of topics, and recorders are relatively inexpensive; video tapes and the associated production and playback equipment have just become generally available, though at high cost. Video disks will probably soon follow.

One suspects that certain sorts of people rely on independent learning much more than others. Perhaps by disposition they
are somewhat averse to organized learning. Some would probably
be closely associated with high technology, such as medical specialists or computer specialists. Another example, associated with
low technology, are the "new ruralists" and other advocates of
"voluntary simplicity" (whose do-it-yourself learning has been suc-
cored in particular by print materials such as the *Whole Earth Catalog* and more recently *The CoEvolution Quarterly*). College professors would be another class of people who, a bit disinclined toward
organized learning for themselves, engage heavily in independent
learning. It is hard to know whether or not subcultures relying on
independent learning will increase in number and size. Three of
the four examples just mentioned probably will.

For the older generation (we have mentioned the youth and
middle generations), many learning-related trends are already well
underway. Past demographic and present medical realities make
for an older population, which for several decades will be expanding more rapidly than the other two generations. Long overlooked
by major social institutions, except for churches and hospitals,
older people will increasingly have their needs attended to through
public policy, if for no other reason than because of their new vot-
ing strength.

Community agencies, including churches, usually operating
with volunteers and shoestring budgets, have long provided modest learning opportunities for the older generation. Schools and
colleges felt no obligation. That is now changed, largely the result
of enrollment and fiscal realities at many colleges. From now on
older adults will be welcomed at almost every college (except perhaps for the traditionally most selective ones). This "graying of the
campus" is surely one of the most notable developments on the
recent higher education scene. Nonschool organizations, such as
certain community organizations, churches, and city recreation
departments, may be harder pressed to retain enrollees in their
educational programs.

What about possible trends in sources of *unintentional* learning? As an agent of unintentional learning, the family is probably
ebbing in significance, with parents—notably working mothers—

spending less time at home with their children. Furthermore, the time parents and children might spend learning from each other is cut into greatly by radio and TV.

As for work, while there is a sprinkling of recent experiments on improving the "quality of work," there are few signs of widespread concern about making employees' work lives more interesting or stimulating. Unfortunately, we can foresee little or no change in work as a source of constructive unintentional learning in the near future.

Friends and acquaintances, however, *will*, we think, take on greater importance as a learning source. This will happen as youth-parent ties weaken, as increasing numbers of middle-generation adults lead essentially single lives—the result of divorce or separation or of never having taken a mate in the first place—and, among the older generation, as spouses die.

The mass media, of course, are not monolithic. In the context of unintentional learning, however, our concern is chiefly with commercial radio and television. During 1977, for the first time in television history, the national TV audience declined (*Time*, January 9, 1978). Perhaps this finding will nudge the industry toward a reappraisal. The population, after all, is less youthful than it has been; it is increasingly better educated; possibly it will be demanding more literate fare. However, whether there will be any change in the mass media is an enormously important question mark.

The trends in use of the various learning sources, which on balance point to greater overall participation, make it tempting to conclude that something akin to a learning society already exists in the United States. While it of course depends on our definition of *learning society,* there is ample reason for doubting that we are soon to become a nation of lifelong learners. When one looks at the society's values as portrayed, for example, in the commercial media, it is evident that the society in general accords rather little value to serious, continuing learning. When one looks at the condition of many families and most workplaces, one sees few signs that these major elements in people's lives will soon become more supportive of continuous learning.

When one looks at participation across all the sources of

education and learning that were described, one sees a clear pattern of class bias. The already well-off disproportionately use almost all the learning opportunities available, as Cross shows further in the next chapter. Although many programs and projects have sought solutions, this fundamental problem of equity nonetheless remains.

When one looks at the "system" of schools and colleges in the country, one finds it to be mostly a nonsystem. Each part goes its own way, marching to its own drummer (funding source). Except in rare instances, there is not much communication between staff of different programs at one level, even less across levels of institutions (between secondary and postsecondary schools, for example), and less still between schools and all the nonschool organizations that provide educational services. With so fragmented an education "system," it is difficult to see how a population of lifelong learners can be served with any measure of efficiency.

This last state of affairs is the one most readers of this volume may be best able to address. Much can be done if planners and other officials can lay aside vested interests and consider how to utilize all the available school and nonschool resources to facilitate learning for all individuals from childhood to old age. Such comprehensive planning is almost unheard of in the United States; maybe it is the only way to resolve the problem of unequal participation by social class. Is it impossible, given jurisdictional and political realities?

Some measure of reform of the nation's educational apparatus so that it can better facilitate lifelong learning is an important aim. But by itself that may not be enough. Renewal of other social institutions that can support continuous, constructive learning— the family, workplaces, the mass media—is equally important. How this can be done is problematic, but as we said earlier, any efforts would be worthwhile. The prospect is a nation of lifelong learners.

CHAPTER TWO

Adult Learners: Characteristics, Needs, and Interests

K. Patricia Cross

Adult learners constitute the most rapidly growing segment of American education. Not only are adults going back to school in ever larger numbers, they are also designing independent learning projects and participating in learning activities sponsored by non-school organizations. Adult learning is a social phenomenon of substantial proportions, requiring coordination and planning of learning resources.

Within the past ten years, more than thirty large-scale sur-

Note: A prior grant from the National Institute of Education to the Center for Research and Development in Higher Education at the University of California, Berkeley, Contract Number 400–76–0107, provided support for some of the work underlying this report.

veys have been made of the preferences and characteristics of adult learners. (See the source list at the end of this chapter.) Most of the studies have been conducted by agencies concerned with educational planning. Interest in adults as a significant market for educational services has been fueled by the knowledge that the low birth rate of recent years promises a reduction in the number of people aged eighteen to twenty-four years old and an increase in the number of older people in the society.

While the surveys, frequently referred to as *needs assessments,* have concentrated on the particular interests of a given locale or state, there is considerable similarity across them. Thus, it is possible to produce a synthesis from them of what we know and do not know about adults who have been engaged in learning activities or who say they would like to continue their learning.

The description of adult learners in this chapter adopts the definition of adult learners used by the National Center for Education Statistics (NCES) and assumed by most of the data-based studies—namely, "persons seventeen or older, not enrolled full-time in high school or college, but engaged in one or more activities of organized instruction."[1]

This definition has the advantage of conforming rather nicely to the common perception of what is meant by adult learners and adult learning activities, but the reader should be aware that definitions limited to "organized" learning activities result in quite conservative statistics. Were we to expand the definition to encompass self-planned or self-directed learning, which has been the subject of several very interesting research studies (Tough, 1971; Penland, 1977), we would include from 79 to 98 percent of the adult population as lifelong learners.

The term *adult learner,* in its broadest sense, applies to almost all of us. The data-based description provided in this chapter rep-

---

[1]Organized instruction, according to NCES, 1972, p.2, includes "correspondence courses and private tutoring; usually at a set time and place; ordinarily under the auspices of a school, college, church, neighborhood center, community organization, or other recognized authority; and generally with a predetermined end result which may or may not be a certificate, diploma, or degree." Sunday school classes, Bible classes, and other activities that could be considered worship service were excluded.

resents only the tip of the iceberg. For every adult participating in organized instruction there are probably nine more who should legitimately be called adult learners. Depending, then, on how learners are defined, estimates of the adult learning force range from the conservative 11.6 percent of the adult population reported in the NCES 1975 preliminary data to the 98 percent found by Tough. Most of this vast difference is attributable to differences between the definitions of *learning* used by NCES (organized instruction) and Tough (deliberate efforts to learn), but there are also methodological differences—the voluntary survey of NCES versus the probing interviews of Tough.

Because the triennial NCES surveys are the most complete available with respect to biographical characteristics of adult learners, the first section of this chapter will rely heavily on them to describe trends and demographic characteristics of learners. Within the last decade, however, college and state planning agencies have collected not only biographical data on adult learners but also data regarding the interests of potential learners and the barriers to their continued learning. The second section of the chapter will concentrate on the needs and interests of adult learners and potential learners gleaned from these needs assessments. The third section of the chapter will then offer some observations about the state of the art in assessing adult learning needs.

Learners: Characteristics and Trends

In 1975 more than seventeen million adults participated in some form of organized learning activity—a figure that is nearly double the number of college students enrolled for degree credit.[2] During the six-year period between 1969 and 1975, the number

[2]Figures in this section are from the NCES triennial surveys for 1969, 1972, and 1975, unless otherwise indicated. It should be kept in mind that these figures represent only participants in "organized instruction." Furthermore, the figures are likely to be an underestimate, since people are more likely to forget to report short courses and the like than to invent them.

of adults participating in organized learning activities increased 30.8 percent, a rate more than double the 12.6 percent increase of their numbers in the total population.

While less than half of the rapid growth of adult education can be accounted for by the demographics of the birth rate, shifting demographics are having a profound effect upon postsecondary education. The post–World War II population bulge is moving into the adult years. People born in 1957, at the peak of the birth rate, are now twenty-one years old, and those born at the beginning of the baby boom are almost thirty. During the present decade, 1970–1980, the number of people aged twenty-five to thirty-four will increase a whopping 44 percent, compared with a modest 8 percent rate of growth for those eighteen to twenty-four. There is every indication that adult participation in organized learning activities will continue to grow faster than the growth rate of the adult population.

A complex interweaving of factors has contributed to the growth of adult education. The shifting of the median age of the population has a noticeable impact on education, just as it has on consumer markets. Then, too, the continuing concern of the nation for equal opportunity has identified age as a discriminatory barrier to educational opportunity, and that barrier is now being challenged along with other discriminatory practices in education. Furthermore, the marketplace continues to require new knowledge and skills, and new job opportunities for women and ethnic minorities have sharply escalated the need for occupational and professional training. Finally, the rising educational level of the populace creates further demand for more sophisticated educational offerings. In short, there are many pressures for increased interest in a concept variously known as nontraditional education, lifelong learning, or adult and continuing education.

Since almost two thirds of the adults in the United States seventeen years of age and older are now high school graduates, the demand for adult education has focused mainly on postsecondary levels of education. This does not mean, however, that the majority of adults are interested in college degrees or even that traditional institutions of postsecondary education will provide the bulk of educational programs for adult learners. Rather, it means that the majority of adults in the United States have completed what is generally regarded as the basic "core" of school learning and, while eligible for postsecondary education, are free to select a varied educational diet consisting of occupational and professional education, education for personal development and family living, social and recreational learning, and so on. Table 1 shows the variety of sponsors of "organized instruction" for adults.

The percentage figures in Table 1 show quite clearly that no sponsor has a corner on the adult learner market. Indeed, the five leading sponsors of adult education were within ten percentage points of one another in 1975, each serving between 10 and 20 percent of the market. Community colleges and vocational-technical institutes, however, are growing very rapidly; they showed a 65 percent growth in adult learners from 1969 to 1972 and an 18 percent increase between 1972 and 1975. Trends clearly discernable from the figures in Table 1 are decreases in the proportion of adults taking part in activities sponsored by public grade and high schools and a decrease in employer-sponsored education. It may be that the commuting locations and low cost of community

**Table 1. Participation in Learning Activities
Provided by Various Sponsors (in percentages)**

	1969	1972	1975
Public grade school or high school	15.1	14.0	10.6
Two-year college or vocational-technical institute	11.9	16.3	17.7
Private trade or business school	11.5	8.9	3.7
Four-year college or university	21.7	21.4	19.1
Employer	17.4	16.6	15.3
Community organization	11.9	12.7	10.5
Labor organization or professional association		5.5	6.1
Private tutor		6.0	6.9
Hospital	.3	.4	
Other	19.3	9.4	7.7
Not reported	.4	.6	.4

Note: Because of multiple activities, percentages will total more than 100.
Source: NCES data for 1969, 1972, 1975. (See full references in the chapter source list.)

colleges have attracted some adults who might otherwise go to public adult schools, while the vocational programs of community colleges have relieved some industries of providing occupational and technical training. Despite the fact that 89 percent of the adults who are currently participating in organized learning activities are high school graduates, two- and four-year colleges and universities are providing only about 37 percent of the educational services for adults. At the same time, it should be noted that colleges and universities are the leading providers of adult education. Indeed, the number of colleges and universities offering adult and continuing education has more than doubled in recent years, increasing from 1,102 institutions in 1967–68 to 2,225 in 1975–76, with an increase in learner registrations from about 5.6 million to 8.8 million (Kemp, 1978). With this brief overview of participation rates and trends, we can turn now to the characteristics of adult learners.

One way to describe adult learners is to simply take the largest frequencies in each category of the 1975 NCES data and construct a modal profile of the characteristics of participants. (The picture that emerges is, of course, dependent upon the particular categories used by NCES.) Such a profile would show the following about adult learners in 1975. Most were white high school graduates, between twenty-five and thirty-four years of age, employed more than thirty-five hours per week, with annual family incomes of $15,000 to $25,000. Female participants were slightly more numerous than male participants. Most participants were taking job-related courses to improve or advance their status in their current jobs. The courses they took were sponsored by two- or four-year colleges and taught in standard classroom format, meeting in school buildings and on college campuses. Learners paid for their courses from their own or family funds, and, while most found that the courses met or exceeded their expectations, the single most common reason given for dropping a course was that it was disappointing or too demanding.

There is nothing at all surprising about this profile of participants in adult learning. It shows that the great bulk of participants come from the great bulk of the American public. There is another way of looking at the national statistics, however, that shows quite clearly that certain groups within the society reap more than their proportionate share of adult education benefits. The profile of those who are disproportionately represented in educational activities, in comparison with their representation in the population, looks a little less like the average American and a little more like a member of the advantaged classes. Those taking the greatest advantage of educational offerings are relatively young, white, well educated, employed in professional and technical occupations, and making good incomes.

Table 2 shows the educational participation rates of various categories of adults over the age of seventeen who were not full-time students in 1975. According to NCES data, 11.6 percent of the adults in the United States were engaged in some form of organized instruction during the year. In order to highlight the underrepresentation of certain segments of the population, groups with a participation rate of 11 percent or lower have been underlined in Table 2.

The message is quite clear that adult education is serving the advantaged classes out of proportion to their numbers in the population. The underlined categories in Table 2 reveal that blacks, the elderly, and those with part-time jobs, low incomes, and low educational attainment are not well served by adult education, as far as access is concerned. Table 2 also shows some interesting regional and population density variations in the accessibility of education, which will be discussed more fully later.

There has been a good deal of discussion and concern about the middle-class bias of adult education. Up to the present time, participation in adult learning activities has been largely voluntary and largely learner financed. This means that well-prepared, highly motivated adults who have access to information about education and who have the wherewithal to support their learning activities are the primary participants. This description of adult learners as an advantaged group—a conclusion supported by almost all of the data—explains the reluctance of some to put more government funding into adult education. In a reanalysis of the 1972 NCES data, however, Froomkin and Wolfson (1977) make the point that the lower classes do get their proportionate share of adult education funds, since groups with the lowest rates of participation are

Table 2. Participation Rates in Organized Instruction in 1975

	Participation Rate[a] (percentages)
Age	
17–24	11.5
25–34	20.6
35–44	15.0
45–54	10.5
55–64	5.8
65 and older	2.3
Race	
Black	6.9
White	12.1
Other[b]	13.4
Sex	
Male	11.7
Female	11.6
Educational Attainment	
Elementary (0–8 years)	2.0
High school (1–3 years)	4.6
High school (4 years)	11.9
College (1–3 years)	17.6
College (4 years)	27.0
College (5 or more years)	30.4
Income (Dollars per Year)	
Under 3000	4.4
3000–4999	5.5
5000–5999	7.5
6000–7499	9.1
7500–9999	11.5
10,000–14,999	12.9
15,000–24,999	15.8
25,000 and over	17.7
Hours Worked May 11–17, 1975	
Less than 10	7.2
10–14	8.6
15–34	11.6
35 or more	15.3
Region	
Northeast	10.0
North Central	11.2
South	10.4
West	16.6

Table 2. Participation Rates in Organized Instruction in 1975
(Continued)

	Participation Rate[a] (percentages)
Metropolitan Status	
In SMSA[c]	12.7
Central city	11.0
Outside central city	14.0
Not SMSA	9.4
Nonfarm	9.8
Farm	6.7

[a] Participation rate is computed from a total population base of the numbers of each category in the population. In 1975 the overall participation rate was 11.6 percent. Groups with an 11 percent participation rate or less are underlined.
[b] The Census Bureau classified Hispanics as either black or white.
[c] Standard Metropolitan Statistical Area (SMSA) is a complex category of population density used in Census Bureau analyses.
Source: Compiled from preliminary data, NCES, 1975.

likely to spend more hours at their educational activities. Thus, the rich enroll more often for courses of shorter duration, whereas the poor enroll less often but for more hours per enrollment. This finding, according to Froomkin and Wolfson, indicates that "compared to the performance of the conventional full-time higher education sector, adult education is certainly more egalitarian" (p. 12). Perhaps from the point of view of government funding, the poor get their proportionate (if not fair) share of the money. Nevertheless, it would still appear that from the learners' point of view, people from the lower classes are numerically underrepresented in organized learning activities; that is, proportionately fewer of them are served. In any event, there is widespread agreement that special efforts should be made to attract the less advantaged classes into learning activities. It may be useful, then, to provide a description of the characteristics of groups that are currently underrepresented in adult education.

Age

Participation and interest in organized educational activities are clear functions of age. Interest, as well as participation, starts to decline in the early thirties and drops sharply after age fifty-five. The study sponsored by the Commission on Non-Traditional Study (CNS) (1974) showed a drop in interest from 74 percent for learners in the thirty-five to fifty-four age bracket to 58 percent for those fifty-five and older.[3] The NCES data on actual participation rates showed a drop from 12.5 to 3.5 percent for the same two contiguous age groups.

Age is an especially interesting characteristic because it reveals so clearly certain socialized perceptions about the role of education in various life stages. Younger people tend to be pursuing credentials and laying the groundwork for later career specialization; those in the age ranges of twenty-five to forty-four are concentrating largely on occupational and professional training for career advancement; and those fifty and older are beginning to prepare for the use of leisure time. Sadly, the data also reveal the socialized perception that learning is for young people. The feeling of being too old to learn increases steadily with age until it becomes a common barrier to education for older people. In most state studies, the proportion of people fifty-five and older who state that their age is a deterrent to learning runs around 15 to 25 percent. The proportion is likely to rise, however, when the motivation for continued education is low for other reasons. In Iowa (1976), for example, where the interest in adult education is generally quite low, a majority (59 percent) of those over sixty-four said they were too old to "go back to school." Similarly, the age factor is more likely to be perceived as a barrier by those who have never participated in continuing education than by those who have (New York, 1977).

Although we have made observations about age as though it operated independently, the fact is that, because of expanding educational opportunity in this country, young people as a group have considerably higher levels of educational attainment than older people. The Maine study found a correlation of $-.23$ between age and educational attainment. Census figures in Maine for 1969 showed that 60 percent of those sixty years of age or over

---

[3]References to surveys will generally be made by sponsor, state, or region in the body of the text. Complete citations may be found in the chapter source list.

had not completed high school, compared with only 24 percent of people between twenty and twenty-nine. The interactions of age and level of educational attainment are among the strongest predictors of adult educational activities and interest. Whereas a younger person with some graduate work is very likely to pursue more education, the likelihood of an older person with less than an eighth grade education expressing an interest in further learning is almost nil.

Lack of mobility also presents a barrier to education for many older people. About one fourth of Kansas adults over sixty could not easily get out of the house once a week, and roughly three fourths of the retirees in the New York survey said they would not travel more than five miles or spend more than thirty minutes in travel to class. It is not surprising to find the elderly overrepresented in most forms of "lonely learning." They tend to learn via TV, radio, and tutors more often than people in other age groups. Yet almost half of those over sixty in the California study said that a primary motivation for their participation in learning programs was to meet new people.

Tutors are more popular with older learners than with any other age group. While those fifty-five and older make up 8.7 percent of the participants in adult education, they constitute 12.1 percent of those learning from private lessons (NCES, 1972). California data showed that one out of five citizens over sixty said that private lessons would be a good way for them to learn; that was the largest proportion of any group interested in the use of private tutors. But private tutors ordinarily cost money, and, when considered in the light of the declining purchasing power of the elderly, the extensive use of tutors would not appear to promise the solution to the mobility problems of the elderly.

Of all groups of learners, the elderly stand out for their intrinsic motivations for learning. They are not interested in degrees or certificates; they are learning because it is enjoyable and personally satisfying. Their major subject matter interests are hobbies and crafts, nutrition and health, and other topics that have practical relevance for their lives.

In recent years there has been an earnest effort on the part of public education institutions to serve older citizens. A recent survey of educational programs for adults fifty-five and older (Atelsek and Gomberg, 1977) showed that over half of the public two-year colleges and public universities surveyed offer instructional programs specifically designed for older adults—courses geared toward a second career, preretirement courses, self-improvement or leisure time courses, short-term residential courses. Community service programs for older adults (special tuition plans, library privileges, recreational programs, and the like) were also common in public institutions, with 70 percent of the public community colleges and 61 percent of the public universities providing some form of service programs. Almost half of the institutions reporting special programs and services are planning to increase the scope of their efforts, whereas only 19 percent of those without such programs are planning to institute them.

In summary, the elderly are among the most underrepresented of all subgroups in adult educational activities. More than for other groups, the major barriers to group participation of the elderly are motivational, in the sense that many contend that they are too old, lack energy, or are not interested in further education. Location is also a serious problem for the elderly, and, although a major motivation for learning is to meet and be with other people, elderly learners are overrepresented in most forms of "lonely learning," presumably because of their transportation difficulties.

Ethnic Minorities

Despite the concern in recent years about educational opportunity for ethnic minorities, information on educational participation and preferences of minority groups is not very complete. The most comprehensive data about race as a variable in adult education appear in the triennial surveys of NCES, but even there categories are limited to black, white, and other. ("Other" includes American Indian and Oriental but not Puerto Rican, Mexican American, and other Spanish-speaking groups, which are classified by the Census Bureau as either black or white.) The common practice in most state studies is to collect data about many ethnic groups but to analyze not more than three categories. The categories in the Colorado study, for example, are white, Spanish American, and other; in the California study, white and Spanish surname;

and in the national Commission on Non-Traditional Study, black and white.

The best, albeit limited, data base on ethnic minorities appears in the NCES data. Therefore we shall use it as the foundation for this analysis, presenting data from other studies when appropriate to confirm, dispute, or elaborate. Since educational needs are known to differ greatly among ethnic groups, analysis based on collections of miscellaneous "others" seems fruitless; hence discussion will be limited to differences between blacks and whites, and where material is available from state studies, Hispanics.

The differences in the participation rates of white and black adults in part-time learning activities are dramatic. According to NCES data, blacks were underrepresented among adult learners in 1969 (7.7 percent to 10.2 percent for whites), and their position has deteriorated over the six years covered by the Triennial Surveys (6.9 percent for blacks to 12.1 percent for whites in 1975). Between 1969 and 1975 the participation rate for whites increased almost three times as fast as their numbers in the population (a 32 percent increase in participation compared to an 11 percent increase in population). For blacks, however, participation did not even keep pace with their expanding numbers in the population (a 5 percent increase in participation but an 18 percent increase in population). There is some evidence, however, that full-time study has increased substantially for blacks. Financial aid may have enabled some blacks to shift from part-time to full-time study.

Nevertheless, concerns about the alleged white, middle-class bias of adult education still seem justified. The bias, however, appears to be more a class than a color bias. If educational attainment is equated, the participation rates for whites and nonwhites are roughly equal, especially at the extremes of the educational attainment scale. Froomkin and Wolfson (1977) show that the participation rate in adult education is the same for whites and nonwhites: 4.1 percent. Likewise, for college graduates, participation rates are similar: 30.5 percent for whites and 29.7 percent for nonwhites.

Other data from the NCES tabulations reveal substantial socioeconomic differences between black and white adult learners in 1975. Black participants have lower levels of educational attainment (53 percent of whites and 39 percent of blacks have had at least some college), earn lower incomes (24 percent of whites and 44 percent of blacks have annual incomes under $10,000), are more likely to be unemployed (4 percent of whites, 10 percent of blacks), and are much more likely to live in the central city (25 percent of whites versus 60 percent of blacks). Clearly, black adult learners are disadvantaged relative to white learners. Remember, however, that both black and white learners are advantaged relative to their counterparts in the general population who are not engaged in learning activities. For example, while 44 percent of the black learning participants have incomes under $10,000, 67 percent of the black nonparticipants do. And while 21 percent of the black participants have not graduated from high school, 58 percent of the black nonparticipants are not high school graduates.

It is well established by this time that socioeconomic indicators are strongly related to participation in educational activities. Low educational attainment, low job status, and low income have a great deal more relationship to low educational participation than race per se. Thus, the needs and interests of nonwhites are generally not very distinguishable from the needs and interests of groups with low educational attainment and low income.

As Table 3 shows, nonwhites are more likely to earn certificates for their learning than are whites, who are more likely to participate in noncredit learning. Would-be learners express interests in the same direction. The California data show Mexican Americans especially interested in certificates of learning completion that could be used for job advancement (29 percent for Mexican Americans compared with 9 percent and 7 percent for whites and blacks, respectively). The desire for credit or certification on the part of ethnic minorities is consistent with their striving for upward mobility through education. The New York study reported that approximately 73 percent of the blacks and Hispanics took courses for job-related reasons, compared with 58 percent for the total sample. The proportions of Asian Americans (64 percent) and Native Americans (69 percent) pursuing learning primarily for upward job mobility were also larger than for the total sample.

Certain assumptions frequently made regarding provision of learning opportunities for ethnic minorities are hard to verify

Table 3. Type of Educational Credit
Earned by Race, 1972
(Percentage of Participants)

	Race		
Type of Credit	Nonwhite	White	Average
No credit	44.1	55.6	54.7
Eighth grade credit	.3	.1	.1
High school certification	8.6	3.3	3.7
Skill certification or license	23.1	15.7	16.2
Two- or four-year college degree	11.9	13.2	13.1
Postgraduate or professional degree	9.3	8.8	8.8
Other	2.8	3.4	3.4
Total	100.0	100.0	100.0

Source: Froomkin and Wolfson (1977).

in the data available. It is commonly thought, for example, that because ethnic minorities make lower incomes than whites, the cost of education might constitute a barrier. While cost is cited more frequently by blacks and Hispanics than by whites in New York, the differences are not very significant in California. Cost data are hard to interpret because they are confounded with age, sources of reimbursement, type of education desired, and so on. Blacks are almost twice as likely as whites to report public funding for their educational activities, and this is especially true for black women, one third of whom received public funds for their educational activities in 1975 (NCES).

Another common assumption is that nontraditional forms of education are not very attractive to ethnic minorities. However, it depends on what kind of nontraditional education is under discussion. General patterns of participation indicate that ethnic minorities are especially concerned about the credibility of the education. They seem to steer clear of unfamiliar innovations, but on-the-job training, which would have high credibility with employers, is a highly acceptable form of nontraditional learning, especially for Mexican Americans (California). Nevertheless, over half of the black learners surveyed in the 1975 NCES poll attended their classes in school and college buildings, and over 70 percent were doing their learning in traditional class formats presided over by classroom teachers (compared with 56 percent for white males and 65 percent for white females).

A distinctive problem for black males is completion of courses. Whereas 74 percent of whites and 62 percent of black women report completing their courses, only 48 percent of the black men do. It is not so much a matter of dropping courses as of reporting courses still in progress (46 percent for black men, as opposed to 29 percent for black women and 25 percent for white men and women). When black men do drop courses (about 9 percent do), their reasons, more than those of whites, seem to be related to job and family. Financial problems, care of family members, and job changes are more likely to plague blacks than whites (NCES, 1975).

Sex

Nationally, the rate of participation in organized learning activities is about the same for women as for men: 11.6 percent for women and 11.7 percent for men (NCES, 1975). The CNS study (1974) reported essentially the same result in a different form: 49 percent of the adult learners are men and 51 percent are women.

Data from state studies, however, seem to vary on the question of sex differences in educational participation. Central New York, Northeastern New York, and Iowa found substantially more interest and participation on the part of women than men; Western New York and Kansas found no difference; and Massachusetts and California found men slightly more active and interested than women. The variation may reflect methodological differences among studies as well as possible regional differences, which would warrant further study. State funding practices for adult education, for example, could have considerable impact on the relative participation rates of men and women. If adult education programs in the public schools were emphasized, more women than men would be expected to participate. If vocational and technical education were plentiful and well funded, the balance would tip in favor of men.

Trend data from the NCES triennial surveys show that women are catching up with and, at some age levels, overtaking men in educational participation. Whereas participation rates for men have remained quite steady over the past six years, the rates for women have steadily increased. The rate of increase for women was 45 percent between 1969 and 1975, compared with an increase of 18 percent for men. Table 4 shows the proportion of men and women of three age groups who reported participation in educational activities in the triennial surveys.

Younger women (age seventeen to thirty-four) have closed the rather substantial gap that existed between men and women in 1969; middle-aged women have come from behind to surpass men in 1975; and older women (fifty-five and older) have retained their lead.

White women, however, seem to account for the increase over the six years, moving from a 9 percent participation rate in 1969 to 11 percent in 1972 and 12 percent in 1975. Black women have shown a modest decrease, moving from 8.7 to 8.6 to 7.6 percent participation rates in the three surveys. The decrease is especially evident for black women in the age range of thirty-five to fifty-four, who dropped from a 10.1 percent participation rate in 1969 to 6.6 percent in 1975.

Table 4. Participation Rates of Women and
Men in Adult Education by Age
(Percentage of Each Population Category)

	Women		
Age	*1969*	*1972*	*1975*
17–34	12.3	15.0	16.0
35–54	10.4	12.0	12.9
55+	3.2	3.9	4.3
Total	9.0	10.8	11.6
	Men		
17–34	16.8	16.9	16.0
35–54	11.8	13.1	12.5
55+	2.5	3.0	3.6
Total	11.2	11.9	11.7

Note: 1969 and 1972 surveys did not ask persons thirty-five years of age and over if they were full-time students. Therefore some persons in this age group were counted as adult education participants although they were full-time students in high school or college.
Source: NCES data, 1969, 1972, 1975.

Although women with a high school education are somewhat less likely than comparably educated men to participate in adult education, women with some college are more likely to participate than their male counterparts. Furthermore, the more education women have beyond high school, the more their participation rate exceeds that of men with comparable educations. The explanation may lie in the fact that advanced education is still a more unusual accomplishment for women than for men and hence requires additional motivation.

Since most studies treat women as a single demographic category contrasted with men, it is easy to fall into the trap of thinking that women represent a homogeneous group with common educational needs. That is far from correct. Data suggest that groups consisting of employed men and women, for example, have more educational needs in common than groups consisting of all women, some of whom are employed and some of whom are full-time housewives. Thus, differences labeled "sex differences" are in fact more likely to be related to employment status than to sex. In most of the studies reviewed, there are thousands of possible cross-tabulations of data. It is important to recognize that conclusions and eventual policy making depend on the choices made.

Despite all of the talk in recent years about women engaging in education for the purpose of entering or advancing in the labor market, studies contrasting the educational interests of men and women still reflect the stereotypes of male and female roles. The California study is typical, showing the following male-female differences in reasons given by potential learners for pursuing further education. Important to at least 5 percent more women than men were these goals: to be better informed and gain cultural enrichment; to gain personal satisfaction; to meet new people and get away from routine; and to be a better parent or spouse. Important to at least 5 percent more men than women, were these goals: to improve income and to meet a job requirement or perform a job better. There were less than 5 percentage points difference between men and women on the following goals: to prepare for a new job; to deal more effectively with personal situations; to work toward a degree; and to solve community problems.

Subject matter choices also reflect sex role stereotyping, with large differences in the expected directions. Men are more interested in trades, women more interested in home and family living and fine arts. Courses in business are usually given a high interest rating by both men and women.

It would be interesting to have better trend data about changing educational goals of women. There is some indication, however, that even the current interest on the part of women in vocational subjects is not presently met (Commission on Non-Traditional Study, 1974). Whereas 40 percent of the women expressed an interest in job-related subjects, only 24 percent were participants. There was no gap between interest and participation rates for men.

It is exceptionally difficult to arrive at a profile of women's educational needs and interests. Women are a very diverse group of people. On the variables showing the greatest relationships to educational participation—age, educational attainment, and place of residence—women range across the full spectrum just as men do. If we are to deal sensitively with the educational needs of women, it would seem necessary to look more carefully at subgroups of women with common educational goals—career women, women entering the labor market, and full-time housewives, for example.

Educational Attainment

Educational attainment is probably a better index to the interests, motivations, and participation of adult learners than any other single characteristic. This observation is consistent across a great variety of studies and is responsible for predictions that adult education will continue to rise as the educational attainment of the populace rises. It is demonstrably true that the more education people have the more interested they will be in further education, the more they will participate, and the more they will demand from state and federal planners.

Table 5 shows the 1975 NCES and 1972 CNS statistics for participation rates of adult part-time learners over the age of seventeen by highest level of prior education. Although the CNS survey found a higher overall rate of participation than NCES, the patterns are similar and show a clear increase in participation with increasing educational attainment. The interest expressed by would-be learners follows the same pattern. In the California study, for example, 35 percent of those with less than a high school diploma expressed interest in further education, compared with 53 percent of the high school graduates and 73 percent of the college graduates.

Policy makers concerned about equalizing educational opportunities will have to assess the special needs and interests of those with less than a high school diploma, a group constituting about one third of the United States labor force. As has already been noted, the poorly educated are not very likely to be participating in organized learning activities. In California, for example, 96 percent of the adults with less than a high school diploma were *not* engaged in educational activities, and 65 percent expressed no interest in getting involved. The statistics from surveys picture a "turned-off" attitude toward further education on the part of poorly educated adults. They are less likely than better educated groups to be willing to spend more than nine hours per week in study (California), although they are less likely to cite lack of time as a barrier to learning. They are less likely to be willing or able to spend time in travel to the learning location (Massachusetts, Northeast New York), more likely to state that barriers to their participation in learning are lack of motivation or lack of self-confidence (Central New York), and less interested in obtaining information about educational opportunity (California), but less likely to know where to go for information (California, Central New York).

Table 5. Participation Rates in Adult Education by Highest Level of Prior Education (Percentage of Each Population Category)

Highest Level of Prior Education	1972 CNS	NCES 1975
Elementary school (0–8 years)	10	2.0
High school (1–3 years)	20	4.6
High school graduate (4 years)	31	11.9
College (1–3 years)	48	17.6
College graduate (4 years)	} 57	27.0
Advanced study		30.4
Average	31	11.6

Source: CNS (Carp, Peterson, and Roelfs, 1974); NCES, 1975.

These cold statistics, however, are cast in a different light by the sensitive observations of Kathleen Rockhill, who recently conducted interviews of adults with less than twelve years of schooling. In her final report to the Division of Adult Education (Rockhill, 1978, pp. ii–iii), she wrote:

> Fundamentally, there is a need for a change of attitude on the part of educational institutions toward people who've completed less than twelve years of schooling. Though some lack basic skills and feel blocked by the lack of a high school diploma, for the most part noncompleters are not a uniformly distinct, "educationally or culturally deprived," population. The "population" is best characterized by its diversity; some are amazingly well educated, though usually self-educated, and most are rich in talents and skills which they've far too often not figured out how to use to their advantage. Indeed, the dominant common characteristic is that most people who've not completed high school disqualify themselves from educational participation, for they are under the impression that they must first complete high school. . . .
> We recommend that: *Legislation be considered which would provide incentives for "postsecondary" institutions to reach out to high school noncompleters, encouraging participation, assuring eligibility, and clarifying admission alternatives to the high school diploma.*

A few words should be said about the general relationship of educational attainment to educational interests. Numerically, the two largest groups taking part in organized learning activities are high school graduates and those with one to three years of college. If those with college experience are contrasted with those without, the better educated are more interested in continuing their education, more able to pay for it (but more concerned about finding time to study), more likely to be pursuing education for intrinsic as opposed to extrinsic rewards, more willing to entertain a variety of methods and locations, but more likely to be pursuing college courses on college campuses. The better educated are also more likely than less well-educated learners to take the so-called luxury courses in social and recreational education and in personal development.

Learners with some college experience are overrepresented in lectures, workshops, and TV courses, whereas high school graduates without college experience favor on-the-job training and, interestingly, are substantially overrepresented in correspondence courses. Whereas those whose highest level of educational attainment is high school graduation make up 38 percent of adult learners, they constitute 49 percent of those enrolled in correspondence study (NCES, 1972). But these preferences are probably related more to course content than to differences in learning styles. Courses offered for college credit, for example, are usually presented via lecture, and lectures are usually the preferred mode of presentation for degree-oriented learners. Professional continuing education is frequently presented in workshops, and workshops are rated high in the preferences of professional learners. Vocational and trades courses are more likely to be offered through correspondence or on-the-job training, and blue-collar workers tend to prefer these modes. Thus, when people are asked about preferred methods, they tend to select those that seem appropriate or familiar ways of dealing with the subject matter that is of interest to them.

Income

Considerable attention has been given to income as a variable in educational participation because potential learners frequently mention the cost of education as a barrier and because there have been some proposals for financial aid to adult learners in the form of entitlements, vouchers, tax incentives, and the like (see Kurland, 1977). From a policy perspective, the relationship between income and educational opportunity is an important one.

Although income is related to participation in adult learning activities, the use of income as a descriptor does not add much information to the analyses by educational attainment. Indeed, in most analyses educational attainment is a more consistent predictor of participation and interest than income—no doubt because the former includes variables such as motivation and ability, which are relevant to educational participation. In most studies, the relationship of income to educational participation and interest follows the same pattern as that previously described for educational attainment, but relationships are somewhat less consistent and less clearly defined.

The data from the NCES surveys show that adult participation rates are related to both income and educational attainment. The participation rates for various income levels rose steadily from 4.4 percent for those with incomes lower than $3,000 per year to 17.7 percent for those with incomes of $25,000 or more in 1975. While such an association lends credence to the notion that lack of money is a major barrier to educational participation for low-income groups, Froomkin and Wolfson (1977) conclude that when age and educational attainment are controlled, income has little influence on the rate of participation.

It does appear, however, that income differentiates somewhat more among older adults than among those under twenty-five years of age. Froomkin and Wolfson (1977) show that among young learners there is only a 4 percent difference in the participation rates for groups at quite different points on the income scale—16 percent for those with incomes of less than $4,000 per year and 20 percent for those with incomes between $10,000 and $25,000 per year. The spread between the same two income groups for adults between twenty-five and thirty-four is 13 percent—from a 12 percent participation rate for the low-income group to 25 percent for the higher-income group. One probable reason for the failure of income level to predict educational participation in the case of young people is that young people with low incomes and low educational attainment are especially likely to be eligible for public funding. For example, over half (60 percent) of the adult learners under the age of twenty-five with eighth-grade educations or less reported receiving public support for their educational activities, compared with only 38 percent of equally educationally deprived learners between the ages of thirty-five and forty-four. These data may demonstrate the potential power of financial aid to encourage the participation of low-income learners, but it is confounded by the age factor because young people express more interest in continuing their education than older people do.

The needs and interests of low-income adults follow the same patterns as those described under low educational attainment. These potential adult learners are primarily interested in learning that will enhance their employability and lead to higher incomes. Although job-related education is a popular form of learning for all income groups, lower-income adults are likely to be pursuing education that will lead to new jobs, whereas higher income groups are more interested in job advancement in their current line of work.

One of the major problems for low-income learners (and for those with low educational attainment, as well) is an excessively high dropout rate. The analysis of NCES data by Froomkin and Wolfson (1977) shows that 78 percent of the learners making an income of $25,000 or more complete their courses, compared to 58 percent for those with incomes between $4,000 and $5,000. Furthermore, there is a steady progression of courses completed as income rises. Data show that high-income learners are considerably more likely to complete their courses than are low-income learners. Froomkin and Wolfson (1977) make a strong argument that courses for the disadvantaged should be repackaged into smaller units, which can be completed more quickly and easily. As it is, low-income adults register for courses, largely publicly supported, that require considerably more time than courses taken by higher-income learners. For example, the contact hours for courses completed by those with annual incomes under $3,000 averaged 139 hours, whereas those completed by adults with incomes over $25,000 averaged only 59 hours. The differences were even greater when comparisons were made for courses *dropped* by the same two income groups. Courses dropped by the lowest income group required 300 hours on the average, compared with an average of 81 hours for the highest income group. While the need for contact hours for low-income learners cannot be denied, it would seem psychologically important to offer shorter units that would permit learners without extensive learning backgrounds to experience the satisfaction of completing a unit before motivation and resolve weaken. Furthermore, the "take-home" value of completed units is likely to be quite important to low-income learners who may be able to convert certificates of completion into job promotions and pay raises.

Place of Residence

National and statewide studies of participation and interest in adult learning show considerable variation by geographical region (see Table 2). For example, educational opportunity is widely conceded to be greater in the western states than anywhere else in the country. In the 1975 NCES data, the rate of participation in adult education in the western states[4] was significantly above the national average—16.6 percent compared with 11.6 percent nationally. Furthermore, the West was the only one of the four Census Bureau regions to show above-average participation rates in all categories of population density—cities, suburbs, towns, and rural areas. Willingham (1970), in his study of access to postsecondary education, wrote, "The West is far ahead of other regions with respect to the number of free-access institutions and the proportion of all entering students enrolled in them."

Data collected for the national Commission on Non-Traditional Study (CNS, 1974) show that westerners not only participate in learning activities more than residents of other regions but nonparticipants also evidence somewhat greater interest in learning than their counterparts in other regions of the country. The difference is especially well illustrated by the state studies of California and Iowa, which used essentially the same interview questions.

In California, 59 percent of adults interviewed said they were interested in participating in further learning beyond high school within the next two years. In Iowa, only 36 percent indicated similar interests. The difference showed up again when prospective learners were asked which of twelve learning support services (counseling, assessment, credit registry, and so on) would interest them. Fifty percent of Iowans, compared with 15 percent of Californians, said they were not interested in any of the services. Similarly, 31 percent of Iowans but only 5 percent of Californians said they were "no longer interested in formal schooling." One can conclude from these figures that California presents a more positive climate for learning than Iowa does.

A number of hypotheses could be advanced for the differences in expressed interest and participation in further education on the part of Iowans versus Californians. Educational accessibility has an obvious and demonstrated impact on participation rates

---

[4]The states included in the Census Bureau's category of the western region were Alaska, Arizona, California, Colorado, Hawaii, Idaho, Montana, Nevada, New Mexico, Oregon, Utah, Washington, and Wyoming.

(Bashaw, 1965; Bishop and Van Dyk, 1977; Koos, 1944; Trent and Medsker, 1965). Willingham (1970) showed that 60 percent of Californians but only 39 percent of Iowans live within a forty-five-minute commute of a free-access college. (Willingham's criteria for a free-access college are that it charge no more than $400 annual tuition, that at least one third of the freshman class be composed of students who graduated in the lower half of their high school class, and that the college be within forty-five minutes commuting time from the students' homes.) Since the Iowa analysis of educational resources found that 82 percent of the programs designed for adult learners used traditional classroom lectures as their principal mode of learning, commuting distance is a matter of considerable significance.

Differences between Iowa and California residents lay, however, not only in participation rates but also in expressed interest. Why should Californians be more interested than Iowans in further education? One possible explanation lies in the consistent research finding that the more education people have, the more they want. Although the high school graduation rate is almost as high for Iowans as for Californians, college attendance in California is higher. Of the adult population in California, 30 percent have had some college, while only 20 percent have in Iowa (Grant and Lind, 1976). Many Californians get some college work through part-time study. Hamilton (1976) reported huge differences in part-time college study—53 percent for California compared with 17 percent for Iowa. This difference no doubt reflects the profusion of free-access community colleges in California.

Much the same kind of analysis can be made with respect to variations in participation and interest based on population density. Table 2 shows that people living in suburban areas are more likely to participate in educational activities than those living in areas of sparse population or in the dense populations of central cities. Farm areas are clearly disadvantaged, with a participation rate of only 6.7 percent, compared with 11.6 percent nationally and 14.0 percent in the suburbs.

Once again, Willingham's analysis of access to colleges would seem related to these findings regarding participation in adult education. He found that 63 percent of the people residing in small cities (population 50,000 to 250,000) lived within a forty-five-minute commute of a free-access college, whereas only 24 percent of rural residents were so conveniently located. Central city residents fell in between, with 38 percent of the population having a forty-five-minute or less commute to a free-access college.

Most of the research that has been done on the impact of accessibility on educational participation has concerned colleges— especially free-access community colleges. Many states are now beginning to collect some data on the broad range of educational resources that exist outside of the so-called educational core. As we begin to think of learning activities extending far beyond traditional schools and colleges, the accessibility of other learning resources becomes an important issue in planning. How accessible, and to whom, are employer-sponsored programs? What kinds of programs and services are offered by community agencies, and what segments of the population are attracted to them? Do televised courses meet the needs of geographically isolated learners?

Systematic study of interactions between the needs of learners and the resources of communities is in its infancy, but the California study attempted to enrich the data from its statewide poll with in-depth studies of seven diverse California communities (Peterson, Roelfs, and others, 1975). Discussions were held with community residents and leaders, and the learning resources of the community were carefully noted. All of the California communities offered multiple forms of educational opportunities. Indeed, a major problem identified by the research team was the lack of information about and lack of coordination among existing programs. In California, a state noted for extensive formal as well as informal learning networks, the problem for adult learners was seen to be more a problem of "brokering" than a lack of provision of appropriate learning opportunities. Brokering involves not only getting potential learners in touch with existing opportunities but also establishing two-way communication in which providers of services can become aware of and respond to learner needs. California's problems in providing learning opportunities for adult part-time learners may be quite different, however, from those of states with more limited educational resources.

It is quite clear from the state studies completed to date that there are regional differences in people's motivation and interest in further education. General patterns, however, are widely recognizable across states. For example, past educational attainment is strongly related to future interest and participation; interest in education declines with increasing age; low-income groups are interested in on-the-job training with the potential for improving their earning capacity, and so on. We may know as much as we are going to know about the characteristics of learners defined by demographic categories. Where regional studies could be of value now is in studying the interrelationships of people and their learning environments.

Conclusions About Learner Characteristics

The existence of a substantial number of state needs assessments (see the chapter source list) permits us to make some generalizations about the characteristics of adult learners and potential learners. The high degree of similarity in survey designs results in studies that are almost replications of one another, and that has advantages and disadvantages. The major advantages are that we can be quite confident that findings that are reported with some regularity in the separate studies are not the biases of particular samples. Moreover, we can conclude, albeit with somewhat less confidence, that there are truly regional differences in the extent of interest in further learning. The disadvantage is that the methodology and even the questions are so similar from study to study that we have not broadened our knowledge much by having thirty studies instead of five. This is not to deny, however, the political and practical advantages of involving people at the local levels in planning for educational change through the collection and analysis of their own data.

The quality and research sophistication vary greatly in the studies reviewed here. Most are reasonably adequate technically, but the differences show up in the thoughtfulness of the analysis and the interpretations of the data. In data collection projects of this magnitude, the choices about how to present the data are seemingly endless. The typical survey may have only twenty questions, but, with multiple responses for each item, there may be hundreds of possible combinations. Five different age groupings may be run against ten subject matter preferences. Blacks may be compared with whites, elderly urban residents with young, learners with potential learners, high school graduates with college graduates, and on and on. The question that has not been given the attention it deserves is what variables should be run against what, and who decides. It is not so much the question of providing the data—which is almost too easy. The problem comes in absorbing it, attending to significant aspects, and developing a focused plan from the information overload. Since decisions about data reporting may literally dictate decisions about policy and planning, the problem is not trivial.

All too many studies take a stereotyped approach to analysis and data presentation. Age, sex, race, and other demographic variables, for example, become the kingpins of analysis because demographic variables are convenient statistics rather than because they necessarily contribute to understanding or to policy decisions.

Let us consider a concrete example. Almost all studies contrast the interests of men with the interests of women, concluding that men show more interest in job-oriented education. Inevitably, this is labeled a sex difference. But because some women are full-time homemakers (and almost no men are), this relatively small group of women homemakers may be responsible for a "highly consistent research finding" that women are more interested in hobbies and personal development than men are—a finding that may or may not be true for most women. Indeed, there is evidence that the difference in interests of employed women and unemployed women is greater than that between men and women.

We would do better in instances such as this to give more attention to the variables underlying the observed "sex" differences—in this case, occupational status or, better yet, educational goals. It is just as easy to obtain a "needs profile" for people who express a common educational goal on the survey as it is to obtain a profile for those indicating a common sex. The needs profile of a group of people wishing to enter the labor market—young and old, black and white, male and female—for example, would provide some very useful information for planning purposes.

A study analyzing data by the educationally relevant variable of learning goals, rather than the demographically convenient vari-

able of sex, could tell us the preferred schedules, locations, subject
matter, and services for a group with some *educational* needs in
common. Such data, while not often presented in the needs assessments reviewed here, could easily be obtained by simple re-
analysis of existing data.

There appear to be three demographic variables, however,
that are highly relevant to educational planning—age, educational
attainment, and place of residence.

The data from the demographic variable of age turn out to
be a commentary on what Best and Stern (1976) have called the
"linear life plan." Young people are interested in laying the foundation for their futures through learning; people in their middle
years are concerned with career advancement and with raising a
family; older people are interested in learning for personal satisfaction, social and intellectual stimulation, and the use of leisure
time. As Best and Stern point out, life does not have to be chopped
into three parts; we could develop "cyclic life plans" whereby each
age period had education, work, and leisure-time components.

Nevertheless, the data from the needs assessments are very
consistent in showing the reality of the linear life plan. Young people are the most eager learners; they want job-relevant education,
preferably with the certificates or degrees that will get them ahead;
and they cite cost as a barrier. Older people seem to have accepted
society's bias that education is for young people. Most people over
the age of fifty-five do not think of themselves as "lifelong learners";
they say they feel too old to learn or lack the energy. For those
who do express an interest, and their number is growing, location
is a major concern. Many colleges are now trying to interest senior
citizens in education by offering free tuition for traditional on-
campus classes. Although the intention is sincere, data from the
needs assessments indicate that such programs are not really very
well designed for most older learners, whose major needs are for
convenient locations (which college campuses usually are not), for
social interaction (which lectures do not provide), and avocational
subjects (which traditional courses are not). Free tuition is nice, but
cost is cited as a barrier more often by young people then by their
elders. The data indicate that there is much that can be done to
plan more effective learning opportunities for older citizens.

A second demographic variable shown by the needs assessments to have high relevance for educational planning is educational attainment. And it is perhaps the most influential variable of all, incorporating as it does many other factors such as income, race, and, to some extent, place of residence. It is very clear that the more education people have, the more interested they are in learning and the more likely they are to engage in formal learning activities. There is no exception to that conclusion in any of the studies reviewed. That fact has powerful implications for educational opportunity. Inevitably, it means that, without governmental intervention, the educational gap between the "haves" and the "have-nots" will widen because the "haves" possess the motivation and the resources to participate in the growing number of opportunities available.

For researchers, the challenge is to ferret out the causes of the high relationship between past participation in education and future interest in learning. Are present educational opportunities geared to the encouragement of certain groups and not others? Does education itself generate an enthusiasm for learning such that longer exposure leads to growing interest? Are there alternative forms of education that would provide reluctant learners with success experiences? It is all too easy to attribute the failure of the "have-nots" to participate in learning activities to lack of money and lack of information. Not enough attention has been given to the unpleasant possibility that many people lack interest in education as they know it.

The third interesting demographic variable, place of residence, needs much more study. From the data presented in the needs assessments, it appears that there are significant regional variations in the extent of interest in continued learning. Some of the variation may be attributed to differences in the populations' educational attainment and in the accessibility of educational resources. But "social climate" may also be a significant factor. More research is needed on the interaction of people and their environments.

In retrospect, the needs assessments have provided a great deal of material for thought as well as some for implementation. The need now is not further broad-scale surveys but rather for careful, thoughtful analyses of what we know and do not yet know about learner characteristics and what that implies for policy making and for further study.

Learner Needs and Interests

The purported purpose of most state studies has been to "assess the educational needs and interests of adults." The methods for doing this have become fairly standard now, consisting largely of asking adults what they want and need and what barriers prevent them from learning whatever they want to learn. Sometimes the questions are open ended, but, more commonly, certain areas of concern are identified and multiple-choice formats presented to respondents. For the most part, adult needs and interests are presented as alternatives to conventional educational programs—for example, options for locations other than school buildings, for schedules other than working hours, and so on. Presented here is a synthesis of information gleaned from many of the studies listed in the chapter source list.

Barriers to Learning

The obstacles that deter adults from participating in organized learning activities can be classified under three headings—situational, dispositional, and institutional. Situational barriers are those arising from one's situation in life at a given time, such as lack of time due to home or job responsibilities, lack of transportation, geographical isolation, lack of childcare, and so on. Dispositional barriers refer to attitudes about learning and perceptions of oneself as a learner—for example, boredom with school, lack of confidence in one's ability, or belief that one is "too old" to learn. Institutional barriers include barriers erected by learning institutions or agencies that exclude or discourage certain groups of learners because of such things as inconvenient schedules, full-time fees for part-time study, restrictive locations, and the like.

According to self-reports in surveys, situational barriers deter the largest number of learners. For many groups, the major barrier to continued education is lack of time. Finding the time for study and learning is usually the major problem for women between the ages of thirty and fifty, when family responsibilities are heavy, and for men of about the same age range, when job demands are likely to be heaviest (California, St. Louis, Northeast New York, Massachusetts, Central New York). Other situational barriers are lack of childcare, usually a problem for between 10 and 20 percent of potential learners (Northeast New York, California, New York, Iowa) and transportation problems, which are especially likely to plague rural and elderly adults.

The barrier of cost can also be considered a situational barrier, operating to the special detriment of younger learners, housewives, and those of low income and low educational attainment (California, St. Louis, Central New York, New York). Taken together, the cost of education and lack of time lead all other barriers by a substantial margin, but they affect different populations. The poor say they have the time but not the money to participate, whereas the professional and better-educated classes say they have the money but not the time (St. Louis, California, Massachusetts, Western New York).

It is difficult to give the percentages of people affected by various barriers because of the variety of reporting formats across state studies.[5] As a rough figure, we can probably assume that the median percentage (across studies) of people who find the cost of education an obstacle to further learning is around one third, and it is approximately the same for the barrier of time, with a range of from 20 to 50 percent. Whether time or cost is the greater problem varies from study to study, but there is rarely any deviation from the finding that time and cost are the two most frequently reported obstacles to adult learning.

One of the more interesting findings to emerge from studies of the barriers to learning comes from the Central New York study, in which respondents were asked not only to cite barriers to their own learning but also to speculate on why other adults of their

[5]Respondents can be asked to name all obstacles or only the major one. Percentages can be computed using people or number of mentions as a base. Time can be considered one barrier or divided into home responsibilities and job responsibilities. Cost can be one variable or separated into tuition costs, books and transportation, lost time from work, and so on. While percentage figures are not comparable, the general ranking of barriers is reasonably consistent across studies.

acquaintance did not participate in educational activities. Lack of interest was a leading barrier (26 percent) attributed to others, but less than 2 percent were willing to admit that lack of interest deterred their own participation. Similar findings were reported in the in-depth community studies conducted by the California research team (Peterson, Roelfs, and others, 1975). When community leaders were asked to estimate what people in their communities would perceive as barriers to their continued learning, the leaders consistently assigned more importance to dispositional barriers than did survey respondents. For example, 18 percent of the leaders but less than 5 percent of adult respondents said that "inability to do the work" would constitute a barrier to continued learning. Findings such as these highlight the problem of social acceptability as a response bias in survey research.

Lack of time and lack of money are both socially acceptable reasons for not participating in adult education. Thus, it is not surprising that they should rank as leading barriers, cited far more often than more personally demeaning barriers such as lack of confidence, lack of ability, or lack of interest. Many adults who cite cost as a barrier may have no idea of the cost of various options, as suggested by the fact that relatively large numbers of respondents (from 20 to 40 percent in the California, Western New York, and Iowa studies) fail to answer or give "don't know" responses to questions about willingness to pay. An investigation into peoples' knowledge about costs would at least provide some basis on which to judge the reality of the cost barrier. It would not, however, resolve the policy issue regarding the funding of adult education, since there is some evidence that willingness to pay is not the same as ability to pay.

The variable of willingness to pay has within it measures of motivation and the anticipated payoff. The Central New York study found, for example, that people were willing to pay more money for courses that would advance their careers than for learning for personal satisfaction, to get away from routine, or to be a better citizen or better parent. Furthermore, while the barrier of cost is related to income, it is also related to measures of interest and motivation and to personal and cultural values. Women, for example, are usually more likely than men to perceive cost as a barrier to their continued education (California, New York, NCES), a finding that probably has its roots in societal mores that make women feel guilty about spending family money for their own educations.

Again, generalizing across data formats that are not completely comparable, it appears that a course fee of more than about $50 would cause the "barrier flag" to be raised for a majority of potential learners (New York, California, Massachusetts, Northeast New York) and that such a fee would work a special hardship on the young, ethnic minorities, women, and the educationally and economically disadvantaged. The policy issue that is not at all clear from the data available through the needs assessments is what difference public funding could make and to whom.

The barriers that can be classified as dispositional—notably, lack of ability or interest—are cited by relatively few potential learners. These barriers fall at the opposite end of the social acceptability scale, however, from the situational barriers just discussed. Thus, their real importance is probably underestimated in the surveys because people do not like to say that they are not interested in learning, are too old, or lack confidence in their ability. These dispositional barriers are typically mentioned by less than 10 percent of the respondents.

In addition to the underreporting of dispositional barriers, there is the methodological problem that respondents who said they were not interested in further education were frequently dropped from further analysis. We might get higher counts for dispositional barriers if we asked those who said they were not interested in further learning the reasons for their lack of interest instead of asking those who want to learn to indicate what obstacles might prevent them. No doubt the largest counts for dispositional barriers are to be found among those who are not participating in educational activities. Indeed, the Northeast New York study found that the only significant discriminators between users and nonusers of educational services were the self-perceptions of the respondents as learners. Nonusers were significantly more likely to cite problems with the enjoyment of studying, feelings of confidence, and knowing what they would like to learn and where to get information about it.

Taking survey results at face value is likely to overestimate the potential gains from financial grants to learners and to underestimate the amount of effort that would be required to overcome dispositional barriers, which are quite likely to be the special problems of some of the groups that social policy makers are most interested in attracting to educational opportunities. The following list is one of the few data sources to provide information about the characteristics of those who say they are *not* interested in further education. The question asked was: "Would you like to engage in some form of further learning beyond high school . . . within the next two years?" and 64 percent of the respondents said, "No" (Iowa, 1976, p. 56).

Respondent Group	Percentage Responding "No"
Farm residents	73
Farmers (occupation)	77
50 to 64 years old	74
65 and older	98
Income less than $5,000	76
Income less than $10,000	74
Grade school education	98
Retired	94

How many people in these groups would become interested in further educational opportunity if the right learning experiences were available at the right cost is not known. But the dispositional barriers to learning are undoubtedly greater than most surveys indicate because most studies concentrate on the barriers identified by *potential* learners—not those identified by adults who say they have no further interest in learning.

Institutional barriers are rapidly being lowered by colleges seeking to serve the adult market. Institutional barriers, of course, exist primarily in that segment of adult education that was originally devised for full-time learners—that is, colleges and universities. The survey of higher education sponsored by the Commission on Non-Traditional Study (Ruyle and Geiselman, 1974) showed that college programs have been made more accessible to working adult students through such devices as scheduling classes when and where working adults can attend, granting credit by examination for noncollegiate learning, and creating more flexible admissions procedures. Nevertheless, there are still substantial numbers of potential adult learners who cite institutional barriers to their continued education.

Each survey seems to have devised its own list of possible institutional barriers, but these barriers can generally be grouped into about five categories: (1) scheduling problems; (2) problems with location or transportation; (3) lack of courses that are interesting, practical, or relevant; (4) procedural problems related to attendance, red-tape, time requirements, and so on; and (5) lack of information about procedures and programs. Of these, potential learners seem to complain most about inconvenient locations and schedules and about the lack of interesting or relevant courses. Generally, each of these three barriers is cited as a problem (although not necessarily the major problem) by up to one fourth of the potential learners (CNS, Iowa, New York, California, Central New York). Relatively fewer respondents cite lack of information as a barrier, although there is good evidence that adults do lack information about the new opportunities available. In the CNS study, for example, 35 percent of those interested in further education said that their desire not to go to school full time was a barrier to further education, yet only 16 percent complained about a lack of information. Surely, had some of those respondents had accurate information, they would have been aware that full-time study is no longer a requirement for adult education in most communities. One wonders if many perceived problems with schedules and locations and courses may not also be due ultimately to a lack of information about the options that do exist.

The Northeast New York study found that less than one third of the respondents had even heard of SUNY's Empire State College and only a handful were aware of the New York State Regents External Degree program. Since these programs were specifically designed to meet the special needs of adult learners, it can be concluded that there is a general lack of awareness of educational opportunities, even on the part of adults who say they are interested in further learning.

Lack of information can be considered an institutional barrier to learning when the assumption is made that it is the responsibility of program sponsors to get accurate information to potential learners. Certainly, as colleges and school systems compete with each other and with an array of other agencies offering learning opportunities, they will have increasing motivation to inform potential customers about learning opportunities. But, more and more, people are discussing the need for centralized information and counseling services, established on neutral ground (that is, not on campuses), to make community residents aware of the whole spectrum of learning resources. (The data on adult perceptions of their needs for information will be discussed later in the section entitled Information and Counseling.)

The central thrust of the adult learning movement has been toward removal of institutional barriers. Perhaps that is because the present movement consists largely of independent entrepreneurial efforts. Institutions and agencies competing to serve adult learners have done a great deal to lower the barriers of inconvenient or impossible scheduling and locations, for example. Public policy decisions may encourage further removal of institutional barriers, but the major challenge for policy makers lies in better understanding of dispositional barriers. And we do not know very much about how to remove these serious barriers to the attainment of equal opportunity.

Motives for Learning

Perhaps the single most important area to understand in planning programs for adult learners is their motives for engaging in learning activities. It is also one of the most difficult areas in which to obtain good and useful data. Most state studies have used a double-pronged approach, asking both *what* and *why* people wished to learn. Both approaches have problems, but together they add something to our understanding of learner motivations.

The problem with asking people *why* they are interested in further education is that the majority tend to give socially desirable responses such as "to be better informed" or "for personal satisfaction." At the same time, when people are asked *what* they wish to learn, most give very pragmatic responses related to their jobs and the practical affairs of life, such as cooking, childrearing, and financial management. While it is, of course, quite possible to want "to be better informed" about one's job or family, the reasons people give for learning do not always provide a very clear picture of the subjects they choose to study. However, the problem with inferring motives from the subjects that people say they want to study is that one adult may take a course (say, typing) for job-related reasons, while another may want it for personal use and enjoyment. Most state needs assessments ask adults about both subject preferences and reasons for learning. Therefore, we will examine in turn both the why and the what of adult learning.

There has been some effort over the years to identify and classify the motives of adult learners. In 1961 Houle identified three motivational orientations—(1) goal orientations (to obtain something); (2) activity orientations (to do something); and (3) learning orientations (to know something). Since Houle's early classification, there have been a number of efforts to factor analyze the reasons adults give for their learning activities and to arrive at a set of relatively discrete dimensions (Burgess, 1971; Dickenson and Clark, 1975; Eggert, 1974; Morstain and Smart, 1977). Although each study identified somewhat different factors, there is considerable similarity of categories. For our purposes in presenting an overview of learning motivations, we have chosen to adopt and adapt the categories identified in previous research that best fit the data from the state studies. Categories rely most heavily on Burgess (1971), the Ontario study (1976), and the CNS study (1974). Following is a typology of learning motivations along with a synthesis of findings from the needs assessments studies.

1. *Desire to achieve practical goals—to get a new job or advance in a current one or to improve income.*

Education is widely perceived as the route to upward socioeconomic mobility. And the desire to improve one's lot in life is clearly the primary motivation for adult education. Those who do not have good jobs would like to get new ones, and those who have fairly good jobs would like to advance. For example, women, factory workers, and the disadvantaged are more likely to be pursuing education in order to prepare for new jobs, whereas men, professionals, and college graduates are more likely to be seeking advancement in present jobs (Kansas, California, Western New York, New York Mid-Hudson). Vocational or professional education is the first choice of about half of all would-be learners (California, Central New York, CNS), and over a third of all adult learners are studying vocational or professional subjects (CNS, Ontario). It is apparent that those who are not currently participating in education (and are less advantaged) are even more interested in job-related education than their more advantaged peers who have the luxury of using education to improve the quality of life off the job as well as on.

2. *Desire to achieve personal satisfaction and other inner-directed personal goals such as personal development and family well-being.*

Typically, about one third of potential learners give personal satisfaction as their main reason for learning (New York, Western New York), but in most studies half or more of the potential learners mention this motive as one of their reasons for learning (California, CNS, Colorado, Northeastern New York). Educational activities falling into this category are often considered luxury items, and it is frequently adults who have no particular desire for economic or career advancement who cite personal satisfaction as a *major* motive—unemployed women, older and retired persons, and the privileged classes.

3. *Desire to gain new knowledge, including the desire to learn for its own sake.*

In one sense, this idealized motivation for learning is so socially acceptable that it is offered by most people as an important motivation for learning. Although it is difficult to obtain any behavioral verification, since almost any subject—from macrame to engineering—could be studied because the act of studying it or knowing more about it is satisfying, nonvocationally oriented learners are more likely to say they are interested in knowledge for its own sake than are career-oriented learners.

The percentage of potential learners seeking new knowledge as their *primary* motivation varies from study to study—10 percent in New York, 28 percent in Long Island, and 39 percent in Florida. Percentages are much higher, but variation is also considerable, for those citing new knowledge as *one* reason for learning—56 percent nationally (CNS), 69 percent in California, and 75 percent in Northeast New York.

Apparently, the average adult learner does not regard traditional liberal arts courses as the foundation subjects that will satisfy his or her need for new knowledge. Only small minorities of adults express a strong interest in traditional-discipline-based subjects, and these learners, predictably, are those with high levels of educational attainment.

4. *Desire to achieve formal educational goals, including degrees or certification.*

To work to obtain an educational degree or certificate is given as a reason (but not usually the main reason) by 8 percent to 28 percent of potential learners (California, Iowa, Kansas, Northeast New York, Western New York). The pursuit of degrees is strongly associated with level of educational attainment and with desire for job advancement. Younger persons and those with one to three years of college are very likely to be degree oriented, whereas the desire for credit or certification declines steadily with increasing age.

While the number of adults wanting formal academic credentials (degree or diploma) is ordinarily quite small, most studies show that about two thirds of adult learners want some kind of recognition (skill certificate, certificate of completion, or degrees) for their learning (68 percent in CNS, 63 percent in California, 63 percent in Iowa). This desire to *use* education to better one's status in life is in keeping with the pragmatic orientation of most adult learners.

5. *Desire to socialize with others or escape from the everyday routine.*

A surprising number of adults (over one third) are frank to admit that escape is, for them, a reason for pursuing course work (California, Iowa, Northeast New York). It is rarely, however, offered as the primary motivation. Nevertheless, there are certain groups of people for whom education serves as escape and an opportunity to meet new people. Such learners are quite likely to be interested in hobbies and recreational subjects, and they are likely to be people who lack other social outlets—the elderly and women confined to home and family, among others. For example, in the Iowa study 90 percent of those interested in crafts (mostly older people, 70 percent female, middle- and lower-income levels, and 40 percent farm residents) said that meeting new people and getting away from daily routine were reasons for their learning interests. Unfortunately, many of those most eager for social contact may live in isolated regions of the country or may lack the mobility to participate in group learning activities. Whether home-delivered education to socially isolated learners can be designed in a way that is satisfying to them remains to be seen.

6. *Desire to achieve societal goals.*

The desire to learn to be a better citizen is not a strong motivation for learning, although about one fourth of potential adult learners cite it as one motivation among others. Those experienced with the market fluctuations for extension and noncredit courses have observed, however, some apparent societal motivations when there is a surge of demand for courses on energy or ecology, for example. The state needs assessments reviewed here offer little information about the reaction of people to particular social concerns publicized by the mass media.

The overall picture that emerges from the data on adult motivations for learning is that adults are pragmatic learners who pursue education for its practical utility to them. A frequently ignored observation is that whereas young people learn more or less what they are told to learn, adults usually learn for a purpose that is clear to them. If we are to serve a "voluntary" learning force, we will need to understand, better than we do now, the real motivations of adult learners.

When potential learners are asked to state their subject matter preferences, about half of them name vocational or professional subjects (California, Iowa, CNS, Central New York). (See Table 6.)

Since most general education is aimed toward a degree or diploma, which is often desired for career advancement, it is fair to add vocational, professional, and general education together

Table 6. First Choice Subject Areas of Potential Learners,
Iowa and National Samples

	Percentage	
	Iowa	*CNS*
Vocational subjects	36	35
Professional	25	19
General education	12	16
Home and family living	11	12
Hobbies and recreation	8	8
Personal development	3	5
Public affairs	3	4
Other	2	1

Source: Iowa, 1976, p. 36.

and to conclude that the majority of adults see education primarily in pragmatic, if not downright economic, terms. Apparently, the only people who can afford to participate in education for enjoyment or other intrinsic motivations are those who are not interested in career advancement—retired people, spouses who are not in the labor market and not seeking to be, and well-educated people who have attained all the career success that education can provide. Viewed from this perspective, there should be no surprise in the generalizations that can now be made across studies of adult subject matter preferences:

• Would-be learners are even more interested in job-oriented education than present learners (who enjoy somewhat higher socioeconomic status already).
• Ethnic minorities are usually more interested in job-oriented education than Caucasians.
• It is usually women and older people, and to a lesser extent well-educated people, who constitute the bulk of learners pursuing non-job-related education such as hobbies and education for personal improvement.
• Interest in traditional-discipline-based liberal arts education is not high among adult learners. Those who do express an interest in studying sociology, history, and the like, are frequently degree oriented. Adults interested in liberal learning, but without degree aspirations, are more likely to pursue noncredit courses

especially designed to meet their needs, such as conversational French, early American art, and similar courses.

- Hobbies, home and family living, and personal development subjects have a wide appeal to potential learners; although few pick these so-called luxury items as first-choice subjects, most express some interest in these areas when they are asked to list all subjects of possible interest to them.
- Few respondents express any interest in studying community or public affairs. Generally less than 5 percent name such subjects as first-choice interests, and only about one third include social responsibilities among their reasons for learning.

Although it is possible to classify the subject matter interests of adults into a reasonable number of major categories, perhaps the most significant finding of the state studies lies in the vast diversity of interests. In the California study, for example, 167 different subjects were mentioned as first-choice selections. In the Massachusetts and Northeast New York studies, one third to one half of current continuing education students expressed interest in more courses across a broad range of topics. The learning interests of adults are not just diverse—they seem almost insatiable. Despite the rich array of course offerings in California, 12 percent of the adults who claimed an interest in further learning said that the available courses were not useful or practical, and 11 percent said that available courses were not of interest to them.

Perhaps one way to meet some possibly rare but important needs would be to provide a national clearinghouse of independent study courses. Whereas few communities can marshall enough interest in certain subjects to warrant the financial investment, a national audience may contain a substantial market for some courses. One of the problems in acting on the data of the regional market surveys is that every region concentrates on marketing courses such as accounting and psychology, which usually show a high demand, while ignoring subjects falling at the low end of the marketing scale. Thus, we find literally hundreds of courses in popular subjects and no courses at all in other subjects of great importance to a few people. The regional approach to course development is especially inefficient in the case of media-delivered courses, which, because of their expense and potential national audience, should be planned on a national data base.

Scheduling

The oldest, and probably still the most common, modification of education to accommodate the special needs of adult part-time learners is scheduling learning activities at times when adults are free to participate. The rather simple idea of the evening college has been expanded now to incorporate a vast array of scheduling possibilities. Whether the sponsor of the learning activity is a conventional educational institution, a community agency, employer, or informal learning group, there is a definable group of scheduling options, which can be categorized as follows: daytime hours, evening hours, block scheduling (ranging from weekends to a residential week or summer), or self-paced scheduling (for example, correspondence courses).

Even with this variety of possible options, scheduling problems are still cited as barriers to education by significant numbers of adults—usually between 15 and 25 percent. Interestingly, scheduling is one of the few areas that presents more problems to well-educated learners than to those with less educational background (California, CNS, Iowa). Yet the better educated are more amenable than other potential learners to a larger number of scheduling options—more seasons of the year, more days of the week, more self-determined schedules (California, Iowa, New York). Only with regard to times of the day do they seemingly lack flexibility. Presumably, job responsibilities prevent traditional daytime schedules.

Despite the rich array of schedules offered, the unanimous finding of the state surveys is that evening hours are the preferred times for learning, preferred by from 40 to 60 percent of the respondents (Northeast New York, 1974, Western New York, Colorado, California, Kansas, Iowa). Ranking second in scheduling preference are mornings, which are usually popular with those not in the labor market, especially young people and retired people (Kansas, Colorado). Rather unpopular with most survey respondents is weekend scheduling. Although there appear to be many successful weekend colleges, the idea of devoting a weekend to scheduled learning activities typically appeals to less than 10 percent of the survey respondents (Colorado, Northeast New York, 1974, Western New York). Part of the resistance to weekend scheduling may be due to a desire to preserve weekends for leisure and family activities, but the spread-out learning that typifies evening colleges is also frequently perceived as more desirable than the compressed learning of weekend activities (Kansas). Most people still think of learning as "courses" dispensed in fifty-minute doses.

Although not often explored in needs assessment studies, subject matter has considerable bearing on scheduling. The typical fifty-minute class period may be quite appropriate for algebra, less desirable for pottery making, and quite inappropriate for an encounter group or a sales conference. Surveys rarely tie subject matter to scheduling or instructional method, and a too-literal interpretation of data can be quite misleading when applied to the broad spectrum of learning activities.

Few studies asked respondents if they would be willing to schedule learning activities in concentrated sessions during summer vacation months or several times a year. Such schedules are used successfully as part of a range of learning methods and schedules employed by nontraditional programs such as Britain's Open University and the University of Oklahoma's Bachelor of Liberal Studies Program. However, in those studies that did give respondents the option of such schedules, very few desired them; in the Commission on Non-Traditional Study survey (CNS), for example, only 2 percent indicated that their first choice would be to learn for short, full-time periods during the summer.

A final schedule alternative is the student-determined schedule. When the schedule is set by the student, learning can be spread out over a longer period of time and can be undertaken at irregular intervals. This option can reduce the problem of lack of time (especially due to job or home responsibilities), which is cited as a major obstacle to learning participation. However, most state surveys failed to question adults about their interest in study schedules worked out in consultation between student and mentor. Because the general public has little knowledge about such schedules, designers of survey questions may have felt that adults would be unable to respond to such queries.

In summary, the evening schedules offered by evening divisions and adult schools appear to meet adult needs for scheduling modifications reasonably well—if one is thinking of rather standard education in classroom format. While a number of interesting scheduling options exist, and most scheduling innovations seem to be well received by adult learners, the surveys have not presented the range of options very well to potential learners, and there is no evidence of strong demand for more unusual or even more individualized scheduling on the part of respondents. There also appears to be relatively little demand for schedules targeted to meet the needs of particular demographically defined groups. With the exception of older—that is, retired people—there is not often much difference in the scheduling preferences of groups defined on the basis of sex, race, income, or educational attainment (New York, Mid-Hudson, Colorado).

Location

A great deal of attention has been given in recent years to location as a vital factor in educational participation. Past studies have documented the fact that establishing a free-access, low-tuition college in a region increases college attendance significantly (Bashaw, 1965; Bishop and Van Dyk, 1977; Trent and Medsker, 1965; Willingham, 1970). Furthermore, adults typically give high priority to the convenience of location when asked to indicate factors that would influence their participation in educational activities. Colleges seeking to attract adult learners have consequently gone out of their way to offer courses in convenient locations.

Given the visibility of the issue of location, it is surprising that the data from the state needs assessments are not more helpful. The major problem seems to be a confounding of location with sponsor. The typical survey, for example, asks for preferred locations—for example, college campus, home, work, or community agency—but respondents, it appears, merge the images of sponsor and location. College campuses almost always emerge as highly favored learning locations, typically leading all other locations by substantial margins (California, Iowa, Northeast New York, Colorado). If college campuses are truly the most popular places to learn, it would appear that colleges are making a mistake in rushing into off-campus programs for adult learners. The California survey attempted to make the issue clear by asking respondents to assume that all of the locations offered as options were "fully creditable toward a college degree or for satisfying whatever reasons you have for pursuing further learning." Nevertheless, 48 percent of the respondents elected a college campus, compared with 13 percent opting for an adult learning center located within five miles of their homes, 8 percent for a work site, and 2 percent for a high school location. As off-campus courses become more familiar and more legitimate in the eyes of learners as well as employers, we would expect more enthusiasm on the part of adults for convenient locations. Certainly, in the abstract, convenience of location is rated as highly desirable by adult learners.

While the probable confusion between sponsor and location argues for extreme caution in interpreting the data on "location" preferences, there are some findings that are universal across studies. First, location is absolutely critical to certain groups of learners. The physically handicapped, the geographically isolated, the aged, and others with restricted mobility cannot participate unless learning opportunities are made accessible. The stereotypes about school buildings as the appropriate places to learn are so strong, however, that it is difficult to introduce people to the potential of new locations for learning unless their options are otherwise limited. The Kansas study, for example, asked respondents to state whether certain locations would be an advantage or a disadvantage to them. Large majorities (over 70 percent) saw advantages to courses "offered locally" or "at the nearest college," but people were generally skeptical about "convenience" locations, such as courses offered by mail, radio, or amplified telephone. For these options, more people found disadvantages than advantages. Television courses occupied a middle ground, with 47 percent finding advantages, 35 percent disadvantages, and 18 percent uncertain.

Second, preference for learning location is strongly associated with past educational attainment and with level of further education desired. Preference for a college location increases consistently with level of formal schooling attained (California, Colorado, Long Island, New York). A college site is also favored by those who wish to undertake "college-level" learning. Similarly, potential learners who want to obtain college credit or to study literature or science or other subjects typically included in a college curriculum are likely to prefer college locations (Central New York, Florida, Iowa).

Third, college sites are more likely to be *used* by learners than to be *preferred* by potential learners (Northeast New York, CNS)—a finding no doubt related to the higher educational attainment of learners. It is important to keep in mind that certain groups, especially the elderly and those with low educational attainment or low income, are likely to prefer public high schools and adult learning centers, in part because these groups tend to favor "noncollege" subject matter such as vocational or recreational topics but also perhaps because their lack of college experience makes them uncomfortable on a college campus.

Somewhat surprising is the low ranking of work sites as attractive places to learn. Typically, work locations, offering one would think exceptional convenience, attract between 5 and 15 percent of those interested in learning. At least, such is the finding of the statewide needs assessments. In a special study of the interests of blue-collar workers, however, Botsman (1975b) found that 57 percent of the respondents indicated that the most favored place of learning was on the job. It is possible that this great disparity regarding site preferences between state needs assessments and Botsman's study is attributable more to the context in which the questions were asked (work site versus home) than to major differences in populations of respondents (blue collar versus others). In general, the profile of learning interests of blue-collar workers is indistinguishable from the profiles of people in the general population of equal educational backgrounds (Botsman, 1975a).

When attention is directed to overall ranking, the range and the diversity of location preferences may be obscured. Few of the studies reviewed showed a *majority* of respondents favoring any particular site. While school buildings are typically the most popular locations, frequently more than half of the respondents prefer other locations, and the diversity is even greater if people are asked about sites they are *willing* to use. The CNS study found that potential learners with at least a high school diploma are amenable to a greater variety of educational sites than their less well-educated peers. In addition, the proportion who say that site makes no difference rises with educational level; in the New York study 10 percent of those with less than eight years of schooling, but 25 percent of those with a college degree, said location made no difference. Perhaps if educated learners blaze the "credibility" trail for more convenient locations, which in the abstract most adults insist they want, *where* one learns will become less important than *what* one learns.

Learning Methods

Surveys indicate that adults favor considerable variety in learning methods—probably more than is available now. As many as 70 to 80 percent of respondents say they would prefer to learn by some method other than classroom lectures (CNS, Western New York, New York, Florida, Central New York). Nevertheless, lectures generally rank first or second in overall popularity out of the five to ten methods that are generally presented in questionnaires.

No doubt familiarity has a great deal to do with the relative popularity of the classroom lecture. In California, 28 percent of would-be learners favored lectures, but 35 percent of the learners were enrolled in lecture classes. Similarly, in Western New York, 47 percent of the learners did their learning through lectures, but only 22 percent of the potential learners selected lectures as their preferred mode. Adult learners appear to be asking for more alternatives and especially for more action-oriented learning. When the New York survey offered the option of "learning by doing," 53 percent of the respondents selected it—by far the largest majority marshalled in any study for any method. On-the-job training, internships, and fieldwork are popular learning methods, showing greater variability from study to study than lectures (from 8 to 41 percent) but generally appealing to around 20 percent of the potential learners (CNS, Western New York, New York, Florida, Central New York). In both the CNS and Western New York studies, the number of learners actually participating in on-the-job learning was far less than the number who expressed an interest in it. Evidently, there are not enough on-the-job opportunities to meet the current demand.

It is not easy to compare preferences in learning methods

across state studies because the lists of methods presented in the surveys differ, and it is hard to tell what people had in mind when they selected "learning by doing," for example, in preference to on-the-job training. More than likely, this is one more illustration of the confounding, in the eyes of the respondents, of methods, subject matter, sponsors, locations, and related factors. Whereas on-the-job training, as a method, is limited to job-related education, learning by doing can apply to jobs, arts and crafts, sailing, languages, or almost anything else adults might wish to learn. In any case, the idea of active learning seems to appeal to many adults, and, outside of the conventional school system, learning by doing is a nearly universal method of learning. If we were to group together all methods in which the learners were interpersonally active (workshops, discussions, internships, group action projects, on-the-job training, private lessons), and compare them with those in which learners were more passive or at least not interacting with others (lectures, correspondence study, TV, radio, records), the interactive modes would be the overwhelming winners in the preferences of adults in almost all studies.

This observation holds especially true for the population that many policy makers are most interested in attracting to educational activities—the economically and educationally disadvantaged. Quite clearly, the nonsocial forms of learning requiring a certain amount of independence or self-direction appeal primarily to those with college educations, high income, and high-status occupations. The data also show that the disadvantaged are more restricted than better educated learners in the modes of learning that they are willing or able to use. While more active learning options would probably benefit the majority of learners, there is reason to think that they would have a special appeal for the educationally disadvantaged.

Information and Counseling

The authors of the California study of postsecondary education alternatives for adults concluded: "Of all the needs for expanded postsecondary opportunities in California, the *most critical is simply information about existing opportunities.* Large numbers of people know that they want to study something, but they have no convenient way or no central location to find out the options available to them" (Peterson and Hefferlin, 1975, p. 56). About one fourth of potential learners confess that they do not know where to go or whom to ask to get information about learning opportunities (Iowa, Western New York). Even when they say they know where to go, many adults lack specific information about courses and programs; for example, 28 percent of the adults surveyed in the Central New York study said they did not know what courses were available in their area. The lack of specific information about educational opportunities presents an obstacle to learning participation for perhaps 15 to 30 percent of potential learners (CNS, New York).

When adults are asked whether they would like more information, the response is overwhelmingly affirmative; 85 percent of the respondents in the Central New York study said they would like to be kept better informed of continuing educational offerings, even though nearly three fourths of them said they knew about courses in their communities.

The unmet need for informational and counseling services is especially great among disadvantaged would-be learners. Adults with low levels of educational attainment are much less likely than other potential learners to know where to get advice (Iowa, Western New York); they are less likely to have specific information about course offerings (Central New York, New York); and they are less likely to have used counseling services in the past (Western New York). Yet potential learners with low levels of schooling express more desire for information and counseling services than do better educated adults; similarly, nonwhites want counseling services more often than do whites (New York, Western New York). Table 7 compares knowledge about advisement services and desire for them, by educational level, for the Western New York survey.

Some of the studies solicited advice about appropriate methods for disseminating information. In Central New York, would-be learners wanted educational providers to make greater use of the media to disseminate information. The popularity of radio and television for receiving adult education information was highest among those with the least formal education and the lowest income levels; 17 percent of those with eight or fewer years of education

Table 7. Knowledge of and Desire for
Advisement Services by Educational Level

Educational Level	Percentage Knowing Location of Advisory and Information Sources	Percentage Desiring to Discuss Adult Learning Activities With Someone
0–7 years	29	} 47
8–11 years	62	
12–15 years	75	37
16 or more years	92	27

Source: Western New York, 1976, pp. 113 and 121.

but only 3 percent of college graduates felt that radio or television was the best method for obtaining information about learning opportunities (New York). But the best method may vary with locale. In the Central New York study, 38 percent most preferred information from newspapers and 27 percent preferred printed bulletins; but in New York as a whole, only 19 percent preferred newspapers, while 50 percent preferred mailed notices.

In addition to impersonal information channels, adults want personal sources of advice. The Central New York study notes that although a majority of respondents named school or college counselors as sources they would seek to use, counselors may be available only during daytime hours. Also, counselors attached to a particular institution may be unaware of educational opportunities in another institution, in a nontraditional program, or in a nonschool organization. And there is always the suspicion, well founded or not, that college-employed counselors may be reluctant to refer an individual to a "competing" organization.

Adults are often unaware of the functions and services of counseling agencies that are available to them. Noting a sense of confusion about the functions of advisement centers, the Western New York study suggests: "It is highly possible that this confusion is shared by persons not interested in using such services. Perhaps their lack of interest is in part due to vagueness about the functions of such services" (p. 125).

When adults are made aware of the opportunities for new kinds of counseling services, many express a high degree of interest. Of the major state studies, only the California, Iowa, and Maine studies specifically queried adults about their interest in new types of educational services, such as assessment of competencies, testing of skills, and evaluation of work experiences for credit. Respondents indicated that they would particularly like assessment and testing of their interests, competencies, and skills (California, Iowa). In California, 31 percent of potential learners were interested in obtaining an assessment of their personal competencies; 28 percent of potential learners wanted to have their strengths and weaknesses in various subjects and skills tested. The desire for assessment and testing services was especially prevalent among less well educated and poorer would-be learners.

In conclusion, there is a widespread desire for more information about learning opportunities. Indeed, the lack of up-to-date information confounds and makes questionable some of the data about barriers. It appears that many adults perceive barriers that may no longer exist. Thus, lack of information becomes the new barrier, operating to exclude those who might stand to benefit most from new kinds of learning opportunities.[6]

Conclusions About Learner Needs

Just as the state studies tend to rely on the same demographic categories to describe adult learners, so, too, they show broad agreement on the variables that describe learner needs. The areas investigated by the surveys can be covered quite well by the topic headings of barriers to learning, learning motives and subject matter preferences, scheduling, location, learning methods, and information and counseling. Since most of the studies were sponsored by agencies concerned about developing the so-called educational core, especially public colleges and universities, "needs" tended to be viewed from the perspective of postsecondary education. (How might colleges modify programs and attract adult learners?) There is not much information available, for example, on how on-the-job training should be modified—only the finding that there should be more of it.

[6]For a comprehensive discussion of the role of counseling and information services for adults, see Cross, 1978c.

The question might be raised whether we settled too early on the standard list of "needs" being emphasized by so-called non-traditional alternatives—flexible scheduling, off-campus locations, community information centers, and the like. There is probably a need for more in-depth research on the candid reactions of adults to the whole concept of continued learning. Present data, and the very topics we choose to gather data about, point our efforts toward tinkering with the mechanisms of traditional education rather than forcing us to take a hard look at some new conceptions of learning opportunities for adults. The problem, of course, is not limited to the questions researchers ask; it is severely restricted by the ability of potential learners to think beyond what they know and have experienced in the educational system. Perhaps we need to spend somewhat more time trying to understand the "natural" learning modes used by adults (see Tough, 1971; Penland, 1977; and Chapter One). Or perhaps we need to ask some questions about the kinds of problems faced by adults that require continued learning.

The data that we have collected to date lead to the following broad conclusions about adult learning needs and to major implications for educational planners and program directors:

- Adults are highly pragmatic learners. Vocationally and practically oriented education that leads to knowledge about how to *do* something is chosen by more adults than any other form of learning, and no study presents data that would offer an exception to that generalization. Traditional-discipline-oriented subjects are not popular with the majority of potential learners. Such subjects are most likely to appeal to degree-oriented learners.
- Adults with low levels of educational attainment and low-status jobs are motivated largely by external rewards—that is, the promise of better jobs or more pay. Adults who have the basic necessities of life are more likely to cite internal rewards, such as personal satisfaction and the desire to learn. Better-educated and higher-income adults are much more likely to pursue so-called luxury learning in personal development or the use of leisure time, whereas disadvantaged learners are more interested in job training and in skill certificates.

- Much of the survey data on barriers to continued learning are suspect for two reasons. First, the tendency of respondents to give socially acceptable reasons for not participating in learning activities underemphasizes motivational factors and overemphasizes environmental factors. It is simply much more acceptable to say that the cost of education prevents one from taking courses than it is to say that one is not interested in learning. Second, lack of information prevents many adults from knowing which barriers really exist and which existed last time they looked into the matter—which may have been never, ten years ago, or whenever they left the formal school system.
- Although there is a great deal of interest expressed in "convenient" locations and schedules, in practice people frequently choose seemingly inconvenient locations and schedules. Home and work sites, which would appear to be highly "convenient" locations, are not usually as popular as school buildings and college campuses. Nor are completely self-determined schedules as popular as evening classes. The explanation seems to lie in the perceived credibility or prestige of the offering or in the perceived appropriateness of the subject matter to the location or schedule.
- There seems to be a need for more active modes of learning. Whereas young people more or less expect to be told what to learn and expect to listen to "experts" dispense information, adults ordinarily want to be able to *use* the knowledge or skills learned. Interactive and active modes of learning are more appealing to most adults than passive listening or watching. The passive mode is especially unattractive to those with low educational attainment.

The State of the Art in Needs Assessments

The thirty large-scale surveys of adult part-time learners reviewed in this chapter together represent probably the most massive collection of data ever made about the needs and interests of any educational constituency. By now, we should know a great deal about adults' learning interests. But it is probably more accurate to say that we know quite a bit about a rather limited aspect of adult learners' motivations and interests. It is only a slight exaggeration to say that what we have are thirty variations of one study. The national study conducted in 1972 by the Educational Testing Service (Carp, Peterson, and Roelfs, 1974) for the Commission on Non-Traditional Study (CNS) seems to have had considerable influence on the general methodology and format of many of the state studies—as has its predecessor, *Volunteers for Learning* (Johnstone and Rivera, 1965), conducted a decade earlier at the National Opinion Research Center (NORC).

There is probably a subtle difference, however, between the purposes of the national studies and those of the state needs assessments that has not been fully recognized. Whereas the national studies were designed to provide a broad mapping of the terrain of adult interests, most of the needs assessments were undertaken in the expectation that they could serve as planning documents—that is, that they would provide an information base from which decisions could be made. While many studies did make recommendations ranging from the general to the specific, it is not clear how helpful the data were in the formulation or implementation of the recommendations. (See Nolfi, 1977b, for an analysis of factors affecting implementation of recommendations.)

Clearly, the design of many of the state studies was not up to the challenging task of delivering solid information on which to base recommendations or decisions. In the majority of the studies, there is no clear rationale for why certain questions were asked, why, out of thousands of possible combinations of data, certain analyses were selected, and what difference the results should make to planners. Consequently, some reports spew forth huge masses of undigested data, hoping, no doubt, that some table will answer a question that someone might want to ask. A few give up any pretense of interpreting the data or making any observations at all.

In contrast, other studies systematically collected and analyzed data to shed light on specific issues (California, for example) or to help colleges identify a potential market (Iowa, for example), or to make some predictions about future demand (Maine, for example). Actually, many of the studies were undertaken, implicitly or explicitly, as "market surveys." Few of the market surveys, however, presented their data as usefully as the Iowa study. Most studies started with biographical data and ended with a series of interest profiles by age, sex, race, income, and so forth. The Iowa study, however, grouped people not solely according to common demographic characteristics but also according to common subject matter interests. The study could then tell a school of education, for example, the age, place of residence, income, profession, educational background, and other characteristics of a group of people who were seriously interested in taking courses in education within the next two years. Furthermore, it could tell planners what instructional methods were preferred, what kinds of services were needed, what other courses would be of interest, and what barriers might prevent enrollment. In other words, colleges in the state of Iowa could build their programs and target their information to rather well-defined target profiles. A similar marketing approach has been used by the media-oriented University of Mid-America (UMA). Basically, the UMA analyses revolve around the variable of location or method rather than subject matter. What the UMA wants to know is what sorts of people are seriously interested in televised educational programs.

While the more common demographically homogeneous profiles are desirable for social policy purposes—that is, for discovering how to attract underserved populations—such profiles are not always helpful in planning educational programs, which usually strive for heterogeneity of demographic characteristics and homogeneity of educational interests. They are not useful because research reveals that grouping people who are homogeneous with respect to demographic characteristics does not result in homogeneity of educational needs. There is no way to plan for the continuing education needs of "women," for example, when women seeking job training for entry into the labor market are lumped together with women engaged full time with home and family. Botsman (1975a) makes the same point emphatically as a result of his study of blue-collar workers—a group that might be somewhat more likely than women to share a common life-style and common educational interests. He writes, "This research has shown that blue-collar factory workers exhibit a very wide range of differences in attitudes, interests, and propensity to participate in adult and continuing education. These differences are so many and so varied that to continue to regard blue-collar audiences as homogeneous would be quite irrational. The data leave no doubt that blue-collar factory workers are far more heterogeneous than they are homogeneous in relation to continuing education" (p. 102).

These observations about some of the weaknesses of the state of the art in needs assessments are not meant to denigrate the contributions of today's studies. Some are superior models, and almost all have made some original contribution. The fact is, however, that for educators and policy makers, most state needs assessments have not added much to the findings of the 1962 and 1972 national studies. While some regional differences in the extent of interest have been demonstrated, the *patterns* of responses are remarkably similar from study to study. There is virtually universal agreement, for example, that the more formal education people have the more interested they are in further learning; that there is a decline in expressed interest in learning with advancing age; and that the majority of adults are pragmatic and interested in learning that has some visible payoff in skill development, job advancement, or practical knowledge. Perhaps the major contribution of the state needs assessments is that, with the high rate of replication, we can be quite sure now that these patterns do not vary from place to place or from sample to sample.

What is needed now is research that goes beyond description into the difficult search for explanations. Why is learning addictive, for example? Until we can answer that question, we will have a very difficult time trying to formulate any kind of public policy that will narrow the educational gap between the well educated and the poorly educated. If the well educated seek out new learning opportunities while the poorly educated avoid them, then the learning gap will surely grow—right along with today's profusion of opportunities. At least, such will be the inevitable result unless we can advance our understanding of the learning motivations of the undereducated.

For almost every data-based observation or "fact" revealed in this synthesis of needs assessments, there is a challenging question waiting to be answered. Thus, the following thirteen italicized observations may serve as a useful summary of what we do know, on the one hand, while the accompanying questions that they raise serve as a chart to what we need to find out, on the other hand. There is no attempt here to incorporate research findings from any domains of adult learning outside the needs assessments, such as adult development or gerontology. The questions are only suggestive of the types of investigations that could be conducted.

1. *Participation and interest in learning increase with educational attainment.* But what are the barriers blocking interest in further learning on the part of those with low educational attainment? What is the relative contribution of factors such as lack of success in school in the past, lack of appropriate courses or teaching methods, lack of information about available opportunities, lack of perceived rewards, lack of funds for tuition, childcare, or transportation, lack of convenient locations, and lack of peer support?

2. *Participation and interest decline with age, sharply after age fifty-five or so.* But what factors are associated with a self-concept of being "too old" to learn? To what extent does lower educational attainment account for the depressed interest of older generations? What roles do impaired vision and hearing play in hindering learning activities for the elderly? How can more adequate opportunities for socially interactive learning be provided for the elderly?

3. *There are regional (including population density) differences in the extent of interest in adult learning.* But what are the environmental factors contributing to a positive climate for lifelong learning? What differences exist between regions in community support and encouragement of adult learning? Are there regional differences in subject matter preferences and in desired delivery systems? What is the interaction between learners and the learning resources of communities—from stimulation of interest, to provision of information, to participation in learning activities?

4. *Cost is cited as a major barrier to participation in adult learning.* But how knowledgeable are adults about costs? What is the relationship between ability to pay and willingness to pay—for

particular subgroups? for various types of learning experiences? for various types of certification? To what extent does cost serve as a convenient rationalization for nonparticipation?

5. *The participation of black men and women in part-time adult education appears to be decreasing.* But what are the reasons for the decrease? Are there compensating increases in other forms of learning? Does the apparent decrease obtain for other ethnic minorities? Does lack of participation handicap black workers in upward economic mobility? What community factors encourage or discourage participation?

6. *Dropout rates from adult education courses are especially high for black males and for adults of low educational attainment.* But what is the impact of course length on dropout figures (see Froomkin and Wolfson, 1977)? What is the real status of people reporting "course in progress"? How many return after what kinds of time intervals? What are the dissatisfactions of non-completers?

7. *Educationally and economically deprived adults are especially interested in job-related learning.* Yet what is the credibility of part-time adult learning with employers? What is the relationship between adult participation in learning activities and job promotion or pay raises? What kinds of educational participation have the highest payoff? What is the role of various kinds of certificiation in job advancement?

8. *Data on learning interests support traditional male-female roles, for example, men are more interested in job-related learning.* But to what extent are women's interests changing? How do the interests of various subgroups of women differ—for example, women entering the labor market, career women, full-time homemakers? Why is cost cited as a barrier to education more frequently by women than by men?

9. *Certain groups of people, especially the elderly and people with low educational attainment, present a "turned-off" profile of learning interests.* But what have been the past experiences of these groups with education? What is their perception of today's opportunities? When not faced by "formal education," what and how do these people learn? What problems do these groups need to solve, and what kinds of learning activities would be helpful?

10. *Advantaged adults are more likely than the disadvantaged to be en-
    gaged in learning activities for intrinsic reasons—that is, for personal
    satisfaction and self-development.* Yet is there a Maslow-type needs
    hierarchy in educational choice; in other words, must basic
    survival needs be fulfilled before life enrichment needs can be
    entertained?
11. *Meeting new people and interacting with people is an important ed-
    ucational motivation for many learners, especially the elderly and
    others with restricted mobility.* But what forms of socially inter-
    active learning are most successful? How can convenience
    of location be combined with social interaction? Can media-
    delivered education be made more socially interactive?
12. *There is much greater diversity of interest within demographically de-
    fined subgroups than between them.* Yet what are some more use-
    ful ways to group respondents than demographic categories
    such as age, sex, and race, so prevalent in existing studies?
    What new questions could be raised by regrouping and rean-
    alyzing existing data?
13. *The major barriers identified by survey respondents are socially ac-
    ceptable barriers such as lack of time and high cost.* But what is the
    real role of less socially acceptable reasons for lack of partici-
    pation in learning activities? What are some new research
    methodologies for ferreting out the attitudes of adults toward
    lifelong learning?

   These items summarize major findings from only a limited
portion of adult learning. Yet the questions raised by these findings
are far more numerous than the questions answered. So far, we
have made reasonable progress in descriptive studies of adult
learners. We now need a directed search for explanatory principles.

Source List: Major National, State, and Regional Studies of Adult Learners and Potential Learners Since 1969

Arkansas

Campbell, M., and others. *New Students: New Markets for the University of Arkansas? Educational Needs and Interests in the Northwest
Arkansas Area.* Fayetteville: University of Arkansas, 1974.

California

Hefferlin, J. L., Peterson, R. E., and Roelfs, P. J. *California's Need for Postsecondary Alternatives* (First technical report, Part I). Sacramento: California Legislature, 1975.

Central New York

Wilcox, J., Saltford, R. A., and Veres, H. C. *Continuing Education: Bridging the Information Gap.* Ithaca: Institute for Research and Development in Occupational Education, Cornell University, 1975.

Colorado

Barlow, B. M., and Timiraos, C. R. *Colorado Adult Needs Assessment* (Final technical report). Denver: Colorado Department of Education and State Board for Community Colleges and Occupational Education, 1975.

Commission on Non-Traditional Study

Carp, A., Peterson, R. E., and Roelfs, P. J. "Adult Learning Interests and Experiences." In K. P. Cross, J. R. Valley, and Associates, *Planning Non-Traditional Programs: An Analysis of the Issues for Postsecondary Education.* San Francisco: Jossey-Bass, 1974.

Florida

Florida Commission on Educational Outreach and Service. *Access to Knowledge* (Vol. 2: Supporting data). Tallahassee: State University System of Florida, 1976.

Genesee Valley, New York

Carlivati, P. A. *Toward Developing a Coordinated System of Postsecondary Continuing Education in the Genessee Valley Region: A Summary Report.* Rochester: Rochester Area Colleges, 1975.

Hayward, California

McCabe, G. E., and Straton, R. A. *University Courses via Cable TV: A Survey of Households Within the Service Area of One Cable Company and Projections for a Statewide Program.* Long Beach: Consortium, California State University and Colleges, 1976.

Illinois

A. C. Nielsen Company. *Adult Educational Interest Survey.* North-brook, Ill.: A. C. Nielsen, 1973.

Illinois

Board of Higher Education. *Summary of Data: Study of Illinois Adult Learners.* Springfield: Illinois Office of Education, 1978.

Iowa

Hamilton, I. B. *The Third Century: Postsecondary Planning for the Nontraditional Learner.* Princeton, N.J.: Educational Testing Service, 1976.

Kansas

Hoyt, D. P. *Appraisal of Interest in Continuing Education Opportunities Among Kansas Adults.* Manhattan: Kansas State University, 1975.

Long Island, New York

Heston, W. M., and Fantz, J. C. *Toward a Comprehensive Coordinated System of Postsecondary Continuing Education for Long Island.* New York: Long Island Regional Advisory Council on Higher Education, 1976.

Maine

Kovenock, D. *The Demand for Adult Education in Maine.* Orono: Social Science Research Institute, University of Maine, 1978.

Massachusetts

Nolfi, G. J., and Nelson, V. I. *Strengthening the Alternative Postsecondary Education System: Continuing and Part-Time Study in Massachusetts* (Vol. 2: Technical report). Cambridge, Mass.: University Consultants, 1973.

Medsker and Others

Medsker, L., and others. *Extending Opportunities for a College Degree: Practices, Problems, and Potentials.* Berkeley: Center for Research and Development in Higher Education, University of California, 1975.

Mid-Hudson New York

Vivona, R., Miringoff, M., and Watsky, C. *Adult Post-Secondary Continuing Education in the Mid-Hudson Region: Increased Access to Improve the Quality of Life.* Poughkeepsie: Associated Colleges of the Mid-Hudson Area; and New Paltz: Mid-Hudson Region Continuing Education Project, 1975.

NCES

National Center for Educational Statistics. *Participation in Adult Education, Final Report, 1969.* Washington, D.C.: National Center for Education Statistics and Department of Health, Education, and Welfare, 1974. (Data collected in 1969.)

NCES

National Center for Educational Statistics. *Participation in Adult Education, Final Report, 1972.* Washington, D.C.: National Center for Education Statistics and Department of Health, Education, and Welfare, 1976.

NCES

National Center for Educational Statistics. *Participation in Adult Education, Final Report, 1975.* Washington, D.C.: National Center for Education Statistics and Department of Health, Education, and Welfare, in press.

New York

New York State Education Department (University of the State of New York), Division of Continuing Education. *New York State Continuing Education Needs Assessment* (Report No. 1: Statewide Analysis). Albany: State Department of Education, 1977.

Northeast California

Treseder, C. *A Survey of Attitudes Toward Higher and Continuing Education in Northeastern California.* San Jose: Diridon Research Corporation, 1972.

Northeast New York

Nurnberger, R. G. *A Profile of Need: A Study of Postsecondary Edu-*

cation Needs in Northeastern New York State. Albany: College of General Studies, State University of New York at Albany, 1974.

Northeast New York

Stelzer, L., and Banthin, J. *A Study of Postsecondary Education Needs in Northeastern New York State: Secondary Analysis.* Latham: Capital Associates, 1975.

Northern New York

Correa, J. M. *Regional Needs and Resources for Postsecondary Education: A Report of the Northern Region Postsecondary Education Group.* Potsdam: Associated Colleges of the St. Lawrence Valley, 1976.

Ontario

Waniewicz, I. *Demand for Part-Time Learning in Ontario.* Ontario, Canada: Ontario Educational Communications Authority, 1976.

St. Louis

Hunter, W. J. *The Non-Traditional Community College Project—Survey of Postsecondary Youth and Adult Learning.* St. Louis: Junior College District of St. Louis, 1974.

SUN

Ross, G. R., Brown, R. D., and Hassel, M. *Clientele Study for the Proposed State University of Nebraska (SUN)—A Multi-Media Off-Campus Collegiate Program.* Lincoln: University of Nebraska, 1972.

SUN

Eggert, J. D. *An Examination of Goals of Potential and Actual Learners: University of Mid-America/State University of Nebraska* (Working paper No. 1). Lincoln: Office of Research and Evaluation, University of Mid-America/State University of Nebraska, 1974.

SUN

Bryan, D., and Forman, D. C. *Characteristics of SUN Learners (First Five Offerings): Statistical Summary No. 4.* Lincoln: University of Mid-America, 1977.

Texas

Neidhart, A. C. (Ed.). *Continuing Education for Texas: Special Studies of Non-Traditional Approaches to Education.* San Marcos: Southwest Texas State University, 1974.

Washington

Randall, M. E., Pailthorp, K., and Bigelow, M.L. *Postsecondary Education in the Tri-Cities.* Olympia: Washington Council for Postsecondary Education, 1976.

Western New York

Robinson, K., and Herdendorf, P. S. *Final Report on the Survey of Public Demand/Need for Postsecondary Continuing Education for Adults (Lifelong Learning Programs) in Western New York.* Buffalo: Project Impact, Western New York Postsecondary Continuing Education Study, 1976.

CHAPTER THREE

Local Programs: Innovations and Problems

John R. Valley

This chapter examines lifelong learning in the United States from a local perspective, concentrating on the relationship between adult learners and their local resources and providers of learning opportunities. In focusing on local services, it does not exclude regional programs and those funded at local levels by federal and state sources. For example, it includes the work of a community college such as Arizona Western College, even though its territory extends about 150 miles north and south of Yuma and covers over 10,000 square miles. It also considers lifelong learning opportunities funded by the Department of Labor in a community on the Connecticut-Massachusetts border.

Indeed, by looking at lifelong learning in local settings, we can gain a genuine sense of what is working and what is not, how things have changed and how they have remained the same, and what the state and national statistics, as presented in the previous chapter by Cross, mean in terms of local learning opportunities. It is in local settings where the policies and funds provided by the federal and state governments are finally translated into learning opportunities, or not, and where the impact of other types of resources on lifelong learning can be observed.

The local realities described in this chapter suggest that we should approach the other chapters with a "Yes, but" attitude. For example, Cross cites California statistics indicating that one out of five citizens over sixty expressed interest in private lessons. Yes, but what local resources are available in different communities to provide the instruction they desire? Similarly, the participation rate of adult part-time learners nationally is 21.6 percent for persons with one to three years of college. But what proportion of the adults in county X or state Y has had from one to three years of college? The U.S. Bureau of the Census reports that 1,114 persons in a particular county in Arizona have less than an eighth-grade education; but how can the director of continuing education in the local community college locate these people?

One problem that affects local learning programs throughout the country is the mobility of the population. The National Center for Educational Statistics (NCES) tells us that in 1975, seventeen million adults participated in some form of organized learning. But also in 1975–76, the Bureau of the Census reports, twenty-five million adults in the country moved—nine million of them to a different county and four million to a different state (U.S. Bureau of the Census, 1977, p. 42). As the census points out, people who tend to move long distances tend also to have attained considerable schooling; as we know from other studies, well-educated Americans tend to seek additional education—resulting in the phenomenon that the most mobile Americans are also among the most interested in lifelong learning. Among the four million movers from one state to another in 1975–76, nearly 80 percent had completed high school and 22 percent had graduated from college. Among the participants in adult education that year, nearly 90 percent had completed high school and fully 30 percent were college graduates.

These data on movers have implications for local providers of learning that seem not to be generally appreciated. In the first place, they tell us that a substantial number of adults will find it difficult to maintain a continuing relationship with a single local provider of education. At least nine million people annually will need to learn once again what educational resources and opportunities are available to them locally because they now reside in a different county. The data also call attention to one factor contributing to the outreach difficulties experienced by local providers of adult basic education: the fact that they are aiming at a shifting target. And the data have implications for educators in rural rather than metropolitan areas. As the census report, from which these statistics were taken, states, "Many 'rural' counties, particularly those with a large state university or a large proportion of older and retired persons, or an especially attractive recreation area, have experienced net migration from other parts of the United States in recent years" (p. 2).

To examine lifelong learning in local settings, this chapter proceeds in three parts. The first section seeks to convey some of the special concerns that arise in local communities by referring to ten locally based studies of lifelong learning, which both support some findings of national and state studies and disagree with others. The second section explores local programs, institutions, and services, using nine major themes as an organizing framework and citing examples of the more innovative or unconventional activities. The third and final section confronts major unresolved issues that follow from the data of the two earlier sections.

Local Concerns

As yet, there has been no systematic review of local surveys of adult learning needs and interests or inventory of local community educational resources. To attempt comprehensive coverage would seem an impossible task: The results of local community assessments often do not reach the stage of formal reports, and, if they do, the reports are known only to agency or organization staff or to community advisory groups. They are neither routinely fed into national information clearinghouses nor published in the professional literature, probably because their authors, as well as journal editors, see them as of local interest only.

However, a good general rule is that wherever you find a

local adult education program, you will find a survey of some sort. The ten examples listed at the end of this chapter and described in the following paragraphs illustrate the wide range of local concerns that such studies address; depict the different methodologies that local planners have found helpful; and confirm the great diversity of needs, interests, and resources from one community to another.

Unequal Community Resources

    Data from four states illustrate perhaps the most widespread local concern about learning opportunities: the dramatic disparities that exist between learning resources in different communities.

    Two contiguous but distinctive areas in Tennessee—rural Monroe County and metropolitan Knoxville, in Knox County—serve as the first example. The following tabulation captures some of the more salient features of the two communities (Peters and Gordon, 1974):

Monroe County	*Knox County*
Located in Southeast Tennessee.	Located in East Tennessee.
Population of 23,475 in 1970, and declining since then.	Population of 177,000 (City of Knoxville) plus 289,000 (metropolitan Knox County).
Average family income, $5,921.	Average family income, $7,893.
75 percent of adults have less than a high school education.	49 percent of adults have less than a high school education.
Educational facilities include 11 public schools, one private military high school, and one private church-related two-year college.	Educational facilities include 111 public schools, 13 private and parochial schools, 6 business schools and various trade and vocational schools, the main campus of the University of Tennessee, plus Knoxville College and the Tennessee School for the Deaf, a zoo, a main library and 20 branches, 4 museums, and 2 newspapers.

It is obvious from these facts that the learning resources in these two communities are substantially different. Learners in the two communities respond differently to questions about their learning activities, according to a survey of a sample of adults in both counties. Although a substantial difference exists in the male-female distribution in the two samples, with 66 percent of the Monroe County sample female, compared with 24 percent of the Knoxville sample—and this discrepancy should be kept in mind in interpreting the following data—responses appear to be related to the availability of learning resources.

In terms of the learning resources that adults in the two communities use, almost twice as many adults in Knoxville are enrolled in programs as in Monroe County—14.7 percent versus 7.4 percent—while nearly a third more are interested in continuing their education: 64 percent versus 46 percent. Experts, books, and magazines are the three most used resources in both samples; but 55 percent of Knoxville's learners report consulting experts, as opposed to 36 percent of those in Monroe County. In contrast, twice as many Monroe people as Knoxville people use family members or television as a learning resource.

Regarding the learning resources that they are aware of, less than half of the Monroe adults can identify any organization or institution offering courses for adults. The leading agencies mentioned are religious groups (45.9 percent), community service groups (38.3 percent), fraternal and social groups (36.7 percent), agricultural associations (30.5 percent), and recreational or sports groups (27.4 percent). By contrast, anywhere from nine out of ten to two out of three Knoxville learners can identify sources of adult education, ranging from college or university adult evening credit classes (91.6 percent) and noncredit classes (85.5 percent) to educational television (78.3 percent), religious groups (71.1 percent), and university- or college-sponsored lectures (69.7 percent).

As to their reasons for not attending adult education classes, Knoxville learners say primarily that they are too busy (48.5 percent) or too tired (34.1 percent), cannot afford them (24.1 percent), are not the studying type (23.6 percent), or find it too hard to get out of the house (19.2 percent), while Monroe learners primarily say that courses are not available (46.8 percent), that they cannot get out of the house (40.3 percent), that they are too busy (37.1 percent) or too tired (36.1 percent), and that they cannot afford them (33.9 percent).

In general we have observed that adults with more schooling tend to participate in education more than those with less schooling. However, despite the higher level of education in Knoxville, twice as many people in Knoxville as in Monroe County cite lack of education as an actual obstacle that they face in planning or carrying out a learning project. Apparently, as one goes up the educational ladder, there is an increased sensitivity to the part that previous education plays in continued learning. Lack of education is seen increasingly as a challenge to be overcome.

These are only the highlights of this study, but they demonstrate how different are the people's interests, knowledge, and needs, as well as the learning resources, in two nearby communities. And they indicate as a consequence how different must be the task of adult educators in these two communities.

The adequacy of adult learning opportunities is also the concern of citizens and government officials in Carter County and the Ardmore area of Oklahoma (Oklahoma State Regents For Higher Education, 1974). Located on Interstate 35 halfway between Oklahoma City and Dallas, Ardmore serves as the county seat of Carter County and has a population of 21,915. But the percentage of adults enrolled in college in Carter County is considerably less than in two other counties—Bryan and Pontotoc—that are part of a ten-county unit making up the Southern Oklahoma Development Association. Only 9 percent of Carter County's twenty- and twenty-one-year-olds were enrolled, compared to 50 percent in Bryan and 57 percent in Pontotoc County. And only 10 percent of its twenty-two- to twenty-four-year-olds were enrolled, compared to 25 percent in Bryan and 21 percent in Pontotoc. Significant for the interpretation of these statistics is the fact that no college is located in Carter County, while Southeastern State College is located in Bryan County and East Central State College is located in Pontotoc County. That adults in Ardmore and surrounding Carter County are interested in taking college-level courses is evidenced by sizable and increasing enrollments in off-campus courses offered in the county by both of these colleges and by a survey of major industrial firms in the county that indicated that over 700 employees were interested in studying some three dozen different subjects, seven of which were of interest to more than thirty-five people each. Some 650 adults each year have been taking courses at the Southern Oklahoma Area Vocational Technical Center, operated by the Ardmore public schools, which serves as a receiving classroom for the Oklahoma Higher Education Television instruction system, linking six state higher education institutions and providing instruction for business and industry personnel. Nonetheless, many employed persons and those with family responsibilities are unable to take advantage of existing courses. This evidence of unmet educational needs has recently led the Oklahoma State Regents for Higher Education to start an innovative pilot program of college-level offerings in Ardmore, using existing state resources and local facilities.

Similar differences of educational opportunity within a local region are evident from other studies. In a four-county area of Minnesota, for example—Stearns, Benton, Sherburne, and Wright—that contains one large city, St. Cloud, but otherwise numerous small rural towns, learning opportunities are heavily concentrated in St. Cloud. Living in the rural areas of the counties constitutes a major barrier to continuing education (Knight, 1976, 1977). And in California, similar differences exist between rural and urban communities as well as between urban centers of similar size, such as Eureka and Santa Cruz. At least in part, these differences reflect differences in effort by local educators, librarians, and public officials to spread educational opportunities throughout their communities and their counties (Peterson, Roelfs, and others, 1975).

Coordination of Efforts

A second area of local concern remains the fragmented and uncoordinated state of adult education, offered as it is by so many agencies and institutions. For example, in the four-county area of Minnesota around St. Cloud, most of the providers of programs agreed that better coordination or "networking" of their offerings was desirable but was so far minimal; both better information and assistance were needed for improved scheduling and service. Few of these providers kept records or gathered data about the participants in their programs or their learning interests and activities, and most of their ideas about past or possible participants and activities are representative of only a "best estimate" figure (Knight, 1976, 1977).

A large metropolitan area, such as Chicago with nearly 150 vocational proprietary schools, has been shown to reflect special problems of coordination. Proprietary schools are relatively free to pursue their missions independently. Their offerings vary not only as a result of such forces as technological changes, new product development, labor market conditions, distribution of student clientele in the area, and competition among themselves for students but also with changes in public education. During Chicago's expansion of its community college system in recent years, for example, the failure rate for both proprietary business schools and data processing schools was approximately half again what it had been before.

Most proprietary schools in Chicago are located near the center of the city, affording some overall convenience for students who commute from outlying areas. A central location is also very important if the school's educational program requires expensive facilities and technical equipment. But one type of school—cosmetology—tends to be scattered throughout the city, serving students more conveniently in the immediate communities in which they live. Some cosmetology schools thus serve predominantly black clienteles, while others serve Spanish-speaking or white clienteles. Different tuition pricing exists in these three submarkets; the highest tuition is charged by black schools and the lowest by the Hispanic schools (Hyde, 1976).

In California, with extensive public adult education and continuing education offerings, a major problem remains that of insufficient coordination among programs and the lack of readily available information for prospective students about these offerings. From an intensive study of seven different California communities, ranging from rural Auburn in the Sierra foothills to central Los Angeles and including the previously mentioned Eureka and Santa Cruz, Peterson and his colleagues reached two major conclusions:

First, the leaders of the various postsecondary programs in the communities are experienced, hard-working, dedicated men and women. In responding to the needs of their communities, however, they have few funds or little time to undertake systematic needs analyses, market surveys, or coordinated planning. As a result, of necessity their programs tend to be reactive rather than progressive: organized after community interest becomes overt and as a result of public initiative, rather than innovative in seeking out need and stimulating demand.

Second, the most immediate problem in adjusting resources to interest does not appear to lie in the creation of new programs but instead in better publicity, information, and distribution of existing programs. Beside their criticisms of red tape, class schedules, and campus location, [community] members noted a lack of readily available information or effective educational counseling about educational opportunities [Peterson, Roelfs, and others, 1975, pp. 15, 21].

Outreach Problems

Poignant demonstration of a third problem—reaching the previously unserved—is illustrated by the work of Mohave Community College in Mohave County, Arizona, in trying to assess and meet the needs of the county's disadvantaged adults. Mohave County witnessed a 234 percent increase in its population between 1960 and 1970, and in 1970 the U.S. Bureau of the Census figures indicated that at least 1,114 of the county's adult residents had received less than an eighth-grade education. For Mohave Community College to locate as many as possible of these people by name, learn their educational interests, and invite or persuade them to participate in further education required a great effort, including contacts with over twenty government agencies, plus service organizations, employers, students, and private citizens, simply to identify and reach them (Jepson, 1974). The college tried a variety of recruiting techniques and expanded the scope of its recruitment effort with volunteers, but it ran into several problems in identifying the prospects (for example, many organizations and agencies believed that ethically or legally they could not give out names), finding them at home (leaving a note, for instance, met with little success), and getting a response from them (the door-to-door salesman approach was a failure). Of the 1,114 persons, the college obtained the names of only 164. Of these, 94 were interviewed, and only 52 were found willing to take adult basic education courses that would provide job-related competence in communication and mathematics. Mohave's experience provides some insight into the challenge facing educators who wish to increase lifelong learning opportunities for disadvantaged adults.

Other difficulties in reaching potential learners involve actual and perceived barriers to further learning. In the California study, for example, prospective students in a predominantly Spanish-speaking area of Los Angeles were deterred both by the absence of Spanish-language books in the local library and by a concern about going to night classes in a downtown location (Peterson, Roelfs, and others, 1975). In a Minnesota study that surveyed both students and nonstudents, it was found that perceptions and attitudes constitute as important obstacles to continued education as do objective conditions. The students were enrolled in a University Without Walls program, and the nonstudents were adults known by these students to be interested in further education. In interviews, the nonstudents typically cited multiple barriers to continued education: For example, an access barrier, such as the lack of a desired program at a nearby institution, was combined with family responsibilities, such as young children at home or limited funds for education. But many of these perceived barriers were related as much to individual values and goals as to purely external factors. Thus, educational planners who deal only with conventional notions of barriers external to the individual, such as class schedules or campus location, may be missing a critical element in the further involvement of adults in learning: In many cases, nonstudents would need help in changing their goals and priorities if they are to decide to become students.

Preferences of Different Groups

That wide variation exists among nonstudents regarding their educational interests is illustrated by a study of blue-collar industrial workers in a five-county region of central New York (Botsman, 1975a). Twenty firms were surveyed, all but four of which employed over 500 workers each. Of these workers, only 19 percent reported having taken a course within the past year, compared with 31 percent of a national sample of adults two years earlier. Their learning interests were somewhat more wide ranging and intense, however, than those of the general population as indicated in the national survey: Fourteen subjects interested at least 20 percent of the blue-collar workers, whereas only nine were of interest to the general population; and the two most popular subjects—building trades and home repairs—attracted 37 percent of the workers, while the two most popular subjects among the general population sample—investments and sports and games—interested only 29 percent and 28 percent of that sample, respectively.

Most interesting, the preferences of these industrial workers in central New York State regarding a desired location for learning activities differed substantially from those of the general population. In contrast to the national sample, which split its preferences somewhat evenly among on-the-job training, public school courses, community college or technical institute courses, and four-year college courses, twice as many of the industrial workers preferred on-the-job training to either public school or four-year college programs, and considerably more preferred two-year colleges, technical institutes, or regional occupational education centers to four-year colleges. Specifically, 57 percent preferred on-the-job programs, compared with 37 percent who expressed interest in two-year college or technical institute courses, 30 percent who were interested in regional occupational education center programs, 27 percent who would take public school courses, and only 23 percent who wanted a four-year college or university course. As Botsman says (1975a, p. 116), "This study has shown that blue-collar workers are not a single homogeneous mass, which can be dismissed as nonparticipant, and conveniently forgotten. . . . It has shown that almost all blue-collar adults say that they wish to continue to learn."

But this study and others also illustrate how different are the learning interests and preferences among groups within the population. In Minnesota, the four-county survey reported earlier (Knight, 1976, 1977) revealed that many more learning opportunities were available in occupationally related fields than in personal development and basic education for adults interested in these courses. And in California, the leaders of postsecondary programs also emphasized vocational programs more than the general education interests of Californians at large would seem to justify (Peterson, Roelfs, and others, 1975).

Unmet Needs of Students

Educators sometimes assume that if adults are enrolled as students, their educational needs are being met. Of course, the fact that significant numbers of adults do not complete their courses suggests that this assumption is not valid. And data from two additional studies point to the needs of enrolled students as an issue of continued concern. A 1976 study surveyed students over twenty-five years of age at the Amherst campus of the University of Massachusetts, where these older students make up over 47 percent of the total student body, to determine their information and assistance needs (Baillie, Eignor, and Averill, 1977). Fully 25 percent of these students reported the following items as either great or moderate needs:

- More information regarding core requirements and major requirements.
- Information on career opportunities in major field.
- Information regarding assessment of abilities and remedial skills.
- Information regarding credit for prior learning.
- Peer counseling in career planning.
- Rent subsidies.
- Information regarding student eligibility for subsidy programs.
- Information on food stamp and related programs.
- More social interaction, including parties, trips to cultural and sporting events, concerts, happy hours, and athletic activities.
- Information on total tuition and fees for one year.
- Information on how and when costs are to be paid.
- Information on specific procedures for applying for aid.
- Information on financial aid application dates.
- Information on how to appeal aid decisions.
- Information on the criteria for aid awards.
- Information on how aid is applied to tuition bills.
- Information on how loans are to be repaid after graduation.

• Information about available grants, fellowships, and scholarships.
• Information about available loans.
• Information about on-campus jobs.

The mundane and reasonable character of most of these needs is striking. What on the surface may appear needs for information of various sorts may, of course, point to more fundamental needs, such as assistance in financing continued studies, locating adequate living accommodations, finding opportunities for leisure, and re-thinking educational and career plans. The extent of these needs suggests that other institutions might well explore similar concerns with their own adult students.

In regard to educational offerings themselves, at the campuses of the University of California significant proportions of full-time students who had been admitted in the fall of 1971 expressed interest the following spring in nontraditional approaches to their academic degrees (Gardner and Zelan, 1972). When asked if they were interested in completing their bachelors' degrees in a program that involved part-time enrollment, instruction at an off-campus location, and lower fees (reflecting the part-time study), 52 percent expressed definite interest in changing to such a program. At the master's or professional degree level, fully 83 percent responded favorably. Whether students at other institutions would react as positively as these at the University of California to a more flexible program and whether nontraditional options would be received as favorably by students now as in 1972 are, to be sure, unanswered questions. But planners of local programs should be prepared to ask such questions, rather than assuming that if students have already enrolled, their educational preferences have already been realized.

Major Themes

What measures have local planners taken to meet the continuing education needs that have been identified? Nine major themes that appear to cover the most significant features of local programming for lifelong learning not only provide an answer but can be recommended as strategies for improving lifelong learning in most local settings during the 1980s:

1. Using educational institutions.
2. Developing the community college dynamic.
3. Modifying institutional roles.
4. Expanding access to credentials.
5. Using new tools.
6. Recognizing student diversity.
7. Meeting individual needs.
8. Adding advocacy to counseling.
9. Relating community and individual needs.

The nine themes have been chosen because collectively they seem to mark out the present boundaries of lifelong learning in local settings in the United States. Each of these themes is sufficiently encompassing that a full treatment of it would require a book-length report, but only selected programs, institutions, or practice can be reported here to illuminate the strategies.

Using Educational Institutions

Traditional educational institutions still remain the primary resource for the instruction of adults and the local school or university building is the facility used for 56 percent of all courses according to 1975 data (Boaz, 1978). This is not to say, however, that the programs conducted at these traditional institutions have not changed over the years.

The evening college has for years represented the main accommodation of higher education institutions to the needs of those whose work, family, or other responsibilities prevent their enrollment as full-time day students. More recently, the weekend college has been increasing in popularity. A survey (Morton, 1977) in 1975–76 of 321 members of the American Association of State Colleges and Universities indicated that twenty-seven institutions had weekend colleges and that fifty-four were planning or developing such units. In addition, eighty institutions offered weekend instructional programming without a special weekend college unit. (A guide to "weekend education" issued in 1976 by W. Cross lists

over 300 weekend residential programs for adults. However, the
providers are not limited to colleges and universities.) It should be
noted that the sponsoring colleges or universities may not regard
the weekend college as one of their regular instructional units, inasmuch as the majority did not offer degrees via weekend colleges.
Then, too, although weekend colleges have been popular where
they were available, in 1974–75 they were available in only eighteen states.

Sometimes, instead of merely shifting schedules, traditional
institutions develop special educational programs for adult students. The development of special degree programs for adults by
small liberal arts colleges was the subject of a doctoral dissertation
by Bunnell in 1974. The study cited eighteen institutions, more
than a third of them in the East, with degree programs that employed "schedules, methods, or techniques to meet the differing
and varying needs of individuals who have a primary commitment
to responsibilities other than their educational activities" (Bunnell,
1974, p. 18). In addition to some forms of schedule modifications,
two thirds of these programs included resident seminars, credit for
learning from life-work experience, independent study, directed
reading, internships, travel study, community projects, credit by
examination, and programs designed by student-faculty negotiation. Of course, special degree programs for adults are not limited
to small liberal arts colleges. This approach to educational programming for mature students has been pioneered by such institutions as the University of Oklahoma, Syracuse University, Brooklyn College, Queens College, the University of South Florida, and
Goddard College.

More recently, the external degree has been instituted by
colleges and universities as an educational option for adult students. A recent study compiled a directory of 244 such programs
offered by 134 accredited or approved institutions (Sosdian and
Sharp, 1977). The external degree program consists of a "formal-
ized but external (meaning that a student with minimum entrance
qualifications can complete it with less than 25 percent of the required work taking the form of campus-based classroom instruction) sequence of studies leading to a particular college level de-

gree." Most, but not all, of the institutions listed in the directory would be regarded as institutions that offer conventional programs of undergraduate instruction in addition to the external degree programs. The local accessibility of external degree programs is difficult to gauge, given that a student need complete only one fourth of the requirements in campus-based instruction. Yet this condition may present a problem for some adult learners.

Degree programs are not the only area in which traditional institutions have been expanding learning opportunities for adults. The Elderhostel, designed for elderly learners, is one interesting innovation (National University Extension Association, 1977). What began in 1975 as a summer program at five New Hampshire colleges, coordinated by the Division of Continuing Education at the University of New Hampshire, has by now grown to thirteen regional Elderhostel organizations spanning the country, with national headquarters located outside Boston. Elderhostels are not routine summer sessions. The courses, usually of a week's duration, are designed to be of particular interest to mature adult learners. Opportunities are also available for participants to pursue highly individualized educational interests. One recent participant, who also happens to have been an adult educator, has written an article on the 1977 Elderhostel at Skidmore College (Brickman, 1978). In it, he offers suggestions for future programs, including arranging for participants to plan some of the program; having instructors available at other than class times; encouraging contacts with regular undergraduates, and arranging financing so that it is not a burden to the sponsor institution.

Colleges and universities are also seeking to attract adults to regular summer sessions on campus. In many such programs, arrangements can be made to accommodate families, with special events for younger members. The number of such programs has grown enough so that *New York Magazine* in the spring of 1978 published a twelve-page directory of those offered in the vicinity of New York City.

Elderhostels and new summer programs for adults may be signaling a broader interest in an adult education form known in Europe, and especially in the Scandinavian countries, as the Folk

College. Folk Colleges are generally small, residential programs that emphasize cultural or social studies rather than vocational subjects; allow faculty to teach what interests them most; and eschew grades, credits, and competition, striving instead for a spirit of fellowship. A good primer on the Folk College is a working paper written by Kathryn E. Parke (1977). The Folk College Association of America, formed in 1976, has as its mission the encouragement of educational opportunities modeled after the Folk Colleges. The leadership of the association and its membership are exploring the potential of this concept in the United States.

Certainly, one of the major educational services provided by colleges and universities is noncredit adult education. In this area there has been a dramatic increase in both institutions offering programs and in registrations for those programs from 1967–68 to 1975–76 (Kemp, 1978). Over 2,000 institutions reported that they sponsored such activities as classes or short courses, conferences, institutes, workshops, independent study or correspondence study, lecture series, closed circuit TV or radio instructions, telelectures, and field studies. Total registrations in 1975–76 reached almost nine million, with public institutions accounting for about 90 percent of them. The question can be asked whether these learning opportunities are equally accessible to all adult learners who wish to study. We can observe, for example, that ten institutions, each with total registrations in excess of 100,000 in 1975–76, accounted for more than one fourth of all continuing education registrations in the country (Kanun and Swanson, 1977).

While a good number of residential continuing education centers are in operation, there is some confusion as to the precise number that exist. The most recent directory, published by Syracuse University in April 1978, lists sixty-eight such facilities, including five that are U.S. Civil Service Commission centers. According to that directory, centers east of the Mississippi outnumber those west of it by better than two to one.

The above recital of programmatic changes within traditional institutions—special degree programs for adults, weekend colleges, noncredit continuing education, and residential centers— should not imply that these are mutually exclusive options. Some institutions are effecting comprehensive accommodations to adult learning requirements by utilizing combinations of these programs. Wayne State University is an example. Its armamentarium of adult programmatic efforts includes a special adult degree program, a weekend college, noncredit and credit continuing education offerings, open-circuit television courses, independent study, off-campus learning sites and registration offices, plus other features. A second example is one pointed to the future. Utah State University is on record with a proposal to build "life-span learning facilities" at a cost in excess of $5.5 million to be integrated with the development of learning opportunities intended to serve both youths and adults in a region embracing Montana, Idaho, Utah, Colorado, Wyoming, and Arizona. The university has already received $3.5 million from the W.K. Kellogg Foundation for this purpose. Included in the plans is a new residential continuing education center (Utah State University, n.d.).

Developing the Community College Dynamic

Community colleges have emerged as major resources for lifelong learning in America. They have (1) recognized and developed programs for special groups, (2) developed flexible organizational forms, (3) applied new educational technology to reach adult students, (4) produced materials and programs suited to adult students, and (5) developed community support relationships. Let us cite examples of each of these developments:

Programs for Special Groups. Community colleges have developed special programs for various sectors of the adult population, recognizing clearly that this student group is not a homogeneous mass to be approached with one general program or service. The following are some examples of programs that have been devised by community colleges for particular populations.

- For the elderly—Emeritus College, College of Marin (California).
- For union members—Monroe County Community College in collaboration with Wayne State University (Michigan).
- For families—Family College, Rockland Community College (New York).
- For commuters—Chabot College Independent Courses For BART Users in San Francisco area.

- For mentally retarded adults—Napa College (California).
- For rural women—Enterprise State Junior College (Alabama).
- For ex-offenders—Florida Junior College, Jacksonville.
- For prisoners—Mercer Community College (New Jersey).
- For deaf adults—Delgado College (Louisiana).

Flexible Organization. Community colleges have demonstrated an amazing array of ways in which they can be organized to offer education. John Wood Community College in Illinois, for example, is an administrative device that utilizes the instructional resources of Quincy College, Gem City College, and Quincy Technical Schools in Illinois together with Culver Stockton College and Hannibal LaGrange College in Missouri. Students, however, receive grades, credits, certificates, and degrees from John Wood Community College. In a similar fashion, the Hudson County Community College Commission in New Jersey acts as a broker to purchase instruction from Jersey City State College, Jersey City Medical Center, St. Peters College, and Stevens Institute of Technology. Another example of special organizational arrangements is WOR–WIC Community College in Maryland, serving students in Worcester and Wicomico counties and using community facilities rather than a central campus. In several large metropolitan areas, the community college systems have also established citywide units to look after special adult education needs in the whole community. Examples would be Chicago City Wide Institute, Pioneer Community College in Kansas City, Missouri, and the Institute For New Dimensions in Los Angeles.

New Uses of Technology. Community colleges have pioneered and in more recent years refined the use of technology to reach adult students. Televised instruction, pioneered by TV College in Chicago, among others, is now offered by the Dallas Community College District, Bergen Community College (New Jersey), Miami-Dade Community College, Coast Community College (California), Milwaukee Area Technical College, and other institutions.

Community colleges have gone beyond television in their search for useful technologies. Recently, a program designed to link Courses By Newspaper to on-campus learning experiences has been implemented under the title Courses By Newspaper Forum.

Twelve colleges are developing community forums based on the newspaper courses, and in at least two instances special efforts to serve handicapped learners will be made. Johnson County Community College (Kansas) will videotape the forums, and these programs will be signed for hearing-impaired viewers. Delgado College in Louisiana will arrange for the forums to be broadcast over local radio for the blind, and a trained interpreter will be present at the forums for the deaf.

Other examples of effective uses of technology by community colleges include the following:

• Foothill College (California)—Phone-A-Course Everyday. Courses on audio cassettes that are available by telephone day or night.
• Consumnes River College (California)—Telelibrary, video cassettes on a wide variety of topics of concern to elderly, delivered through local libraries.
• Bunker Hill Community College (Massachusetts)—Modularized, individualized approach to its entire curriculum.
• ACCESS—Association of Community Colleges For Excellence In Systems and Services, based at College of DuPage in Illinois. Technology for rapid transmission and storage of instructional materials, which permits the recording of a complete two-term course on a single TV tape.

Materials for Adult Students. Community colleges are producing instructional materials, counseling materials, and other aids directed particularly to adult learners. These materials are not restricted in their use to a single institution. For example, the materials distributed under the banner of Career Education For Nontraditional Students by Northern Virginia Community College are print-based career skills packages designed to help adult students evaluate and implement career goals. Moreover, as noted above, several community colleges are engaged in the actual production of television courses (Luskin and Zigerell, 1978). These courses require the writing, procurement, and distribution of collateral materials like study guides, texts, workbooks, and tests to form complete instructional packages. The availability of such instructional packages may be one of the important factors in the acceptance of television courses.

Community Support Relationships. Community colleges are also increasing their effectiveness in working with various constituencies in the local community. A good discussion of the range of relationships that are possible is to be found in *Five Community-Based Programs That Work* (Owen and Fletcher, 1977). The kinds of activities discussed in this reference include assessment of community needs, use of community advisory committees, joint planning with local agencies, joint scheduling, registration, cross-registration, and cooperative use of facilities with other providers of education in the community.

For a statistical treatment of the provision of community services by community colleges, the reader is referred to a survey of 1,275 institutions in the United States and Canada conducted in May 1976 by Fletcher, Rue, and Young (1977). The tabulation in this study of the community colleges' offerings from among close to two dozen different community services shows substantial variation. At the top of the list, more than three out of four colleges included the provision of library facilities, assistance to business and industry in identifying educational needs, programs to upgrade job skills, cultural events, courses and services in health care, and programs for women, minorities, and other special interest groups. Services of lowest frequency were the provision of computers and technical facilities for use by the community, outreach counseling centers, and courses by television, newspapers, and other media. (Still, more than four out of ten colleges offered media courses.) This study also indicates the uneven distribution of educational services: more than one third of the total institutions reporting provisions for community education were concentrated in the states of California, North Carolina, Texas, Illinois, New York, and Virginia.

The community college dynamic has owed much to the leadership and assistance provided by the American Association of Community and Junior Colleges (AACJC). Special units sponsored by AACJC that serve to keep its membership alert to lifelong learning developments include the Center for Women's Opportunities,

Community College CbN Forums, Community Education–Work Councils Program, Task Force on the Use of Mass Media For Learning, the Center for Community Education, the National Council on Community Services and Continuing Education, Offender Assistance Through Community Colleges, and the Service Center for Community College–Labor Union Cooperation. With that kind of interest and support coming from the national association, it is easy to see why local community colleges have a special dynamic in lifelong learning.

While it has been easy to find examples of particular community colleges to illustrate their outreach to adult students, it is equally important to recognize that the particular programs, services, or arrangements described here are not uniformly available to adult learners throughout the country. A fine program may operate at one or more colleges and yet not be available to any and all learners who may be interested. The program providing vocational preparation for educable mentally retarded adults at Long Beach City College obviously does not help an adult in similar circumstances in Norfolk, Virginia. By and large, one needs to live in the community where a program is offered to take advantage of it.

Modifying Institutional Roles

Communities are increasingly recognizing that lifelong learning resources are not limited to educational institutions. And organizations whose primary function is not education are becoming aware that they have educational roles. Such institutions as libraries, museums, the professions, industry, and government can provide important learning opportunities, as the following examples show.

Libraries. What began in 1970–71 as a project sponsored by the College Board to support a few libraries interested in helping adults prepare for the College Level Examination Program (CLEP) evolved into the Library Independent Study and Guidance Projects (LISGP) in the period from 1972 to 1974 and is today being continued as the Consortium for Public Library Innovation, headquartered in Minneapolis (*College Board News,* 1976). The College Board provided coordination, staff, and financial support for

LISGP with the assistance of the Council on Library Resources, the National Endowment For the Humanities, and the Division of Library Programs, U.S. Office of Education. The focus of the project gradually shifted from preparation for CLEP to concern for adults who for any reason had an interest in independent study. The project therefore addressed the general question of what needed to be done by libraries to meet this kind of need effectively (Office of Library Independent Study and Guidance Projects, 1974a).

Ten libraries participated in the project: Atlanta, Denver, Portland, St. Louis, Salt Lake City, Tulsa, Cleveland, and Miami-Dade Public Libraries, as well as Enoch Pratt Free Library (Baltimore) and Free Public Library of Woodbridge (New Jersey). In general, the project resulted in constellations of some of the following kinds of services being provided by the libraries:

- Educational consulting services to assist with learning plans.
- Clearinghouse and referral of independent learners to resources in the community.
- Expanded library holdings and materials for independent learners.
- Training of staff in counseling and adult learning styles.
- Development of specific resources for independent learners, such as study guides.
- Services to those who could not come to library, including books by mail and telephone counseling.
- Suitable space and physical facilities.
- Publicity.
- Contacts with community agencies or programs, such as advisory councils and, in one instance, an external degree program.

Library services for adult learners are by no means confined to the projects listed. Especially noteworthy is the development of collaborative arrangements between libraries and local higher educational institutions. Through a program called Studies Unlimited, public libraries in Chicago make available video tapes of courses offered by Chicago TV College. Students can study the tapes, take exams, and receive credit from TV College. The University of Wisconsin at Oshkosh and the Oshkosh Public Library have also joined in a project called Public University, which features short one-credit undergraduate mini-courses available at the library as slide-tape programs or cassette tape lectures.

A particularly useful reference on library services for adult learners is the entire April 1975 issue of the *Drexel Library Quarterly*, devoted to "Library Services and the Open University."

Museums. Despite the disclaimer in a recent reference work on museum education that "an art museum is not a school, a day-care center, a business, a library, a university, or a settlement house, however many of these functions it may sometimes have" (Newsom and Silver, 1978), museums nonetheless have significant educational roles. They offer the following kinds of services:

- Exhibits
- Special courses for adults.
- Special outreach programs for segments of the community not inclined to come to the museum.
- Training of docents.
- Special programs for professional artists.
- Books, reference works, and other materials.
- Programs for those interested in professional museum careers and opportunities for scholars.

In fact, art museums resemble conventional educational institutions in their educational service to adults. A wide range of adults may be served by a particular art museum, for example, the University of Rochester Memorial Art Gallery has a membership of roughly 9,000, the Museum of Modern Art in New York City a membership of 30,000. However, a survey of the membership of the Memorial Art Gallery suggests that members may be somewhat older than adult college and university students. (27.7 percent were twenty-six to thirty-six, 39.5 percent were thirty-six to fifty years of age.) Most prominent among the reasons cited for becoming members were a general interest in art (63.9 percent) and a desire to take art classes (32.2 percent).

Museums share with conventional education institutions the fact that they recognize needs of special adult populations. For example, the Philadelphia Museum of Art has a four-year program that combines the use of the museum's collection with a studio course in sculpture designed specifically for blind and partially blind students. Examples of other programs for special adult student clienteles include the following:

- Everson Museum, Syracuse—A penitentiary art workshop.
- Virginia Museum of Fine Arts, Richmond—An artmobile for rural populations.
- Metropolitan Museum of Art, New York—Programs for senior citizens.
- Albright-Knox Gallery, Buffalo—Sculpture program for the blind.
- Anacostia Neighborhood Museum, Washington, D.C.—Special program for low-income adults.

A particularly interesting outreach project started in 1974 by Museums Collaborative, Inc. (1977) in New York City is the Cultural Voucher program, designed to broaden the participation of the adult population in the cultural resources of the city. The program permits community organizations to propose cultural programs of their choice and then via a voucher system arranges for the reimbursement to the museum (zoo, botanical garden, or other institution) for the services provided. Annual grants in the form of vouchers ranging from $3,000 to $8,000 are awarded to the community organizations participating in the program. During the period September 1975–August 1977, more than 600 separate projects were undertaken by twenty-four cultural institutions and community organizations. The bulk of these projects consisted of lessons in the arts, including poetry, music, and dance (53.3 percent) and courses in art, anthropology, and the like (22.6 percent).

In general, art museums may seem more oriented toward young learners than adult learners. According to Newsom and Silver (1978, p. 32), "Slightly over half of America's art museums regularly provide guided tours, gallery talks, lectures, clubs, classes for adult visitors, compared with 70 percent that regularly provide similar services for school children." Nonetheless, within art museums there is a unique adult learner population—the docents. Of the 23,900 museum volunteers, 30 percent worked in education programs as docents or teachers, many receiving intensive weekly training. Docents generally are well educated, prosperous white women—"the single most museum-educated audience in the nation." Although no studies have assessed the impact of continuing museum education on this self-selected audience, museums judge it substantial.

A special resource for information regarding museum education is the Center For Museum Education at George Washington University. Its 1978 publication *Lifelong Learning/Adult Audiences, Sourcebook #1* is one that readers of this chapter with an interest in museum-based adult education will find especially informative.

Private Industry. Learning opportunities provided under the sponsorship or encouragement of employers are another major category of adult educational resources. *Education In Industry* (Lusterman, 1977) was commented upon from a national perspective in Chapter One. However, a particularly useful feature of this Conference Board report is its inclusion of specific examples, such as Eastman Kodak, Mobil Oil, Butt Grocery Company, American Airlines, General Electric, and General Motors, as well as more detailed profiles for Cincinnati Milacron, John Breuner Company, and John Hancock Mutual Life Insurance Company. In reading these profiles one cannot help but be impressed by how the fact of being an employee of a particular organization influences the learning opportunities available to an individual. At Eastman Kodak, for example, vocational training services provide apprentice training in sixteen skills ranging from carpentry to glass blowing; the professional services training emphasizes computer-related and information systems courses, statistical and mathematics courses; management training services offer training for supervisors, courses related to evaluating job performance, writing and reading skills; and photographic training services emphasize developing an understanding of photography. The learning opportunities at the two other companies for which detailed profiles were provided are substantially different.

Another aspect of company training and education is that provided to nonemployees. Whirlpool Corporation is an example of a company that offers home study courses on the repair and maintenance of major home appliances. The twelve courses are open to anyone who wishes to take them. These courses are complete instructional packages including tests that can be returned to Whirlpool for grading. The graded test directs the student to specific places in the study material for questions not answered correctly. Since 1973 over 16,000 persons have enrolled in the courses, which are offered for a surprisingly low tuition charge—under $30 for most courses. For students completing the courses successfully, a record of their learning is maintained. Continuing Education Units (CEU) are awarded, and students can request transcripts of their CEU records.

Several examples of industry cooperation with public education institutions have also been noted. A study completed in 1975 (Winkfield, Granger, and Moore, 1975), which the authors admitted was incomplete, listed more than 100 such programs. They covered such areas as adult basic education, General Educational Development Test preparation, skills training, English as a Second Language, preretirement seminars, courses for college credit, and leadership seminars for women. This study also produced case studies of five selected programs, three of which have been selected for comment here to provide a general indication of the kinds of collaboration effected.

One program brings together Wharton County Junior College and Johnson Testers, Inc. in Texas. The college provides machinist training at the company plant from 10 P.M. to 12 midnight one night per week for fifty weeks; the employer provides time off for the first hour and time and a half for the second hour. The employer reimburses the college for tuition and provides for purchase of books and the use of company equipment at no charge. The college provides and pays for the instruction.

A second illustration involves the Grand Rapids Schools and the Fisher Body Plant of General Motors. This arrangement permits employees to complete the requirements for a high school diploma and also take vocational and college courses at the plant. The company provides class facilities, teaching equipment, and storage space. The Community Education Program covers the tuition charges, teachers, materials, and supervision.

A third illustration involves the Lancaster-Lebanon Intermediate Unit 13 and the Walter W. Moyer Company in Pennsylvania. The program provides basic skills instruction designed to assist people to pass the General Education Development (GED) tests. A particularly interesting feature is that the program is open to nonemployees as well. Classes are offered twice a week at night. The company provides space, desks, chairs, storage, and a TV cable hook-up. The schools provide the instructors. Participants do not pay anything for the program.

Government. Governments, as well as industry, provide local learning opportunities for employees. The educational resources available to government employees are indeed quite extensive. For example, the Government Education Center in Los Angeles makes assessments of the education and training needs of all levels of government. There are over 1.3 million government employers in 3,000 agency sites of the ten-county area served by the Center, which began operations in September 1975. The center looks to the available resources in the community for instructional purposes, and it has encouraged the development of career counseling services. It is sponsored by the Los Angeles Federal Executive Board and the College Federal Council For Southern California. The budget for the first two years of operation was about $540,000.

The ten regional U.S. Civil Service Training Centers also offer extensive learning opportunities to employees at all levels of government—federal, state, local, and, in the case of the Denver Regional Office, tribal units. The Denver Center's mission includes responsibility for two resources that are national in scope. The National Indian Training Center located in Utah provides educational opportunties for Indian people and government employees who work with them. The National Independent Study Center, established in 1976, provides correspondence courses for government employees in all parts of the country. By 1977 nine courses were available. As more courses are made available, this service will become especially valuable for government employees drawing overseas assignments.

The Federal Regional College in Chicago arranges for classes to be offered by City Colleges of Chicago (Loop College) and Northeastern Illinois University in classroom space provided by the federal government. Courses are scheduled on employee time or shared time (before work, including some work time; extended lunch period; after work, including some work time). The colleges contracting to offer the courses grant the credits and degrees.

The Civil Service College, an operation of the San Francisco Community College District, offers courses both for people who wish to prepare for public service occupations and for people in those occupations who need additional training. This program was inspired by the simple observation that one sixth of all jobs are public service positions. The program is tuition free. Courses run from 7 A.M. to midnight except Sundays. All classes are open to the public. About 150 courses were listed in the Fall 1976 catalog.

Professional Associations. The professions are another source of continuing education in local settings. State-mandated continuing education requirements are increasing. As of 1977, optometrists faced the most state regulations mandating continuing education, with forty-five states having relicensure requirements (Phillips, 1977). For other professionals, the situation was as follows:

Nurses	9 states
Lawyers	4 states, 3 additional with specialty requirements
Realtors	11 states
Veterinarians	18 states
Social Workers	6 states
Pharmacists	14 states
Nursing Home Administrators	38 states
Physicians	17 states
Certified Public Accountants	23 states
Dentists	8 states

The connection between such requirements and local adult education learning opportunities is fairly obvious. The requirements generate learning needs, and the adult with these needs tends to seek out local resources to meet the needs. For example, Phillips (1977) notes that in Ohio pharmacists are joining professional organizations in record numbers and showing particular interest in

meetings with continuing education on the agenda; pharmaceuti-
cal manufacturers, for their part, are developing low-cost educational programs for their pharmacist customers.

The professional societies themselves are becoming increasingly active in assisting their members to meet mandated continuing education requirements. Phillips indicates that most associations conduct their own continuing education programs as well as
assisting local chapters. Magazines are a popular device for bringing instructional content to the learner. Associations may also offer
learning packages and home study materials, including self-
assessments.

Expanding Access to Credentials

Since credentials are so important in our society, facilitating
access to credentials has become a key function of adult education.
In the 1970s several state and national developments have made
it easier for adult learners to earn credentials. Three state programs now offer adults the opportunity to qualify for undergraduate degrees on the basis of demonstrated learning: New York's
Regents Degree, New Jersey's Thomas A. Edison College, and
Connecticut's Board for State Academic Awards. In addition, the
College Proficiency Examination Program and the College Level
Examination Program have increased their examination offerings
and the number of students they serve. In 1976–77, for example,
the latter program administered approximately 385,000 tests, including over 145,000 to servicemen and women via the Defense
Activity For Nontraditional Learner Support. The 1970s also saw
the development of the American Council on Education project,
through which academic credit recommendations for noncolle-
giate-sponsored instruction are published by the Office on Educational Credit. In the early 1970s, the Cooperative Assessment of
Experiential Learning project administered by Educational Testing Service focused national attention on a variety of approaches
to assessing and crediting adult learning acquired prior to enrollment in college. This project resulted in a new national postsecondary educational association known as the Council For The Advancement of Experiential Learning (described in Chapter Six).
There have been similar developments at lower educational levels,

such as the Adult Performance Level Tests from the University of Texas and competence-based approaches to the high school diploma in New York State and elsewhere.

Local developments have also increased access to credentials. Most notable of these developments are (1) new institutions, (2) new programs in existing institutions, and (3) new linkages between institutions and services. Community-oriented educational institutions serving adults emerged in the 1970s in sufficient numbers to prompt the establishment of the Clearinghouse For Community Based Free Standing Educational Institutions (CBFSEI) in Washington, D. C. The Clearinghouse is a membership organization serving educational institutions that are community based and community controlled, free standing and independent of state support, involved actively in community development, and serve disadvantaged and minority people. There were thirty-five member organizations in 1978. These organizations are attempting to reach and serve adults who by and large are not being reached by any of the programs or institutions mentioned earlier in this chapter. Their clienteles include adults with some of the following characteristics: low income, self-taught, rural, migrant, seasonally employed, black, Spanish speaking, Puerto Rican, Navaho Indian, and, frequently, craft or skill oriented. While each member of the Clearinghouse is unique, a common purpose of many of the members is facilitating access to educational credentials.

In 1977, when the Clearinghouse had twenty-six members, it indicated (CBFSEI, 1978) that its membership provides "direct educational services to over 100,000 individuals and reaches another 250,000 through a variety of support services." Member organizations are seeking to be accorded recognition as legitimate and responsible educational institutions. Those whose educational programs warrant it are seeking accreditation from regional accrediting associations (Campus Free College, Vermont Institute For Community Involvement, Hoosuck Institute, Colegio Cesar Chavez). Some, such as the Malcolm King: Harlem College Extension, are receiving support and cooperation from established educational institutions—in this case, Marymount Manhattan College, College of Mount St. Vincent, and Fordham University.

New programs have also emerged within existing institutions that are facilitating access to credentials. One example is the external degree, mentioned earlier in this chapter. Most external degree programs are offered by established institutions. However, a new service is being offered in the Twin Cities metropolitan area by the six local community colleges. This service, known as the Metropolitan Assessment Services, conducts assessments of competencies acquired prior to enrollment, which are accepted by all members of the consortium. A service generally comparable in nature is one offered by the Life Experience Center, whose assessments of learning acquired in nonacademic settings are recorded as credits on Edinboro State College transcripts. More comprehensive services are available in Vermont through a unit of the state colleges known as the Office of External Programs.

The Women's Career Program at Northeastern University tackles the credentials issue in a different manner. This program analyzes jobs in local industries in terms of competencies required rather than credentials. The service then offers short (one-year) academic programs to develop the job-linked competencies as rapidly as possible.

New linkages between institutions and services also serve to facilitate access to credentials. The East Central College Consortium, consisting of seven small liberal arts colleges in Ohio, West Virginia, and Pennsylvania, is now offering an external degree program. It has developed independent study materials, procedures for the assessment of prior learning, and trained faculty for new roles and responsibilities with adult students.

In the Midwest, several centers for off-campus teaching have been established cooperatively by colleges and universities to improve access to instruction, particularly at the graduate level (Quad Cities Graduate Studies Center, Rochester Postsecondary Education Center, University Consortium Center). A program of a different character, yet one that serves the same end, is a joint project by the University of Missouri School of Medicine, the University of Nebraska, and the University of Kansas to offer a Health Services Management Program. The consortium will develop curricular materials and then use the three state universities and community and private colleges to provide instruction. Finally, in Indianapolis is a program called Learning In The City, a project of the Consortium For Urban Education, which unites the educational resources of universities and colleges, business, and city government. It arranges for courses at convenient times and places in the downtown area, for which some companies and governmental units grant employees released time. More recently, it added an Adult Education Information Center. The reader is also reminded that an example cited earlier in this section, namely Malcolm King: Harlem College Extension, is a linkage arrangement among three New York City private colleges.

Perhaps one of the more complex linkage arrangements is that represented by the Union for Experimenting Colleges and Universities. Some two dozen or more institutions have joined forces to develop and sponsor the University Without Walls program, which is executed through instructional facilities at individual colleges and universities. A unique feature of the program is that the student's degree may either come from the individual institution where the course work was done or, under certain circumstances, may be awarded by the Union. What the future holds for the Union and its programs at this moment is in doubt because of financial difficulties. In July 1978, students and faculty of the Union petitioned the federal courts to place the institution in receivership and an accrediting team of the North Central Association of Colleges and Schools recommended accreditation be withheld because of the Union's financial problems (*Chronicle of Higher Education,* July 17, 1978, p. 2).

There are three references that address many of the ideas discussed in this section. One of them is *Extending Opportunities For A College Degree: Practices, Problems and Potentials* (Medsker and others, 1975). This work, an analysis of extended degree programs (extended campus, liberal studies adult degrees, individualized study, or degree by examination), includes, among its special features, guidelines for implementing extended degree programs. More recently, new guidelines have been issued for planners based on a review of the original work in a policy seminar (Medsker and Edelstein, 1977). The third reference is a text on open learning systems (MacKenzie, Postgate, and Scupham, 1975). While it is international in its orientation and has more than a dozen case studies, it includes discussions of Empire State College, Metropolitan

State University, and the Community College of Vermont. This work also has a chapter specifically addressed to issues that confront planners of open learning systems.

Using New Tools

Innovative adaptations of technology represent one of the strategies available to planners who recognize that rigidly scheduled classroom instruction may not meet the needs of many adult learners. The 1970s have witnessed not so much the appearance of new technologies as the development of new competence in applying various technologies to expand educational opportunities for adults. Here, again, we can call attention to only a few of the many technologies and cite local examples of their use.

To what extent radio and television are used for adult education in local settings is difficult to say. A report prepared for the Corporation For Public Broadcasting's Advisory Council of National Organizations (Witherspoon, 1974) contains some information, but its current reliability is not known. The report notes that from 1968 to 1972 the proportion of broadcast hours of instruction by television intended for college and adult students dropped from 22.6 percent to 14.6 percent. Educational radio stations in 1972 reported only 5 percent of their instructional broadcasts were intended for continuing adult education and continuing professional audiences. However, since these data were published we have seen several exceedingly popular television courses broadcast nationwide and offered for academic credit by local colleges and universities. Typically, credit students are expected to register with a local institution, partake in a limited number of on-campus seminars, and take an end-of-course proctored examination. Following is a partial listing of television courses offered in recent years.

Course	*Year First Offered*
"The American Presidency"	1974
"Science and Society"	1975
"Ascent of Man"	1975
"Transformation of American Society"	1976
"Adams Chronicles"	1976
"Latin America: The Restless Colossus"	1977

"Age of Uncertainty"   1977
"Classic Theatre"   1977
"Paradox of Power: U.S. Foreign Policy" 1978
"The Growing Years"   1978
"The Long Search"   1978

A number of colleges and universities are making use of Instructional Television Fixed Service (a system of television transmission making use of microwave frequencies for limited point-to-point coverage at costs comparatively lower than required for VHF or UHF facilities). By 1973, twenty-nine higher education institutions had such facilities, which were being used typically to carry instruction from campuses to classrooms located in business and industry. Institutions utilizing such arrangements, usually for individuals pursuing degrees in engineering or management, include Illinois Institute of Technology, University of Southern California, Case Western Reserve University, University of Michigan, University of Pennsylvania, University of South Carolina, and Stanford University.

Applications of cable television for adult education purposes are being made by several institutions, including City University of New York, Flathead Valley Community College in Montana, and Purdue University in Indiana. A particularly interesting experiment, which will bear watching, is a two-way cable communication system being developed by six communities in the Dayton, Ohio, area. Such a system could bring about substantial changes in communications in practically all facets of community life (Brown, 1978). However, it obviously holds special promise for education.

The telephone is another technology that has had diverse applications in adult education. Its use in actual instruction for home-bound adults has been demonstrated by the University of Wisconsin, the Kansas Regents Continuing Education Network, and the Los Angeles Unified School District, among others. In the latter case, about 500 adults, handicapped and confined to hospitals, were reported in 1974 to be receiving instruction by phone (*Education Training and Market Report*, 1974). A unique instructional application of the telephone, Phone-A-Course, which combines the telephone with recorded audio cassettes, was cited earlier.

The Rhode Island Career Education Project has also demonstrated that the telephone can be used effectively for educational counseling of adults. In Kansas, adults may call a special WATS line for information about post–high school learning opportunities and careers. SUNY College at Purchase, New York, has designed, pilot tested, and implemented a system that handles registration for adults completely by telephone. That system began when a staff member observed that course registrations really should be no more complex than airline reservations.

Courses By Newspaper, which originated at the University of California, San Diego, are dependent on the readiness of local colleges and universities to support the program by offering whatever orientation may be required, plus examinations. The arrangement calls for the college rebating $5.00 out of the tuition charges to Courses By Newspaper for each student who takes the course for credit. These monies are then used by Courses By Newspaper to help develop succeeding courses. Courses By Newspaper began in 1972, and now two courses are regularly offered each academic year. By 1976 there were 5,000 readers registered per course. Between 200 and 300 colleges participate in this program, which provides opportunities for adults to secure academic credit. In 1977 a new community college program called Courses By Newspaper Forum came into being. Participating institutions offer a regular forum series on campus to parallel the materials presented in their local newspapers. The most recent extension of Courses by Newspaper is an arrangement through which these courses will be made available through business and industry company newspapers and magazines.

The idea of using the newspaper as a vehicle for instruction has had other extensions. In Vineland, New Jersey, a General Education Development Program series called "Its Never Too Late" is carried by the local newspaper in cooperation with the adult education program in that community. The newspaper course serves as a partial basis for helping adults prepare for the General Educational Development Tests.

Several institutions have harnessed a variety of technologies—audio cassettes, video tapes, film strips, films, slides, and computers—to create personalized programs of instruction that enable adults to pursue their educational objectives much more independently. These arrangements permit adults to set their own schedules and to pursue their educational interests at their own pace. One example is the program of modularized courses available through the University of Southern California's Flexible Education Program, which makes use of audio cassettes. Another example is the program at Central Nebraska Technical College that uses taped lectures, demonstrations on film, and programmed assignments.

Finally, to return to another aspect of educational television, in the late 1970s several institutions have become quite involved, either singly or in various consortial arrangements, in the production of televised courses for adults. The courses may be broadcast on open-circuit channels, leased or sold to other institutions for use in closed-circuit internal transmission, or used in special training contexts. The newer institutional producers of television courses have also acquired substantial marketing expertise. They not only produce a technically fine TV course but they also simultaneously arrange for the production, sale, and distribution of study guides, texts, and other supplementary learning materials. Typically, an administrative manual is also made available, which provides complete guidance to the administrator as to how to proceed to have the course offered for credit on a local campus. The names of some of the institutions particularly well known for their expertise in producing complete media instructional packages are Miami-Dade Community College, Coastline Community College, Bergen Community College, Wayne State University, and Massachusetts Institute of Technology. The latter now offers over 450 16mm film or video tape lectures on sciences, engineering, and management, which include study guides, reading assignments, and problem sets as well.

For a general overview of how colleges and universities are using media, especially television, the reader can do no better than to consult *Media and the Adult Student* (Carlisle, 1976). This reference focuses on eleven very different institutions around the country whose media-related program budgets range from $45,000 to $7 million.

A second overview, dealing with the use of multi-media programs in industry as well as colleges and universities, is available in a report prepared for the Directorate For Science Education, National Science Foundation (Biedenbach, 1977). This report also contains an extensive bibliography and lists names and addresses of people conversant with programming in continuing engineering education, as well as video publishers and providers of packaged materials. In his commentary on industry use of multi-media programs, Biedenbach says, "Industry and government have probably made the most efficient use of multi-media programs of any of the major institutions in our society. The reason is that they have specific requirements which are very well defined, indicating which employees need a particular educational experience. The military has probably led the way in the development of multi-media materials to train their personnel. The major reason, of course, is that they encompass large numbers of people who need the same kind of educational or training experience and also are widely dispersed" (p. 108).

Recognizing Student Diversity

The development of programs for particular categories of adults suggests that increased attention is being paid to the theme of recognizing the diversity of adult learners. The essence of this theme is that adults are exceedingly varied in their social circumstances, needs, and educational development and that for educational purposes they cannot be approached as though they were a homogenized mass. It seems safe to say that adult learners represent a substantially greater range of differences on more significant dimensions for education than we would find among traditional school-age learners. This elementary fact is increasingly being recognized. As a consequence, we see lifelong learning programs being planned not for adults in general but for a variety of subgroups within the adult population.

It is fairly commonplace for local program planners to recognize the major conventional categories of adult learners—women, minorities, elderly, and handicapped. Yet even this fairly basic classification hints at some of the problems of local program implementation. Some adults fall into more than one of these categories—minority women and elderly handicapped, for example.

Below are some categories of adult learners together with some examples of institutions offering special programs for those groups.

Adult Group	*Program*
Women	Barat College—Regular college classes opened to adult women.
	Saint Mary of the Woods—Women's External Degree.
Handicapped	Metropolitan State College—"College For Living" for mentally retarded adults and coordination for similar programs operated by Mesa College, University of Southern Colorado, University of Northern Colorado, and University of Colorado.
	Long Beach City College—Vocational preparation program for educable mentally retarded adults.
Union Members	College of New Rochelle—New Resources Program for members of District Council 37, American Federation of State, County, and Municipal Employees, AFL-CIO in New York City area.
	University of Michigan, Dearborn Campus—Project REACH, offering courses on audio cassettes for union members.
Minorities[1]	Experimental and Bilingual Institute, New York City—Program for Spanish-speaking residents of East Harlem.

[1]For descriptive information on several programs directed to minorities, see Pantoja, Blourock, and Bowman (Eds.), *Badges and Indicia of Slavery* (Lincoln, Nebr.: Study Commission on Undergraduate Education and the Education of Teachers, 1975).

	Watts Skill Center—Program for black residents of South Central area of Los Angeles.
Elderly[2]	University of Kentucky—Donovan Scholars Program, open to any retired adult who wishes to take courses. One of the pioneering programs of its type.
	Fairhaven College—Bridge Project, a residential program that integrates older students with regular enrolled students.
Midcareer change	Metropolitan State University—Life and Career Planning For Adults.
	University of South Florida—Re Focus Program.
Employees	St. Mary's College, Minnesota—Employee Learning Program.
	Hartford Graduate Center, Connecticut—Working Professionals.
Low Income	DeAnza Community College—Women's Re-Entry Educational Program.
Apprentices	Women Apprentices—YWCA of metropolitan Denver, Better Jobs for Women Program.
Rural	Oklahoma State Department of Vocational and Technical Education, "Mobile Career Development Programs"—Counseling services delivered by mobile vans that travel from community to community.
	North Central Technical Institute—

[2]For a summary of institutional programs for the elderly, see Florio, *Collegiate Programs For Older Adults* (New York: Academy For Educational Development, 1978).

	"Career Education For Persons in Rural Areas."
Commuters	Chabot College, California—Courses for BART Commuters in San Francisco area.
	Adelphi College—Graduate Courses In Business Administration, taught in Long Island Railroad commuter cars.
Prisoners[3]	Jackson Community College Prison Program, Michigan.
Adults With Families	Rockland Community College, New York—Activities offered for entire family unit.

The list of special programs suggests one of the problems in dealing with the diversity of adult learners. How adequate for educational purposes are the conventional ways of grouping adults? There are all kinds of ways to classify people, but what systems can be derived from theory or from more empirical or analytical approaches to the question? The reader is directed to two sources for assistance in this regard. The first is a paper titled *Different Strokes For Different Folks* (Appalachian Adult Education Center, n.d.). This paper proposes four categories of adults with less than a high school education and then goes on to suggest the general characteristics of educational programs that would be effective with each of the groups. For example, one group is the stationary poor, described as so "fatalistic that they do not believe they can have any control over their own futures. Thinking it is the only thing to do, they often exhort their children not to hope or set a model for not hoping—thereby perpetuating the cycle of poverty. They are unemployed and unemployable." This group is further described as needing clearly articulated subgoals on which they can work and as being less likely to interpret their problems as information needs.

[3]For a reference on college-level prison education, see Seashore and others, *Prisoner Education Project New Gate and Other College Programs* (1976).

The second resource is the emerging literature on the psychosocial development of adults. A synthesizing article on this subject has been written by Arthur W. Chickering (in Keeton and Associates, 1976).

Meeting Individual Needs

The literature of psychology and sociology and the tenor of recent decades have moved the learner to an increasingly central position in adult education. We see this in curricular developments that have been referred to as contract learning and competence-based education, in new institutional arrangements such as learning exchanges and free universities, in individualized and independent study programs, and in re-entry counseling. These developments seem to be captured by the theme "meeting individual needs."

Traditionally, degree requirements have been measured in precisely defined semester-hour credits. More recently, competence measures have emerged as an alternative basis for academic recognition. Competence refers to specific behaviors the student is expected to demonstrate in order to qualify for academic credit or a degree. For example, the New York Regents Associate degrees in nursing require that the candidate be observed and evaluated for two and one half days while extending real patient care and performing simulated laboratory exercises in actual hospital settings. Competence-based education is, of course, not confined to the postsecondary level. In New York State a performance route to a high school diploma was initiated in 1972, and in 1975 eighteen high school diplomas were presented to the graduates of the Central New York External High School Diploma Program (Nickse, 1975).

Contract learning is a development that has paralleled competence-based education. In contract learning, the student defines the learning outcomes to be attained. The student and a mentor or facilitator representing the college or university then develop a written agreement incorporating the learning objectives, the resources to be used, and the methods and criteria for assessing the learning. While contract learning and competence-based education are concepts that are not restricted to adult learners, they have been programatically implemented in institutions serving adult clienteles (Trivett, 1975b). Empire State College, Metropolitan State University, and Community College of Vermont offer examples.

Learning exchanges (now called *learning networks*) illustrate another aspect of an increased attention to individual needs and requirements. The idea of a learning exchange is beguiling in its simplicity. Someone wishes to learn something, someone else is prepared to teach something. The problems are practical ones. How does the learner describe his or her needs? How does the teacher describe his or her competence? What mechanism brings these two basic pieces of information together? What does it cost to do this? Who pays for it?

The Learning Exchange in Evanston, Illinois, established in 1971, is now incorporated as an independent not-for-profit organization. It derives its income from members, who receive information about the exchange, including a list of over 2,500 subjects for which instruction is available, a newsletter, and a private telephone number at the exchange for members only (*The Learning Exchange News*, 1977). By 1975 it had a full-time staff and reportedly its services were used by 20,000 people in and around Chicago (*Psychology Today*, 1975). From the learner-teacher perspective, its operation is as follows: Members who wish to learn call in and receive referrals to people prepared to teach and then contact those people directly. Members who wish to teach call in and describe what they are prepared to teach, what background they have, whether they will teach in groups or individually, what compensation they expect, where they are prepared to teach, and so on. Learner information and teacher information are recorded and maintained on card files.

An extension of the learning exchange concept is the free university (an organization offering ungraded, unaccredited classes to the general public). As noted in Chapter One, free universities began in 1964 and by 1976 they numbered over 200. Initially, they were campus based and college student oriented (*Adult and Continuing Education Today*, 1976). The University of Man, a free university headquartered in Manhattan, Kansas, is of particular interest because of its efforts to bring free university type programs to twelve rural communities in Kansas. This was done during the period between 1975 and 1977 with the assistance of twenty-four VISTA volunteers. In that period of time about 12,000 rural residents took 700 courses. One of the useful by-products of the project is the *Kansas Community Education Manual,* a very practical how-to-do-it reference that covers all the basics of establishing and operating such a program (Dwyer and others, 1978).

Independent learning opportunities represent another way of attending to individual needs and requirements. Collectively, these opportunities include all efforts made to assist learners proceeding on their own, at their own pace. The Bachelor of Arts in Humanities program at California State University, Dominguez Hills, is an illustration. The program features study guides, faculty contacts with students in communities where they reside and via telephone, a weekend seminar at the beginning of the program, newsletters, optional seminar, informal study groups, and use of radio, television, records, tapes, and films. Other examples of this approach include the External Studies Program of the University of Pittsburgh and the College-At-Home Program of Northampton County Area Community College, headquartered in Bethlehem, Pennsylvania.

A major expansion of independent study opportunities will occur when the Carnegie Corporation–funded Committee on Institutional Cooperation project is completed. This project, which started in 1976, will provide upper-division correspondence courses needed by students who intend to qualify for a degree via home study. Credits for such courses would be accepted for a degree at Indiana University, the University of Wisconsin, and the University of Iowa.

Individualized learning is a further variant of the strategy of attending to individual needs and requirements. Here the student has the opportunity to proceed relatively independently in the direction of his or her own learning interests. Miami-Dade Community College's Life Lab Program is an example. The essence of the program has been captured in the title of a program report, *On Your Own—But Not Alone* (Johnson and Ross, n.d.). This program uses a contract system, but in addition there is extensive use of media-based materials (recorded interviews, documentaries, TV programs, an extensive audio tape library, a reprint library,

TV cassettes), competency-based study guides, comprehensive testing, and counseling.

There are increasing signs that adult education program planners are beginning to recognize that adult students cannot function well if they are simply turned loose in an instructional program without first having had substantial individual or group counseling. Re-entry counseling, therefore, could logically have been treated here as part of the theme of attending to individual needs and requirements. However, counseling is treated in the discussion of educational brokering immediately following.

Adding Advocacy to Counseling

Educational brokering[4] emerged as a significant concept in the early 1970s, when several counseling agencies added student advocacy to their traditional counseling, advising, information, referral, and assessment functions. The National Center for Educational Brokering (1976) describes advocacy as placing learners' interests and needs above those of institutions. It can take two forms: intercession on behalf of individual students or efforts to change institutional policies that hamper adult learners' progress.

In 1978 the first directory published by the National Center for Educational Brokering listed 215 locations in 41 states "where information and advice on educational and career decisions are available to people not currently in educational institutions." Included in the listing were 44 nonprofit independent agencies, 42 public libraries that have advisory services for adults, and 31 interinstitutional arrangements involving colleges and sometimes libraries and school systems. In addition, 8 Educational Opportunities Centers were listed, even though they were based at a degree-granting institution. Probably the most extensive service geograph-

---

[4]Educational brokering is not to be confused with the commercial operations of education brokers. The latter term has been used on occasion to refer to profit-making organizations whose services include the location, identification, and recruitment of students; program development; records processing; and to a lesser extent faculty recruitment and faculty review. Brokers apparently offer a service of value to local providers of adult education. How extensive the operations or the degree to which brokers' services are being used by colleges and universities or other providers of education is not clear at this time (Johnson, 1977).

ically is the program of Community Based Counseling for Adults of the University of Wisconsin Extension, which offers services in 40 counties in the state. New York State also has over 40 sites where brokering services are available, with the majority of these offered through libraries (National Center For Educational Brokering, 1978). With close to 40 percent of the brokering services listed in this initial directory located in but two states, we have another instance of uneven distribution of educational services for adults.

In 1978 we will see the initiation of a service that may combine the functions of educational brokering and commercial education brokers. The Learners' Cooperative, funded by a grant from the Fund For The Improvement of Postsecondary Education, will both offer educational advisory service and negotiate lower tuition rates than those charged to individual students by contracting with colleges and universities through agreements much like those made available to employers, trade unions, and other groups. Learners' Cooperative will function as a typical cooperative. Members will direct the operation; each member will vote; and any savings or benefits will redound to the users (Fund for the Improvement of Postsecondary Education, 1977).

A similar operation already exists for nurses in Illinois (Marcec, 1977). EDUCARE is a modified form of prepaid continuing education for nurses operated by the Southern Illinois Health Manpower Consortium (SIHMC), which includes 32 hospitals, 6 community colleges, and Southern Illinois University, Carbondale. For an annual membership fee of $20, SIHMC guarantees to produce 12 contract hours of continuing education for professional nurses. EDUCARE provides a constellation of services for its more than 500 members: a career profile plus counseling services from member community colleges, a newsletter announcing topics of current continuing education programs, an annual printout of Continuing Education Units earned, and programs that meet requirements of the American and Illinois Nurses Associations. In arranging these services, EDUCARE not only assures nurses of continuing education at times and places they will find convenient and at costs lower than they would pay otherwise but also assures the providers of student customers, reducing their financial risks and record keeping.

Matching learners and resources for learning requires access to information about the learning opportunities that are available. Various models of information services have emerged in local settings. They range from independent community agencies (Regional Learning Service of Central New York), to libraries (Lifelong Learning Center, Free Public Library of Philadelphia), to state higher education systems (Education Hotline in New Jersey), to telephone counseling and information services (Career Counseling Service, N. Kingston, Rhode Island), to computer-based guidance systems (System of Interactive Guidance and Information developed by Educational Testing Service), to computer-based information systems operated especially for low-income groups (Computer Based Educational Opportunity Center in New York City). It is expected that statewide education information services will become commonplace as the provisions of recent federal legislation are implemented.

Relating Community and Individual Needs

In all of the previously discussed themes of adult education in local settings, the underlying rationale for educational service has assumed the services were directed to the needs, interests, and goals of individuals. However, the community itself may have needs and requirements for the further education of its adult citizenry, and advancing the educational development of the individual may be seen not only as a way of enriching the individual but also as a way of improving the community. McMahon wrote in this vein in 1972 as follows: "The total educational needs required to solve or reduce a major community problem are different from the individual educational needs of those who comprise the community. . . . Historically the focus of adult education was on the individual and his needs. It is only in recent years that attention has turned to community needs as such" (p. 27). Community education programs are specific expressions of this concept.

Community education is generally regarded as having six major components: the kindergarten through twelfth grade instructional program, programs for children outside the formal K–12 curriculum, plus four additional components particularly relevant to local adult education. These components are use of facilities as community education centers, programs for adults, use of community services, and community involvement (Charles Stewart Mott Foundation, 1978b).

As noted in Chapter One, substantial support for community education has come from two sources. One is the Community Schools Act of 1974, through which in FY 1977 approximately $3.5 million was awarded to ninety-two local education agencies, state education agencies, and institutions of higher education (Federal Community Education Clearinghouse, 1978b). The second is the Charles Stewart Mott Foundation, which now dedicates a major portion of its total grants each year to its support of community education projects. In addition to grants directed to particular communities, the foundation also supports fifteen regional community education centers training programs, which offer master's and doctoral programs.

Some federally funded community education programs seem overly ambitious at the local level of implementation. One program listed as its objective to foster understanding of drug abuse, to increase enrollment in general education development programs, to assist unemployed and underemployed in career planning, to assist in developing proficiency in business and vocational education, plus several other goals including reducing crime and delinquency. All this was to be accomplished by a project funded at $28,000 (Federal Community Education Clearinghouse, 1978b).

Three specific examples will be used to illustrate aspects of the relationship of community needs to individual adult learning needs in local settings. One is the Urbanarium, a project being sponsored by a consortium of nine institutions in the Rochester, New York, metropolitan area: the Center for Governmental Research, Monroe Community College, Nazareth College of Rochester, Rochester Institute of Technology, Rochester Museum and Science Center, Rochester Public Library, St. John Fisher College, State University College of New York at Brockport, and WXXI-TV-FM. Membership in the Urbanarium will be open to nonprofit organizations whose aims are consistent with those of the Urbanarium. The mission of the Urbanarium is to improve the civic competency of citizens in the Rochester community to make well-informed policy decisions on selected issues. It hopes to do this via a wide-ranging program that will include assessment of major community problems, forums, development of information on solutions to problems, stimulation of interinstitutional cooperation, facilitation of interdisciplinary approaches, and ongoing evaluations of programs and activities that are undertaken (Urbanarium Coordinating Office, 1977).

Programs directed to improving public leadership are another way of relating community needs and individual adult education needs. These have emerged in several communities. The oldest, apparently, is Leadership Atlanta, which began in 1969. In this program, sixty persons participate in annual retreats, monthly programs, and task force assignment as they receive an in-depth orientation to decision making in Atlanta, extending over a nine-month period. Leadership Atlanta is a nonprofit organization and is supported mainly by participant tuition and funding from the Atlanta Chamber of Commerce. These programs are reported to be in operation in about thirty communities (Bigham, 1977).

Our third example is the Nebraska Vietnamese Physicians Educational Program, which was operational during the period June 1975–December 1977. The example is interesting in and of itself, and it calls attention also to the transitory nature of certain community needs to which adult education can be responsive. The problems being addressed in this instance were the combined needs of twenty-one rural communities in Nebraska that were without physicians and displaced Vietnamese physicans who did not have the credentials to practice in this country. The program provided a constellation of educational support services needed by the physicians to develop competency in English and the additional training required to pass medical licensure examinations. The result was twenty physicians practicing medicine in rural Nebraska (National University Extension Association, 1978).

A more inclusive definition of the term *community* will contribute to the reader's understanding of this theme. A community may refer to people with common interests living in a particular area. However, it may also refer to a group of people with a common characteristic or interest living together in a larger society. Consequently, we can have urban-rural communities, but we can also have communities of ethnic groups or occupations. In any event, a sense of community tends to develop among adult members of a population who recognize that advancing the learning interests of its members serves the needs of the community as a whole. This is an important focus of the local members of the Clearinghouse For Community Based Free Standing Institutions, discussed under the theme "expanding access to credentials." As a group, the institutions that are members of the Clearinghouse offer educational programs that attempt to serve identifiable community needs as well as adult learning needs. Thus, lifelong learning in local settings in the 1970s has seen the emergence of new organizational forms to accomplish these dual purposes.

Unresolved Issues

From the multitude of issues surrounding lifelong learning in local settings, four have been chosen for comment here. The first is the uncertainty that plagues educational innovations. The second is the overriding problem of coordination of local programs and resources. The third is the related issue of goal setting at the local level. And the fourth is the question of how to maximize the utility of local studies, surveys, and research.

While in local settings in the 1970s we have seen many innovations in adult education, the field has not been without its failures. Some ideas for new programs died during studies preliminary to proposals (Iowa Commonwealth University would be an illustration). Some ideas emerged as formal proposals only to die because of lack of support in critical quarters (for example, Pennsylvania Open College). Sometimes a plan is actually implemented but in very different form than originally conceptualized and then fails under unusual circumstances. Perhaps the prime example is Lincoln Open University: Conceived as a public institution in Illinois, it was chartered finally as a private college and failed amidst bizarre educational and financial frauds.

In some instances, an idea is implemented as a demonstration project but no provision is made for continuing the operation after its demonstration is concluded. A classic example is Project Communi-Link, set up in Colorado in the early 1970s to demonstrate how communities could develop and maintain coordinated comprehensive adult education programs. It was based on the concept of establishing a communications network among groups in a community concerned about adult education. After the network was established, the project tried to demonstrate a systems approach to adult education planning. The project expanded to thirty-two communities in fourteen states. When it was completed, a report was issued, but there was no organization or resources for continuing the project (Project Communi-Link, 1973).

Of course, some plans are implemented as conceived and still fail. Examples would include one of the early brokering services, Capital Higher Education Service in Hartford, Connecticut; the very popular and highly regarded clearinghouse on postsecondary innovations, known as NEXUS, sponsored by the American Association For Higher Education; and the Extended University Program of the University of California, which began in 1972, admittedly as an experiment and pilot program, but was being phased out during 1976.

These and other efforts that have not succeeded need to be recognized as part of the general climate surrounding lifelong learning in America. Of course, during the same period in which these educational experiments failed there were also failures of traditional institutions serving traditional student populations. Yet there is a subtle distinction. The adult learner tends to greet new educational programs and opportunities with some degree of skepticism—and to be especially sensitive to their demise. If innovative programs and institutions acquire a reputation for impermanence, interest and support for lifelong learning may be weakened. It may be too limiting on new programs to ask they have built-in disaster plans. Nonetheless, the planners of innovative adult learning programs have a special obligation to find ways to share the risks of those they encourage to participate.

Certainly a major issue that surfaces in local education settings is that of coordination. What can be done at the local level to minimize raw competition for the same students on the part of programs and services that are not appreciably different? More to the point, how can all the resources of a community be coordinated to make available the maximum of educational service and opportunities for all?

The models of local coordination range from very simple to very complex, and communities themselves seem to differ in the extent to which local coordination is regarded as an issue of sufficient magnitude to merit serious attention. However, there is reason to suspect that coordination problems usually exist, whether or not circumstances have brought them to the community's attention. Sometimes the problems of coordination begin within an institution. A recent study at the University of Michigan observed that there were "no less than 38 separate continuing education units on the Ann Arbor campus" (Eisley and Coppard, 1977, p. 129).

It is not difficult to find illustrations of cooperation, collaboration, and mutual support at the local level. The examples that follow will progress from simpler to more complex but with no implication that it was necessarily easy to arrange the less involved coordination efforts. For example, Cooperating Raleigh Colleges in North Carolina joins together six higher education institutions in a variety of mutually supportive efforts. Most of these are programs that would go on even if no adult students were involved, such as cross-registration agreements or faculty development programs. However, the six institutions are also the joint sponsors of an adult learning information center, which is physically located in the local county library.

In New Jersey it was recently announced that community colleges and county vocational-technical schools are about to offer joint degree programs in various technological trades. Bergen Community College and Vocational-Technical Schools of Bergen County will offer the degree of associate of applied sciences in electrical technology, for example. The program provides that students will take technical courses at the technical schools and general education and less job-related courses at the community colleges (Hanley, 1978).

In Denver, Colorado, the Adult Education Council, a nonprofit membership organization, provides information about educational and cultural opportunities. The Council supports the Community Information and Resource Center For Lifelong Education (CIRCLE). Three times a year CIRCLE publishes *Educational Opportunities,* containing over a thousand of the most requested courses and a list of more than fifty educational centers that offer adult programs. At a still higher level of coordination, the seventy-one colleges in Pennsylvania Region I (the five counties around Philadelphia), of which as many as fifty offer continuing education, have undertaken a study funded by the Kellogg Foundation to plan a delivery system for higher education in the region. Task force reports are presently being assembled, on the basis of which it will be decided what activities the institutions will undertake jointly. (Incidentally, this project came about because of a strong negative reaction to a coordination plan conceived at the state education department level.)

The *Employment and Training Report of the President* (1977) contains an interesting discussion of aspects of coordination of federal programs that impact at the local level. As is now well appreciated, all training and education activity resulting from federal initiatives is not assigned to a single department in the federal bureaucracy. Administration of the Comprehensive Employment and Training Act (CETA) is assigned to the Department of Labor, whereas the Department of Health, Education, and Welfare (HEW) has responsibility for many other federal education programs. The issue is how to coordinate these federal efforts in local communities. In appreciation of this underlying problem, HEW Regional Manpower Coordination Units designated a number of CETA prime sponsors to whom HEW would provide coordination assistance. For example, in Lafayette parish, Louisiana, an agreement was reached whereby the local welfare agency sends clients to CETA prime sponsors for training. The agency provides social services to CETA at no charge. The local school board provides basic education and General Education Development (GED) courses. CETA prime sponsors make public service employment slots available to the school board. A local health planning agency makes assessments of shortage occupations in health fields. The CETA prime sponsor trains enrollees in these fields.

In Vermont, CETA supplies tutors for an adult education program through which home tutoring was provided to 3,411 students in fiscal year 1976. These students were located in areas where class instruction is not feasible. They are people with transportation and childcare problems.

In 1975 we saw the publication of a comprehensive study of the interrelations of education and work entitled *The Boundless Resource* (Wirtz, 1975). The study, done under the auspices of the National Manpower Institute, called for "local communities and states to bring together manpower and education planning, to provide career advising within the content of the realities of the longer-term labor market, and to relate systematically business managements, labor organizations, and our formal educational institutions with the arrangements for private training and skill acquisition" (Wirtz, 1975, p. xi). More specifically, the study called for the establishment of Community Education-Work Councils. Pilot councils were established in 1976 under a project funded by the U.S. Department of Labor and coordinated by the National Manpower Institute. The American Association of Community and Junior Colleges also supported five councils selected because of their potential for development of distinct models. One council is used as a basis for discussion here because this council involves collaboration among diverse educational providers, including schools, business, industry, and colleges. It also shows some of the adult education ramifications of the Comprehensive Employment and Training Act. In addition, the example shows that it is sometimes difficult to confine problems within local boundaries. In this instance, the needs being addressed crossed state lines. The source of the following information is the final report for 1977 and progress reports for two periods in 1978 (Education-Work Council, 1978).

The Education-Work Council in Enfield, Connecticut, was sponsored by Asnuntuck Community College and started in the spring of 1977. It recruited a broad membership in the Hartford, Connecticut, and Springfield, Massachusetts, area by inviting 112 persons and organizations to join. By the fall of 1977, there were 87 members distributed as follows:

	Number	*Percentage*
Manufacturing	11	12.6
Public Service	22	25.3
Education	20	23.0
Labor	4	4.7

Business	13	14.9
Associations	9	10.3
Media	0	0.0
Youth	2	2.3
Others	4	4.6
Independent	2	2.3
	87	

In its short life the council has gotten a number of significant projects underway. It has also appreciated some of the limitations or barriers that had to be overcome. The council reported that "collaboration is not as easy to achieve as one reading the Wirtz publication might anticipate" (p. 61). We will come back to this point in a moment. Let us look first at the council's progress. Since the province of the council includes school-to-work transitions, activities are not all necessarily directed to adult learners. They include the following:

- Development of a career resource directory.
- Manpower planning seminars.
- Student survey completed in schools in Connecticut and Massachusetts.
- Research on barriers to youth employment.
- A Future Machinist Film.
- A senior citizens' project including a Widow's Center, A Peer Career Counseling program, a retired senior volunteer program, and a Senior Citizen College.
- Remedial Instruction Centers for Adults.
- Alternative Ways of Learning—a referral service to learning opportunities, support services, and counseling services.

The last four of these are part of five CETA projects funded at $387,000.

By being located on Interstate 91, the council discovered that employment opportunities and problems, educational resources, and people to be served along this highway were not limited to Connecticut but extended to the Springfield area of Massachusetts as well. Therefore, questions arose about developing a collaborative relationship with the Community Council in the Springfield area and possibly the Massachusetts Occupational Information System. The council discovered that regional manpower data for this area were not routinely available, though they would be extremely useful.

The final report of the Education-Work Council listed the following items as significant elements in developing collaboration among its members:

1. Vested interests assume an important role. As members were recruited for the council, the question was constantly raised, "What's in it for me?"
2. A self-determination process in goals clarification was quite time consuming but also very important. With this conclusion has come the discovery that collaboration is not just communication but a process involving trade-offs.
3. There is a need for a smaller group to serve as a catalyst—a group prepared to make decisions and to move ahead.
4. The Council wishes to be independent of the federal and state governments. It feels sufficiently strongly about this that the Council is considering incorporating itself as a nonprofit corporation.
5. Who legitimizes the actions of the Council is a very important issue. This Council has learned that simply because it has influential opinion leaders on its board, it is not automatically legitimate. The Council is sensitive to the absence of a direct representation of teachers, counselors, and parents in its membership and would like to find a solution for the problem.
6. The Council senses a need for forums through which interests not represented on the Council can be heard and can hear the Council.
7. Implementors must be involved in planning. Local support at participating institutions is vital if initiatives undertaken by the Council are to succeed.

The author believes that the Council's sensitivity to these matters may in itself be a critical factor in the success that it has enjoyed to date.

One of the basic problems of local coordination is the absence of any authority for assigning and defining responsibility for coordination. Coordination of local efforts seems highly dependent upon local leadership and initiative. Such seems to have been the case with regard to all of the examples discussed above. One of the consequences is that what is seen as requiring coordination or collaboration is defined quite differently from one local setting to another.

An issue related to local coordination of learning opportunities is the issue of local goals. Ordinarily, individual providers of adult learning opportunities set their own goals. However, in the absence of effective coordination, individual organizational goals may be in conflict with each other. Moreover, needs and interests of individuals or groups of learners go unattended. The author is unaware of any local study, including those conducted in communities with seemingly varied and comparatively plentiful educational resources, that reported that all learning needs and interests have been attended to.

Should every local community try to provide for every adult learning need and interest? If the practical answer is no, this cannot be done, then which needs or whose interests should be given priority through local resources, which needs and interests should be referred to services, agencies, or resources beyond the local community, and which needs and interests are either set aside or remain as assignments to be handled by individuals as best they can? This is a critical general issue at the local level for which we have neither the mechanisms nor the rationale for deciding.

In regard to rationale, for example, is it the number of people sharing a common learning interest that should serve as the deciding factor? Is it the severity of the learning deprivation without particular regard to the numbers affected? Is it learning directed to practical ends that is to be favored over learning for "personal" satisfaction or leisure? Is it learning that people are willing and able to pay for out of their own pockets? Is it the age of the learner with younger adults favored over older or vice versa?

In regard to mechanisms, what local agency or organization do we recognize as the adult education authority at the local level? Perhaps some day in the future, local governments will turn to establishing such authorities, which appear to be virtually absent today. However, the current absence of an effective voice on the part of many unserved learners has been responsible for the emergence of new local educational organizations and agencies that are now seeking to establish their legitimacy in the local community at large. This seems to account for and characterize most, if not all, of the membership of the Clearinghouse for Community Based Free Standing Educational Institutions. However, when we project the limited resources of the Clearinghouse against the vastness of local communities in the country, we really have not found the ways to deal with the issue of local goals.

Finally, the last issue is how we can maximize the benefits from local studies of adult education. As was noted earlier, such studies have contributions to make beyond the settings in which they were conducted. However, at the present time we have not exploited them as effectively as perhaps we might. Three types of problems need to be addressed: (1) accessibility of local studies, (2) methodological concerns, and (3) cross-community data comparisons. The first problem, learning about the local studies that have been done, may suggest another clearinghouse, but perhaps we can avoid that step. Perhaps the many professional associations concerned with adult education could be encouraged to suggest to their respective constituencies that local studies should be written up and the reports submitted to the Educational Resources Information Center (ERIC) Clearinghouses. This comment is directed not just to the conventional adult education associations but to associations of all groups involved in the education of adults—industrial human resource developers, museum education directors, librarians, military service training units, and so on. Secondly, the many professional associations might encourage the discussion of local studies at their annual forums.

The second problem concerns methodology and limited resources. That is, what methodologies are most appropriate for what purposes in local settings? The background problem here is that local planners do not have the resources to commit to local studies despite their need for good information. The average funding for the ninety-two community education projects was only slightly in excess of $38,000 during fiscal year 1977, for example.

Local planners have limited funds, and frequently they are under time pressures that limit their ability to engage in research of lengthy duration.

The third problem is our current inability to make cross-community comparisons. How do we define and measure learning experiences? How do we define and measure needs? How do we define and measure educational resources? Are there criteria for evaluating programs that have general applicability? The absence of such measures or agreement as to which measures are appropriate suggests the barriers that exist to cross-community comparisons.

To summarize a chapter on lifelong learning in local settings is as much of a challenge as writing the chapter itself. We began by saying that we can learn a great deal about lifelong learning in America if we will listen to the people. Local studies give us insights that are not provided by national or state studies because they pursue different concerns or issues. We then looked at lifelong learning from a local perspective and noted the new developments that have occurred in the 1970s—new institutional forms, new services, new programs. We are beginning to recognize that adult learners exist who are different from those previously served. Efforts are being made to reach out to them. We have noted, too, that there is a climate of change and innovation in local adult settings but that not all innovations succeed. Lifelong learning implies that the services or learning opportunities an individual requires will be available whenever and wherever he or she wants them. It is here that the local perspectives on lifelong learning differ from federal or state perspectives. It is in local settings that the uneven distribution of learning opportunities or the mismatch between learners' expectations and available resources occurs. In the local communities there remains the challenge of how best to achieve what may be an impossible dream.

Source List: Illustrative Studies of Lifelong Learning in Local Settings

Arizona

Jepson, P. *Assessment of Training Needs of Adults in Mohave County.* Kingman: Mohave Community College, 1974.

California

Gardner, D. P., and Zelan, J. *A Strategy for Change in Higher Education: The Extended University of the University of California.* Paris: Organization for Economic Cooperation and Development, 1972.
Peterson, R. E., Roelfs, P. J., and others. *Community Needs for Postsecondary Alternatives.* Sacramento: California legislature, 1975.

Illinois

Hyde, W. D., Jr. *Metropolitan Vocational Proprietary Schools.* Lexington, Mass: Lexington Books, 1976.

Massachusetts

Baillie, D., Eignor, D., and Averill, D. *Nontraditional Student Needs Assessment Project.* Amherst: University of Massachusetts, 1977.

Minnesota

Klinger, K., and Marienau, C. "Barriers to Adult Learning." *Delivery,* 1978, *1* (2), 3–4.
Knight, D. *Alternatives for Lifelong Learning in Minnesota: The Nonformal Educational Sector, Summary Report.* St. Paul: Minnesota State Planning Agency, 1976.
Knight, D. *Lifelong Learning in Minnesota: The Nonformal Educational Sector, Final Report.* St. Paul: Minnesota State Planning Agency, 1977.

New York

Botsman, P. B. *An Analysis of the Continuing Education Interests and Needs of Blue-Collar Factory Workers.* Ithaca: Cornell Institute for Research and Development in Occupational Education, 1975a.
Botsman, P. B. *The Learning Needs and Interests of Adult Blue Collar Factory Workers.* Ithaca: New York State College of Human Ecology, Cornell University, 1975b.

Oklahoma

Oklahoma State Regents for Higher Education. *Postsecondary Education in the Ardmore Area: A Study of Needs and Priorities.* Oklahoma City: Oklahoma State Regents for Higher Education, 1974.

Tennessee

Peters, J. M., and Gordon, R. S. *Adult Learning Projects: A Study of Adult Learning in Urban and Rural Tennessee.* Knoxville: University of Tennessee, 1974.

CHAPTER FOUR

State Policies: Plans and Activities

Susan A. Powell

To describe the range of state plans and activities in the area of lifelong learning requires an overview of a wide variety of educational programs initiated and funded by the states, including extension, adult, and continuing education programs, literacy programs, outreach and off-campus programs, and external degree programs—as opposed to those that are privately, federally, or institutionally backed.

This chapter offers such an overview under five general headings: (1) statewide policy studies, (2) counseling and other brokering services, (3) external degree and related programs, (4) consortia and other regional arrangements, and (5) instructional programs for specific target groups, such as the elderly, the unemployed, and the functionally illiterate. It *illustrates* these plans and activities without attempting to *inventory* every last one of them or evaluate any of them as ideal models for other states to copy. The chapter is based on the examination of several hundred state documents, including those cited in the chapter source list, and on interviews with educators and political leaders in four states selected for their different demographic, fiscal, social, and historical backgrounds: Massachusetts, Florida, Illinois, and Pennsylvania.

Statewide Policy Studies

By far the most common state activity in the postsecondary sector of education with regard to lifelong learning is planning: the holding of planning conferences, the undertaking of policy research, the drafting and publishing of master plans. The hundreds of recommendations stemming from this planning and embodied in the documents listed at the end of the chapter range from specific proposals for legislative and institutional action to vague requests for changes in public attitudes. And evidence indicates that the vast majority of these suggestions for change are never implemented.

Recently, state planning activities for lifelong learning have taken three basic forms: conferences, research projects, and master plans.

Conferences

As part of their planning processes, several states have sponsored major conferences on the problems and promise of lifelong learning, bringing together people knowledgeable about the topic and influential in affecting state policies and practices. Three recent ones—in New York, Pennsylvania, and Florida—illustrate the process.

New York. In May 1974 the Bureau of Post-Secondary Continuing Education of the State Education Department sponsored a meeting on "Lifelong Learning: Diagnosis and Prognosis," to elicit from participants "specific recommendations which could be translated into useful actions" (New York State Education Department, 1974, p. 1). The participants were drawn primarily from academic and governmental institutions, and their recommendations dealt basically with four areas of concern: (1) articulation of planning and programming, (2) credentialing, evaluation, quality, and the management of human resources, (3) historical and economic views of the role and structure of postsecondary education, and (4) individual, institutional, and governmental responsibilities for the financing of programs and of student participation.

Pennsylvania. In December 1976 the Pennsylvania Department of Education held a meeting on "Merging Educational Innovations With the Concept of Lifelong Learning: Making the Pieces Fit." Conferees discussed topics ranging from the role of libraries in lifelong learning and alternative programming for lifelong learning to the educational needs of such groups as prisoners and older adults and the varieties of possible new client services, including information systems for potential students, brokering networks, educational entitlements, alternative assessment procedures, the educational credit bank, and individualized degree programs (Ziegler, 1976).

Florida. In February 1977, Orlando, Florida, was the setting for a conference on "State Planning for Lifelong Learning: Improving Access For All Citizens," sponsored jointly by the Florida Postsecondary Education Commission, the Education Commission of the States, the Postsecondary Education Convening Authority of the Institute for Educational Leadership, the National Center for Educational Brokering, and the State and Regional Higher Education Center of Florida State University. It examined recent federal initiatives affecting lifelong learning, including the Education Amendments of 1976, state planning dealing with adult education and nontraditional postsecondary systems, and educational brokering services. In terms of brokering, it addressed three questions in depth: (1) What is the federal Educational Information Center's program? (2) Where are adult information and counseling services located and how are they financed? And (3) How can states plan educational information and counseling services? (Florida Postsecondary Education Commission and others, 1977).

The impact of such conferences as these has seldom been studied. Some concrete outcomes undoubtedly evolve from them, in that policies or programs actually do get implemented; but their greatest benefit may be political, in terms of bringing together interested and concerned policy makers and lifelong learning specialists for at least one time in the planning process.

Research Activities

Many states have recently conducted statewide studies related to lifelong learning, and results from some thirty of them are discussed by Cross in Chapter Two. Three such studies—from California, Iowa, and Oregon—are briefly described here for illustrative purposes.

California. In 1974 the California State Legislature commissioned a study of "postsecondary alternatives" as a result of its earlier report by the Joint Committee on the Master Plan for Higher Education (1973), which recommended that a new postsecondary education segment be created to serve nontraditional clientele needs not being met by the state's three systems of public higher education: the University of California, the California State University and Colleges, and the California Community Colleges.

The California study had as its primary focus the question, "How can California most effectively structure its educational options beyond the high school level to meet the legitimate learning needs of all its citizens?" The study addressed four basic questions: (1) What are the present and forseeable educational needs of adult Californians? (2) What educational resources already exist or are being planned to meet these needs? (3) Where are there gaps between needs and resources? And (4) How can these gaps most effectively be narrowed?

The report of the study, *Postsecondary Alternatives To Meet the Educational Needs of California's Adults* (Peterson and Hefferlin, 1975) was released in September 1975. In the 1975–76 legislative session, legislation was introduced to implement major recommendations of the report, including the creation of "Golden State College," which, operating on a statewide basis through regional centers, would use individually oriented educational programs to reach adults and have the authority to grant degrees at the associate and bachelor's level. The legislation passed the Assembly's Education Committee but died in the Ways and Means Committee.

Iowa. One of the most recent examples of a state attempt to explore lifelong learning comes from the Iowa College Aid Commission (formerly called the Iowa Higher Education Facilities Commission). Following up its 1976 analysis of the need for lifelong learning opportunities reported in Chapter Two (Hamilton, 1976), in 1977 the Commission surveyed existing continuing education programs and issued its *Recommendations for Lifelong Learning in Iowa in the Third Century, The Final Report* (McLure, 1977b). These twenty-nine recommendations encompassed nine major topics: institutional missions; structure; needs assessment and programs; guidance; communicating opportunities; faculty, credit by examination, and assessment of experiential learning; professional standards; cooperative and consortium arrangements; and finances.

During 1978, this study led to the voluntary creation of regional clusters of postsecondary institutions in each of the state's five areas as well as to cooperative planning of programs within each cluster and to coordinated publicity about existing programs within each region. The Commission has not required legislative action for these initiatives; instead, it has used federal funds to provide mini-grants to the regional clusters and to hire a statewide coordinator for further voluntary effort. It is also encouraging the Iowa Coordinating Council for Post High School Education to develop additional policies for lifelong learning in the state and the Iowa Coordinating Committee for Continuing Education to take leadership in implementing these policies.

Oregon. Using funds from Title I of the Higher Education Act of 1965, the Oregon Educational Coordinating Commission initiated a project in 1976 having as its general purpose "expansion of communication between taxpayers and educators on increasing access to postsecondary education to nontraditional students." Three somewhat more specific objectives guided the effort: (1) to identify and communicate information about existing programs in Oregon aimed at the nontraditional learner, (2) to identify and communicate *needs* for filling gaps in programs for nontraditional learners, and (3) to bring taxpayers, consumers, educators, and policy makers together in a constructive policy formulation process to recommend ways to improve utilization of current programs and to recommend new programs to fill existing gaps in ways both academically sound and cost effective.

As described in the project's final report (Fehnel and Mc-Intyre, 1977), a wide range of activities was undertaken: limited survey research; numerous conferences involving consumers, educators, and policy makers; publication of the *Oregon Inventory of Postsecondary Educational Programs for Lifelong Learners, 1976–1977* (Oregon Educational Coordinating Commission, 1977a); production of a film and video tape on the needs of nontraditional learners; mass media presentations; publication of *Lifelong Learners Newsletter;* and development of a host of tentative recommendations in five key areas of lifelong learning.

State Master Plans

State planning documents generally include in their review of postsecondary education some discussion of continuing education and public service programs of colleges and universities. Illustrative are recent master plans from fifteen states—Arizona, California, Connecticut, Kansas, Kentucky, Michigan, Minnesota, Mississippi, New Hampshire, New Jersey, Ohio, Oklahoma, South Carolina, Utah, and Washington. (State agencies in two other states currently have master plan studies under way but the results are not included here: Louisiana's Board of Regents is examining the responsibility of institutions of higher education in providing lifelong learning, and Maryland's State Board for Higher Education is examining adult education needs and participation.) Few planning documents employ the term *lifelong learning;* instead they address facets of lifelong learning under other topics, such as "community service."

The first and most consistent theme in most of these planning documents is the need for additional revenues to finance almost everything, but particularly improvements in continuing education, which traditionally has been self-supporting. Thus, in Oklahoma the State Regents have recommended that "the practice of extension and public service activities 'paying their own way' be revised to provide a budgetary base sufficient at least to support the administrative costs of staff maintenance for those charged with the responsibility of program development and administration" (Hobbs, 1976, p. 120). Kentucky's Council on Public Higher Education states, "Sufficient resources are usually not available—and usually not committed—for supporting continuing education programs. Additional funds would permit flexibility for meeting continuing education needs in the most pressing areas" (1976, p. 19). And the Utah State Board of Regents urges that "the Utah Legislature should provide funds to establish financial support programs in Utah Divisions of Continuing Education to assure needy, disadvantaged, and culturally different students access to existing offerings" (1976, p. 45).

Directly linked to the financing of lifelong learning is the issue of part-time students in postsecondary education. Long neglected because of the long-standing institutional orientation toward residential students, part-time students are usually ineligible for most forms of state student aid and denied other student services available to full-time students.

Among numerous attempts to alter this situation, the New Jersey Board of Higher Education in Phase II of its Master Plan (1974, p. 21) predicts and recommends:

> With increasing social, intellectual, technological, and economic change, larger numbers of people will undertaken part-time undergraduate and graduate studies. It is imperative that they receive the quality of faculty and programs available to full-time students. . . . Colleges that secure resources from the state by enrolling part-time students should make sure that an adequate share of those resources, such as advisory services and faculty, is devoted to part-time students.

The Utah State Board of Regents (Continuing Education/Community Service Task Force for Lifelong Learning, 1976, p. 45) advocates that:

> Eligibility criteria for participation in student financial aid programs—federal, state, or institutional—should be established to include part-time students in all credit programs, and financial assistance should be proportionate to the course load taken and consistent with student needs.

And to reduce discrimination against part-time students in terms of tuition and fees, it recommends that:

> Student tuition and fees should be equalized within institutions to ensure that there is no discrimination against part-time students. Students should be charged for courses and credit ac-

tually taken. Any mandatory fees charged for services and facilities other than instruction should be proportionate to the part-time student's course and credit load.

In Connecticut, the Commission for Higher Education (1976, p. 33) proposes:

- That continuing education policy guidelines be developed for the benefit of part-time as well as full-time students.

- That the Commission for Higher Education seek equitable funding for continuing education programs in order to remove inequities in charges made to part-time students.

- That part-time students be provided supporting services equivalent to those provided for full-time students.

Similarly, the Board of Regents of the University of the State of New York in its *Statewide Plan for the Development of Postsecondary Education* (1976, p. 39) specifies that, "as a long-term goal, and if funds become available, state financial aid be extended to part-time students."

Beyond advocating greater state funding of continuing education and more equitable treatment of part-time students, many states are attempting to eliminate the distinction between credit received on campus and that obtained off campus in continuing or extended education. The Kansas Board of Regents (1972, p. 36) recommends that:

> To the greatest degree possible, the distinction between off-campus extension credit and on-campus resident credit should be eliminated *when the same quality of instruction is offered in the two settings* [emphasis added]. Such courses should be staffed and financed on essentially the same bases as on-campus instruction, and the same principles regarding reciprocity of credit among the Regents' institutions should apply.

However, the Regents do not define *quality.*

In Oklahoma (Hobbs, 1976, p. 120) it was recommended that:

> The State Regents review the policy on off-campus credit and eliminate the "dual" credit system of residence and extension

credit and provide guidelines and standards so that all credit offered in Oklahoma be residence credit.

Another common theme is new forms of teaching and programs. In *University Development in the Mid-Seventies: A Long Range Plan,* the Arizona Board of Regents recommended (1974, p. 19):

Consideration should be given to using the divisions of continuing education for creative programming, that is, external degree programs, statewide television-based programs, the micro campus, and other examples, as well as a facilitating organization of continuing education.

In a similar vein, the Utah State Board of Regents (Continuing Education . . . , 1976, p. 42) suggested the following:

Each institution should explore new methods of instruction and design new programs to reach nontypical student populations as well as traditional on-campus students. Means should be provided to encourage and support faculty interested in developing alternative forms of instruction. Faculty and institutional renewal can be enhanced by explorations in nontraditional education and participation in continuing education and community service.

Case Examples: Florida and Massachusetts

The perils and problems faced by all these conferences, research activities, and master plans can be exemplified by the fate of two recent projects: the work of Florida's Commission on Educational Outreach and Service and the proposals in Massachusetts for financing adult learning through a selective entitlement or voucher program.

Florida. Florida's Commission on Educational Outreach and Service was appointed in January 1975 by the chancellor-designate of the nine-campus State University System of Florida. Shortly thereafter, the Florida Division of Community Colleges, which operates twenty-eight colleges, joined the State University System as a cosponsor of the study. Both the State University System and the Division of Community Colleges in theory operate under the jurisdiction of the State Board of Education, which has statutory authority for reviewing individual institutional budgets and making consolidated budget recommendations to the governor and legislature for all public senior and junior institutions. But both of them have statutory responsibility for planning and approving programs, reviewing budgets, and submitting consolidated budget recommendations for their own systems. And the Board of Regents of the State University System appoints the chancellor of its system and the presidents of the nine universities in the system.

The Commission on Educational Outreach and Service consisted of thirty-three Florida citizens, including representatives from business and industry, government agencies, labor unions, senior citizens, media, the military, public and private higher education institutions, and public service organizations. The commission was charged with examining the totality of the instructional, research, and service needs of the state of Florida and its citizens; identifying the needs that could be met by higher education institutions; and determining what part of them the State System should meet. More specifically, the commission attempted to do the following:

- Assess Florida citizens' outreach needs.
- Inventory existing outreach efforts.
- Determine outreach roles of various postsecondary institutions.
- Suggest improvements for the delivery of outreach programs.
- Develop a plan for continued reassessment.

The need for the study was evident. Florida, with over 8.3 million residents, ranks eighth among the states in total population, and its growth rate is second only to that of Arizona—a 21.9 percent increase between 1970 and 1975, according to the Bureau of the Census. More important, Florida's proportion of residents aged sixty-five years or older is the highest of any state in the nation and steadily climbing. In 1977 it was estimated to be close to 20 percent. Moreover, Florida ranks above the midpoint of the states in per capita income—twentieth among the fifty, as of 1974–75—and near the midpoint in expenditures for elementary and secondary education—twenty-sixth of all fifty, in proportion to percapita personal income. But its aid to higher education falls significantly below the national average, ranking only thirty-eighth among the fifty.

The tangible result of the commission's work was an extensive report, entitled *Access to Knowledge,* released in the summer of 1976 in four volumes: I. *Preliminary Report;* II. *Data Collection and Analysis;* III. *Annotations of Selected Literature;* and IV. *Recommendations From Selected Literature.* In the *Preliminary Report,* the Commission presented thirty recommendations for action. Significant among these recommendations were the following two:

- It is recommended that the Florida Legislature mandate a public policy which enables the state's adult learners to have the educational resources and services of public and private postsecondary educational institutions accessible to them throughout their lifetime and that such access be made available without regard to race, age, sex, or place of residence.

- It is recommended that the Florida Legislature provide the resources and/or the reordering of priorities to enable adult learners and the state's postsecondary institutions to fulfill the above lifelong learning policy.

Almost no action has been taken by the Florida legislature on the commission's recommendations. A number of reasons have been brought forth to explain this inaction. First, the economic situation in the state is such that there is little support for *any* new social programs. Florida has been functioning on a "bare bones" budget for several years. In FY 1974 and FY 1975, the designated funds were held back, and while there has recently been a tax increase, those dollars are not likely to be directed toward adult education.

Second, there was voiced the broader philosophical question of just "where the buck stops." Does the state owe everyone a B.A., an M.A., a Ph.D.? Further, should the state be paying for those who can afford to pay for themselves? These unresolved issues will probably impact greatly on state action regarding lifelong learning in Florida.

Third, a primary argument used to support lifelong learning is the need for retraining of manpower for employment purposes. Because of the industrial make-up of Florida, however, the need for retraining is currently said to be minimal.

Fourth, apparently the internal legislative priorities are such that primary and secondary education should receive additional revenues before any additional revenues are directed toward postcompulsory schooling.

Fifth, some concern was expressed regarding what role the University of Florida (the primary sponsor of the report) should have in various of the recommended special adult programs. The core of this concern seems to lie in the question of what functions (or "role and scope") each Florida institution of education will have in the future. More simply, who should do what? This set of issues is far from being resolved, although the systemwide office of the university system has been conducting a "role and scope" study for over a year, and the role of the university system has been reviewed by the Constitutional Review Commission, which meets every ten years to review the State Constitution.

Sixth, state legislators appear particularly reluctant to support expansion of educational programs or the creation of new ones that require new dollars. While this reluctance comes, in part, from concern over limited resources, there is also concern about the institutional motives behind the push for more education programs. This skepticism stems from the fact of stabilizing and declining enrollments. Legislators suspect that the push for programs for adults is an attempt to obtain more funds to make up for declining enrollments of younger students.

Seventh, and finally, legislative concern reflects experience with previous educational programs that were judged to be ineffective or inefficient. For example, during FY 1975 a Community Instructional Services (CIS) Program was granted $11.3 million to "support . . . educational activities, courses, and programs based on significant community problems related to: the environment, health, safety, human relations, government, childrearing, and consumer economics" (Florida Legislature, 1977). In FY 1976 the program's funds were cut to $4.4 million, and during FY 1977 they were further cut to $2.3 million. In one year the governor threatened to abolish the program entirely. The primary reason cited for the reduced funding was that an audit revealed that program records kept on students were inadequate, that many classes existed mostly on paper, and that the District Coordinating Councils, which were required to meet to fulfill the requirements of the program, were in fact not meeting. As a result of this unfavorable audit, funds were reduced and more legislative restrictions were placed upon the CIS programs.

More recently, legislative confidence in the programs has increased. Twenty-eight regional coordinating councils were revitalized; each developed priority problem statements and fiscal agent agreements. Governing boards of community colleges and school districts developed interboard agreements through the offices of the respective coordinating councils. The state CIS appropriation was upped by 42 percent in 1977–78 over 1976–1977. But by then the momentum for action on the commission's recommendations was lost, and it seems doubtful that it will be regained in the near future.

Massachusetts. In 1972 the Massachusetts Advisory Council on Education contracted with University Consultants, Inc., an independent consulting firm in Cambridge, to conduct a study of continuing and part-time education programs and needs in the commonwealth. The study had a two-fold purpose: (1) to generate a comprehensive data base for a detailed analysis of continuing and part-time education in Massachusetts and (2) to develop a set of recommendations for public and private institutional policies for the 1970s.

This study resulted in a comprehensive two-volume report entitled *Strengthening the Alternative Postsecondary Education System: Continuing and Part-Time Study in Massachusetts* (Nolfi and Nelson, 1973). Among the major findings, the study found that current students in part-time and continuing education programs are predominately middle and upper class; concentrated in the twenty-five to thirty-five age bracket (45 percent); disproportionately males (66 percent); and professionally and managerially employed (60 percent). The conclusion of the study was that "the current education system is not operating as a second chance system. Although open admissions is standard, psychological and financial barriers inhibit many people from attending" (Syracuse University, 1974).

A number of recommendations were made by the study group regarding the improvement of continuing and part-time education in Massachusetts. Foremost among these recommendations was a proposal that a program of continuing education vouchers for adults with low income or low previous education be established and funded by the state. This entitlement proposal provides an individual subsidy for part-time postsecondary study, its amount depending on the recipient's income, previous educational attainment level, and the actual course fees.

While Massachusetts does even better than Florida in supporting elementary and secondary education—ranking fourteenth out of fifty in per-capita expenditures and nineteenth out of fifty in terms of personal income per-capita expenditures—its support of higher education is extremely low relative to the rest of the states. It ranks forty-ninth out of fifty in terms of per-capita expenditures and only slightly better—forty-seventh—in terms of personal income per-capita expenditures. The chief reason for this low ranking, of course, is the many private colleges and universities in the commonwealth. As in most of the northeastern states, higher education in Massachusetts is highly influenced by a large and prestigious private sector. In fact, more than twice as much state student financial aid per student goes to students attending private institutions as those enrolled in public colleges and universities: $52 per student, in contrast to $22.

Some kind of need-based voucher program in Massachusetts has been requested by a number of organizations and individuals in the state. Letters and supporting testimony have come from a widely divergent constituency, including the Massachusetts Social and Economic Opportunity Council; the AFL-CIO; the Massachusetts College of Art; the Associated Industries of Massachusetts; and various women's organizations.

As yet, however, Massachusetts policy makers have not committed the state to the establishment of a need-based voucher system for adults. Bills were introduced to implement the plan in the 1975, 1976, and 1977 sessions of the legislature; but so far the legislation has always failed to pass. The coordinating agency for higher education in the commonwealth—the Massachusetts Board of Higher Education—formally supported the 1977 bill, but the board's staff expressed several concerns about the legislation. First, there is concern that the cost of such a program could be much higher than currently estimated by supporters of SB 197. Part of the reason for concern is that the number of persons likely to take advantage of such a program may be greatly underestimated. Second, the provisions of the bill are such that people *now* in school would not benefit immediately; those persons currently attending and paying could not participate in the first one to three years, depending on the length of the start-up demonstration. Finally, there is reluctance in the state to support any new education programs. Because of economic realities, the program lacks government support. More specifically:

- Education is not a priority of the current administration.
- Higher education is in its third year of "leveling off" in funding; the only funding increase in 1977 was for faculty salaries.
- It is too early in the game to talk about adults. State policy makers are primarily concerned with educating the young. It is assumed that adults can and should take care of themselves.
- What little support exists for adult education is for adult basic education.

Conclusions

The hundreds of recommendations to be found in recent state planning and research documents, illustrated here and reviewed in Volume IIIB of *Access to Knowledge* by Florida's Commission on Educational Outreach and Service, clearly reflect state-level concerns about expanded adult learning opportunities. But their rhetoric must be distinguished from action. First, many of the suggestions are vague and rhetorical in nature, and implementation is difficult. Second, realization of part or all of a master plan usually rests upon a series of delicate political negotiations between the institutions representing state government and education. Any one or all of the following factors could hinder action:

- Changes in the state's economic situation, resulting in fewer dollars for education.
- Changes in the state government's administrative structure.
- Changes in the organization of the legislature.
- Changes in the state's education administration structure, and of key officials.
- Changes in postsecondary education governance.

Furthermore, the ability to implement policy and planning recommendations depends in large part on who does the recommending. Some policy and planning studies are developed by systemwide boards and state agencies with a great deal of statutory authority over budgeting, planning, and program review. Other studies are conducted by boards or agencies with advisory powers only. While, in the last analysis, it will be the quality of staff work and staff abilities for persuasion that will determine policy change, those agencies with statutory authority, *if exercised,* are more likely to be able to implement comprehensive changes.

Counseling and Other Brokering Services

Most state master plans for postsecondary education suggest some improvements in counseling and information systems, but rarely do they deal with the specific needs of adult or part-time students. Most of them seem to assume that these needs can be met by developing a single type of advisory system for *all* students, traditional and nontraditional.

Some states, however, have proposed specific services for continuing education students. In Connecticut, for example, the Commission for Higher Education (1976) supports the "development of regional information and counseling centers, using and supplementing existing organizations and resources where possible, to gather, share and disseminate information about continuing education programs." (p. 33). And in Utah the following recommendations were made in the report of the Continuing Education/ Community Service Task Force for Lifelong Learning (1974, p. 44), part of the master planning effort by the Utah State Board of Regents:

> A strong, well-informed, coordinated counseling and guidance service should be maintained on the campus of every postsecondary institution with some expertise for advising and counseling the mature adult learner. This service should evaluate the student and direct him to that program or institution which best fits his purposes, aptitudes, abilities, and interests. Information should be provided on the variety of programs available, where they are located, costs involved, and methods of instruction employed.

Deans of continuing education and counseling personnel should coordinate and administer programs so that guidance and counseling services are available to part-time and evening students as well as to traditional full-time day students.

Central to these counseling and information services for adults is the concept of *educational brokering,* which is the name newly given to a network of noninstructional adult learning services that includes information giving, counseling, assessment of individual capabilities, and advocacy (aid in coping with institutions). In general, "brokers" act as go-betweens, offering individuals impartial advice on learning opportunities available to them.

The concept of brokering seems to be spreading, and a National Center for Educational Brokering (NCEB) was established in 1976 (see Chapter Six). Although some of the component services of brokering have been provided at educational institutions and community agencies for many years, independent, "freestanding" brokering units are more recent. Many of them have been launched with grants from the Fund for the Improvement of Postsecondary Education. Perhaps the best known of them is the Regional Learning Service of Central New York, located in Syracuse, but others are now in operation in localities across the country.[1] Thus far, however, support has been primarily local or federal: only a handful of state agencies have considered or tried to implement comprehensive brokerage services for adult learners— among them, agencies in California, Massachusetts, and Rhode Island.

California. California is an instance in which extensive policy research has not yet led to program implementation by the state. As noted earlier, in 1974 the legislature commissioned the Postsecondary Alternatives Study—a comprehensive analysis of adult learning needs and needed new services. The study found counseling and information (about area learning opportunities) to be

[1]For descriptions of many of these agencies, see the October 1976, September 1977, and other issues of the National Center for Educational Brokering *Bulletin.* A general overview of the organization and functioning of brokering services has been prepared by Heffernan, Macy, and Vickers (1976).

among the highest priority needs, and recommended regional networks of small, community-based brokering units throughout the state, beginning with a pilot network of four units ("Educational Services Centers") in one region (Peterson and Hefferlin, 1975).

In 1976 legislation was introduced to establish ten Postsecondary Educational Services Centers throughout the state between 1977 and 1980. This bill passed the Assembly's Subcommittee on Postsecondary Education and the (full) Assembly Education Committee before being killed by that house's Ways and Means (finance) Committee. A modified version of the bill calling for three pilot "Community Advisement Centers" in different parts of the state was passed by both houses of the legislature in 1977 but was subsequently vetoed by the governor.

Massachusetts. One of the earliest and still most significant of the state agency–initiated brokering programs is the Massachusetts Regional Educational Opportunity Center (REOC) Program. It originated in 1972 with the idea that the State Education Department could develop community-based counseling, testing, and other brokering services for welfare recipients. Further support for the concept came from recommendations in a comprehensive statewide study of adult learning needs and resources conducted for the Massachusetts Advisory Council on Education (Nolfi and Nelson, 1973).

Located in areas of high unemployment, five REOC's became operational in 1974 with (and because of) state funds available for reducing welfare dependency. In 1975 modest federal funding was secured through the Comprehensive Employment and Training Act (CETA) and the U.S. Office of Education's "TRIO" Program (the unit then administering the Upward Bound, Talent Search, and Equal Opportunity Centers programs). Two centers are operated by community agencies, two by consortia of area colleges, and one by a single community college. This last— the single institution—model proved ineffective (National Center for Educational Brokering, Summer 1976). While each center operates independently, there is coordination statewide from the Executive Office of Educational Affairs.

In general, each REOC identifies economically disadvantaged adults who can benefit from further education, inventories and maintains contact with educational resources in its region, assesses academic and vocational potentials of clients, and—with assistance from other social service agencies—assists clients to enroll in schools or colleges, or otherwise act to achieve their career goals.

Rhode Island. Another early brokering service was the Career Education Project, which was established in Providence with funding from the National Institute of Education (NIE). When NIE funding ended in 1975, the program was reconstituted as the Career Counseling Service with funding from state appropriations and from a variety of federal sources channeled through state agencies (National Center for Educational Brokering, September 1976). Under a recent "Cooperative Agreement," which sets forth management and resource responsibilities of each organization, the Career Counseling Service is jointly operated by a consortium of four state agencies, including the Department of Education, Division of Job Development and Training, Department of Employment Security, and Department of Social and Rehabilitation Services.

Planned for FY 1978 is an expanded "occupational and educational information system, linking secondary schools, post-secondary institutions, and human service agencies to a centralized information base, to provide technical assistance to participating agencies in meeting the identified needs of their clients, and to maintain a follow-up and monitoring program to assess client outcomes" (Rhode Island Department of Education, 1977). The new information component will have three major dimensions—information development, information delivery, and user services—together intended to fulfill five major objectives: (1) to develop and maintain an information base that realistically reflects the employment and educational opportunities for the people of Rhode Island, (2) to provide a wide variety of individuals and guidance personnel with opportunities to use one or more information delivery systems (hard copy, telephone, computer application, and so on), (3) to create a way that the identified informational needs of participating agencies can be met by the centralized information base, (4) to provide in-service training for guidance personnel and technical assistance to participating agencies in the establishment and maintenance of career resource centers, and (5) to establish and maintain a follow-up monitoring system to assess client outcomes and to provide feedback to participating agencies and institutions.

Developments in Brokering

Among encouraging developments in brokering is the potentially highly useful computer-based educational (and occupational) information system. A good example is Oregon's Career Information System (CIS). While it contains educational, occupational, and manpower needs information, the CIS also has an interactive counseling component. Its central storage unit is at the University of Oregon, and terminals are located throughout the state in schools, prisons, shopping centers, libraries, and other public places.

The U.S. Department of Labor, which funded the Oregon project, is currently supporting development of computer-based information systems in eight states: Alabama, Colorado, Massachusetts, Michigan, Minnesota, Ohio, Washington, and Wisconsin. Papers by Franklin (1978a, 1978b) summarize activities in these and several other states.

The most important recent development affecting brokering at the state level, however, has been passage of the Educational Information Centers (EIC) provisions of the federal Education Amendments of 1976 (the full text of which appears at the end of Chapter Five). The EIC program makes grants to states "to pay the federal share of the cost of planning, establishing, and operating Educational Information Centers to provide educational information, guidance, counseling, and referral services for all individuals, including individuals residing in rural areas." The federal share is no more than two thirds and not less than $50,000. A total of $3 million has been appropriated for Educational Information Centers for FY 1979. Forty-four states and territories submitted EIC proposals (plans).

Preparation of proposals for EIC grants can afford states a good opportunity for innovative planning. For example, in North Carolina a nongovernmental agency, the North Carolina Adult Education Association, created a Task Force on Educational Brokering Services, which has released an extremely provocative report (Knowles, 1977). In Connecticut, the structure for implementing the EIC's will be the state's regional planning districts. In Vermont, planning and operating the Centers will be accomplished by a consortium including the University of Vermont, the State

College System (including the Community College of Vermont), and the Vermont Student Assistance Fund. The Summer 1977 and April 1978 issues of the NCEB *Bulletin* have overviews of state EIC planning efforts, and the report *State Planning for Lifelong Learning* (Florida Postsecondary Education Commission and others, 1977) has a useful discussion of relevant issues.

In terms of increasing access to education, good information and counseling services are even more critical for adult students than for students in the traditional "college-age" bracket. Improved advisory services should mean better career and educational decisions for all. Yet the critical variable will not simply be the creation of sophisticated information and counseling systems but the means by which nontraditional students are put in touch with these systems. If new methods of approaching and informing heretofore unserved populations are not used, the new brokering agencies will serve those persons least in need: middle- and upper-class white-collar Americans. Given the severe economic and psychological problems faced by those who have been left out of the mainstream of American society, it is unlikely that those people would be able—without special assistance—to utilize the new information and counseling services any better than they now utilize other American institutions (business, government, and so forth).

External Degree and Related Programs

Far more common than state-sponsored information and counseling services for adult learners, as illustrated by the brokering centers described above, are nontraditional instructional programs and external degree programs sponsored by the states. State postsecondary education agencies and institutions often look on external degrees and other nontraditional approaches, such as television, radio, and tape cassette instruction, as strategies for expanding access to education. For example, according to the Connecticut Commission for Higher Education (1974, p. 77), the two most critical aspects of nontraditional education are (1) "developing alternative methods of delivering quality programs at times and places convenient to students on or off campus" and (2) "devising ways to measure each individual's knowledge and skills, irrespective of the means by which the learning was acquired, in order to award academic credit and 'external' degrees."

New York, New Jersey, and Vermont illustrate successful state efforts to establish external degree and nontraditional education programs. But because there have been as many unsuccessful as successful efforts to establish such programs in other states, several abortive plans will also be discussed here.

New York. Probably one of the first, and certainly one of the best known, of any external degree program in the United States is that of the New York Regents. Since 1971 more than 22,000 students have enrolled in programs leading to Regents External Degrees at the associate and baccalaureate levels in the arts, sciences, nursing, and business administration; and as of the end of 1978 more than 8,000 of these students throughout the country have received Regents External Degrees.

Ewald B. Nyquist proposed this innovative program at his inauguration as President of the University of the State of New York and Commissioner of Education in September 1970. The Board of Regents endorsed the proposal and created the External Degree Program to enable independent students with college-level knowledge to earn degrees without attending college. The degrees are awarded by the Regents through the State Education Department, which evaluates the students. The program has no campus, resident faculty, or resident students.

Many types of educational activities can be used to satisfy the Regents External Degree requirements, including the following:

- College courses taken from accredited institutions either on campus or through correspondence.
- Proficiency examinations.
- Study under the auspices of the Defense Activity for Nontraditional Education Support (formerly the United States Armed Forces Institute).
- Military service school courses.
- Certain noncollegiate study programs offered by police and civil service agencies, business and industry, and government.
- Oral, written, and performance "Special Assessment" examinations to assess on-the-job experience and literacy, artistic, or musical skills, as well as other academic areas where existing proficiency tests are not appropriate.

Candidates for the Regents External Degree are reviewed by the faculty committee that oversees the degree program in which they are enrolled; those who have met the requirements are recommended to the Board of Regents for conferral of the degree by the University of the State of New York. Other program services include a network of 150 volunteer advisors; the Higher Education Library Advisory Service (described in Chapter Six); the Inmate College Advisory Project; and the Regents Credit Bank, an evaluation and recordkeeping service for people not interested in earning an external degree.

New Jersey. Thomas A. Edison College is one of New Jersey's nine state colleges. Like the other eight, it is authorized by the State Board of Education to grant college credit and to award college degrees. Like them, it depends upon academic councils (committees made up of college instructors and administrators) to determine its degree requirements. But unlike the others, it offers no instruction.

Created in 1972 by New Jersey's State Board of Higher Education, Thomas Edison's mission is to "develop flexible methods of evaluating college-level knowledge, regardless of how that knowledge has been acquired: and make use of these methods to award valid college credits and degrees to individuals who have not met—or have not chosen to meet—the requirements of a traditional college or university" (*Thomas A. Edison College Catalog 1977–78,* p. 7). As of January 1977, more than 5,000 students had enrolled in Thomas Edison College and more than 1,000 had earned degrees.

In carrying out its mission, the college performs four specific functions:

- It provides free academic counseling.
- It awards baccalaureate and associate degrees.
- It grants college credits, which may be applied toward an Edison degree or transferred to another college. These credits are earned in three ways:
    1. By transfer of credit from another institution;
    2. By passing college-equivalency examinations; or

3. By receiving an Individual Assessment of college-level knowledge, performed by an academic consultant engaged for that particular evaluation by the college.

• It acts as a catalyst for adult education by giving college credit for approved in-service training courses sponsored by employers, labor organizations, and community or government agencies (*Thomas A. Edison College Catalog 1977–78,* p. 8).

Another, quite different type of external college program was started in New Jersey in the summer of 1974, when an act of the New Jersey State Legislature made it possible for a county that lacked a community college to establish a community college commission. Under the new law such a commission could be funded like a community college, could enter into contracts with existing educational institutions to provide services for its students, and could grant diplomas, certificates, and associate degrees. When the New Jersey Board of Higher Education approved establishment of a Community College Commission in Hudson County (HCCC) in September 1974, it became the first agency of its kind in the country.

The commission contracts for whole programs from three senior institutions and other educational institutions, including the Hudson County Vocational Technical School. It has no full-time faculty or campus of its own. It assists the cooperating colleges, schools, and hospitals to develop a new range of career offerings appropriate to the needs of community college students. However, the commission does provide certain direct services. For instance, it conducts an evening college program with adjunct faculty in five locations in Hudson County. It also provides academic and financial aid counseling for students through a federally funded Educational Opportunity Center, which it sponsors jointly with three other educational institutions.

Basically, the community college, through four centers in different parts of the county, provides interviewing, career counseling, testing, program planning and related services to accommodate the interests and needs of potential students. The primary function of the commission's staff is to develop a program for a student that uses the resources of the contracting institutions to meet student goals. Certificates or associate degrees can be awarded by the commission or by the contracting institutions, depending upon the specific plan developed between the student and the commission, acting as the "broker" (Bender, 1977).

The commission takes a realistic stance toward its present contribution to the community and its potential for the future. In a memo to the chancellor of the State Department of Higher Education, HCCC's president stated: "It should be recognized that the commission's structure represents a significant, but not a total, response to the community college needs of Hudson County. The commission is not a comprehensive community college. It is, given the financial constraints of a heavily taxed community, a reasonable alternative to one . . . . What of the students whom we cannot reasonably expect these colleges to serve—the new immigrant with limited English language ability, the recent high school graduate who is reading at a sixth-grade level; the thirty-year-old high school dropout who now realizes that education is the key to career mobility? As the commission begins to address these problems, it moves away from its pure brokering role."

Vermont. Certainly one of the most innovative external degree programs in the United States is the Community College of Vermont (CCV). The college has no buildings: classes are held anywhere space is available within a community—churches, libraries, meeting halls, garages, or schools. It has no paid, full-time faculty· individuals are hired from the community to teach their own career specialities. It has no set course offerings, no grades, no credits, hours, or requirements. Two-year degrees are awarded on the basis of demonstrated skills and completion of individual contracts instead of number of courses taken or amount of time spent in study.

The history of the college goes only as far back as 1970. In that year the governor of Vermont issued an executive order initiating CCV's forerunner, the Vermont Regional Community College Commission. In 1972 the Commission was merged with the Vermont State College system and became the Community College of Vermont.

In the state of Vermont, fewer high school students enter college than in any other state. In the Community College of Vermont, more than 43 percent of the students enrolled have low incomes; a third of them are high school or college dropouts; and over two thirds hold regular jobs.

To determine community needs, three times a year "regional site teams," of which there are seven, make contact with potential students at union meetings, church events, and other gatherings to gain information on the types of courses people want. (Regional site teams are groups of teachers and student support personnel whose job is to bring together those who have information with those who need it.) Students already in the program are polled also and if there is no instructor available to teach a requested program, CCV staff seek someone from the community.

CCV bases its curriculum on competency-based concepts, which focus on outcomes of the learning process—the learning itself—rather than inputs to it—the teaching. The college produces sets of guidelines indicating the clusters of competencies (or "goals") that must be met in order to qualify for the degree. Students are expected to address themselves to a minimum of fifteen of the following twenty goals (Daloz, 1975):

Social Competence
1. Has significant degree of awareness of self in relation to society.
2. Can establish a productive, helping relationship with another person.
3. Can develop a personally consistent set of beliefs that can be acted upon.
4. Can make a clear, positive, and demonstrable impact on the local community.
5. Can act within situations of uncertainty and complexity.
6. Can relate effectively to people from a variety of different backgrounds and ages.
7. Knows local resources and can use them.
8. Can recognize potentially coercive forces in the environment and act accordingly.
9. Can develop autonomy in defining and pursuing goals.

Physical Competence
1. Can work skillfully with the hands.
2. Can take part in activities that require a significant degree of physical coordination.

Intellectual Competence
1. Has a significant level of knowledge in and about a chosen field of study.
2. Can relate own field to other areas of study.
3. Can think critically and analytically.
4. Can carry out a systematic problem-solving sequence.
5. Can carry out a systematic evaluation sequence.
6. Can plan and carry out a systematic sequence of inquiry.
7. Can communicate effectively in oral and written form.
8. Can communicate effectively in nonverbal form.
9. Can think imaginatively and act creatively.

The framework through which these goals are realized is the learning contract. The contract has five parts (Daloz, 1975):

1. A narrative written by the student and providing an overview of the student's background, learning history, goals, and aspirations.
2. A "program outline sheet" detailing the goals addressed, the specific ways in which the student met the goals, and keys to lists of learning experiences and documentation.
3. A list of "learning experiences" outlining the context in which the particular learning occurred.
4. Documentation used to confirm that the learning did occur.
5. A portfolio of papers ranging from samples of student work to letters attesting to the student's accomplishment of the goals in question to transcripts from other colleges.

Quality control rests with Local Review Committees. These groups, made up of peer students, teachers, practitioners in the student's field, and the CCV staff, provide guidance during the preparation of the contract and final confirmation upon demonstration of contract completion. After recommendation for the degree, the contract is forwarded to a committee for review at the all-college level. There it is examined to see that "no outstanding problems that would question the integrity of the contract" exist. If approved by this group, the degree is conferred.

Enrollment was 635 students in 1972–73. By 1975–76 the enrollment was 2,200, and CCV graduates numbered 196.

Wisconsin. Among more limited and more typical nontraditional degree programs is the University of Wisconsin's Extended
Degree Programs, which have resulted from the failure of the university system to develop a totally "open university." In 1973 a
Planning Task Force within the University of Wisconsin System
had issued a report entitled *A Planning Prospectus for the Open University of the University of Wisconsin System.* On the basis of demographic data, various market surveys, and reports from other surveys on the needs of adult learners, the task force report, like many
other such reports, indicated that a substantial number of prospective students were not being reached by traditional campus-
based approaches to postsecondary education. The Planning Task
Force recommended that open education programs be initiated,
which should incorporate alternative modes of learning, including
competency-based concepts.

In 1974, in a supplemental budget bill, the legislature supported the Regents-approved proposal for the Regents Statewide
University by granting *legal* sanction to proceed. However, because
of Wisconsin's recessionary fiscal climate and overall state budget
retrenchments, funding was withheld (University of Wisconsin,
1976b). As a consequence, the university inaugurated its more limited Extended Degree Programs and is testing ten of these pilot
programs at eight learning resource centers with the help of grants
from the Fund for the Improvement of Postsecondary Education.

This set of programs is designed specifically "for people
with some college experience who possess the necessary motivation, basic learning skills, and maturity to accept responsibility for
their own progress" (University of Wisconsin, 1976b, p. 1). Long-
range objectives are "to meet more fully the needs of a wide diversity of learners," through (1) "increased opportunity to receive
degree credit for the educational value of prior learning through
competency-based evaluation of learning achieved," and (2) "encouragement of alternative educational delivery systems and teaching techniques aimed at populations now unserved or poorly served,
including working adults and those isolated from the possibility of
long-term campus residence" (University of Wisconsin, 1976b,
p. 4). There appears to be some contradiction between reaching
"a wide diversity of learners" and at the same time requiring these

learners to possess "some college experience." Nonetheless, the Extended Degree Programs have the following aims (University of Wisconsin, 1976b, p. 6):

- To develop at one campus a competency-based Bachelor of General Studies Degree, which would be open to adults throughout the state.
- To provide extended degree programs adapted from existing individualized majors in the liberal arts so that adults unable to take advantage of campus-based instruction may be served on a regional basis.
- To develop methods of making certain curricular elements of existing professional degree programs more accessible to those who need them.
- To develop in the University Center System a sophomore-year completion program for those persons who have some college experience but have not been able to complete courses for an associate degree or to transfer to an upper-division baccalaureate program.
- To develop in appropriate University of Wisconsin System institutions learning resource centers that will have statewide responsibility for selected support areas within a competency-based learning network.

The following steps define for campus administrators the process for planning a University of Wisconsin extended degree and also contain criteria for the evaluation of proposed Extended Degree Programs (University of Wisconsin, 1976b):

1. Emphasize upper-division work.
2. Place degree programs in a competency-based format.
3. Individualize learning programs.
4. Establish a contract procedure for extended degree programs.
5. Establish a procedure for assessment of prior knowledge.
6. Establish procedures for prior assessment of learning situations, for example, work experience, internships.
7. Identify available faculty resources for extended degree programs.

8. Identify learning resources.
9. Evaluate use of alternative learning modes, for example, formal course work, tutorials, self-paced instruction, cooperative internship.
10. Identify counseling (brokering) resources both on and off campus.
11. Establish a procedure for ongoing evaluation of quality standards.
12. Establish extended degree program efforts as part of the normal teaching load.

Wisconsin's inability to create a full-fledged open university for adults is far from unique. While numerous studies have been conducted, recommendations made, and legislative support sought, attempts to develop new nontraditional delivery systems are frequently met, for political and economic reasons, with skepticism and eventual defeat. In 1972, for example, the Illinois Board of Higher Education recommended Lincoln State University, and in 1974 the Massachusetts Commonwealth Task Force on the Open University recommended a statewide external degree program. Both attempts failed to be realized. More recently, legislation was introduced in California during 1976 to create "Golden State College" and reappropriate various amounts of money from specified future fiscal-year appropriations to the University of California, the California State University and Colleges, and the California Community Colleges to operate the new college; but, as mentioned earlier, the legislation died in the Ways and Means Committee. And in that same year the California legislature failed to re-fund the pilot Extended University program of the University of California, which had operated for three years as an effort to expand the university's teaching services to part-time and adult students.

Colorado. The legislative story was more fleeting in Colorado. In 1976, Senate Bill No. 486 specified that:

> There is hereby established an institution of higher education to be known and designated as "Colorado Centennial Open University" . . . which shall be governed by the Board of Trustees for Colorado Centennial Open University and conducted according to regulations promulgated by the Colorado Commission on

Higher Education. The open university shall provide postsecondary educational opportunities to adult citizens of the state who, by reason of circumstances such as limitations on their time, the locations of their homes, or personal handicaps, are unable to take advantage of traditional campus-based instruction. Colorado Centennial Open University is intended to meet the lifelong learning needs of the adult population who may not have completed their education, who have been bypassed, who want midcareer changes, who require professional continuing education courses or programs, or who are interested in pursuing other life-style impacting noncredit programs whether avocational, cultural, or recreational in nature.

It is the intent of the general assembly that the open university shall provide the following services: counseling and tutoring, credit evaluation, and the educational programs to meet the needs of the adult citizens of this state as set out in this section. The open university may grant credentials and degrees as recommended by the Board of Trustees and approved by the Colorado Commission on Higher Education.

Nothing came of the bill, however.

Michigan. Details of a more recent study regarding an external degree program in Michigan reveal the conflicting pressures such program proposals generate. In 1975 the Michigan State Board of Education established a task force to study the need for and possible structure of an external degree program for Michigan. The task force report, which was based on somewhat scanty information and rather heavily laden with questionable assumptions regarding population growth and educational needs, concluded (Task Force to Study the Feasibility. . . , 1977a, p. 17): "It appears the most feasible response to the External Degree need would be to initially offer an external degree that makes use of the existing system, represents a limited departure from the present baccalaureate degrees, and does not include features that inflate the cost-effectiveness of the enterprise." Further, the report asserted: "All institutions interviewed felt that an External Degree Program at the statewide level should be developed by coordinating and expanding existing college and university offerings to serve the citizens of the entire state. It was felt by all but two of the institutions that funding for a statewide External Degree Program should be provided by a combination of state, institutional, and student fee revenues. Finally, there was general agreement that the concept of lifelong learning should incorporate both on-campus and off-campus learning opportunities."

The task force report recommended that the President's Council of State Colleges and Universities be the agency to implement the External Degree Program in Michigan. Further, the report suggested that each state college or university indicate by official action a desire to, or not to, participate in all or selected External Degree Programs. To develop the program to be administered by an Office of the Executive Director of the Program in three area offices, the following two stages were recommended:

> 1. The CSCP [Michigan Council of State College Presidents] appoint a task force with representatives from each member college or university to determine:
>   a. Degrees to be offered.
>   b. Curriculum content.
>   c. A temporary administrative structure common to multiple institutions.
>   d. Alternate sources of funding.
>   e. Permanent administrative structure.
> 2. Concurrently, the legislature should be approached for a special account to make the program operational, including funding for a program director along with support for staffing the proposed three out-state educational service centers which would handle student advising, appraisal, evaluation and coordination [Task Force to Study the Feasibility . . . , 1977a, p. 23].

The Task Force emphasized the need for new monies to implement the new program, "so that universities can adequately serve their new constituencies." However, a minority report appended to the Michigan study expresses reservations about just how "new" these constituencies will be. As stated in *The Minority Report* (Task Force to Study the Feasibility . . . , 1977b, pp. 2 and 5): "It seems to us, in effect, that the report of the Task Force, taken at face value with respect to description of need and promise, must lead one to an exactly opposite set of conclusions from those presented. If a need can be identified, then it must be that it is not now being well satisfied by traditional structures or devices. . . .

One of the major weaknesses of the report of the Task Force is the general underlying assumption reflected therein that the presently established state colleges and universities are doing all that can be done, or need be done, to serve adequately the special educational needs and interests of off-campus students, or nontraditional learners."

Conclusions

The trend of the past decade to advocate and create various external and nontraditional degree programs through state agencies or institutions appears to be slowing. One reason, of course, is that such programs usually require substantial amounts of additional state revenues. But another reason is that it is still unclear to what extent such programs increase nontraditional students' access to education. Certainly, many external degree programs serve traditional clienteles more conveniently than the regular programs for full-time students; but these new programs may be of little help to nontraditional groups whose social, psychological, or economic backgrounds prevent use, or even knowledge, of services within the "system." Merely offering the educational facilities is not sufficient.

Moreover, external degree and other nontraditional programs have often emphasized the importance of "delivery systems" rather than students. Quite frequently, as an unintended consequence, institutional and system interests take precedence over student or individual interests. It is relatively easy to integrate a new delivery system into an existing traditional structure. It is much harder to make an institution, with its firmly established services and curriculum, responsive to individual student needs. Thus, nontraditional students who have widely divergent educational, psychological, and financial needs make demands upon the traditional structure that often the institution is not equipped to meet. For these reasons, if states rely in the future primarily on existing colleges and universities to offer these programs, rather than following the example of New York, New Jersey, and Vermont and creating totally new agencies to offer them, their impact on nontraditional students will remain minimal.

Consortia and Regional Arrangements

While state efforts at educational brokering are only beginning and external degrees programs seem to have peaked, state
initiatives in the direction of consortia and regional cooperation
for lifelong learning appear to be gaining ground. The consortium
concept is very loosely defined and can include many types of
structural and programmatic arrangements. According to Webster, "consortia are partnerships, unions, or marriages." In higher
education, the word *consortium* has usually meant an ad hoc voluntary interinstitutional arrangement, often regional in nature. To
be listed in the *Consortium Directory,* a consortium must meet four
criteria: (1) it must be voluntarily formed, (2) it must have a full-
time professional director, (3) it must have multiple programs, and
(4) it must report tangible member support for the central consortium office.

A 1976 survey conducted for the Kansas City Regional
Council for Higher Education (Averill, 1976) found that 122 vol-
untary consortia representing 1,200 institutions exist in the United
States. The "typical consortium" was depicted as follows:

> The typical voluntary educational consortium in the United
> States is located east of the Mississippi River, most likely west of
> Erie, Pennsylvania; consists of between nine and ten institutional
> members, whose membership fee is assessed on a variable scale;
> has a 1976–77 budget of $381,802; is led by a chief executive of-
> ficer called Executive Director; and has a full-time professional
> staff of three or more persons.

Numerous observers believe that continuing education will
be a growing area for interinstitutional cooperation. Cooperative
programs operate on the premise that several institutions can increase accessibility to courses and programs for continuing education students, at a cost savings. Continuing education may be
coupled with nontraditional delivery systems in order to realize
economic benefits and to avoid unnecessary duplication.

Illustrative of state-sponsored consortia and regional arrangements are programs in Illinois, Iowa, Minnesota, New York,
and Virginia.

Illinois. One of the most extensive systems of consortia exists in Illinois. The Illinois Board of Higher Education, in *A Master Plan — Phase III* (1971, p. 14), recommended:

> a new pattern of delivery . . . a Collegiate Common Market that utilizes the total resources of higher education, public and private. . . . Inherent to the common market concept is the diminution of traditional barriers among the institutions. It can also be the vehicle for the university without walls pattern, which calls for, among other things, an ease of transfer among campuses and the development of new criteria for the evaluation of an individual's educational progress. Ideally, the student in the Illinois integrated system, whatever his age, whatever his educational background, would have access to the resources of the entire system.

As a result, the Illinois legislature passed the Higher Education Cooperation Act (HECA) in 1972. It established:

> A program of financial assistance to programs on interinstitutional cooperation in higher education . . . to implement the policy of encouraging . . . cooperation in order to *achieve an efficient use of educational resources, an equitable distribution of educational services, the development of innovative concepts and applications, and other public purposes.* . . . In awarding grants to interinstitutional programs under this Act, the Board shall consider in relation to each such program whether it serves the public purposes expressed in this Act, whether the local community is substantially involved, whether its function could be performed better by a single existing institution, whether the program is consistent with the Illinois master plan for higher education, and such other criteria as it determines to be appropriate.

Between FY 1973 and FY 1976, the state of Illinois contributed over $1.3 million to three regional study centers, fourteen consortia-sponsored programs, and twenty-nine institutionally sponsored programs. The Illinois programs differ dramatically. Some examples are the Graduate Studies Center at Millikin University, the Council of West Suburban Colleges, the Illinois Regional Library Council, the Consortium for Judaic Studies, the Community College Learning Resource Center and the Quad-Cities Graduate Study Center.

These HECA programs vary so widely that it is difficult indeed to generalize about them. For example, one program was developed among four private education institutions with the idea of *upgrading* existing services cooperatively and serving a new clientele without creating new services. Another program is specifically designed for the "lifetime learner," in that it conducts in-service training programs that are basically continuing education. This program is also currently developing a new component on the aging, in cooperation with the local Department on Aging, to train health care providers for the elderly.

The Quad-Cities Graduate Study Center, perhaps the best known of all HECA programs, is a publicly funded consortium of ten colleges and universities around the cities of Moline and Rock Island in Illinois and Davenport and Muscatine in Iowa, such as Augustana College, Western Illinois University, Marycrest College, and Iowa State University. It started in 1969 with seed money from the four cities four years before full funding came from the Iowa and Illinois legislatures, and developed because of a combination of local pressure from the business community for trained managers and the unwillingness of either state to commit the necessary fiscal resources to develop a wholly new graduate school in the area. Its Articles of Incorporation specify the following objectives:

- To develop in the Quad-Cities coordinated programs of study at the graduate level which are applicable toward degrees from member academic institutions.
- To expand continuing education opportunities for individuals who desire to extend their education without qualifying for an advanced degree.
- To consider the feasibility and the means of establishing residence degree programs.
- To encourage experimentation in the pooling of resources of the member institutions to achieve the objectives stated above.

Through the center, students may take graduate-level degree and nondegree programs and credit or noncredit courses. The center does not admit students, nor does it award degrees; rather, it acts as an "agent" for the member institutions in coordinating course offerings so that students may pursue degree work in locations near their homes or places of work. Students may take courses from any member institution. Institutions geographically distant from the Quad-City area send faculty to the area, and some institutions have assigned a full-time faculty member to the center. Course offerings are frequently supplemented by video tape and other electronic devices. Students have access to eight area libraries through one center card (Quad-Cities Graduate Study Center, 1976).

Some HECA programs, like the Quad-Cities Center, are geared toward and basically serve an already educated clientele, while others are targeted toward "nontraditional" students. Nevertheless, many programs not specifically designed to serve new clienteles are in fact now doing so.

The HECA programs are not without their problems. Two evaluations of them by the Illinois Board of Higher Education have shown a number of them to be relatively weak (1974, 1976a), although a subsequent in-depth examination of several of them produced more positive results (Wood and Patterson, 1976). Problems, judging from interviews with state officials and educators, generally fall into two major categories: stability of funding and disagreements between institutions.

First, these programs are funded year by year by the Illinois State Legislature. Since there are no guarantees of long-range financing, long-range planning is difficult. Representatives from the HECA programs tend to feel that this funding uncertainty leaves their programs "more fragile" than those in the traditional educational institutions in the state.

Second, as with virtually all consortium arrangements, there are frequently disagreements between the institutional members of the HECA consortium. These disagreements often stem from the differently perceived levels of "academic prestige" among the cooperating institutions. However, many interinstitutional problems that were present at the inception of these programs have apparently been resolved.

The strength of the HECA programs seems to lie largely in their regional or local orientation and their capacity to be highly responsive to community needs. Each was designed very differently to meet local demands. This suggests another strength of these programs: The fact that each was designed with different purposes in mind suggests that the programs provide the state with greater educational diversity than would otherwise be provided.

Iowa. An example of a regional or consortium program for adult education is Iowa's program involving cooperative relationships among area community colleges, vocational-technical schools, county school systems, higher education institutions, community agencies, and the Iowa State Department of Public Instruction. This program originated from a 1965 legislative act that authorized regional community colleges or area schools in fifteen specified areas in Iowa. The role of the Adult Education Unit of the Department of Public Instruction is to provide leadership for statewide programs in adult basic education, high school completion, general adult and continuing education, and career supplementary education.

In addition to adult basic education and programs for veterans, there are offerings in such areas as agricultural production, consumer education, alcoholism, and selected apprenticeship trades. One particular use of the system is in the state's corrective institutions; courses have been conducted in the Iowa Women's Reformatory, Iowa Training School for Boys, the State Reformatory, and the Iowa State Penitentiary (Russell and Sumner, 1975).

Minnesota. A program similar to the Quad-Cities Center but at the undergraduate level is the Rochester Consortium in Minnesota. The Rochester Consortium is one of three regional projects authorized by the 1973 Minnesota Legislature to be administered by the Minnesota Higher Education Coordinating Board. The main objective of the program was to improve accessibility to postsecondary education in the Rochester area. Like the Quad-Cities Center, the Rochester Consortium does not offer degrees. Rather, through the use of a joint schedule, joint advising services, and other means, students may select courses and obtain degrees from among institutions that bring their resources to Rochester. Institutions from four public systems of postsecondary education and three private colleges participate. Now in its fifth year of experimentation, it has increased its registrations from 1,500 for the entire 1973–74 school year to about 2,300 for fall 1976 in the credit classes presented. Many additional students participate in noncredit classes and community service offerings. As with most proposals for new educational programs in other states and institutions, the Rochester program has been constrained by tight budgets and other resource limitations, which inhibit the growth and development of new programs (Wakefield, 1977).

Another notable consortium in Minnesota is the Minnesota Intergenerational Education Consortium. Largely the creation of Daniel Ferber, it has been funded by the HEW Administration on Aging and is now (mid 1978) a line item in the state budget. Particular programs for or about older persons are provided by eight cooperating institutions, including the Colleges of St. Benedict, St. Thomas, and St. Catherine, Mankato State University, Minneapolis Public Schools–Community Education Services, North Hennepin Community College, St. Paul Vocational-Technical Institute, and the University of Minnesota. New schools scheduled to join in FY 1979 include Inver Hills Community College, Dakota County Vocational-Technical Institute, St. Paul Open School, Bemidji State University, Hamline University, and the University of Minnesota at Crookston. The work of the consortium is conducted in the context of "intergenerational education," which seeks new learning opportunities for older persons toward continued personal growth, reduced intergenerational tensions, and increased "senior citizen power" on behalf of constructive change. In an even larger framework of what Ferber (1977, n.d.) calls "inventive federalism," Minnesota is viewed as a "statewide demonstration model" in which lifelong learning activities in that state (described in Chapter Six) may be catalytic of a "national learning society."

New York. One of the more noteworthy regional organizations in New York is the Council for the Advancement of Lifelong Learning (CALL), sponsored by the Northeastern New York Committee on Continuing Higher Education—a group of twenty-two colleges and universities. Funding is from participating colleges and from Title I of the 1965 Higher Education Act. CALL seeks to promote lifelong learning in Northeastern New York, coordinate continuing education activities of area institutions, improve accessibility to programs, act as liaison between institution and consumer, and assist in matching needs of consumers with capabilities of continuing education providers.

Among its activities, CALL operates a telephone Lifelong

Learning Referral Service, which provides information on courses offered by a variety of collegiate and noncollegiate providers in the region. Three times a year it publishes a *Guide* to credit courses offered in the late afternoon or evening and on Saturday. It publishes a five-volume *Directory* of all types of continuing education providers in the sixteen-county Northeastern New York area. The council also conducts a program to train so-called "linkers"—human service workers, library staff, training officers, union leaders, for example—to serve as a bridge between individuals in the community and continuing education programs. And CALL also maintains a Faculty Registry, a listing of individuals interested in teaching continuing education courses in the area.

Virginia. In 1966 the General Assembly of Virginia instructed the State Council of Higher Education to coordinate "off-campus extension and public service of all state-controlled institutions of higher education including all credit and noncredit courses." In 1972 the General Assembly urged that the council and the state-supported institutions "increase their attention to and efforts in continuing education, and work towards the end that the quality and prestige of continuing education be comparable to that of regular degree programs, that full degree credit be given in place of extension credit, that meaningful programs be devised, answerable to the needs of the communities in which they are offered, and that facilities and resources be used fully and economically," and it called for "the immediate establishment of a cooperative center or consortium for continuing education with main offices at George Mason University." The intent of the legislature was to use this initial consortium as a model for future joint programs in other areas of the state.

As a result of this legislative activity, the state was divided to form six regional consortia districts. Each district contains a number of state-supported institutions of higher education, and a senior state-supported institution is to serve as the focal point for development of each regional consortium. The senior institutions are encouraged to develop nontraditional degree programs at the baccalaureate and master's levels. "Such programs should be designed to provide maximum higher educational opportunities for the earning of degrees by continuing education students" (Virginia State Council of Higher Education, 1972, p. 2).

Responsibilities of each consortium include the following:

1. To assess the needs for continuing higher education programs in the consortium region.
2. To provide maximum higher education opportunities for continuing education students.
3. To encourage mutual acceptance and interchangeability of course credits among participating institutions.
4. To facilitate the earning of degrees at all levels by continuing education students.
5. To make efficient and appropriate use of the resources of all state-supported institutions offering courses within the consortium region.
6. To approve or disapprove specific course offerings by member institutions engaged in continuing higher education activities in the consortium region.
7. To publish periodically an announcement listing offerings available in the consortium region for continuing education students.
8. To ensure counseling services by participating institutions for continuing education students.
9. To ensure the maintenance of academic records by participating institutions for continuing education students.
10. To facilitate interinstitutional cooperation in the development of community service programs for the consortium region.
11. To evaluate, where appropriate, the effectiveness of continuing education offerings and activities conducted through the consortium.
12. To report semiannually to the State Council of Higher Education the ongoing activities of the consortium.
13. To report to the State Council of Higher Education on the desirability and need for educational services from state-supported institutions not engaged in continuing higher education within the consortium region when educational expertise is not available within the member institutions of the consortium.

The Virginia consortia reflect a good example of groups that interact regionally to increase cost effectiveness and increase access. Further, these consortia serve as information and counseling centers. Often in other states that do not have formal consortia, such services are performed by other consortium-type groups gathered together to perform one consortium function.

Programs for Specific Target Groups

The most common state programs geared to particular nontraditional clienteles are the adult basic education programs provided for educationally disadvantaged adults. Next most common are statewide programs for the elderly, perhaps because citizens over sixty or sixty-five years of age are a relatively easily defined population. Other state programs for such groups as women, the unemployed, veterans, and ethnic minorities are minimal, although local programs may exist for these groups.

Adult Basic Education

Most adult basic education programs at the state level operate pursuant to the federal Adult Education Act of 1966, which deals with basic literacy and high school equivalency diplomas (see Chapter One). A recent publication from the National Advisory Council on Adult Education (1977b) contains up-to-date information on adult basic education as well as secondary adult education for all fifty states, including the nature of state governing documents, the extent of federal, state, and local financial support over the past decade, the numbers of students served during 1976, and the number of General Education Development (GED) credentials issued during the same year. Rather than repeating these data here, the following paragraphs illustrate recent programmatic innovations by various states.

In New Hampshire, the State Office of Adult Basic Education has designed a volunteer tutorial program to help functionally illiterate adults in one pioneering county in the state. On a restricted and experimental basis, the State Office has organized, trained, and coordinated several corps of volunteer tutors in the Concord area.

In a significant innovation, the New York State Education Department has developed an External High School Diploma Program. This is a competency-based, life skills assessment program in which adults are granted diplomas by their local school boards for demonstrated ability in certain required areas, including communication, computation, self-awareness, social awareness, consumer awareness, scientific awareness, and occupational preparedness, regardless of where, when, or how the learning occurred. As of late 1978, over 1,000 adults in New York State had earned their diplomas through this alternative program (New York State Education Department, 1979). Although the diploma is currently awarded by local school districts, assessments can be conducted by trained personnel in many different agencies. Learning is done at home, not in classes; it is self-paced and competency oriented. To qualify for a diploma, candidates must pass five tests, which deal with competencies in sixty-four basic "life skills." Tests are mostly of the take-home variety, though they also include oral interviews. Candidates must also demonstrate occupational or vocational skills, advanced academic skills, or specialized skills in community organization, art, or music. A portfolio is prepared attesting to the candidate's ability to do college work. The average person takes three months to go through the program (Regional Learning Service of Central New York, 1976).

North Carolina's governor is actively supporting implementation of a pilot program to convince the state's nonreading adults to enroll in special reading programs in the community colleges. Tentative proposals call for the use of state and federal money to hire community recruiters and new reading teachers at the community colleges and technical institutes. According to the governor, "North Carolina must mount all its resources in the war against illiteracy . . . and the community colleges should be in the forefront of that fight" (Governor's Office News Release, 1977).

In Rhode Island, the Department of Education is attempting to obtain funding for a program for improving basic education for disadvantaged adults. The program would have three main objectives: (1) to design a new high school diploma program for adults based on life-coping skills, (2) to design and launch a public information campaign aimed at increasing the enrollment in adult education programs at both the state and local community levels, and (3) to raise the level of state funding to increase support for current basic education programs and to allow for more intensive development of innovative adult education programs. The Board of Regents of Rhode Island presented a supplementary budget request to the General Assembly, which the General Assembly did not approve for FY 1977. According to a position paper prepared by the Regents, "It is expected that it [the request for additional funding] will be included in the Board of Regents' budget for 1978–79 and that the General Assembly will be receptive at that time." (The Regents' paper does not explain why the Assembly would be receptive in 1978 when it was not in 1977.)

In South Carolina, the Office of Adult Education in the State Department is using newspapers to teach adults and children to read. The department has developed a reading program that consists of 180 lessons run in a local newspaper. No classrooms or certified teachers are required. The series of lessons is based on a vocabulary of words frequently used in newspapers. Reading specialists analyzed lists of words appearing twenty-five or more times in a typical newspaper, and then determined the degree of difficulty for each word at different grade levels.

Programs for the Elderly

In Arizona, an innovative program to help elderly people cope with their problems is conducted by a consortium of six community college districts. Funded under Title I of the Higher Education Act, it is called "Six Dimensions for People Over Sixty." There are twenty centers that offer semester classes in consumer health, consumer economics, drawing and painting, ceramics, home repair, nutrition, clothing construction, decoupage, leathercraft, sculpturing, woodworking, embroidery, and community involvement.

A practice that is becoming more common in all states is some form of tuition waiver for the elderly; at least some institutions in every state have such tuition reduction policies (*PER* Editors, 1978). For example, in 1976 the Tennessee Legislature passed Senate Bill 70, which specified that:

> persons sixty years of age or older, who are domiciled in
> Tennessee, may audit courses at any state-supported college or

> university without paying tuition charges, maintenance fees, student activity fees, or registration fees; however, *this privilege may be limited or denied by the college or university on an individual classroom basis according to space availability* [emphasis added].

Later the act was amended to allow the colleges and universities to charge a "service fee" for record keeping, not to exceed $75 a semester.

In 1977 the General Assembly of North Carolina passed a similar piece of legislation regarding the attendance of persons over sixty-five at state-supported institutions of higher education. Its House Bill 842, however, was even more specific than the Tennessee legislation.

> State-supported institutions of higher education, community colleges, industrial education centers, and technical institutes shall permit legal residents of North Carolina who have attained the age of sixty-five to attend classes for credit or noncredit purposes without the required payment of tuition, provided, however, that such persons meet admission and other standards deemed appropriate by the educational institution, and provided further that such persons shall be accepted by the constituent institutions of the University of North Carolina only on a space-available basis. . . . Persons attending classes under the provisions of this act, without payment of tuition, shall be counted in the computation of enrollment for funding purposes.

The Minnesota State Legislature in its 1977 session also passed legislation that permits "senior citizens," sixty-two years of age and over, to attend tuition-free all publicly assisted institutions on a "space-available" basis.

Interestingly, in Florida, where the "over sixty-five" age group is approaching 20 percent of the state's population, a bill that would have waived tuition for persons over sixty-five failed to pass the legislature. However, with the aid of a federal grant under Title I of the Higher Education Act of 1965, the Central Florida Institute of Lifetime Learning at Valencia Community Colleges is offering no-fee courses to citizens aged fifty-five and over. Classes include personal enrichment, recreation, vocational up-grading, and life skills.

North Carolina is relatively active in programs for persons over sixty-five, although the state ranks thirty-seventh in its percentage of people over sixty-five—9 percent (1975 Census). There exists a Governor's Coordinating Council on Aging, and in July of 1977, the Office of the Governor, the North Carolina Medical Society, the North Carolina Conference for Social Services, the Center for the Study of Aging and Human Development, and the North Carolina Department of Human Development, Division of Aging, sponsored The Governor's Conference on the Quality of Life for Our Senior Citizens.

Wisconsin has also recently held a Governor's Conference on Aging. Six regional follow-up "Mini Conferences on Problems of the Elderly" were also held, which focused on four problems: (1) community involvement and volunteerism, (2) claiming and handling retirement monies—Social Security, VA benefits, and pensions, (3) coping with medical costs in old age—health insurance, Medicare, and Medicaid, and (4) cutting the red tape in wills and probate.

Wisconsin's Gateway Technical Institute, serving the southeastern corner of the state, has proposed a model for a senior citizen bureau. In the proposal, it cites four main objectives: (1) to create a senior citizen bureau that would provide comprehensive services at Gateway Technical Institute, (2) to improve the delivery system for course offerings to senior citizens, (3) to improve the needs assessment for senior citizens, and (4) to provide a model for other vocational, technical, and adult education districts for use in the development of senior citizen bureaus.

A great many programs have been instituted in many states to train persons to assist the elderly with specific problems. For instance, again in Wisconsin, a workshop entitled "Leadership: A Workshop for Leaders in Senior Citizens' Groups" was organized to train persons to work with senior citizens' organizations. Funded by the State's Division on Aging, the workshop had four goals: (1) to acquaint participants with leadership skills and talents that are possessed by themselves and others, (2) to share ideas and techniques for solving problems and answering questions that are important to the participants, (3) to explore how to set goals and make decisions that involve others in a way meaningful to them, (4) to develop action plans that can be used to achieve the goals of the organization.

Programs for Women

Very few documents were forwarded to us regarding state-initiated programs for adult women. Several states reported programs funded by Title I (A) of the Higher Education Act. For example, at Kansas State University, a Kansas Women's Outreach Program, supported by Title I, sponsored (1) preparation of a resource handbook of educational institutions and their offerings in Kansas and (2) workshops in assertiveness training. The university was handicapped, in this program, by having no vocational-technical classes, little prospect of offering such classes for credit, and no state support for extension classes at this level. Other Title I programs dealing with women's problems exist in other states, but most such programs are developed at the institutional level.

One exception is the Continuing Education for Women program in Hawaii, which was funded from various sources, including Title I of the Higher Education Act, revenue receipts, and state general funds in 1976–77. This program is worth noting because it is a rare instance of federal monies working as a catalyst for a program that was later picked up by the state. The state, in other words, saw the program's importance and was willing to fund it.

The Continuing Education for Women program provides a number of services for adult women in Hawaii. First, in an attempt to assist both young and mature women who want to return to education or who require "alternative life-styles," individual educational, vocational, and career counseling is offered. Also, information and referral services are offered via telephone. In 1976–77, 1,604 women from eighteen to sixty years of age were helped. Their educational backgrounds ranged from elementary and high school dropouts to those working towards graduate degrees, and they were from diverse economic, social, and ethnic groups.

A second program in Hawaii is geared specifically toward helping the disadvantaged woman. The target population consists of women who are housebound, displaced homemakers, offenders, and other disadvantaged women. The emphasis of this program has been individual counseling through a pilot program entitled "Everywoman." Part of the project consisted of a needs assessment of the types of services women want. Sixty-five women have been served by the program: Twelve were from Habilitat (the state prison), one was an offender on probation, and four were unwed mothers referred by the YWCA.

Third, the Continuing Education for Women program in Hawaii has taken on the task of trying to educate the public to the needs, potentials, and contributions of women as human resources. To this end, conferences, workshops, media publicity, and public speaking are common activities. Workshops and seminars for the women cover such subjects as personal growth, employment, and career and financial planning and management. Such groups as the American Federation of State, County, and Municipal Employees–AFL-CIO, the American Women's Business Association, and the Navy Public Works Women's Program have become involved. In FY 1978 the program was able to serve 4,500 women in Hawaii. Yet, as with many other programs in the country, "the primary external trend affecting the program is the austerity of the budget and the release of part/total funds by the Department of Budget and Finance" (Hawaii State Postsecondary Education Commission, 1977, p. 1).

Programs for the Unemployed

Information was received on only one program that was specifically targeted to the chronically unemployed. This was the Human Resource Development (HRD) Program in North Carolina, which is "an intensive effort to restore to permanent employment the economically disadvantaged and the chronically unemployed." It consists of three primary components:

1. Identification and recruitment of the individuals within the community who are in greatest need of the service.
2. Enrollment in an eight-week (240 hours) class in which the individual re-evaluates his self-concept; interacts in a group; learns the rudimentary disciplines associated with obtaining and retaining regular employment; and, when necessary, takes remedial instruction in basic education. Throughout the training period and post-training follow-up period, emphasis is placed

on individual counseling in an effort to help each trainee resolve the sociological, emotional, or economic barriers impeding
his vocational progress.

3. Placement in a job commensurate with the individual's abilities
and interests.

The concept of HRD training was originated by the North
Carolina Manpower Development Corporation and was first introduced into the community college system as a pilot project at
one community college in 1969. During FY 1974, nearly $1.5 mil-
lion provided by the General Assembly supported HRD programs
in twenty-eight technical institutes and community colleges. In FY
1975 an appropriation of $2.1 million enabled the program to be
offered in thirteen additional schools. In FY 1975, enrollments
exceeded 4,000.

Programs for Vietnam Veterans

Well over twice as many Vietnam veterans have died since
coming home as were killed in the war. According to Veterans
Administration figures, 46,498 American troops lost their lives in
combat in Southeast Asia, but 113,000 Vietnam-era vets have died
since returning. Some experts believe that the deaths are due to
a disproportionate number of suicides and drug- or alcohol-related
problems. Nevertheless, it appears that there is little educational
activity at the state level for the purpose of reintegrating the veteran into the American mainstream. Possibly, too much reliance
has been placed on the GI Bill, which helps the veteran financially
but does little to help him to readjust socially.

With these problems in mind, the University of the State of
New York, through the State Education Department, produced a
report entitled *The New York State Vietnam Veteran: His Immediate and
Continuing Needs in Post-Secondary Education* (Comly, 1975b). The
primary purpose of the report was to determine the unmet educational needs of Vietnam veterans. The report noted that about
80 percent of New York State Vietnam veterans are high school
graduates and could therefore benefit from postsecondary education. Yet the number of veterans in New York who have applied
for benefits was found to be well below the national average. Less

than one third of the community colleges provide their own veterans' counselors.

In New York, a variety of programs are available for veterans, but none of them is designed to "maximize their participation in educational opportunities." The New York report points out that "those who work with Vietnam-era veterans note their apathy towards mailed information, their desire to be associated with fellow veteran colleagues, and their dependency on outreach and special programs designed to increase motivation (Comly, 1975b). (These characteristics of veterans may well apply to *most* nontraditional clienteles.)

The needs of veterans, according to Comly's report, fall into three categories:

1. The need for a coordinated program of educational outreach and counseling—personal, academic, and career-oriented.
2. The need for increased interagency cooperation, coordination, and support in order that veterans may readily have access to available educational and training opportunities and information.
3. The need for state legislative support and programs enabling veterans to partake of educational programs during a period of rapidly rising costs.

To meet the first need, the State Education Department's Bureau of Post-Secondary Continuing Education has proposed a series of regional workshops designed to provide veterans with outreach and counseling for postsecondary programs.

Unfortunately, it appears that one of the primary motivations for New York's concern for the Vietnam veteran was the revenues lost from their nonparticipation. According to Comly (1975b), "New York State will lose $703 million in 1974 potential revenues because these eligible high school graduates do not participate in GI educational training benefits. These nonparticipants constitute a large potential student body at the very stage of declining college enrollments."

While we received no additional information from other states regarding veterans' programs, the New York report indicated that, according to the Veterans Administration, successful veterans programs exist in Cleveland, Dayton, Denver, and Los Angeles. It is not known if these programs are state based or institutionally based. Finally, according to the report, a "model program" to assist veterans through an extensive counseling program is in existence at Southern Illinois University.

Conclusion

Apart from components of adult basic education programs, state-directed learning programs for particular target groups of adults are not widespread. At least three factors seem to be involved: (1) entrenched institutional interests, (2) the decentralized academic governance structure, and (3) academia's traditional isolation from the American mainstream. Entrenched institutional interests make attempts at changes difficult. Functioning under a growth syndrome during the past several decades, postsecondary education institutions are currently trying to adjust to a more stable environment. The conflicting demands of maintaining current human and physical resources while adjusting to new student needs and demands can lead to difficulties. Managing decline is quite different from managing growth.

The traditional decentralized governance structure in the academic world makes reevaluation and reform difficult. The diffusion of responsibility in postsecondary education has often led to: inadequate long-range planning; poor coordination with external needs and priorities; and poor internal management of resources. The strength of the system, its decentralized grass-roots character, can be a weakness when initiating systemwide change.

The education sector has by and large failed to integrate its goals with the needs and goals of the larger society. The academic community has generally not balanced internal needs with external needs and priorities. The failure to integrate these priorities raises the question whether traditional systems are able to meet new external needs—in this instance, the needs of lifelong learners.

Current Outlook

What impact has the movement toward lifelong learning so far had on the states? Is there, in fact, a movement toward state policies supporting lifelong learning? While there are probably fifty answers to these questions, in general new state initiatives in postcompulsory education have been limited. Policy makers have adopted few statewide policies for lifelong learning, and they show little sign of doing so in the immediate future. This does not necessarily reflect a lack of concern on the part of decision makers; more likely it reflects a number of ongoing social and economic trends. The state documents and case studies reveal a number of political and educational constraints common to all the states.

None of the fifty states illustrates these constraints more graphically than Pennsylvania, in particular through the problems encountered in funding the Office of Lifelong Learning in its Department of Education.

Pennsylvania is the only state to our knowledge that has formally incorporated the concept of lifelong learning into its governance structure. Under the leadership of Jerome Ziegler, then Pennsylvania Commissioner of Education, an Office of Special Programs was created within the Department of Education. In 1976 the office was renamed the Office of Lifelong Learning. Although never officially recognized by the governor, the Office remained as part of the Department of Education under Pennsylvania's new commissioner, Edward C. McGuire. The Office of Lifelong Learning has been involved in a wide range of activities, some new and some initiated by its predecessor (The Office of Special Programs). Currently, a number of both instructional and noninstructional programs are administered from the Office. These include: a library program; a minority counseling program; a continuing education program for senior citizens; a program for correctional institutions; a field-work program; a staff development program; an internship program; and an information collection and analysis service.

In addition, the Lifelong Learning staff concerns itself with legislation that may affect adult learning in the state. Three such bills, in particular, have been introduced in the last four years. First, Senate Bill 1472, which would have created an open college administered by the State Department of Education, was introduced in 1974. Second, two bills (SB 926 and SB 729), introduced in 1975 and 1976, sought to create educational brokerage centers and an educational credit bank. None of these measures passed.

By the next year, 1977, Pennsylvania was deep in a major fiscal crisis. State revenues were insufficient to meet next year's fiscal needs; many state legislators had recently been elected on a "no tax hike" ticket; they refused to support a tax increase requested by the governor. The deadlock resulted in numerous state employees being "furloughed" for a period of time, including six of the twelve-member staff of the Office of Lifelong Learning. Although a budget for Pennsylvania was eventually passed, missing from that "balanced budget" was nearly $300 million for state-related (four) and state-aided (thirteen) higher education institutions. It was not until December 1977 that these seventeen institutions, which have been borrowing to stay in operation, were funded.

With this fiscal crisis as a backdrop, it may be of no surprise that issues such as "lifelong learning" are not seen as top priority in Pennsylvania. When 100 employees were furloughed from the Department of Education, the Office of Lifelong Learning suffered a 50 percent loss of staff—the highest percentage cut in the department. Although the staff was subsequently restored to its initial complement after the budget was passed, the severe cut is indicative of the department's priorities.

From information gathered from legislative staff, there appears to be little support in the legislature for adult or lifelong learning programs. Reasons most frequently cited for legislative inaction include the following:

- Many, perhaps most, legislators do not feel that education is a priority area.
- Traditionally, basic education receives priority funding, and postsecondary education gets what is left over.
- Since enrollments are declining, costs should also be declining; instead, they are still escalating.
- The state is already contributing a very large proportion of its tax dollars to education.
- Legislators question the productivity of the education community; while costs are increasing, the quality of education seems to be declining (judging from declining test scores).
- Many legislators were educated in traditional modes and ques-

tion the validity of nontraditional approaches, including awarding credit for such things as "life experience."
- Numerous policy makers feel that the move toward adult education is a "grab" for money occasioned by declining enrollments
  of traditional college-age youths.

In summary, while Pennsylvania has, over the past several
years, been in the forefront of educational policy making in the
area of lifelong learning, the present fiscal support from the state
is small and prospects for the future are not bright. Pennsylvania
is probably particularly instructive in that many other states may
well face a fiscal crisis in the future, which will force state policy
makers to distribute limited state revenues among an increasing
number of public services. Education, clearly, does not receive top
priority in an era of fiscal retrenchment.

Across the fifty states, more seems responsible for the low
priority given lifelong learning than the current budgetary constraints and the competition from other public services such as
unemployment compensation, health, social security, and environmental protection. Changes in public attitudes toward education
also play a role. While public support for education rose dramatically in the 1950s and 1960s and was accompanied by increased
financial support, disenchantment with the performance of the
education establishment has set in during the 1970s. Moreover, the
overabundance of underemployed and unemployed highly educated persons, particularly teachers, has led many people to question the need for yet more postsecondary education. This is particularly true of political leaders. Declining enrollments in the
education sector and the subsequent decline in average daily attendance (ADA) and full-time equivalent (FTE) funding have led
state policy makers to regard new education programs with caution. Many feel that the call to expand adult enrollments is motivated primarily by the need for additional revenues and the need
to fill empty classroom spaces. Were adult learners themselves,
rather than educators, calling for expanded services, state leaders
might be less suspicious. Just as they may be less leery of calls from
patients than from hospital administrators for more hospital construction, so they may await public demands for state-supported
lifelong learning services rather than only those of educators.

Source List: Illustrative State Documents
Related to Lifelong Learning

Arizona

Arizona Board of Regents. *University Development in the Mid-Seventies: A Long Range Plan.* Phoenix: Arizona Board of Regents, 1974.

California

California Legislature. Assembly Bill No. 4324 (Appropriations for Golden State College and the Educational Opportunity Center). March 29, 1976.

California Postsecondary Education Commission. A Proposal for Establishing Community Advisement Centers. Sacramento: California Postsecondary Education Commission, 1976 (Draft).

California Postsecondary Education Commission. *The Adequacy of Opportunities for Californians to Receive Credit for Prior Learning.* Sacramento: California Postsecondary Education Commission, 1977a.

California Postsecondary Education Commission. *Planning for Postsecondary Education in California: A Five-Year Plan Update, 1977–1982.* Sacramento: California Postsecondary Education Commission, 1977b.

Clark, R. L., and Rubin, D. P. *Instructional Technology and Media for Postsecondary Alternatives* (Fourth Technical Report). Sacramento: California Legislature, 1975.

Deegan, W. L., and Maynard, J. B. *Establishing Community Advisement Centers: A Proposal.* Sacramento: California Postsecondary Education Commission, July 1975.

Del Buono, X. A., and Riles, W. *Status Report and Recommendations for the Administration of Adult Education in California.* Sacramento: California State Department of Education, Adult Education Division, 1975.

Hefferlin, J. L., Peterson, R. E., and Roelfs, P. J. *California's Need for Postsecondary Alternatives* (First Technical Report, Part One). Sacramento: California Legislature, 1975.

Hodgkinson, H. L., and Shear, W. M. *Noninstructional Services as Postsecondary Alternatives.* Sacramento: California Legislature, 1975.

Joint Committee on the Master Plan for Higher Education. *Report of the Joint Committee on the Master Plan for Higher Education.* Sacramento: California Legislature, 1973.

Martin, W. B. *Alternative Forms of Higher Education for California.* Sacramento: Joint Committee on the Master Plan for Higher Education, California Legislature, 1973.

Peterson, R. E., and Hefferlin, J. L. *Postsecondary Alternatives to Meet the Educational Needs of California's Adults.* Sacramento: California Legislature, 1975.

Peterson, R. E., Roelfs, P. J., and others. *Community Needs for Postsecondary Alternatives* (First Technical Report, Part Two). Sacramento: California Legislature, 1975.

Salner, M. B. *Inventory of Existing Postsecondary Alternatives* (Second Technical Report). Sacramento: California Legislature, 1975.

Colorado

Barlow, B. M., and Timaraos, C. R. *Colorado Adult Needs Assessment.* Denver: Colorado Department of Education, 1975.

Colorado Legislature. 51st General Assembly. Senate Bill No. 486 (To establish Colorado Centennial Open University). 1977.

Colorado Commission on Higher Education. *Education Centers: A Rationale and Estimated Budget for Establishment of Education Centers in Colorado.* Denver: Colorado Commission on Higher Education, 1977.

Community Service and Continuing Education Program. *Outreach and Community Service Programs: Annual Report for 1975–76 (Title I, Higher Education Act of 1965).* Denver: Colorado Commission on Higher Education, 1977.

Connecticut

Connecticut Board of Education. *Adult Basic Education Annual Program Plan for Fiscal Year 1978.* Hartford: Connecticut Board of Education, 1977.

Connecticut Commission for Higher Education. *Master Plan for Higher Education in Connecticut, 1974–1980: Quality and Equality.* Hartford: Connecticut Commission for Higher Education, 1974.

Connecticut Commission for Higher Education. *Connecticut Master Plan Update: Biennial Supplement.* Hartford: Connecticut Commission for Higher Education, 1976.

Smith, T. A., and others. *In Support of Lifelong Learning: A Report to the Connecticut Commission for Higher Education by a Resource Group on Continuing Education and Community Service.* Hartford: Trinity College, 1975.

Florida

Florida Commission on Educational Outreach and Services. *Preliminary Report (Access to Knowledge,* Vol. 1). Tallahassee: Florida Commission on Educational Outreach and Services, 1976a.

Florida Commission on Educational Outreach and Services. *Data Collection and Analysis: An Appendix to the Report (Access to Knowledge,* Vol. 2). Tallahassee: State University System of Florida, 1976b.

Florida Commission on Educational Outreach and Services. *Educational Outreach and Non-Traditional Programs in Post-Secondary Education: Part One–Annotations of Selected Literature, (Access to Knowledge,* Vol. 3A). Tallahassee: State University System of Florida, 1976c.

Florida Commission on Educational Outreach and Services. *Educational Outreach and Non-Traditional Programs in Post-Secondary Education: Part Two–Recommendations from Selected Literature (Access to Knowledge,* Vol. 3B). Tallahassee: State University System of Florida, 1976d.

Florida Department of Education. *Status of the Community Instructional Services Process in Florida.* Tallahassee: Florida Department of Education, 1977.

Florida Legislature. *Conference Committee Report on House Bill 10-A,* House/Senate Committee on Appropriations. Tallahassee: Florida Legislature, June 15, 1977.

Florida Postsecondary Education Commission, and others. *State Planning for Lifelong Learning: Improving Access for All Citizens.* Tallahassee: Florida Department of Education, 1977.

Hawaii

Government Organization Commission. *Government Organization Commission Report.* Honolulu: Government Organization Commission, 1976 (Draft).

Hawaii State Postsecondary Education Commission. *Continuing Ed-*

ucation for Women: Program and Budget Plans, FY 1977–78. Honolulu: Hawaii State Postsecondary Education Commission, 1977.

Idaho

Trump, C. M. *A Report on the Continuing Education Correspondence Study and Extended Day Program Review.* Boise: Idaho Board of Education, Office of Academic Planning, n.d.

Worldwide Education and Research Institute. *Recommended Action Emerging from the Idaho Governor's Conference on Educational Needs.* Salt Lake City: Idaho Department of Education, 1973.

Worldwide Education and Research Institute. *Needs Assessment Manual for Local Education Agencies.* Salt Lake City: Idaho Board of Education, School Needs Assessment Project, 1976.

Illinois

Committee on Community Services and Continuing Adult Education for Master Plan—Phase IV. *Public Service–Non-Degree Programs and Activities.* Springfield: Illinois Board of Higher Education, 1975.

Council of West Suburban Colleges. *Reporter,* Vol. 4, No. 2. Lisle: Council of West Suburban Colleges, 1977.

DeRolf, J. J., and Pringle, R. A. "One Major Step Forward—The Board of Governor's BA." *Adult Leadership,* January 1975, *23,* 214–220.

Dungan, R. A., and Furman, J. M. "The State's Role in Non-Traditional Education: Two Contrasting Viewpoints." In Postsecondary Education Convening Authority, *Nontraditional Education: State Level Issues and Concerns.* Washington, D.C.: Postsecondary Education Convening Authority, 1977.

House, R., and Ragan, J. *Master Plan I: Directions for Cooperative Post-Secondary Education in Southern Illinois.* Springfield: Regional Council of the Southern Illinois Collegiate Common Market, 1976.

Illinois Board of Higher Education. *A Master Plan for Higher Education in Illinois: Phase III–An Integrated State System.* Springfield: Illinois Board of Higher Education, 1971.

Illinois Board of Higher Education. *Survey of Interinstitutional Co-*

operation in Illinois. Springfield: Illinois Board of Higher Education, 1972.

Illinois Board of Higher Education. *Adult Educational Interest Study.* Springfield: Nielsen Marketing Service, 1973.

Illinois Board of Higher Education. *Progress Through Cooperation: A Report on the Illinois Higher Education Cooperation Act (HECA).* Springfield: Illinois Board of Higher Education, 1974.

Illinois Board of Higher Education. *Public Service–Non-Degree Programs and Activities* (A Report Submitted by the Committee on Community Services and Continuing Adult Education for Master Plan—Phase IV). Springfield: Illinois Board of Higher Education, 1975.

Illinois Board of Higher Education. *Higher Education Cooperation Act: A Staff Evaluation of Programs Funded via the Higher Education Cooperation Act.* Springfield: Illinois Board of Higher Education, 1976a.

Illinois Board of Higher Education. *Inventory of Adult Educational Interests.* Springfield: Illinois Board of Higher Education, 1976b.

Illinois Board of Higher Education. *A Master Plan for Postsecondary Education in Illinois.* Springfield: Illinois Board of Higher Education, 1976c.

Illinois Board of Higher Education. *Moving into the Third Century: Toward Lifelong Learning.* Springfield: Illinois Board of Higher Education, 1976d.

Illinois Board of Higher Education. *Report on Off-Campus Credit Activities.* Springfield: Illinois Board of Higher Education, 1976e.

Illinois Board of Higher Education. *Survey of Off-Campus and Cooperative Degree Credit Activities in Illinois.* Springfield: Illinois Board of Higher Education, 1976f.

Illinois Board of Higher Education, Committee on Nontraditional and Cooperative Programs. *Background Paper on the Recommendations of the Committee on Nontraditional and Cooperative Programs.* Springfield: Illinois Board of Higher Education, 1973.

Illinois Board of Higher Education, Educational Television Commission. *A State Plan for Educational Television in Illinois.* Springfield: Illinois Board of Higher Education, 1977.

Illinois Collegiate Common Market Task Force. *Report.* Springfield: Illinois Board of Higher Education, 1973.

Illinois Higher Education Cooperation Act Program. *An Assessment of the Higher Education Cooperation Act Program by Its Participants.* Springfield: Illinois Board of Higher Education, 1976.

Illinois Legislature. 77th General Assembly. House Bill No. 4528 (The Higher Education Cooperation Act). 1972.

Metro East/St. Louis Regional Council on Interinstitutional Cooperation. *Newsletter.* December 1974, June 1975.

Metro East/St. Louis Regional Council on Interinstitutional Cooperation. *Executive Director's Report, No. 10.* Edwardsville: Metro/East St. Louis Regional Council on Interinstitutional Cooperation, 1976.

Millikin University, Graduate Studies Center. *Annual Report 1977.* Decatur: Millikin University, 1977a.

Millikin University, Graduate Studies Center. *Course Catalog Spring 1977.* Decatur: Millikin University, 1977b.

West Suburban Intercollegiate Council. *Evaluation of Cooperative Programs of the West Suburban Intercollegiate Council Developed Under Provisions of the Higher Education Cooperation Act.* Lisle: West Suburban Intercollegiate Council, 1976.

Illinois and Iowa

Quad-Cities Graduate Study Center. *Annual Report 1975.* Rock Island: Quad-Cities Graduate Study Center, 1975a.

Quad-Cities Graduate Study Center. *Survey Questionnaire, April 1975.* Rock Island: Quad-Cities Graduate Study Center, 1975b.

Quad-Cities Graduate Study Center. *Survey Questionnaire, October 1976.* Rock Island: Quad-Cities Graduate Study Center, 1976.

Quad-Cities Graduate Study Center. *Annual Report 1976.* Rock Island: Quad-Cities Graduate Study Center, 1977a.

Quad-Cities Graduate Study Center. *Newsletter.* Vol. 6, No. 2. Rock Island: Quad-Cities Graduate Study Center, 1977b.

Wood, H., and Patterson, L. D. *Quad-Cities Graduate Study Center: Comprehensive Evaluation and Recommendations.* Rock Island: Quad-Cities Graduate Study Center, 1976.

Indiana

Bruce, L. *Study of Continuing Education and Non-Traditional Programming.* Indianapolis: Commission for Higher Education, 1976.

Iowa

Hamilton, I. B. *The Third Century: Postsecondary Planning for the Nontraditional Learner.* Princeton, N.J.: Educational Testing Service, 1976.

McLure, G. T. *Lifelong Learning in the Third Century: Gaps, Problems, and Cooperative Efforts in Postsecondary Planning in Iowa.* Des Moines: Higher Education Facilities Commission of the State of Iowa, 1977a.

McLure, G. T. *Recommendations for Lifelong Learning in Iowa in the Third Century, the Final Report.* Des Moines: Higher Education Facilities Commission of the State of Iowa, 1977b.

Russell, K., and Sumner, J. "An Adult Education Delivery System: The Iowa Model." *Adult Leadership,* May 1975, *23,* 339–344.

Kansas

Hoyt, D. P. *Appraisal of Interest in Continuing Education Opportunities Among Kansas Adults.* Manhattan: Kansas State University, 1975.

Kansas Board of Regents. *Guidelines for Increasing Efficiency at State Colleges and Universities.* Topeka: Kansas Board of Regents, 1972.

Kansas State University, Council of Deans and Directors of Continuing Education and Council of Chief Academic Officers. *Continuing Education Study in Kansas Regents' Institutions.* Manhattan: Kansas State University, 1977a.

Kansas State University, Council of Deans and Directors of Continuing Education and Council of Chief Academic Officers. *Results: Off-Campus Instructional Appraisal Program FY 1977.* Manhattan: Kansas State University, 1977b.

Kansas State University, Division of Continuing Education. *Roles and Objectives of Continuing Education: Research Summary.* Manhattan: Kansas State University, 1977.

Kentucky

Council on Public Higher Education. *Kentucky and Comprehensive Planning for Higher Education.* Frankfort: Council on Public Higher Education, 1976.

Louisiana

Louisiana Board of Regents for Higher Education. *Directory of Post-*

secondary Opportunities in Louisiana. Lafayette: University of Southwestern Louisiana, 1977.

Maryland

Butkiewicz, L. K. (Ed.). *1977 Conference Highlights.* Bel Air: Maryland Association for Publicly Supported Education, 1977.

Massachusetts

Baker, C. O., and Knerr, A. D. "Planning Continuing Education: A Key Bay State Study." *Planning for Higher Education,* 1973, 2 (6), 1–2.

Fischer, S. J., and Nolfi, G. J. *Needs Analysis and Instrument for Measuring Crisis Proneness.* Cambridge: University Consultants, Inc., n.d.

Massachusetts Commonwealth Task Force on the Open University. *Toward an Open Learning Network for the People of Massachusetts: Preliminary Report.* Wellesley: Massachusetts Commonwealth Task Force on the Open University, 1974.

Massachusetts Governor's Commission on the Status of Women. *Your Chance to Return to School.* Boston: Massachusetts Governor's Commission on the Status of Women, 1976.

Massachusetts Legislature. Senate Bill 197/House Bill 2132 (An Act Creating the Adult Recurrent Education Entitlement Voucher Program). 1976.

Nolfi, G. J., and Bush, J. W. *Design and Implementation of Community-Based Information Counseling and Referral Centers to Serve Adult Learners: Lessons from the Massachusetts Experience.* Cambridge: University Consultants, May 1976.

Nolfi, G. J., and Nelson, V. I. *Strengthening the Alternative Postsecondary Education System: Continuing and Part-time Study in Massachusetts,* Vols. 1 and 2. Cambridge: University Consultants, 1973.

Nolfi, G. J., and others. *Identification and Recommendation of Target Clienteles for the Proposed Open University in Massachusetts.* Cambridge: University Consultants, 1974.

Michigan

Eisley, J. G., and Coppard, L. C. *Extending Opportunities for Graduate Studies in Michigan: A Preliminary Report on the Feasibility of Exter-*

nal Graduate Programs. Ann Arbor: Horace H. Rackham School of Graduate Studies, University of Michigan, 1977.

Task Force to Study the Feasibility of an External Degree Program in Michigan. *Report to the Michigan State Board of Education.* Lansing: Task Force to Study the Feasibility of an External Degree Program in Michigan, 1977a.

Task Force to Study the Feasibility of an External Degree Program in Michigan. *The Minority Report.* Lansing: Task Force to Study the Feasibility of an External Degree Program in Michigan, 1977b.

Minnesota

Ferber, D. A. *On Inventing the Process of "Inventive Federalism" and Its First Product, "Lifelong Learning."* St. Paul: D. A. Ferber, 1977.

Ferber, D. A. *An Abstract and Introduction of an Administration on Aging Competitive Extension Proposal: Toward Minnesota as a Statewide Systematic Demonstration Model of Intergenerational Education.* St. Paul: Macalister College, n.d.

Minnesota Higher Education Coordinating Board. "Regional Center Approach Serves Residents Effectively." *Mhecb Report,* May 1977, *3,* 1–3.

Minnesota Higher Education Coordinating Commission. *Making the Transition: Report to the 1975 Minnesota Legislature* (Comprehensive Plan—Phase IV). St. Paul: Minnesota Higher Education Coordinating Commission, 1975a.

Minnesota Higher Education Coordinating Commission. *The Rochester Postsecondary Education Center: An Experiment in Meeting Regional Needs Through Cooperation and Coordination.* St. Paul: Minnesota Higher Education Coordinating Commission, 1975b.

Minnesota State Planning Agency. *Alternatives for Lifelong Learning in Minnesota: The Nonformal Educational Sector.* St. Paul: Minnesota State Planning Agency, 1976.

Minnesota State Planning Agency. *A Proposal for Comprehensive Educational Brokering in Minnesota.* St. Paul: Minnesota State Planning Agency, 1977.

Wakefield W. L. " 'The Rochester Consortium': A Developmental Program on Improving Post-Secondary Educational Accessibility Through Inter-Institutional Cooperation in the Southern

Minnesota Area." In Florida Postsecondary Education Commission and others, *State Planning for Lifelong Learning: Improving Access for All Citizens.* Tallahassee: State of Florida Department of Education, 1977.

Mississippi

Board of Trustees of Institutions of Higher Learning. *Long Range Plan: Mississippi State Institutions of Higher Learning.* Jackson: Board of Trustees of Institutions of Higher Learning, 1975.

Nebraska

Gessner, S. *Terminology: Adult and Continuing Education.* Lincoln: Nebraska Coordinating Commission for Postsecondary Education, 1977.

Nebraska Coordinating Commission for Postsecondary Education, Adult and Continuing Education Committee. *Preliminary Staff Report to the Commission.* Lincoln: Nebraska Coordinating Commission for Postsecondary Education, 1977.

Nebraska Coordinating Commission for Postsecondary Education. *Goals and Recommendations for Adult and Continuing Education Instructional Programs of Nebraska Postsecondary Institutions.* Lincoln: Nebraska Coordinating Commission for Postsecondary Education, 1978.

New Hampshire

New Hampshire State Office of Adult Basic Education. *Volunteer Tutorial Program to Help Functionally Illiterate Adults in Hillsborough County.* Concord: New Hampshire State Office of Adult Basic Education, n.d.

Sideris, J. E., and Whalen, R. E. *An Alternative to Secondary Education: A Position Paper.* Concord: New Hampshire Office of Adult Basic Education, 1973.

New Jersey

Bender, L. W. "A Third Version of the Community College: The Contract College—An Analysis for State Planners." In Florida Postsecondary Education Commission and others, *State Plan-*

ning for Lifelong Learning: Improving Access For All Citizens. Tallahassee: Florida Department of Education, 1977.
New Jersey Board of Higher Education. *A Development Plan for Higher Education in New Jersey—Phase II of the Master Plan.* Trenton: New Jersey Board of Higher Education, 1974.
O'Neill, J. P. *Memorandum: The Community College Commission, Its Structure and Operation.* Jersey City: Hudson County Community College Commission, December 1975.
Thomas A. Edison College. *Thomas A. Edison College Catalog, 1977–78.* Princeton: Thomas A. Edison College, 1977.

New York

Adult Learning Services Committee. *Adult Learning Services: A Status Report on Programs of the State Education Department.* Albany: New York State Education Department, 1978.
Ambach, G. M. *Changing Stages of Learning* (Inaugural Address of the President of the University of the State of New York and Commissioner of Education). Albany: Office of the Commissioner of Education, 1977.
Board of Regents, University of the State of New York. *The Regents Statewide Plan for the Development of Postsecondary Education, 1976.* Albany: Board of Regents, University of the State of New York, 1976.
Comly, L. T. *The Demography of the New York Population of Educationally and Economically Disadvantaged Adults.* Revised, June 1975. Albany: Bureau of Post-secondary Continuing Education, New York State Education Department, 1975a.
Comly, L. T. *The New York State Vietnam Veteran: His Immediate and Continuing Needs in Post-Secondary Education.* Revised, January 1975. Albany: Bureau of Post-Secondary Continuing Education, New York State Education Department, 1975b.
Comly, L. T., and Kurland, N. D. *Adult Lifelong Learning Information Directories for New York State: A Feasibility Study, April 12, 1976.* Albany: New York State Education Department, 1976.
Folsom, M. B., Gardner, J. W., and Heald, H. T. *Meeting the Increasing Demand for Higher Education in New York State: A Report to the Governor and the Board of Regents.* Albany: New York State Education Department, 1960.

Heston, W. M., and Fantz, J. C. *Toward a Comprehensive Coordinated System of Postsecondary Continuing Education for Long Island.* New York: Long Island Regional Advisory Council on Higher Education, 1976.

Kurland, N. D., and others. *Postsecondary Continuing Education and Lifelong Learning.* Albany: New York State Department of Education, 1976.

MacKenzie, K. M. *Reports on Continuing Education, 1975–76.* Albany: State University of New York, 1976.

New York State Education Department. *Guidelines for Awarding Academic Credit for Knowledge Gained from Work and Life Experience* (and) *Bibliography on Crediting Knowledge Gained Through Work and Life Experience.* Albany: New York State Education Department, n.d.

New York State Education Department. *Lifelong Learning: Diagnosis and Prognosis* (Conference on Postsecondary, Part-time, Continuing, and Adult Education). Albany: New York State Education Department, 1974.

New York State Education Department. *New Opportunities for New Learners.* Albany: New York State Education Department, 1976.

New York State Education Department. *Federal Legislation and Education in New York State.* Albany: New York State Education Department, 1977.

New York State Education Department, Bureau of General Continuing Education. *Compilation of Statistical Data Concerning Public School Continuing Education in New York State, 1975–76.* Albany: New York State Education Department, n.d.

New York State Education Department, Office of Higher and Professional Education. *The Higher Educational System of New York State: A Summary of Major Changes in the State's Higher Educational System and Funding in Recent Years.* Albany: New York State Education Department, 1977.

New York State Education Department, Office of Postsecondary Research, Information Systems and Institutional Aid. *Study of Adult Education, March 25, 1977.* Albany: New York State Education Department, 1977.

New York State Education Department. *Adults Learning Here.* Albany: New York State Education Department, 1979.

Nolan, D. J. "Open Assessment in Higher Education: The New York Regents External Degree." *International Review of Educa-*

tion, 1977, *23*, 231–248.

Project on Noncollegiate Sponsored Instruction. *A Guide to Educational Programs in Noncollegiate Organizations.* Albany: University of the State of New York, Office on Noncollegiate Sponsored Instruction and American Council on Education, Office on Educational Credit, 1976.

Regional Learning Service of Central New York. *New York State External High School Diploma Program.* Albany: Division of Continuing Education, New York State Education Department, 1976.

North Carolina

Eason, J. "Memorandum on Brokering Services for North Carolina." Greensboro: North Carolina Adult Education Association, April 1977.

Governor's Coordinating Council on Aging. *Education for Older Persons: Action on Aging.* Raleigh: Governor's Coordinating Council on Aging, 1973.

Jones, E. W. *Needs of Senior Citizens: Emphasis Education.* Fayetteville: Fayetteville State University, 1977.

Knowles, M. S. *Report to the North Carolina Adult Education Association from the Task Force on Educational Brokering Services.* Raleigh: 1977.

North Carolina Legislature. General Assembly. House Bill No. 842 (Tuition waiver for persons over 65). 1977.

North Carolina Manpower Development Corporation. *Human Resources Development Program.* Raleigh: North Carolina Manpower Development Corporation, 1975.

Office of the Governor. *Governor's Conference on the Quality of Life for Our Senior Citizens.* Raleigh: Office of the Governor, 1977.

Tart, J. *Proposal: For Improving and Increasing the Level of Education for Under-Educated Adults and Decreasing the High School Dropout Rate in North Carolina.* Smithfield: Johnston Technical Institute, 1977.

Ohio

Ohio Board of Regents. *Higher Education in Ohio Master Plan: 1976.* Columbus: Ohio Board of Regents, 1977a.

Ohio Board of Regents. *Higher Education in Ohio Master Plan: 1976, Summary.* Columbus: Ohio Board of Regents, 1977b.

Smith, D. H. *Lifelong Learning in Ohio: A Report of Credit and Non-credit Continuing Education and Extended Learning Programs in Post-secondary Institutions.* Columbus: Ohio Board of Regents, 1975.

Oklahoma

Hobbs, D. S. *A State Plan for the 1970s: Revision and Supplement.* Oklahoma City: Oklahoma State Regents for Higher Education, 1976.

Oregon

Fehnel, R. A., and McIntyre, V. L. *Nontraditional Learners and Post-secondary Education Policy* (Report to the Oregon Educational Coordinating Commission). Eugene: University of Oregon, 1977.

Oregon Educational Coordinating Commission. *Adult Continuing Education in Oregon: Staff Report, August 12, 1976.* Salem: Oregon Educational Coordinating Commission, 1976.

Oregon Educational Coordinating Commission. *Oregon Inventory of Postsecondary Educational Programs for Lifelong Learners, 1976–77.* Salem: Oregon Educational Coordinating Commission, 1977a.

Oregon Educational Coordinating Commission. *Title I-A Project Award Recommendations: Exhibit 8.* Salem: Oregon Educational Coordinating Commission, 1977b.

Pennsylvania

Barcus, V. F. *Pennsylvania Adult Education and Training Programs and Services.* Harrisburg: Pennsylvania Department of Education, August 1976.

Brehnan, G. E. *A Preliminary Evaluation of the Tutoring and Counseling Effectiveness of Act 101 Program A of 1973–74.* Harrisburg: Pennsylvania Department of Education, 1975.

Flautz, J. *Position Paper on Lifelong Learning—What, How and When?* Harrisburg: Pennsylvania Department of Education, 1976.

Haller, E. S. *Images of Women: A Bibliography of Feminist Resources for Pennsylvania Schools.* Harrisburg: Pennsylvania Department of Education, Bureau of Curriculum Services, 1973.

Kline, C. M. "Log Cabin Education in a Jet Age." In *Merging Educational Innovation with the Concept of Lifelong Learning: Making the Pieces Fit.* Harrisburg: Pennsylvania Department of Education, 1976.

Martinko, A. *Educational Counseling Services for Nonschool Adults.* Harrisburg: Pennsylvania Department of Education, 1977.

Pennsylvania Department of Education. "Adult Continuing Education Activities in Institutions of Higher Education in Pennsylvania, 1973–74." *Our Colleges and Universities Today.* 1975a, *12* (6).

Pennsylvania Department of Education. *Postsecondary Degree-Granting Institutions and Planning Regions of Pennsylvania: Guide Supplement.* Harrisburg: Pennsylvania Department of Education, 1975b.

Pennsylvania Department of Education. *Lifelong Learning* (Newsletter). Harrisburg: Pennsylvania Department of Education, 1977.

Pennsylvania Department of Education, Bureau of Equal Opportunity. *Higher Education Equal Opportunity Act 101 Guidelines, 1976–77: Application Information and Program Manual.* Harrisburg: Pennsylvania Department of Education, n.d.

Pennsylvania Legislature. General Assembly. Senate Bill No. 926 (Adult Education Career Opportunity Act). 1975.

Pennsylvania Legislature. General Assembly. Senate Bill No. 729 (Adult Education and Career Opportunity Act). 1977.

Pennsylvania State Board of Education. *The Master Plan for Higher Education in Pennsylvania.* Harrisburg: Pennsylvania State Board of Education, 1971.

Pennsylvania State Library, Bureau of Library Development. *Evaluation of District Library Center System in Pennsylvania.* Harrisburg: Pennsylvania State Library, 1975.

Raymond, B. *A Guide to Postsecondary Educational Programs and Services for the Elderly: Resource Materials.* Harrisburg: Pennsylvania Department of Education, 1977.

Reardon, F., and others. *View of the Agents' and Consumers' Needs of the Lifelong Learner.* Harrisburg: Pennsylvania Department of Education, 1977.

Ziegler, J. "Memorandum on Continuing Education and Lifelong Learning." Harrisburg, Penn.: Office of the Commissioner of Higher Education, October 22, 1975.

Ziegler, J. "From the Commissioner's Desk." *Higher Education Planning*, July/August 1976, *3* (3).

Ziegler, W. L. "Conference Synthesis." In *Merging Educational Innovation with the Concept of Lifelong Learning: Making the Pieces Fit*. Harrisburg: Pennsylvania Department of Education, 1976.

Rhode Island

Basner, S., and others. *A Curriculum Guide for Adult Education Based on the Adult Performance Level Study*. Kingston: Curriculum Research and Development Center, University of Rhode Island, 1976.

Goldman, F. H. *Toward a Master Plan in Continuing Education* (Continuing Education Master Plan Series, Vol. 1). Providence: Division of Organization and Management, Rhode Island Department of Education, 1973.

Rhode Island Department of Education. *Improving Fundamental Education for Disadvantaged Adults: A Position Statement of the Board of Regents for Education*. Providence: Rhode Island Department of Education, 1975.

Rhode Island Department of Education. *Program Proposal* (for an Occupational and Educational Information System). Providence: Rhode Island Department of Education, 1977.

Rhode Island Department of Education, Bureau of Research, Planning, and Evaluation. *Purposes of Postsecondary Education*. Providence: Rhode Island Department of Education, 1977.

Rhode Island Public Commission on Fundamental Education for Disadvantaged Adults. *Progress Report*. Providence: Rhode Island Department of Education, 1977.

South Carolina

"'Bird Cage Liner' Also Teaches Reading." *The Greenville News*, May 23, 1977.

South Carolina Commission on Higher Education. *Discussion and Recommendations* (Goals for Higher Education to 1980, Vol. 1). Columbia: South Carolina Commission on Higher Education, 1972.

Tennessee

Tennessee Higher Education Commission. *Guidelines for Awarding and Reporting CEUs.* Nashville: Tennessee Higher Education Commission, 1977.

Texas

Champagne, J. E. *Higher Education, Lifelong Learning, and Community Service: A Profile of Action and Responsibility.* Houston: Center for Human Resources, University of Houston, 1975.

Neidhart, A. C. (Ed.). *Continuing Education for Texas: Special Studies of Non-Traditional Approaches to Education.* San Marcos: Southwest Texas State University, 1974.

Texas College and University System Coordinating Board. *Annual Program Plan, Fiscal Year 1978* (Texas State Plan for Community Service and Continuing Education Programs). Austin: Texas College and University System Coordinating Board, 1977.

Utah

Continuing Education/Community Service Task Force for Lifelong Learning. *Master Planning for Postsecondary Education in Utah.* Salt Lake City: State Board of Regents, 1976 (Draft).

Vermont

Bobowski, R. C. "College Model for the Grass Roots." *American Education,* June 1976, *12,* 15–19.

Carnegie Corporation of New York. "Education for 'New' Students: How It's Done in Vermont." *Carnegie Quarterly,* Fall 1973, *21,* 1–3.

Community College of Vermont. *The Local Review Community Handbook.* Montpelier: Community College of Vermont, n.d.

Community College of Vermont. *The Community College of Vermont: Product and Progress.* Montpelier: Community College of Vermont, 1974.

Daloz, L. A. "Giving Education Back to the Learner." *International Journal of Career and Continued Education,* Fall 1975, *1,* 97–102.

Hochschild, S. F. *Postsecondary Education Access Study: Vermont Postsecondary Education Access Study Project.* Montpelier: Vermont Commission on Higher Education Facilities, 1974.

Hochschild, S. F., and Johnston, J. G. *Vermont Adult Aspiration Study. Postsecondary Education Access Study.* Montpelier: Vermont Commission on Higher Education Facilities, 1974.

Virginia

Byrd, P. *Direct Instruction for Adult Learning: Teaching by Telephone.* Richmond: Virginia State Department of Education, 1977.

Consortium for Continuing Higher Education in Northern Virginia. *Realigning Educational Resources in Northern Virginia.* Fairfax: Consortium for Continuing Higher Education in Northern Virginia, 1976.

Virginia Legislature. General Assembly. Senate Joint Resolution No. 44. 1972a.

Virginia Legislature. General Assembly. Senate Joint Resolution No. 67. 1972b.

Virginia State Council of Higher Education. *Introductory Statement on Continuing Higher Education: Regional Consortia–Policies and Procedures.* Richmond: Virginia State Council of Higher Education, n.d.

Virginia State Council of Higher Education. *Coordination of Continuing Higher Education in Virginia: A State Plan for Regional Consortia for Continuing Higher Education.* Richmond: Virginia State Council of Higher Education, 1972.

Virginia Tidewater Consortium for Continuing Higher Education. *Undergraduate Student Cross-Registration.* Newport News: Virginia Associated Research Campus, 1977.

Washington

Chance, W. *Recommendations for the Coordination of State College and University Programs of Off-Campus Instruction.* Olympia: Council for Postsecondary Education, 1976.

Kenny, E. *The Upside-Down or Inverted Curriculum and the Career Ladder Concept in Washington Postsecondary Education.* Olympia: Washington Council for Postsecondary Education, 1978.

Washington Council for Postsecondary Education. *Planning and Policy Recommendations for Washington Postsecondary Education: 1976–1982.* Olympia: Washington Council for Postsecondary Education, 1976.

Washington Council on Higher Education, Select Commission on Non-Traditional Study. *Dynamics of Change: Alternative Educational Opportunities.* Olympia: Washington Council on Higher Education, 1974.

Wisconsin

Gateway Technical Institute. *Development of a Model for a Senior Citizen Bureau.* Madison: Gateway Technical Institute, 1977.

University of Wisconsin. *A Planning Prospectus for the Open University of the University of Wisconsin System.* Madison: University of Wisconsin, 1973.

University of Wisconsin. *A New Way to Complete a University Degree.* Madison: University of Wisconsin, 1976a.

University of Wisconsin. *University of Wisconsin–Extended Degree Programs: A Brief History and Description.* Madison: University of Wisconsin, 1976b.

Waukesha County Technical Institute. *Governor's Southeastern Mini-Conference on Problems of the Elderly.* Pekaukee: Waukesha County Technical Institute, n.d.

Wisconsin Board of Vocational, Technical, and Adult Education. *Legal Aid for the Elderly.* Madison: Wisconsin Board of Vocational, Technical, and Adult Education, 1977.

Wisconsin Department of Health and Social Services, Division on Aging. *Aging in the News.* July and December 1976.

Wisconsin VTAE District One Technical Institute and Lakeshore Technical Institute. *A Workshop for Leaders in Senior Citizen's Organizations: Facilitators' Manual.* Eau Claire: Wisconsin VTAE District One Technical Institute and Lakeshore Technical Institute, n.d.

Wisner, S. M. "Can an Entire State System Move Nontraditional Study?" *Alternative Higher Education,* Summer 1978, *2*, 314–317.

Wyoming

Wyoming Higher Education Council. *A Proposal for State Funding for Adult Literacy, Vocational, and Continuing Education: 9th Budget of the Community College Commission.* Cheyenne: Wyoming Higher Education Council, 1977.

CHAPTER FIVE

Federal Policies: Programs, Legislation, and Prospects

Terry W. Hartle
Mark A. Kutner

Lifelong learning offers hope to those who are mired in stagnant or disadvantaged circumstances—the unemployed, the isolated elderly, women, minorities, youth, workers whose jobs are becoming obsolete. All of them can and should be brought into the mainstream of American life . . . lifelong learning . . . is a necessary step toward making the lives of all Americans more rewarding and productive [Walter Mondale, 1975].

The federal government has for many years supported and stimulated educational innovation and reform. Recently, lifelong learning—an innovative educational philosophy regarded by many as the cutting edge of American education—has attracted federal attention. "The Lifelong Learning Act" (Public Law 94-482), proposed by Senator Mondale and enacted by the Congress as part of the Education Amendments of 1976, is perhaps the clearest statement of federal interest in lifelong learning.

This chapter examines the current federal role in lifelong learning by considering (1) the context of federal aid to education, (2) federal programs that support lifelong learning, (3) the Lifelong Learning Act of 1976, (4) current proposals concerning lifelong learning, and (5) the status of federal policy for lifelong learning.

A key issue is the absence of a widely accepted definition: No one knows exactly what lifelong learning is. Most people take the term in its literal sense, to mean the learning process from cradle to grave. This chapter, however, uses the term *lifelong learning,* as is commonplace in Washington, to describe educational opportunities designed to meet the varied needs of Americans past compulsory school age, with special emphasis on those not served by existing educational programs. (Sometimes confusion arises from the fact that the same phrase is used to refer to both a broad philosophy of education and a set of statutory provisions in the Higher Education Amendments of 1976. To avoid such confusion, this chapter uses "lifelong learning" when discussing the philosophy of education, and "Lifelong Learning" when referring to the Higher Education Amendments of 1976 and the Lifelong Learning Project.)

The central theme of this chapter is that the federal government is extensively involved in lifelong learning but that the impact of this involvement is diluted by an absence of coordination among federal activities. Recent studies identify hundreds of federal programs that provide extensive opportunities for lifelong learning experiences, but each program travels its own track and lacks central direction. Proposals for an expanded federal role must begin by recognizing the extent of current activities and indicating how these programs might complement new ones.

The Federal Context

A complex series of historical, social, and political factors determine federal involvement in any area of American life. Although the calculus differs among areas, certain aspects of American political culture usually prompt federal program activity. To understand the emergence of lifelong learning as a federal initiative as well as to assess the likelihood of its further growth, one must keep in mind the historical and the procedural traditions of federal action in education. Several key traditions involve the governance of education; the development of educational policy; and the division between elementary/secondary and postsecondary education.

Governance of Education

Responsibility for framing and administering educational policies and programs is divided among federal, state, and local levels of government—the accepted roles for each depending on constitutional and historical factors, fiscal and administrative capacities, and philosophical values.[1] Almost invariably, public education is the responsibility of state and local agencies. The federal role has traditionally been to encourage improvements in education by financing innovation, capacity building, and research. In recent years this role has drawn increasing criticism. The lack of a coherent set of intergovernmental relationships in education has prompted a call for a more formal partnership among federal, state, and local governments, which would replace "marble cake federalism" with a distribution of real power among several centers that must negotiate cooperative arrangements with one another to achieve common goals (Elazar, 1972). A partnership implies that "in planning and initiating actions each of the partners will take account of the obligations and responsibilities of the other partners, their customary modes of operation, their administrative capabilities, and their financial capacities" (Honey and Hartle, 1975b). Proponents of such a partnership, while recognizing the administrative, planning, and financing role of the states, argue that states cannot address the national interest without federal leadership.

Development of Educational Policy

Public policies and programs in the United States generally rest on the base laid by previous policies. Some legislation is gen-

---

[1]For a further discussion of issues addressed in this section, see Honey (1977) and Chapters 10 and 11 in Gladieux and Wolanin (1976).

uinely pioneering—for example, the National Defense Education Act of 1958 and the Elementary and Secondary Education Act of 1965—but most expansions or alterations of the federal role have been incremental. That is, they emerge from a long series of precedents.

Public policy issues and concerns emerge from a complex process involving more than the demonstration of simple public needs (see Gladieux and Wolanin, 1976). A research study documenting social problems that need resolution is no guarantee that the problems will be addressed. Gerald Grant (1972) has concluded that even seminal studies such as the Coleman Report generally come to the attention of congressional policy makers through an informal "word-of-mouth" network. Moreover, as Gladieux and Wolanin (1976, p. 258) point out, "the least examined part of the policy making process is its initial stage, the recognition of social aspirations and needs as public problems." In education, events and issues outside the mainstream of education itself disproportionately influence public policy. The Stanford Research Institute (1974) has commented: "Changes in educational policy are not normally initiated within the education system. External pressures—Supreme Court decisions, the 'baby boom,' Sputnik, the war on poverty, the movement for community control, the movement of women into the labor force—have resulted in more and more basic changes in the educational system than have the pedagogical studies of professional educators."

Policies and programs usually take shape out of a complex series of interactions among individuals and organizations with stakes in the outcome. Special interest groups are important actors because they define the issues and propose solutions according to the needs of those they represent. Products of the policy process are usually marked by compromise; although no group gets precisely what it wanted, most get enough to be reasonably satisfied with the final product (Honey, 1977).

Division Between Elementary/Secondary Education
and Postsecondary Education

Traditionally, compulsory (elementary and secondary) education and higher (or postsecondary) education have been organized and treated separately in public policy. People concerned

about elementary and secondary education are a different group
from those whose primary interest is higher or postsecondary education. To some extent, this separation is a function of the sheer
size of American education and the large number of individuals
involved. However, it is also a function of the cultural values placed
upon "higher education" and the status attached to the credentials
of the people who purvey it. Different popular images of "high
school teacher," "junior college teacher," and "university professor" may, for example, not only rigidify our definitions of education but affect the ability of these educators to recognize their
potential common interests. While this separation assures that the
needs of each educational sector will be considered, lines of communication between the sectors are tenuous at best. Consequently,
potentially useful political cooperation and sharing of information
and resources to address common interests such as lifelong learning rarely occur.

These dimensions of federal education policy development
will emerge frequently in the analysis of current Washington perspectives on lifelong learning. They are not the only factors of importance, but recent interviews suggest that these themes must remain central concerns of those interested in encouraging greater
federal support for lifelong learning.

Federal Antecedents of Lifelong Learning

The incremental nature of the policy process means that
new policies and programs are shaped largely by existing or past
programs. Thus, a brief historical look at existing programs may
be useful in assessing federal lifelong learning activities and pre-
dicting further initiatives. The relatively recent vintage of most of
these programs reflects the fact that, despite important early initiatives such as the creation of the Agriculture Extension Service
in 1847 and the Smith-Hughes Act of 1917, the federal government's interest in increasing educational opportunities for all
Americans has been primarily a phenomenon of the past thirty
years.

The Servicemen's Readjustment Act of 1944, commonly
known as the GI Bill (Public Law 78-346), represented the government's efforts both to help servicemen readjust to civilian life

and to defer the entrance of ten million soldiers into the job market. The act encouraged servicemen to begin or continue their education in both traditional and nontraditional institutions. Eligible veterans received payments for tuition, books, and living expenses for up to four years of schooling. The impact of returning veterans upon education was tremendous. College and university enrollments jumped from 400,000 in the fall of 1946 to 1.5 million in the fall of the next year (Levin, 1973).

A recent social history of the postwar years summarizes the GI Bill's impact:

> The most important feature of the GI Bill was higher education. . . . It marked the polarization of higher education in America. After the 1940s, a college degree came to be considered an essential passport for entrance into much of the business and professional world. And mass America, once the GI Bill afforded it a glimpse at higher education, demanded no less an opportunity for successive generations. Pushed beyond their prewar capacity by the glut of veteran students, colleges and universities vastly expanded their physical plants. Once the space existed academia filled it, and the educational boom was on [Golden, 1976, p. 67].

This legislation entitling veterans to educational assistance is the germ of existing proposals to extend educational entitlements to all citizens.

International events as well as domestic issues pressed the federal government to become more involved in education. The Korean War, the Cold War, the "baby boom," the civil rights movement, and Vietnam each encouraged the federal government to expand its education investment.

The 1957 launching of Sputnik and widespread concern that Soviet technological advances would dwarf those of the United States encouraged passage of the National Defense Education Act, which authorized student loans and institutional purchase of instructional equipment, awarded graduate fellowships, and encouraged guidance and counseling programs.

The Vocational Education Act of 1963 expanded a federal role in vocational education that began with the Smith-Hughes Act of 1917. The 1963 act was directed at all individuals, including the handicapped, who wish to develop or improve job skills in areas where there are reasonable expectations of employment (Public Law 90-576).

Later that same year, the Higher Education Facilities Act authorized a five-year program of federal grants and loans for constructing and improving public and private higher education facilities.

The landmark Elementary and Secondary Education Act of 1965 somewhat obscured the Higher Education Act of 1965. In both pieces of legislation, however, the federal government assumed important responsibilities. Title IV of the Higher Education Act contained several major provisions for student assistance. For the first time, Congress approved federal scholarships for undergraduates through the Educational Opportunity Grant Program. Another program, the Guaranteed Student Loans, insured loans with federal subsidies on interest payments. The loans and scholarships, together with a work-study program originally enacted as part of the Economic Opportunity Act of 1964, were expected to help students from middle- and low-income families attend college.

Title III of the 1966 Amendments to the Elementary and Secondary Education Act created the Adult Education Act, which established the federal presence in adult basic education and sought to assist individuals over eighteen years of age who had not completed high school or its equivalent (Public Law 89-750).

The 1968 Amendments to the Adult Education Act expanded the scope of the original legislation by including private, nonprofit agencies among eligible grant recipients. In 1970 the legislative purpose was extended to include the expansion of opportunities available for adults wishing to complete high school (Public Law 89-750). Additionally, a fifteen-member National Advisory Council on Adult Education replaced the eight-member Advisory Committee mandated in the original legislation.

Indian tribes and local and state educational agencies were added to the list of authorized grant recipients in 1970. Special projects for the elderly, state advisory councils, and a clearinghouse on adult education were established by the 1974 Amendments.

Each set of amendments further expanded the purposes and scope of the federal role in adult education, although the program remains focused on the needs of people over eighteen who have not completed high school. The Adult Education Act, in acknowledging the federal interest in adult learning and recognizing the importance of the concept, is a precursor of current federal lifelong learning initiatives.

The seeds of lifelong learning are also found in other significant pieces of legislation. After several years of debate and extensive study, Congress enacted the 1972 Amendments to the Higher Education Act, which contained a variety of provisions expanding educational activities and programs supported by the federal government. As Gladieux and Wolanin (1976, p. 226) note:

> The Education Amendments of 1972 encourage and in some ways mandate a broadening of the educational mainstream to include types of students and institutions that have generally been excluded or given second-class status in the past. The new term is *postsecondary education.* The intent is to break the stereotype that education beyond high school means a four-year academic program leading to a baccalaureate degree. Explicit federal recognition and legitimacy are accorded to programs of career preparation and occupational education, to proprietary institutions and community colleges, and to students who attend less than full-time.
>
> The broad significance of these changes is that Congress now conceptualizes education beyond high school as a range of options that are equally appropriate depending on an individual student's needs and interest. As a spokesman for the proprietary schools noted, the Education Amendments of 1972 finally "illuminated the whole horizon." The legislation recognizes that sound policy must address all segments of the system.

This significant shift clearly illustrated that Congress recognized the role of nontraditional education at the postsecondary level. It was only a short step from this recognition in 1972 to passage of the Special Projects Act, part of the Education Amendments of 1974, which created programs such as Community Schools, Career Education, and Arts in Education. The purposes of the Special Projects Act were to experiment with new educational and administrative methods, techniques and practices; to meet special or unique educational needs or problems; and to place special emphasis on national educational priorities (Public Law 93-380).

Against this background of federal aid to education and growing federal interest in nontraditional education, Title I,

Part B of the 1976 Amendments to the Higher Education Act, known as the Lifelong Learning Act, seeks to encourage lifelong learning opportunities and further their planning, assessment, and coordination. This act mandates a study of the current state of lifelong learning to identify ways to advance the concept. In addition, demonstration projects are authorized to test lifelong learning delivery systems. This legislation and its implementation are considered in some detail at a later point.

Federal Administration of Education

We have outlined the historical background of lifelong learning and indicated the complex context of federal education policy. Another dimension of federal involvement, the administrative structure, cannot be ignored. Almost all federal agencies and departments administer some education programs. Most are administered by the Education Division of the Department of Health, Education, and Welfare (HEW), established in 1972 under an Assistant Secretary for Education in response to congressional concerns over the administration and management of education programs. Within the Education Division are the National Institute of Education (NIE) and the U. S. Office of Education (OE). NIE, the research and demonstration arm of the division, has no operational authority; OE, directed by the U. S. Commissioner of Education, administers federal programs and has few research responsibilities.

The Assistant Secretary for Education (ASE) has responsibility for the direction and supervision of the Education Division. Within the Office of the Assistant Secretary are the Deputy Assistant Secretary of Education for Policy Development (ASE-PD), the Fund for the Improvement of Postsecondary Education (FIPSE), the National Center for Education Statistics (NCES), and the Federal Inter-agency Committee on Education (FICE).

Although efforts have been made to improve coordination of federal education programs since the establishment of FICE in 1972, and by centralizing authority in the Office of the Assistant Secretary for Education, effective coordination and program administration remain elusive. One recent study of federal education programs noted that the Office of Education "has failed in nearly every program to give adequate guidance, support, and consistent enforcement of policies to the states" (Education Coalition, 1977).

These structural concerns are often omitted in discussions of possible federal lifelong learning activities. They are likely, however, to be crucial to the effective implementation of any new federal policy. Previous experience with Great Society programs suggests that new programs are solidly grounded only if administrative arrangements and constraints have been considered.

Federal Programs

The shifting social context of education in the 1970s has altered the perspectives of educators and policy makers with respect to the learners they serve and the kinds of programs these learners need. The following factors have contributed to the changing view of American education:

- The decline in the number of students in traditional student age groups and the increase in "older" students.
- Increased leisure time.
- Rapidly changing technologies, which make some fields obsolete and create new ones, thus increasing the need for retraining.
- The growth of egalitarianism and the opening of doors to previously excluded Americans.
- A growing concern about the number of Americans who lack the basic skills to function in our society.

Federal policy has increasingly recognized these developments by creating programs to encourage "nontraditional" education.

Federal programs for lifelong learning are both direct and indirect. In *direct* programs, specific types of lifelong learning experiences or activities are provided by the federal government or by an outside agency. In *indirect* programs, no specific training is offered but federal involvement provides incentives that encourage states and local areas to develop their own programs. Examples of such programs are the Adult Education Act, the Lifelong Learning Act, and the Special Projects Act, all of which focus increased attention on nontraditional education and encourage adult participation in educational activities. The indirect programs are more visible; the direct programs are more common and involve greater sums of money.

This section summarizes federal government programs and policies that support lifelong learning. First, some of the direct programs are analyzed; second, the major indirect programs are reviewed; finally, an assessment is made of the level of federal investment in lifelong learning.

Direct Federal Programs

Although direct federal support for lifelong learning is extensive, it lacks a central focus. Adult basic education programs, for example, are sponsored by eleven cabinet-level agencies and departments, including the Office of Education, the Department of Agriculture, the Department of Transportation, the Department of Health, Education and Welfare, and the Bureau of Indian Affairs. Most of these programs are operated through public school systems, although some are sponsored by libraries, museums, and other community organizations. Federal funds for adult basic education have increased from less than $19 million in fiscal year (FY) 1965 to $80.5 million in FY 1978.

Following are examples of other representative lifelong learning programs in various government agencies.

Department of Agriculture. The Cooperative Extension Service offers programs in the broad subjects of agriculture, natural resources and environment, and community resource development. In 1978 the federal contribution to Extension programs was $269 million. In addition, the Secretary of the Department of Agriculture appoints the governing board of the Graduate School, a private, nonprofit institution whose objective is to improve government services through continuing education and training. The Graduate School has an Evening Program, an Independent Study Program, a Special (day) Program, an International Program, and a Career Planning and Development Program.

Department of Health, Education, and Welfare. Within HEW, most lifelong learning programs are administered by the Education Division. However, other educational programs can be found in HEW's health and welfare agencies. The Public Health Service offers grants to private, nonprofit organizations that conduct community drug abuse education clinics, workshops, and institutes. Similar programs exist for alcohol abuse. The Office of Child Development mounts technical assistance programs for handicapped and retarded children, unmarried mothers, and communities that request programs for youth development. Numerous Office of Education programs serve lifelong learning goals through training programs for teachers, counselors, and administrators.

Department of Labor. The Department of Labor offers most federal training and employment programs geared to increase skills and employment opportunities for both individuals already in the work force and those who seek jobs but lack vocational preparation or face other employment barriers. Programs support activities such as skill training, rehabilitation, transitional employment experience, job placement assistance, and related support services. In FY 1976, of the $8.5 billion spent on training and employment programs, slightly over $6 billion of that was spent by the Department of Labor. Most of these programs were aimed at low-income individuals and others who confront great barriers to employment and who, unassisted, are least likely to improve their employment (Budget of the United States Government, 1977, pp. 187–201). The Work Incentive Program, for example, provides job training for welfare recipients. In FY 1973, 354,000 individuals who needed training in basic or vocational skills participated in this program.

Department of the Interior. Interior's Bureau of Indian Affairs offers a variety of programs to assist American Indians in developing the skills and competencies needed to function in today's society. Indian Agricultural Extension provides individualized assistance in farming, family economics, and consumer education. The Indian Employment Assistance Program provides vocational training for Indians in marketable skills.

Department of Justice. The Justice Department's Immigration and Naturalization Service distributes textbooks on U. S. history, English, and citizen responsibility to immigrants who seek U. S. citizenship. The Law Enforcement Assistance Administration (LEAA) offers the Law Enforcement Education Program (LEEP), which aims to improve criminal justice courses through the "development of criminal justice education programs of selected colleges and universities." The program also provides assistance to students who are preparing for careers in criminal justice.

Department of the Treasury. Treasury's Internal Revenue Service (IRS) offers counseling services and assistance in filing income tax returns to individuals who request it. The IRS develops tax courses for groups such as small business associations and conducts tax institutes, which train citizens to help others prepare tax returns.

Department of Defense. Of all government agencies, the Department of Defense has the most comprehensive learning program for employees. The GI Bill was a landmark piece of American education legislation. In order to attract recruits today, the armed forces continue to offer substantial education benefits. These include (1) training connected with military service occupations, (2) professional training, not necessarily related to military job-related training, primarily for officers, and (3) voluntary education consisting of recreational and leisure courses. Seventy-five percent of expenditures for voluntary education go toward tuition assistance (Postsecondary Education Convening Authority, 1977c).

One particularly innovative program for military personnel is Defense Activity for Non-Traditional Education Support (DANTES). Established in 1974 to replace the United States Armed Forces Institute (USAFI), DANTES (1) conducts nationally recognized credit by examination and certification programs, notably, the College Level Examination Program (CLEP), DANTES Subject Standardized Test (DSST), and the General Education Development Test (GEDT), and (2) facilitates independent study by making college courses available to military personnel through a single application (*PER* Report, April 11, 1977).

Direct programs are not limited to the cabinet departments. Numerous federal agencies sponsor educational activities such as the following. The Civil Service Commission offers training courses for federal, state, and local government employees. (In FY 1976 there were nearly one million instances of training for federal employees at a total cost of $237 million.) The Library of Congress offers public bibliographic and reference materials to individuals unable to obtain the information from other sources. The Smithsonian Institution assists local communities to develop museums through curatorial training programs and programs to improve research. The Small Business Administration helps businessmen through advisory services, managerial counseling, training, and information dissemination.

Indirect or Incentive Programs

The federal government sponsors a wide variety of indirect programs that address the objectives of lifelong learning. These programs are of two types: (1) federal categorical aid or project grants, which are administered by states and local organizations, and (2) discretionary programs awarded through competitive grants.

Categorical and Project Grant Programs. A variety of federal categorical programs pursue lifelong learning goals. The Christoffel study identifies sixty-four categorical programs administered by the U. S. Office of Education alone (Christoffel, 1978c). Perhaps the most visible of these categorical programs relating to lifelong learning are activities sponsored under the Adult Education Act.

As previously noted, the Adult Education Act seeks to expand educational opportunity and encourage new education programs that will enable adults to continue their education at least through secondary school. Among its mandated provisions are service to institutionalized persons; cooperation with manpower development and training programs; assistance to persons of limited English-speaking ability; and training of adult education personnel. This program is designed for the 52.5 million adults over age sixteen who have not completed and are not currently enrolled in high school. In FY 1976 this program was serving 1.65 million people; of these, 55 percent were women, 35 percent were unemployed, and 9 percent were on public assistance (U.S. Office of Education, 1978).

The program has encouraged states to initiate basic education programs. A 1975 study summarized the positive and negative effects of the program this way:

> Since it began in 1965, the Adult Basic Education Program has expanded educational opportunities by establishing broadly available programs for those adults who want to continue their formal education through completion of the eighth grade and in some cases through high school. Although the Adult Education Program has had positive achievements, as currently funded and operated it is successfully reaching only a small fraction of those needing it—particularly among the more educationally deficient [Comptroller General of the U.S., 1975].

While the Adult Education Act represents a major lifelong learning effort, it is only one of several federal indirect programs. Other notable programs are the following:

- *Vocational Education Personnel Development.* This program seeks to meet the need for qualified vocational education leadership personnel by making awards to experienced vocational educators for up to three years of graduate study in leadership development programs.
- *Teacher Corps–Operation and Training.* Among other objectives, this program seeks to encourage institutions of higher education and local education agencies to improve programs of training and retraining for teachers and teacher aides.
- *Environmental Education.* This program seeks to educate citizens on the problems of environmental quality and ecological balance. Project grants under this program are used to offer community education projects, environmental education centers, and in-service training projects for both noneducational personnel and educational personnel.
- *Child Welfare Training Grants.* The Social and Rehabilitation Service (SRS) funds projects under this program for training workers in the field of child welfare.

Of course, these are not the only federal projects or categorical grants designed to stimulate states and other organizations to provide specific types of education. They illustrate, however, the wide variety of federal activities that are currently available, though not necessarily identified as lifelong learning programs. Calculating the total dollars invested in these and other federal programs is quite complicated.

Discretionary Programs. The Community Schools program seeks to promote greater use of public education facilities as well as to provide educational, recreational, cultural, and other community services wanted or needed by a locality. The Consumer Education program is similarly designed to develop programs, curriculums, and materials to prepare consumers for knowledgeable participation in the marketplace.

Both programs are authorized by the Special Projects Act and are funded at extremely low levels. The competition for grant money is therefore fierce, and many worthwhile projects are not funded. To most advocates of lifelong learning, discretionary programs such as these remain on the periphery of attention. The low level of attention to discretionary programs tends to eliminate discretionary programs as potential vehicles for advancing lifelong learning.

Federal Investment in Lifelong Learning

Federal support of education is both complex and diverse. Table 1 presents an overview of federal education aid in FY 1979, "including programs that provide aid to state and local education agencies, to institutions of higher education, to individuals, and direct federal activities" (Budget of the United States Government, 1977, p. 171).

This estimated total of $22.7 billion is better understood in terms of how closely each program's purpose is tied to education. According to the Budget Special Analysis for FY 1979 (Budget of the United States Government, 1978), $14.1 billion of federal education outlays will go to programs whose primary purpose is education; $8.2 billion will go to programs beneficial to education but not primarily educational; and $.4 billion will go for salary supplements, or educational allowances.

The $22.7 billion total, although it illustrates the extent of federal education activity, is misleading. Not included, for example, are nearly $15.2 billion in Federal Training and Employment programs and nearly $1.3 billion in Health Training and Education programs (*Budget of the United States Government,* 1978).

Given the difficulty of determining exactly how much federal money is spent on education, it follows that no simple calculation exists to determine the federal monetary commitment to lifelong learning. While the appropriation for each program can be summed to determine an aggregate investment figure, the total is misleading because not every program devotes 100 percent of its money to education and training activities. Indeed, the percentage spent for education and training programs will vary from year to year. If the final appropriation differs from what was anticipated, more or less may be devoted to education and training. Further, the number of programs supporting some form of lifelong learning may shift considerably, depending on what definition of the

Table 1. Federal Aid for Education by Agency

Agency	1979 Estimate Outlays (Millions)
Legislative Branch:	
Library of Congress	$ 107
Funds Appropriated to the President:	
International Development Assistance	129
Appalachian Regional Commission	45
Agriculture	3,090
Commerce	21
Defense—Military	1,343
Defense—Civil	11
Health, Education, and Welfare:	
Office of Education	10,087
Other HEW	4,070
Housing and Urban Development	54
Interior	281
Justice	62
Labor	619
State	11
Transportation	48
Treasury	14
Energy Research and Development Administration	3
Environmental Protection Agency	5
General Services Administration	16
National Aeronautics and Space Administration	5
Veterans Administration	2,341
Other Independent Agencies:	
ACTION	22
Corporation for Public Broadcasting	120
National Foundation of the Arts and Humanities	53
National Science Foundation	51
Smithsonian Institution	74
United States Information Agency	63
Other	1
TOTAL	$22,746

Source: *Budget of the United States Government*, 1978.

term one chooses. If lifelong learning is defined in "cradle to grave" terms rather than (as in this chapter) in terms of adult learning needs, the total number of programs increases.

Despite these difficulties, several efforts have been made to determine the total federal investment. In 1972 the National Advisory Council on Extension and Continuing Education identified 208 federal programs that supported continuing education; $2.6 billion of the $8.2 billion appropriated for these programs was estimated to have been spent for adult education (National Advisory Council on Extension and Continuing Education, 1973, p. 24). In a new study, Christoffel (1978a) tries to specify the level of federal involvement by determining the percentage of each program spent on lifelong learning activities. She concludes that the federal government spends $13 billion for education and training programs past the compulsory school age, and allows another $900 million in tax expenditures. Other knowledgeable observers believe federal support to be approximately $20 billion, but they hesitate to make specific estimates for fear that the figures will be so high that Congress will refuse future authorizations and appropriations.

The federal government is widely involved in lifelong learning. Christoffel's 275 federal programs supporting adult education and training are 27 percent of the 1,026 federal domestic assistance programs. Yet the absence of a widely accepted dollar total, whatever the precise figure, suggests the lack of a clear federal focus or detailed accountability. The federal involvement in lifelong learning has evolved piecemeal and today is a melange of programs and activities widely scattered throughout the government. The lack of a clearly coordinated federal interest reduces the visibility of the federal investment as well as blunting its stimulative impact on other potential sponsors in state and local government and private industry.

The Lifelong Learning Act

Despite the high level of federal support for lifelong learning activities through direct and indirect mechanisms, there is no coherent federal lifelong learning policy. Current government activities lack clearly articulated and widely accepted goals and definitions. The 1976 enactment of Part B of Title I of the Higher Education Act ("The Lifelong Learning Act") authorized a planning study to investigate lifelong learning in the United States. Its demonstration grants to advance lifelong learning have been seen by many as the first step toward a more coherent policy. The background and implementation of this key legislation deserve attention.

Legislative History

During a speech opening Hunter College's Brookdale Center for Research in Human Aging on April 7, 1975, Senator Mondale (D. Minn.) announced that he would introduce a "Lifetime Learning Act." Speaking of the importance of learning throughout one's lifetime, Mondale noted that "all of us, regardless of age, encounter a series of demands, and we must shape education in its broadest sense to help us meet these demands."

Mondale's bill, S. 2497, was introduced on October 8, 1975 as an amendment to Title I of the Higher Education Act (U.S. Congress, Senate, 1975a).

At a single day of hearings on the Lifetime Learning Act on December 18, 1975, witnesses were virtually unanimous in their praise. Stephen K. Bailey, vice-president of the American Council on Education, spoke of the need to develop public policies for lifelong learning, citing emerging demands and uncoordinated resources, and warned that "unless a new emphasis is placed on education as a lifelong pursuit, I doubt that our society will be capable of renewing itself" (U. S. Congress, Senate, 1975b). Lloyd Davis, executive director of the National University Extension Association (NUEA), in a statement submitted to the subcommittee, expressed hope that studies authorized by the legislation would suggest how the federal government can more adequately support lifelong learning activities. In addition, he suggested that Congress needed basic information on the current "patchwork quilt" of programs and policies supporting lifelong learning (U. S. Congress, Senate, 1975b).

The only witness opposing the legislation was Harold Hodgkinson, director of the National Institute of Education. Speaking for the Ford administration, Hodgkinson recognized the barriers that confront adults who seek further education. Nonetheless, he opposed the proposal because it "confused the responsibilities of the Office of Education and the National Institute of Education" and authorized activities that were already provided by federal agencies and state and local organizations under existing legislation (U.S. Congress, Senate, 1975b).

Despite the Ford administration's opposition, the Senate committee recommended passage of the bill, emphasizing that its focus was adults. The committee approved legislation

> to build on the existing programs, to attempt to monitor and assess them, and to make recommendations which would assist in the implementation of a coherent lifelong learning policy [U. S. Congress, Senate, 1976a].

The committee's bill paralleled Mondale's original proposal with three differences: (1) "lifetime learning" was retitled "lifelong learning," (2) the controversial proposal for an Office of Lifetime Learning within the Office of Education was eliminated, and (3) a broader definition of lifelong learning was included, emphasizing the role of education in assisting citizens' adjustment to "social, technological, political, and economic changes."

To win political support, legislative provisions were expanded to include:

> review [of] the lifelong learning opportunities provided through employers, unions, the media, libraries and museums, secondary schools and postsecondary educational institutions, and other public and private organizations to determine means by which the enhancement of their effectiveness and coordination may be facilitated [U. S. Congress, Senate, 1976a].

Authorizations for the Lifelong Learning Act were set at $40 million annually for the fiscal years 1977 through 1982. The legislation required that the first $5 million appropriated under this title be spent on federal monitoring, assessment, and planning activities; the next $4 million were to be spent on state demonstration projects.

Most lobbyists found Lifelong Learning difficult to oppose but saw it as an unnecessary addition. They were primarily concerned with other parts of the omnibus legislation, especially the sections on vocational education and student financial aid.

Ellen Hoffman, a Mondale staff member, directed the formation of an ad hoc group to lobby for passage of the Lifelong

Learning provisions. The group consisted of representatives from the Coalition of Adult Education Organizations (CAEO), the American Federation of Teachers (AFT), the National University Extension Association (NUEA), the National Association of Retired Persons (NARP), and the Adult Education Association (AEA). This coalition collectively and individually lobbied for the Lifelong Learning legislation. Under Lloyd Davis, NUEA assumed leadership of the interest groups pressing for passage of the Lifelong Learning provisions.

This broad-based coalition benefited from the traditions surrounding Senate operations. A Senator's numerous committee assignments often limit his attention to any one committee. Thus, if a Senator develops a specific interest, such as lifelong learning, senatorial courtesy usually requires that other Senators not oppose it until it is debated on the floor. Senate tradition thus helped assure Lifelong Learning's place in the committee bill despite Senate Education Committee Chairman Pell's (D. R.I.) belief that the 1976 Amendments should be limited in order to allow Congress additional time to evaluate the effect of innovations enacted as part of the 1972 Amendments.

In the House, representatives have greater opportunity for specialization; any new proposal receives closer initial scrutiny than is generally possible in the Senate. The support of several key members of the relevant committee can be crucial to the fate of new proposals. For education in 1976, the central figures included Carl Perkins (D. Ky.), John O'Hara (D. Mich.), John Brademas (D. Ind.), and Albert Quie (R. Minn.). These representatives shared Senator Pell's feelings about the 1976 Amendments, and they were most interested in obtaining committee agreement on the vocational education and student aid provisions. After agreement was reached on these provisions, the House committee decided against hearings on Lifelong Learning and other Senate initiatives, choosing instead to resolve in conference the differences between the House and Senate versions of the Education Amendments.

The Conference Committee convened on September 1, 1976, with Lifelong Learning a low priority for nearly everyone. The higher education lobby was preoccupied with the Basic Grants and Guaranteed Student Loan Program. The Community and Junior

College groups were largely interested in the Vocational Education Amendments. One House staff member would later estimate that, of the fifty-nine hours the Conference Committee was in session, less than fifteen minutes were devoted to the Lifelong Learning provisions.

Since Senator Mondale was campaigning for the vice-presidency, responsibility for passage of Lifelong Learning fell largely on Ellen Hoffman. Her efforts, together with those of Ken Fischer and Marilyn Kressel of the Postsecondary Education Convening Authority, Norman Kurland of the New York State Department of Education, and Dan Ferber of the Minnesota Learning Society, were largely responsible for maintaining sufficient visibility for Lifelong Learning to win its inclusion in the 1976 Amendments. While Mondale's absence made Hoffman's work more difficult, some conference members were loath to eliminate "Fritz's pet" and run the risk of antagonizing the future vice-president.

House conference members, however, did have some objections to the Lifelong Learning provisions in the Senate proposal. Led by Rep. Quie, they argued:

- The provisions were a policy statement more suitable to an HEW position paper.
- The concept was largely undefinable.
- There was no need to create another small categorical program whose main beneficiaries would most likely be higher education institutions.
- Lifelong learning was already a reality, so the legislation was unnecessary.
- The Lifelong Learning provisions were no more than an adult or continuing education bill.

To meet these objections, the Senate provisions were redrafted more narrowly. For example, the Congressional Declaration in the Senate version:

> It is the policy of the United States that (1) opportunities for lifelong learning shall be available to all persons without regard to previous education or training [U. S. Congress, Senate, 1976a].

was rewritten in conference to read:

> American society should have as a goal the availability of
> appropriate opportunities for lifelong learning for all its citizens
> without regard to restrictions of previous education or training,
> sex, age, handicapping condition, social or ethnic background, or
> economic circumstance [Public Law 94–482].

The conference deleted appropriation restrictions in the
Senate bill, which mandated specific percentages for research and
state demonstration projects. In addition, the authorization levels
were reduced to $20 million (from $40 million) in FY 1977, $30
million in FY 1978, and $40 million in FY 1979.

Unlike many federal education programs, the Lifelong
Learning Act provides no apparatus for a complete federal program. It has two components: (1) a study of how existing federal
programs can help produce a coordinated lifelong learning effort
and (2) demonstration grants to test lifelong learning delivery systems. The study, to be conducted by the Assistant Secretary for
Education (ASE), was to investigate various alternatives, including:

• Tax incentives to encourage business and labor support.
• Entitlement proposals or voucher plans.
• Modification of current student aid programs to make them
  more applicable to lifelong learning.
• Modification of existing federal manpower, unemployment compensation, and other programs to assist lifelong learning
  programs.

The second component, demonstration grants, was substantially reduced by the Conference Committee, although the law em-
powers the Assistant Secretary to fund a few demonstration projects under the direction of "appropriate state agencies, institutions
of higher education, and public and private nonprofit organizations."

Implementation

The implementation of the Lifelong Learning Act was de-
layed by three factors: (1) organizational disputes within the Ed-

ucation Division of the Department of HEW, (2) the lame duck status of the Ford administration following the Carter election in November 1976, and (3) the lack of appropriations to make the law a reality, such that staff and office space had to be borrowed.

In a December 1976 speech before the Monthly Dialogue on Lifelong Learning sponsored by the Postsecondary Education Convening Authority (PECA), then Deputy Assistant Secretary of Education for Policy Development, Philip Austin, outlined implementation activities under way:

> We in HEW thought that there were two issues that were reasonably straightforward with respect to congressional intent. The first was that it was not the intent of Congress to have this legislation delegated from the Assistant Secretary to OE, to NIE, to the Fund [for the Improvement of Postsecondary Education], or any other agency but that it was, at least for the time being, to remain in ASE.
>
> Secondly, we interpreted legislative intent to be that, at least for the first several months, the type of activity that was envisioned was largely conceptual in nature rather than immediately putting programs on track and start funding the programs.
>
> Now, to carry this out, the Assistant Secretary determined that someone who was rather senior in the bureaucracy should head this activity up and also someone who was familiar with the substance of what is generally known as lifelong learning [Postsecondary Education Convening Authority, 1976].

What Austin's remarks did not reveal was the competition within the education bureaucracy—among such interested agencies as the National Institute of Education, the Bureau of Postsecondary Education, and the Office of Adult Education in the Bureau of Occupational and Adult Education—for control of the program. Rather than "give" the program to one agency or another within the Education Division, the Assistant Secretary's Office determined that the "someone who was rather senior in the bureaucracy" was Virginia Smith, Director of the Fund for the Improvement of Postsecondary Education. Smith's appointment was viewed as desirable for two reasons: First, it kept responsibility for lifelong learning within the Office of the Assistant Secretary for Education, and second, Smith had a reputation as a "conceptual thinker" with extensive experience in nontraditional forms of education. Smith viewed her task as building a framework for future program development:

> We are calling it "the lifelong learning project," and I insist upon calling it "the lifelong learning project" because I don't want to have it lost as a perspective or as a concept or as an idea or as a coordinating mechanism. It is much more important and much more real than any of these things.
>
> I would hope that for every information-gathering mandate that exists in the act, that we will have, you will excuse the jargon, a "pro-active process" in which we do not gather information without disseminating information, that every gathering of information activity will itself be an educational process [Postsecondary Education Convening Authority, 1976].

When Smith left Washington in the summer of 1977 to become president of Vassar College, administrative responsibility for direction of the project fell to Chuck Bunting, the Deputy Director of FIPSE. Penny Richardson coordinated the day-to-day activities of the project staff.

Enacting a bill into law is only the first battle; winning appropriations to finance its implementation is another, often more significant, struggle. The coalition that was successful in getting Title I, Part B enacted was unsuccessful in efforts to get it funded. Since no funds had been appropriated for Lifelong Learning, the study was supported by OE, NIE, and FIPSE, which each assigned to it one staff member and some funding. Given Mondale's interest in lifelong learning, Austin and Smith believed that the project was likely to be funded in future budgets, possibly the 1977 supplemental appropriation.

Educators were dismayed that the 1978 budget released by President Ford three days before he left office contained no funds for Title I of the Higher Education Act. This marked the sixth consecutive year in which Republican administrations had asked no money for Title I—a reluctance based on their belief that states and local governments are responsible for community service and continuing education. Yet supporters of Title I were optimistic that a Democratic administration would be more generous. They were unhappily surprised by the announcement of January 31, ten days after the administrative transition, that President Carter would generally accept the Ford administration's budgetary recommendations: "It will be a Ford budget with Carter amendments." In the wake of this announcement, the education lobby began to rally support for Title I funding. On February 9, 1977, the National Advisory Council on Extension and Continuing Education (NACECE) urged a broad group of legislators and officials to support funding for Title I, primarily Part A, by means of a letter to all members of the House and Senate Appropriations Committee, the Senate Labor and Public Welfare Committee, the House Education and Labor Committee, the President, the Assistant Secretary for Education, and the Commissioner of Education.

On February 15, NACECE, backed by other higher education organizations, released a detailed budget and argued for funding Title I at the following levels:

	FY 1977	FY 1978
Part A, Community Service and Continuing Education	$20,000,000	$40,000,000
Part B, Lifelong Learning	500,000	5,000,000

The budget justification for Lifelong Learning read:

> A funding level of $500,000 for FY 1977 will enable the Assistant Secretary for Education to identify the possible sources for the data needed to conduct the studies mandated by the legislation and to design the procedures for filling gaps in knowledge about lifelong learning. In addition, a FY 1977 appropriation would provide funds to design and test the effectiveness of procedures for the broad-based information sharing activities that are essential components of a lifelong learning program.
>
> For FY 1978, $5,000,000 will be required to begin work on the twenty major research and information gathering studies specified in the legislation and to analyze the findings and interpret their significance. These activities will provide the major substantive data for the report that the Assistant Secretary is required to transmit to Congress on January 1, 1978 [National Advisory Council on Extension and Continuing Education, February 22, 1977a].

When President Carter announced his FY 1978 budget on February 21, it included a $12 million request for Community Service and Continuing Education Programs (Title I, Part A) but no request for Lifelong Learning (Title I, Part B). Supporters of Lifelong Learning, shut out of the FY 1978 budget, assumed they would receive from $3 to $5 million as part of FY 1977 supplemental appropriations and were surprised when that too contained no mention of Lifelong Learning.

While some feel that Lifelong Learning was a victim of Carter's campaign promise to balance the budget, more optimistic supporters believe it was simply lost in the crush of events that fell upon the new administration. Other explanations include the following:

• Lifelong Learning was low on the list of priorities given to the Congressional Appropriation Committees by education organizations. While no organizations opposed Lifelong Learning, few gave it wholehearted support, as we have seen.
• Vice-President Mondale lost interest in the program. Those who believe this point out that a word from Mondale to the chairmen of the Congressional Appropriations Committees would most likely have led to an appropriation.
• The feeling prevailed on Capitol Hill and in the Office of Management and Budget (OMB) that many federal programs already deal with lifelong learning, making additional money superfluous.
• Interest in lifelong learning in the private and nonprofit sector had been sufficiently aroused merely by passing the program; funding it became unnecessary.

Of course, we lack a precise calculus for determining which new programs are funded and which are not; in the case of Lifelong Learning, however, there is a measure of truth in every reason noted above.

Because no funds were appropriated to Title I, Part B in FY 1978, the Lifelong Learning Project relied on the limited staff and funds contributed by the agencies. (The $200,000 budget for the project came from the Office of Education, the Assistant Secretary for Education, the National Institute of Education, and the Fund for the Improvement of Postsecondary Education.) Its activities were confined to a mandated report to the President and Congress submitted on February 1, 1978.

The final report consisted of two documents: (1) a short report for Congress and the President and (2) a compendium of background reports on selected topics intended for a wider audience. The short report, *Lifelong Learning and Public Policy,* defines lifelong learning as "the process by which individuals continue to develop their knowledge, skills, and interests throughout their lifetimes" (p. iv). The report notes that most federal adult learning support is concentrated on college-age individuals and is directed at activities taking place in traditional postsecondary institutions. It recommends:

> Future federal policy should have as a priority the availability of learning opportunities for all citizens. Public policy should also emphasize meeting learning needs as well as certification needs, through supporting learning opportunities in a range of formal and nonformal settings (universities, community colleges, public schools, workplaces, community centers, public libraries, museums, public broadcasting) that are attractive to and appropriate for all adults, particularly those with special learning needs. Steps in this direction would include program analysis and coordination, basic and applied research, and demonstration and dissemination of effective learning practices [p. v].

The report focuses on learners (rather than on governmental or educational structures) over age sixteen who are not presently served by existing educational systems. Among the specific target groups who need special attention are workers, urban youths, women and older adults. The document is notable for its restraint. Among its recommendations, the report urges the federal government to initiate realistic and modest coordination efforts; support research and experimentation; support demonstration projects and dissemination of information; emphasize the needs of disadvantaged groups in all activities; provide incentive grants for state leadership activities; reduce duplication; assist states in improving information and assessment efforts; encourage the establishment of interstate and regional services for adults; and support programs that develop new learning approaches for adults. Notably, there are no proposals calling for the initiation of new large-scale federally operated programs. (See Chapter Six for additional details.)

The future federal role in Lifelong Learning under Title I, Part B is unlikely. Although the Carter administration requested $5 million in the FY 1979 budget for demonstration activities, but Congress failed to appropriate any funds. The President's FY 1980 budget did not request any funding for Title I, Part B.

Current Proposals

This section assesses the present climate of thinking about federal involvement in lifelong learning: what people say about it, what aspects are likely to win further support, and which forms of support are considered possible. Before exploring alternative federal roles, we will review proposals for federal action from several important and widely cited lifelong learning studies.

Background Studies and Proposals

Norvell Northcutt (1975), whose work on functional competencies has influenced Washington thinking on lifelong learning, identifies several deficiencies in existing programs:

• Current programs are narrow. Their content and delivery systems must be made attractive, especially to people who function only with difficulty.
• With minor exceptions, few programs attract the people who need them most. "Have-nots" are attracted only by innovative programs, since traditional education usually arouses painful memories.
• Although employers may give employees the opportunity to improve their job-related skills, basic education is rarely a part of the employer programs.
• Federal manpower programs such as the Comprehensive Employment and Training Act (CETA) do not provide participants with adequate skills.

Northcutt has urged the establishment of a national organization to coordinate lifelong learning delivery systems, eliminating duplication of services and providing the basic organizational framework needed to satisfy the special needs of the poor, minorities, and the undereducated.

In a similar vein, Michael O'Keefe (1977) identifies several basic deficiencies of current lifelong learning opportunities:

- There exists an underserved population desperately in need of educational assistance.
- The geographical distribution of lifelong learning programs is uneven.
- The unique problems and needs of adults have not been adequately considered.

He identifies several areas where knowledge of the sociological and governmental systems involved is inadequate to assess lifelong learning:

- The unique educational needs of subgroups.
- The role of education in minimizing job and career dissatisfaction.
- The existing methods used to finance adult education (subsidies, grants) and their varying degrees of success.
- The reasons why more employees do not take advantage of employer-sponsored education benefits.
- Potential tax incentive benefits to employers who mount lifelong learning programs or encourage employees to seek further training.

O'Keefe urges the development of federal programs to eliminate obstacles to adult education by (1) expanding student aid programs, (2) expanding Manpower Training Programs to cover people seeking to change jobs, and (3) including target groups in addition to the disadvantaged. He considers broader possibilities of federal support and concludes that at present only a limited, incremental approach is realistic.

The 1976 Wingspread Conference on Lifelong Learning sponsored by the Coalition of Adult Education Organizations suggested that "the appropriate role of government at all levels regarding lifelong learning is to provide affirmation, leadership, and critical support" (Wingspread Conference on Lifelong Learning in the Public Interest, 1976). Several areas vital to a federal policy were specified:

- Adult counseling and information services should be expanded to allow for the users' limited time, unique needs, and special interests.
- Adult learners' needs should take priority over those of educational institutions.
- Lifelong learning opportunities should be better publicized.
- Financial support must have top priority.
- Adult education research and development should be expanded.
- More efficient use should be made of existing adult education resources—human, fiscal, programmatic.
- An ongoing and mutually beneficial relationship among the federal, state, and local levels of government and various sectors of the adult education community should be developed.
- Interactions among national education groups and other interested organizations should be encouraged.

In their study *Lifetime Distribution of Education, Work, and Leisure,* Fred Best and Barry Stern argue that work sharing, in the form of more "cyclical" (as opposed to "linear") life patterns, should be considered as a partial solution to unemployment. This approach would create job vacancies by allowing individuals to leave their jobs temporarily to engage in leisure, education, or community service activities (Best and Stern, 1976). Lifelong learning, they contend, requires an active federal role that would help create a larger number of informal, variously structured opportunities for education, learning and leisure. They suggest several federal steps toward such a society:

> Expand research to assess the kinds of life-scheduling patterns which appeal to people as well as serve the collective public interest.
> Help states establish occupational and educational information systems as well as (education consumer) brokering services which would help individuals of all ages make more intelligent choices about careers and educational and leisure activities.

> Consider legislation which would enable more workers to take a temporary leave of absence from their jobs in order to participate in activities which might facilitate career or life improvement, renewal, or redirection [Best and Stern, 1976, pp. 59–60].

Best and Stern want a reorientation of the social structures of work, leisure, and education, while Northcutt and O'Keefe seek to direct federal lifelong learning efforts especially toward the underprivileged.

Norman Kurland, Director of Adult Education for New York State, thinks we must also change our patterns of secondary education, arguing that education must evolve away from "the emphasis on terminal degrees and toward the concept that each stage of education should be, first, in itself valuable as a learning experience, second, useful as preparation for further study, and third, helpful in achieving one's career and personal goals" (Kurland and others, 1976). Kurland proposes modifying current federal financial assistance programs and starting an entitlement plan to give adult students federal financial support for their education.

The broad policy proposals outlined in these studies are a source for emerging lifelong learning initiatives, particularly in the areas of (1) improving the information available to prospective learners, (2) increasing the financial resources available to nontraditional students, and (3) encouraging private sector activities in lifelong learning.

Several of these initiatives will be analyzed here. Some are carefully drawn proposals with widespread approval, while others are "study" proposals or "think" pieces, which have little chance of enactment.

Improving Information

Two types of information dissemination are of concern here: information for policy makers and program administrators about the operation of adult learning programs nationwide (a clearinghouse service) and information to potential learners about educational opportunities in local areas (a brokerage service). Supporters of the clearinghouse approach argue it has a variety of benefits. First, it would enable the federal government to assist federal, state, and local agencies involved in lifelong learning activities at minimal cost. In addition, it would help identify existing resources and encourage the development of citizen information networks. Finally, it would allow the federal government to promote lifelong learning without creating another federal program and without imposing standards on lifelong learning delivery systems.

Several clearinghouses have already demonstrated the potential of this mechanism. The Clearinghouse for Community Based Free-Standing Educational Institutions, for example, is composed of community-based organizations such as museums and libraries. It serves as a central coordinating agency for resource development, information dissemination, technical assistance, and evaluation.

The Regional Learning Service of Central New York (RLS) is a highly visible example of an educational brokerage that offers adult learners noninstructional services such as counseling and educational information. Funded by the Carnegie Corporation, RLS is "an advocate for individuals seeking new vocational and educational directions in their lives" ("What Is the Next Thing . . ." 1977).

In 1976 the brokering concept became more visible when the National Center for Educational Brokering opened in Washington, D.C. The center, which received initial funds from several sources, including the Carnegie Corporation and FIPSE, seeks the expansion and improvement of career and adult education information and advisory, referral, and advocacy services (see Chapter Six).

A related development is the creation of Education Information Centers authorized by the Education Amendments of 1976. Part A of Title IV of the Amendments calls for the federal government to:

> make grants to states to pay the federal share of the cost of planning, establishing, and operating Educational Information Centers to provide educational information, guidance, counseling, and referral services for all individuals, including individuals residing in rural areas.

Three million dollars was appropriated for this program during FY 1979; however, no money is included in the President's

1980 budget. Various proposed implementation strategies from the states are described in Chapter Four.

The federal government has already encouraged the development of clearinghouses and the provision of better information to potential learners. The sixteen Educational Resources Information Centers (ERIC), which are supported by the National Institute of Education, disseminate information regarding educational research. In addition, the Clearinghouse ADELL (Adult Education and Lifelong Learning), currently located at Informatics, Inc., in Rockville, Maryland, seeks to coordinate information on adult education and manpower programs and convey that information to interested individuals and groups.

Financial Alternatives

A variety of proposals to extend or modify existing financial aid for the adult or part-time learner have been put forward. Federal initiatives fall into several categories:

- Tax relief.
- Modified Basic Educational Opportunity Grants (BEOG).
- Entitlement or voucher plans.
- Institutional incentives.
- Private sector incentives.

Tax Relief. In recent years, numerous proposals have been introduced to allow students (or their parents) some form of tax relief for educational expenditures. There are three basic types of proposals: credits, deductions, and exemptions. Tax *credits* would allow the taxpayer to deduct money from taxes owed to the federal government. Credits are more powerful and costly to the government than simple tax *deductions,* which are subtracted from the taxpayer's gross income. The *exemption,* a somewhat less popular idea, would allow the taypayer to claim an extra personal exemption for education purposes.

Tax credit and deduction bills have received increasing support. Over eighty bills that would have provided some form of tax relief for tuition expenses were introduced in the first session of the 95th Congress. One proposal introduced by Senators Roth (R.

Del.) and Ribicoff (D. Conn.) providing a tax credit of $250 for each student passed the Senate as part of the Social Security refinancing. In December 1977 the provision was dropped in the House-Senate Conference only after extensive lobbying by the White House and strong resistance to the idea by House conferees.

In 1978 the Carter administration, seeking to avoid enactment of higher education tuition tax credits, proposed expanding the existing student assistance programs to aid middle-income students. Although the Senate and House approved higher education tax credits despite the threat of a presidential veto, the provisions were eliminated during the House-Senate Conference in favor of a modified version of President Carter's plan.[2]

An alternative tax measure has been proposed by Representatives Mikva (D. Ill.) and Ketchum (R. Calif.). Their proposal would permit their students or their parents to *defer* from their taxes a percentage of the eligible educational expenses and to repay in full the deferred amount over a ten-year period after completion of the educational program. The repayment provision would protect federal revenues while giving taxpayers a larger credit than a traditional tax credit program could provide. During its first year, the Mikva-Ketchum program would be very expensive, costing as much as $8 billion. This sum would be reduced as the deferred taxes are repaid. The sponsors have also indicated a willingness to speed up the repayment period or charge minimal interest. Opponents of such a plan note that the default rate on student loans (currently about 13 percent) illustrates the danger that such a funding proposal might eventually require vast sums of money.

Modified Basic Education Opportunity Grants (BEOG). The BEOGs tend to discriminate against working adults because recipients must be at least half-time students. This usually disqualifies the adult learner who works during the day and enrolls in only one

---

[2]In 1978 the New York State Legislature enacted a tuition tax deduction and deferral. It is estimated the deduction, ranging from $120 to $1000 for each student, and the deferral, a maximum of $750 per year, will cost the state $25 million in the first year. It is unclear whether other states will follow New York's lead.

or two courses per semester. Modifying the legislation to include part-time students would eliminate this inequity. Removal of income ceilings, inappropriate for adults supporting families, would eliminate a second obstacle to adult eligibility for BEOGs and would facilitate lifelong learning.

Another modification was recently proposed by Dallas Martin, Executive Secretary of the National Association of Student Financial Aid Administrators. Martin recommended increasing the personal asset reserve limitation from the present $12,500 to $17,500 and increasing the farm and business asset reserve from the current $25,000 to $50,000. These changes would somewhat relieve middle-income families and make more adults eligible to participate in the program.

Critics who object to modifying the BEOG program argue that such changes would dramatically increase the program's budget. A simple increase in the maximum BEOG award from $1,400 to $1,600 in FY 1978, for example, was estimated to have increased the program budget by about $400 million. Proposed changes in the program are strongly resisted by higher education interest groups.

Entitlements. A more radical approach to financing lifelong learning is an entitlement or voucher program. Under such a program, the target population would receive a predetermined amount of money for continuing education. Entitlements would give learners complete freedom to determine where to spend their educational dollars.

A number of limited entitlement programs are currently operated by federal and state governments as well as private industry. These include the BEOG, the GI Bill, the Social Security survivor benefits, the New York Tuition Assistance Program, and Employee Tuition Benefits. (For a discussion of these and other programs see Honey and Hartle, 1975a, and Kurland, 1977.) Most of the many entitlement proposals debated in recent years have been strongly criticized for being too costly or superfluous.

There are a variety of prominent entitlement proposals. One example is George Nolfi's Adult Recurrent Education Entitlement Voucher plan (Nolfi, 1974). Aimed at persons over twenty-five who have not completed four years of college, it provides greater benefits for individuals with low income and low educational attainment.

The Generalized Educational and Social Entitlement Plan (Cartter, 1973), prepared for the Carnegie Commission, would pay half of college tuition for full-time students over eighteen years of age and give students monthly tax-exempt payments based on their educational costs. This plan would be funded both out of general revenues and by regular employee-employer contributions through payroll taxes.

Herbert Striner's National Economic Security Fund would be supported through a federal takeover of state unemployment funds and the imposition of additional payroll taxes. It would provide total expenses and income support for a period of two years for all workers over seventeen years of age (Striner, 1972). Kurland and Comly's Age Neutral Educational Entitlement program would place $200 per year in an interest-bearing account for each person over twenty-five. Without time restrictions, this money could be used for counseling, tuition, and income maintenance (Kurland and Comly, 1975).

In early 1977 Senator Edward Brooke (R. Mass.) announced his intention to introduce entitlement legislation in the 95th Congress. The Brooke assistance programs would be modeled on the GI Bill and include a system of vouchers, grants, and loans. However, the proposal was never introduced.

Enactment of any entitlement plan in the near future is, at best, a slim possibility.[3] Robert C. Andringa (1977), former Minority Staff Director of the House Committee on Education and Labor, identifies "21 Political Factors Standing in the Way of Federal Education Entitlements for all American Adults." The factors inhibiting entitlements include the following:

• No evidence of sufficient public support for such a massive new federal program.

_____

[3]See O'Keefe (1977) for a graphic presentation of various entitlement plans. Honey and Hartle (1975b), also summarize several proposed plans.

- President Carter's commitment to balance the budget by 1981 from a current $60 billion annual deficit.
- Extreme difficulty of passing *any* new entitlement program under the new Budget Control and Impoundment Act.
- Perception, based on recent trends, that general entitlements would be used most by white middle-income people who already have more education than the average American adult.
- Increasing doubt about the "value added" by ad hoc formal education.
- Taxpayers' vexation over increasing costs for declining enrollments.
- Poor track records of adults taking advantage of current employee tuition remission programs.
- The tendency of many legislators to discourage major new proposals by pointing to the 275 federal statutory authorizations that already support adult education.
- Extreme difficulty in getting the federal-state coordination necessary for a nationally equitable general entitlement program.
- Fear that a federal entitlement program would bring about even greater regulatory control over institutional decision making than current government policies.
- The almost impossible task, in an age of interest group politics, of reducing or eliminating current financing schemes for higher education, which most entitlements supporters say should be done.
- Failure of the president or any key congressional leader to promote entitlements.

Asked about a specific entitlement scheme, one Senate staffer quickly dismissed the idea and went on to say that too many other worthwhile causes need public money. Summing up his opposition to entitlements, he remarked, "not now; not next year; not ever." But he suggested that one possible way to finance lifelong learning is to expand the BEOG program incrementally (Honey and Hartle, 1975a).

While there is good reason to seek some federal financial support for lifelong learning, too much emphasis has been placed on entitlement schemes. For the immediate future, such schemes are politically, financially, and administratively unrealistic.

Institutional Incentives. There is some interest in making post-secondary institutions more accessible to adult learners through financial incentives to institutions that begin lifelong learning programs. Institutional support, however, is not a popular method of financing education except among those who speak for education institutions (that is, the higher education lobby) because it runs counter to the current direction of student assistance, which is geared toward helping the student rather than the institution. Unlike institutional support, student assistance programs force institutions to compete for enrollment by offering more attractive programs.

The most frequently cited example of institutional aid is the "cost of education" provisions authorized by the Higher Education Amendments of 1972. These would provide direct institutional aid for every student receiving federal student assistance. This provision has never been funded, although the *New York Times* recently encouraged an appropriation to offset the high cost of college. The *Times'* editorial position was intended as an alternative to the increasing proposals for tax relief (*New York Times,* 1977).

Private Sector Incentives. There is substantial interest in encouraging the private sector to support lifelong learning by giving employees tuition benefits and educational leaves. Through a program of tax incentives, it has been suggested the federal government could encourage corporations to begin such programs.

Tax deductions are already available to employers who invest in employee training and education. Allowing deductions for expenses such as the cost of salaries while employees take educational leaves, or for the company's contribution to tuition reimbursement programs, would encourage such programs. O'Keefe (1977) suggests taxing corporations that do not offer employee educational benefits and using the revenues from this tax to assist corporations that do have such programs.

Since it is impossible for the federal government to be the main provider of lifelong learning services, federal encouragement of private support is an important, desirable step. Many unions and corporations have already made major commitments to lifelong learning (see Chapter One); their potential support amounts to billions of dollars. While the use of tax incentives to facilitate lifelong learning is attractive because it involves the private sector, the potential costs to the federal government make enactment of such a program unlikely.

Washington Views on Lifelong Learning

A number of important themes emerged from nearly fifty interviews and conversations with Washingtonians who are professionally interested in lifelong learning. Most of our interviews focused on lifelong learning as a philosophy of education as well as on the prospects of an increased programmatic role for the federal government in lifelong learning. Because few interviewees were willing to speak for the record, we guaranteed anonymity to all as the most effective means of obtaining candid opinions.

Gleanings from our interviews are grouped in this section according to the agency or interest group represented by our sources: Congress, the executive branch, community organizations, adult and continuing education groups, higher education, and labor unions.

Congress

There is no evidence of congressional support for additional lifelong learning programs. Staff aides report little obvious public support, pointing out that attendance decreased steadily at the Postsecondary Education Convening Authority's Monthly Dialogue on Lifelong Learning as it became clear that there would be no new money for lifelong learning. Moreover, a primary mover behind the Lifelong Learning Act—Senator Walter Mondale —has moved on.

Little support for the Lifelong Learning Act emerged in the FY 1978 appropriations process. Education interest groups gave the program a low priority on the "shopping lists" they presented to the appropriation committees. Congressional aides note that Carter administration support will be essential if any money is to be appropriated during future budget deliberations.

In the near future, any congressional action that would af-

fect lifelong learning will probably be confined to tax relief measures or the 1979–80 revisions of the student aid programs. Any
specific federal initiatives in lifelong learning—such as Brooke's
entitlement plan—will probably emerge in the Senate. The likelihood of this, however, is small.

The congressionally mandated report of the Lifelong Learning
Project was released in February 1978. While the Carter administration's FY 1979 budget included $5 million for the Lifelong
Learning Act, Congress did not appropriate funds. The lack of
funds (none are requested by Carter for FY 1980) indicates that Lifelong Learning—*as a separate federal policy initiative*—will disappear.

Executive Branch

Program managers in the Office of Education have conflicting concerns. They fear that a broad philosophy like lifelong learning will overwhelm their particular education specialties; yet if
there is to be any federal lifelong learning program they want a
piece of it. It is therefore not surprising that we found little consensus in OE, or indeed within the executive branch as a whole,
regarding potential or desirable next steps toward federal support
of lifelong learning.

In general, OE officials feel that, since lifelong learning is
already a reality, the federal government should refrain from becoming extensively involved. OE staff fear that the development
of a coordinated federal lifelong learning policy will decrease their
autonomy. Perhaps as a result, they view lifelong learning as a
broad concept that lacks cogency for government agencies or other
institutions. There is a consensus that if the federal government
does decide to become more involved with lifelong learning, its role
should be limited to categorizing the learning needs and availability
of resources for the disadvantaged. The key to any federal involvement in lifelong learning, they believe, is to encourage the development of learner-centered programs and mechanisms such as
educational brokerages and regional learning services—programs
that do not require the development of a Lifelong Learning Office.
One official noted candidly that OE is frequently seen as "an administrative disaster area," and any major program would be difficult, if not impossible, for the agency to administer effectively.

One government official close to the HEW Lifelong Learning Project commented that the concept is "all things to all people." As a result, Lifelong Learning raises serious, perhaps insoluble, planning problems. If Title I, Part B is funded, this official does not expect the states to receive much money for demonstration grants. The lion's share of appropriated funds would be spent on planning and research.

Within the bureaucracy, the work of the Lifelong Learning Project is not seen as having gone smoothly. While most interviewees praised Virginia Smith, her tenure was brief and problems such as lack of funds and staff, complicated by an uncertain agenda, produced shakedown difficulties for the project. Although the project's report was favorably received, the project was not funded.

One important variable within the executive branch is the role that the Assistant Secretary for Education (ASE), Mary Berry, chooses to play in regard to lifelong learning. The legislation gives her clear authority over the project, and Berry's interest in centralizing Education branch activities within ASE suggests that she might use Title I, Part B to expand the responsibilities of her office. Reportedly, Berry regards lifelong learning as a major priority.

In April 1978, the Federal Interagency Commission on Education (FICE) noted that while the learning needs of all adults require attention, many subgroups require specific attention because of special needs. The FICE report urged strong federal efforts to assure adult literacy. The report also encouraged the federal government to "support the implementation of vocational and avocational lifelong learning activities with emphasis on research and information dissemination and on building increased state and local capacity to develop and implement programs that meet community needs." (Federal Interagency Committee on Education, 1978, p. 78).

Several executive branch officials suggested that a desirable goal for the federal government in lifelong learning would be to improve coordination among programs—a traditional suggestion whenever improving OE/HEW program administration is discussed. Another source suggested a federal program of incentive grants to the states for assessing needs, conducting an inventory of available resources, and planning lifelong learning programs.

Community Organizations

Community groups such as libraries, museums, the "Y," and churches are, in general, critical of federal education policy for its excessive reliance on traditional providers of education. They argue that, although community groups can offer extensive educational and training opportunities, they are ignored by policy makers. Their perspective on lifelong learning may best be summarized as "interested, but wary."

People from these groups argue that they have been providing lifelong learning programs for preschoolers, school children, adults, and senior citizens for years. In the words of one, "we've been providing special learning opportunities for adults since Sputnik—long before it became fashionable." While they applaud the increased emphasis on learning throughout one's lifetime, they fear that increased federal activity in this area would flow toward traditional education institutions and neglect the important contributions made by community groups.

The only federal activity most community organizations would support is some form of an entitlement, although they acknowledge the political infeasibility of such a program and recognize that the higher education lobby would be reluctant to support a plan that provides money for nontraditional programs.

Adult and Continuing Education Groups

Given the close relationships among adult education, continuing education, and lifelong learning, we anticipated strong support for lifelong learning from these groups. But, while our interviewees acknowledged lifelong learning as an important concept, they too were unenthusiastic about new activities, given the underfunding of existing programs. One source admitted that many adult educators hope that Title I, Part B dies quickly and quietly since "it gets in the way of existing programs and could take money away from already operational adult education programs."

Most adult and continuing educators fear being lost under a lifelong learning umbrella and are anxious that any federal activities in this area be narrow in scope. Several suggested, for example, that the most important contributions the federal government could make would be to study issues such as unmet educational needs, the interests of the learning population, and the programmatic and fiscal barriers that confront potential learners. Assuming that unmet needs and educational barriers are problems, the adult and continuing education representatives felt the proper federal role would be to assist or encourage states, local governments, and private organizations to solve problems. They did not think that a large federal program would be an appropriate response.

Higher Education Organizations

Almost no support for lifelong learning can be found among higher education interests. Originally, colleges and universities viewed the concept favorably, as a way to attract adult learners to replace the disappearing traditional student, but their ardor has cooled as the prospects for abundant government funding have dimmed.

Interviewees from higher education organizations admit that, while not opposing lifelong learning, they are not pursuing federal support. They see no need for an organized lifelong learning program and are reluctant to modify the student assistance programs to assist adult learners until they know how this change would affect higher education's interests.

One prominent higher education official compared lifelong learning to career education, in that both are struggling with the problem of conceptualization. He felt that senior citizens offer a large untapped market for postsecondary institutions and suggested that states have a potentially more important role to play in lifelong learning than does the federal government. Considerable support exists among higher education interests for the operation of information networks (Education Information Centers) to link potential learners with education opportunities.

Several people noted the proliferation of "special interest education"—career education, consumer education, women's equity education, and so forth. They argued the necessity to define more clearly the goals and objectives of "lifelong learning." Presumably, such a definition would indicate the primary target groups and methods of lifelong learning. In its present form, higher educators note, lifelong learning is a "catchall concept"—it lacks specific objectives or target groups. There is, of course, a penalty for specifying goals and target groups because, while this encourages political support, it is inherently limiting.

Community and junior college officials generally support lifelong learning, although one interviewee was openly skeptical, remarking, "I feel lifelong learning doesn't have much focus. People have a hard time drawing a line, and I get a little impatient when people draw in early childhood education along with everything else. It seems to me that 'lifelong learning' will have to be given an operational definition which sets its territory and distinguishes it from other territories involved in the lifestream of individuals, or else it will be necessary to forget about it."

Community college representatives argue that their institutions form the ideal delivery system for adult education because they have historically done more for the adult student and tend to be both more accessible and more flexible in hours and curriculums. Private nonprofit and proprietary schools generally favor the idea. Like the community colleges, they argue that their institutions have offered lifelong learning programs for years.

Labor Unions

Union leaders are skeptical of federal lifelong learning programs. They oppose tax relief to businesses that mount lifelong learning programs, believing that unions would spend the same money more effectively on lifelong learning activities. Some union representatives favor the establishment of a labor extension service patterned after the Agriculture Extension Service:

> To this end, organized labor itself is engaged in what may well be the largest continuing education program in the nation. In a four-year period, something like 100,000 union members have participated in the programs conducted by the AFL-CIO Education Department, the education departments of the individual unions, and the labor extension centers which have been established by 41 major universities [National Advisory Council on Extension and Continuing Education, 1977b].

At the National Advisory Council on Extension and Continuing Education's "Invitational Conference on Continuing Education, Manpower Policy, and Lifelong Learning," representatives from labor, industry, government, and education met for two days to discuss the relationship of education to work. Although no clear agreement was reached, interest was expressed in (1) a White House conference on lifelong learning, (2) a cabinet-level Department of Education, and (3) a labor extension program similar to the Agriculture Extension Act (Postsecondary Education Convening Authority, 1977b).

Teachers' Unions

Although teachers' unions have a potential dual interest in lifelong learning as both deliverers and recipients of educational services, we found them surprisingly unconcerned about the future federal commitment.

The American Federation of Teachers (AFT) joined an ad hoc committee of interest groups to support the Mondale Bill in early debate. While recognizing the importance of the concept, the AFT has not been involved in any further lifelong learning lobbying efforts since the ad hoc committee disbanded when the 1976 Amendments passed.

The National Education Association (NEA) favored the 1976 Lifelong Learning legislation, although unsure of its exact meaning. While a spokesperson for NEA claims the association supports placing all lifelong learning programs that provide educational (as opposed to technical) assistance in a cabinet-level Department of Education and supports the development of Teacher Centers, some observers are dubious of NEA's commitment to lifelong learning.

> You can read all nine pages of a well-written wrap-up memo release on the National Education Association's 1977 convention without finding a hint there is a concept called lifelong learning.
> While NEA is not officially against adult education, it sure is not for it in any active way. There is a suspicion that a good many NEA members do not really desire to associate with any adults who do not have a baccalaureate degree [Brightman, 1977].

In Washington, lifelong learning is very popular in the abstract, but few people in positions of influence like it well enough to actively seek new federal initiatives. A common theme in our interviews was the "desirability" and "value" of lifelong learning. It is an "eminently sensible concept" with roots that can be traced to the writings of Dewey and Mann. Expressions such as "it's an important and worthy concept" and "that's what education is all about" punctuated our interviews. Lifelong learning is regarded as a "motherhood" issue—impossible to oppose. Yet despite overwhelming approval, there is no interest in massive federal programs and little agreement regarding incremental changes in existing educational delivery or support systems. There is little agreement at present on needed or desirable next steps to advance the concept of lifelong learning.

There is a small minority in Washington who regard lifelong learning as simply the latest fad in educational policy—one that will simply fade away in time. The weight of evidence, however, is that they are wrong. The shifting context of education suggests that educational institutions will increasingly concentrate on serving the needs of individuals throughout their lifetime, if for no other reason but to assure institutional survival.

The challenge for lifelong learning is not simply to supply additional learning opportunities but rather to win participation of those Americans who remain underserved—the poor and disadvantaged. We predict that education will evolve toward lifelong learning out of economic necessity, whether or not the federal government encourages this evolution.

Federal Role in Lifelong Learning: Summary

Lifelong learning has aroused considerable interest in Washington during the past few years, and there is general agreement that over the next decade educational programs and policies will devote more attention and resources to the needs of nontraditional adult learners.

The government is already involved in lifelong learning. As noted earlier, almost all federal departments and agencies offer adult education and training programs. One careful compilation of federal lifelong learning activities (Christoffel, 1978c) identified 275 separate programs; other studies, using different definitions, have identified even more. The cost for these programs lies in the vicinity of $15–19 billion annually.

Despite federal interest, lifelong learning notably lacks organized political support and enthusiasm among those individuals and groups who might be expected to endorse it. The primary barrier to increasing support is the broad focus and orientation of lifelong learning, one of its most distinguishing characteristics. "Lifelong learning is an emerging philosophy of education," noted one individual we interviewed. "How do you implement a philosophy?"

Washingtonians who work with domestic policy issues tend to have a professionally parochial outlook. Thus, as we noted at the outset, educators are usually in either elementary/secondary or postsecondary categories, and rarely the twain shall meet. Within these categories there are subcategories—postsecondary, for example, includes institutional subgroups such as public, private, proprietary, two-year, four-year, faculty groups, and student groups. Effective communication among the diverse groups is infrequent, and interaction with other groups—such as industry or health care organizations—is limited and superficial.

Grafting a broad lifelong learning philosophy onto such a structure is extremely difficult. By focusing on their narrow concerns, interest groups tend to be skeptical supporters of new programs unless they clearly see what is in it for them. Advancing lifelong learning in Washington will require advocates to campaign for acceptance and support among interest group representatives. Presumably, this should include demonstrations of how specific concerns of interest groups relate to lifelong learning.

Even if such political support could be identified, serious fiscal difficulties would restrict the development of any lifelong learning program requiring federal dollars. Although the Carter administration requested funds for the Lifelong Learning Research and Demonstration grants in the FY 1979 budget, no interest group has emerged as a strong supporter, and the Congress failed to appropriate any funds for them. Moreover, the Carter administration's budgetary concern with terminating or limiting existing federal programs rather than creating new ones does not augur well for further support of lifelong learning. Then, too, generating support for a new program when many existing programs are underfunded and when the nation faces other pressing social needs (for example, welfare and social security reform, health insurance) is an almost impossible task.

While political and fiscal issues are important contextual barriers to a greater federal role in lifelong learning, they are not the only critical concerns. Our interviews identified another set of issues that raise concerns about program implementation and delivery.

1. *Definition.* Exactly what is lifelong learning? Who are the primary beneficiaries? How does lifelong learning relate to existing federal education and training programs? These questions remain unanswered in the minds of many. Until the answers to such basic questions come easily, increased federal interest is unlikely.

2. *Scope and Form.* The extent and precise nature of federal programs to encourage or support lifelong learning should be discussed in some detail. As noted previously, there are a wide range of suggestions for federal activity, and those concerned with lifelong learning need to set priorities among the alternatives. For example, which groups of potential lifelong learning recipients should receive priority attention and in what form?

3. *Organization.* Who should administer lifelong learning programs? Several units, such as the Bureau of Higher and Continuing Education and the Office of Adult Education, within the Education Division have operational authority for programs that would make them potential candidates for administering any new lifelong learning program. Neither of these units, however, has the broad outlook or the potential connections with other agencies that other groups within the Office of the Assistant Secretary of Education (ASE) have. Yet ASE lacks the operational authority or staff to administer a lifelong learning program. The most effective mechanism for operating the program—be it an existing or a new agency or department—should be specified clearly.

4. *Federal-State-Local-Institutional Relationships.* Intergovernmental relationships are vitally important to the success of all education programs. Although federally funded, most education programs are administered at the state, local, or institutional level. Proposals for a "partnership" have been suggested, but to date no mechanism has been established to make consistent the roles and responsibilities of governments with respect to American education. The roles of federal, state, and local government as well as school districts and postsecondary education institutions need to

be carefully analyzed to identify planning, financing, and operational lifelong learning capabilities.

5. *Accreditation and Eligibility.* Organizations that provide lifelong learning activities must be judged "eligible" by some criteria in order either to receive federal funds or to allow individuals to enroll with federal student assistance funds. Recent criticisms of accreditation procedures suggest that the present system inadequately provides for nontraditional institutions such as profit-making schools, libraries, museums, and open universities. Given the wide range of institutions that may well be able and willing to provide lifelong learning, it is important that the eligibility procedures be flexible enough to allow all interested groups to participate but tight enough to protect both the student and the federal funds. Striking such a delicate balance with existing mechanisms is probably impossible, but it must be attempted.

Forecasting the policy process is always risky, given the unpredictable factors that may influence policy concerns. For lifelong learning, however, we do not foresee any new federal programs in the near future, given its cloudy definition, fiscal pressures, and the absence of both political support and salable proposals. While the lifelong learning concept may benefit indirectly from federal initiatives in other areas, there is currently little support for specific new programmatic measures. We can see no compelling need for a specific lifelong learning program being articulated. The federal government is already heavily involved in lifelong learning, and many vagaries of definition, focus, delivery systems, and so on prevent specific recommendations for new lifelong learning activities.

This is not, of course, to suggest that federal activity in this area will cease. The existing federal programs encouraging lifelong learning will be continued. In addition, efforts like those of the Lifelong Learning Project are important and should be continued. This approach permits a detailed consideration of specific issues such as improving coordination of existing federal programs and improving the relationship among professionals concerned with related but distinct issues such as lifelong learning, adult, continuing, and recurrent education. Nor does our view suggest that efforts, including legislative initiatives, to modify existing programs to address adult needs be abandoned or receive less attention.

While the existing political environment is not ripe for federal programmatic activity, lifelong learning experts should continue their efforts to increase visibility and public interest. Building ties with other interest groups and encouraging modifications of existing programs to better serve the needs of lifelong learners are important activities, usefully served, for example, by the Monthly Dialogue on Lifelong Learning sponsored by the Postsecondary Education Convening Authority (PECA). Professionals who want greater federal activity in lifelong learning should now be practicing what Nelson Polsby calls "policy incubation"—that is, keeping a proposal alive and seeking support until the political and financial climates are more favorable (Polsby, 1969).

We have suggested throughout this chapter that education will evolve in the direction of lifelong learning and that public policy will follow that shift through mechanisms such as tax credits and through instruments such as Education Information Centers to serve the nontraditional student. Those seeking a greater federal role in lifelong learning would be well advised to identify and urge incremental changes that will draw support from many individuals and organizations.

The federal government can encourage lifelong learning by supporting the activities and programs currently in place, or it can seek to speed its evolution by creating mechanisms and programs to advance the concept. Speeding evolution is a risky business, and, from a Washington perspective, there is no evidence of a pressing need to do so. While lifelong learning will shift the boundaries and reshape our concepts of educational policy, these changes will be gradual. It is through such incremental change that lifelong learning will evolve into a new force in American education.

Education Amendments of 1976

Following are the complete texts of four 1976 amendments to the Higher Education Act of 1965 (Public Law 94-482, October 12, 1976) relevant to lifelong learning: (1) Title 1, Part A, concerning Community Services and Continuing Education; (2) Title 1, Part B, concerning Lifelong Learning; (3) Title IV, Part A, concerning Educational Information Centers; and (4) Title X, Part A, concerning the Expansion of Community Colleges.

TITLE I—HIGHER EDUCATION

Part A—Community Services and Continuing Education

extension and revision of program

Sec. 101. (a) Section 101 of the Higher Education Act of 1965 (hereafter in this title referred to as "the Act") is amended to read as follows:

"appropriations authorized

"Sec. 101. (a) For the purpose of (1) assisting the people of the United States in the solution of community problems such as housing, poverty, government, recreation, employment, youth opportunities, transportation, health, and land use by enabling the Commissioner to make grants under this title to strengthen community service programs of colleges and universities, (2) supporting the expansion of continuing education in colleges and universities and (3) supporting resource materials sharing programs, there are authorized to be appropriated $40,000,000 for the fiscal years 1977, 1978, and 1979.

"(b) For the purpose of carrying out a program for the promotion of lifelong learning in accordance with the provisions of part B, there are authorized to be appropriated, $20,000,000 for fiscal year 1977, $30,000,000 for fiscal year 1978, and $40,000,000 for fiscal year 1979."

(b) Title I of such Act is amended—

(1) (A) by amending the heading of section 102 to read as follows:

"definition of community service program and continuing education program";

(B) by inserting "(a)" after the section designation of such section 102; and

(C) by inserting at the end thereof the following new subsections:

"(b) For purposes of this title the term 'continuing education program' means postsecondary instruction designed to meet the educational needs and interests of adults, including the expansion of available learning opportunities for adults who are not adequately served by current educational offerings in their communities.

"(c) For purposes of this title, the term 'resource materials sharing programs' means planning for the improved use of existing community learning resources by finding ways that combinations of agencies, institutions, and organizations can make better use of existing educational materials, communications technology, local facilities, and such human resources as will expand learning opportunities for adults in the area being served.";

(2) by amending section 103 (a) to read as follows:

"SEC. 103. (a) From the sums appropriated pursuant to section 101 (a) for any fiscal year which are not reserved under section 106 (a), the Commissioner shall allot to each State an amount which bears the same ratio to such sums as the population of such State bears to the population of all the States, except that, for any fiscal year beginning on or after October 1, 1976, no State shall be allotted from such sums less than the amount which such State received during the fiscal year beginning July 1, 1975."

(3) by striking out "community service programs" in section 104 and inserting in lieu thereof "community service and continuing education programs, including resource material sharing programs,";

(4) by striking out so much of section 105 (a) as precedes paragraph (1) and inserting in lieu thereof the following:

"SEC. 105. (a) Any State desiring to receive its allotment of funds under this part for use in community service and continuing education programs, including resource material sharing programs, shall designate or create a State agency or institution which has special qualifications with respect to solving community problems and which is broadly representative of institutions of higher education in the State which are competent to offer community service and continuing education programs, including resource material sharing programs, and shall submit to the Commissioner a State plan. If a State desires to designate for the purpose of this section an existing State agency or institution which does not meet these requirements, it may do so if the agency or institution takes such action as may be necessary to acquire such qualifications and assure participation of such institutions, or if it designates or creates a State advisory council which meets the requirements not met by the designated agency or institution to consult with the designated agency or institution in the preparation of the State plan. A State plan submitted under this part shall—."

(5) (A) by inserting "or combination" after "and institution" in section 105 (a) (2); and

(B) by striking out "community service programs" each place it appears in such section and inserting in lieu thereof "community service and continuing education programs, including resource materials sharing programs,";

(6) (A) by inserting "and combinations thereof" immediately after "institution of higher education" each place it appears in section 105 (a) (3);

(B) by striking out "community service programs" each place it appears in such section and inserting in lieu thereof "community service and continuing education programs, including resource materials sharing programs,"; and

(C) by striking out "in the light of information regarding current and anticipated community problems in the State" in subparagraph (C) of such section;

(7) by striking out "community service programs" in section 105 (a) (4) and inserting in lieu thereof "community service and continuing education programs, including resource materials sharing programs,";

(8) by inserting "or combinations thereof" after "institutions of higher education" in section 105 (a) (5);

(9) by striking section 105 (a) (6) and inserting in lieu thereof the following:

"(6) assurances that all institutions of higher education in the State have been given the opportunity to participate in the development of the State plan."; and

(10) by inserting immediately after section 105 (b) the following new subsection:

"(c) The Commissioner shall not by standard, rule, regulation, guideline, or any other means, either formal or informal, require a State to make any agreement or submit any data which is not specifically required by this part."

(c) Section 107(a) of the Act is amended by striking out "$25,000" and inserting in lieu thereof "$40,000."

(d) Section 109 of the Act is amended to read as follows:

"JUDICIAL REVIEW

"SEC. 109. If a State's plan is not approved under section 105 (b) or a State's eligibility to participate in the program is suspended as a result of the Commissioner's action under section 108 (b), the State may within sixty days after notice of the Commissioner's decision institute a civil action in an appropriate United States district court. In such an action, the court shall determine the matter de novo."

(e) Title I of the Act is further amended by redesignating sections 111, 112, and 113, and any references thereto, as sections 112, 113, and 114, respectively, and inserting immediately after section 110 the following new section:

"TECHNICAL ASSISTANCE AND ADMINISTRATION

"SEC. 111. (a) The Commissioner is authorized to reserve not to exceed 10 per centum of the amount appropriated for any fiscal year pursuant to section 101 (a) in excess of $14,500,000 for the purpose of this section.

"(b) From funds reserved under subsection (a) of this section, the Commissioner shall provide technical assistance to the States and to institutions of higher education. Such technical assistance shall—

> "(1) provide a national diffusion network to help assure that effective programs are known among such States and institutions;

> "(2) assist with the improvement of planning and evaluation procedures; and

> "(3) provide information about the changing enrollment patterns in postsecondary institutions, and provide assistance to such States and institutions in their efforts to understand these changing patterns and to accommodate them."

"(c) The Commissioner shall provide for coordination between community service and continuing education programs (including resource materials sharing programs) conducted by him with all other appropriate offices and agencies, including such offices and agencies which administer vocational education programs, adult education programs, career education programs, and student and institutional assistance programs."

(f) (1) Section 112 of the Act (as redesignated by subsection (e)) is amended—

(A) by striking out "the Commissioner, who shall be Chairman." in subsection (a); and

(B) by striking out "through June 30, 1975" in subsection (f) and inserting in lieu thereof "until the programs authorized by this part are terminated."

(2) The text of section 113 of the Act (as redesignated by subsection (e)) is amended to read as follows: "Nothing in this section shall modify any authority under the Act of May 8, 1914 (Smith-Lever Act), as amended (7 U.S.C. 341–348)."

(g) Title I of the Act is further amended—

(1) by inserting before the section heading of section 101 the following:

"Part A—Community Service and
Continuing Education Programs";

(2) by striking out "this title" each time it appears in section 102 through section 112 of such title, and inserting in lieu thereof "this part"; and

(3) by adding at the end thereof the following new part:

"Part B—Lifelong Learning

"findings

"Sec. 131. The Congress finds that—

"(1) accelerating social and technological change have had impact on the duration and quality of life;

"(2) the American people need lifelong learning to enable them to adjust to social, technological, political and economic changes;

"(3) lifelong learning has a role in developing the potential of all persons including improvement of their personal well-being, upgrading their workplace skills, and preparing them to participate in the civic, cultural, and political life of the Nation;

"(4) lifelong learning is important in meeting the needs of the growing number of older and retired persons;

"(5) learning takes place through formal and informal instruction, through educational programs conducted by public and private educational and other institutions and organizations, through independent study, and through the efforts of business, industry, and labor;

"(6) planning is necessary at the national, State, and local levels to assure effective use of existing resources in the light of changing characteristics and learning needs of the population;

"(7) more effective use should be made of the resources of the Nation's educational institutions in order to assist the people of the United States in the solution of community problems in areas such as housing, poverty, government, recreation, employment, youth opportunities, transportation, health, and land use; and

"(8) American society should have as a goal the availability of appropriate opportunities for lifelong learning for all its citizens without regard to restrictions of previous education or training, sex, age, handicapping condition, social or ethnic background, or economic circumstance.

"SCOPE OF LIFELONG LEARNING

"SEC. 132. Lifelong learning includes, but is not limited to, adult basic education, continuing education, independent study, agricultural education, business education and labor education, occupational education and job training programs, parent education, postsecondary education, preretirement and education for older and retired people, remedial education, special educational programs for groups or for individuals with special needs, and also educational activities designed to upgrade occupational and professional skills, to assist business, public agencies, and other organizations in the use or innovation and research results, and to serve family needs and personal development.

"LIFELONG LEARNING ACTIVITIES

"SEC. 133. (a) The Assistant Secretary shall carry out, from funds appropriated pursuant to section 101 (b), a program of planning, assessing, and coordinating projects related to lifelong learning. In carrying out the provisions of this section, the Assistant Secretary shall—

"(1) foster improved coordination of Federal support for lifelong learning programs;

"(2) act as a clearinghouse for information regarding lifelong learning, including the identification, collection, and dissemination to educators and the public of existing and new information regarding lifelong learning programs which are or may be carried out and supported by any department or agency of the Federal Government;

"(3) review present and proposed methods of financing and administering lifelong learning, to determine—

"(A) the extent to which each promotes lifelong learning,

"(B) program and administrative features of each that contribute to serving lifelong learning,

"(C) the need for additional Federal support for lifelong learning, and

"(D) procedures by which Federal assistance to lifelong learning may be better applied and coordinated to achieve the purposes of this title;

"(4) review the lifelong learning opportunities provided through employers, unions, the media, libraries, and museums, secondary schools and postsecondary educational institutions, and other public and private organizations to determine means by which the enhancement of their effectiveness and coordination may be facilitated;

"(5) review existing major foreign lifelong learning programs and related programs in order to determine the applicability of such programs in this country;

"(6) identify existing barriers to lifelong learning and evaluate programs designed to eliminate such barriers; and

"(7) to the extent practicable, seek the advice and assistance of the agencies of the Education Division (including the Office of Education, the National Institute of Education, the Fund for the Improvement of Postsecondary Education, and the National Center for Education Statistics), other agencies of the Federal Government, public advisory groups (including the National Advisory Councils on Extension and Continuing Education, Adult Education, Career Education, Community Education, and Vocational Education), Commissions (including the National Commission on Libraries and Information Sciences and the National Commission on Manpower Policy), State agencies, and such other persons or organizations as may be appropriate, in carrying out the Commissioner's responsibilities, and make maximum use of information and studies already available.

The review required by clause (3) of this subsection shall include—

"(i) a comparative assessment of domestic and foreign tax and other incentives to encourage increased commitment of business and labor;

"(ii) a study of alternatives such as lifelong learning entitlement programs or educational vouchers designed to assist adults to undertake education or training in conjunction with, or in periods alternative to employment;

"(iii) review of possible modifications to existing Federal and State student assistance programs necessary to increase their relevance to the lifelong learning needs of all adults;

"(iv) the organization and design of funding for pre- and post-retirement training and education for the elderly; and

"(v) modifications to Federal and State manpower training, public employment, unemployment compensation, and similar funding programs so as to better facilitate lifelong education and training and retraining, for employment.

"(b) After consultation with appropriate State agencies, the

Assistant Secretary is authorized—

"(1) to assist in the planning and assessment, to determine whether in each State there is an equitable distribution of lifelong learning services to all segments of the adult population;

"(2) to assist in assessing the appropriate roles for the Federal, State, and local governments, educational institutions and community organizations; and

"(3) to assist in considering alternative methods of financing and delivering lifelong learning opportunities, including—

"(A) identification of State agencies, institutions, and groups that plan and provide programs of lifelong learning,

"(B) determination of the extent to which programs are available geographically,

"(C) a description of demographic characteristics of the population served,

"(D) analysis of reasons for attendance in programs of lifelong learning, and

"(E) analysis of sources of funds for the conduct of lifelong learning programs, and the financial support of persons attending programs of lifelong learning.

"(c) The Assistant Secretary is authorized, with respect to lifelong learning, to assess, evaluate the need for, demonstrate, and develop alternative methods to improve—

"(1) research and development activities;

"(2) training and retraining people to become educators of adults;

"(3) development of curricula and delivery systems appropriate to the needs of any such programs;

"(4) development of techniques and systems for guidance and counseling of adults and for training and retraining of counselors;

"(5) development and dissemination of instructional materials appropriate to adults;

"(6) assessment of the educational needs and goals of

older and retired persons and their unique contributions to
lifelong learning programs;

"(7) use of employer and union tuition assistance and
other educational programs, educational and cultural trust
funds and other similar educational benefits resulting from
collective bargaining agreements, and other private funds
for the support of lifelong learning;

"(8) integration of public and private educational
funds which encourage participation in lifelong learning,
including support of guidance and counseling of workers
in order that they can make best use of funds available to
them for lifelong learning opportunities; and

"(9) coordination within communities among educators, employers, labor organizations, and other appropriate
individuals and entities to assure that lifelong learning opportunities are designed to meet projected career and occupational needs of the community, after consideration of
the availability of guidance and counseling, the availability
of information regarding occupational and career opportunities, and the availability of appropriate educational and
other resources to meet the career and occupational needs
of the community.

"(d) In carrying out the provisions of this section the Assistant Secretary is authorized to enter into agreements with, and to
make grants to, appropriate State agencies, institutions of higher
education, and public and private nonprofit organizations.

"(e) In carrying out the provisions of this section, the Assistant Secretary shall issue reports summarizing research and analysis conducted pursuant to this section, and shall develop the resources and capability to analyze and make recommendations
regarding specific legislative or administrative proposals which
may be considered by the President or by the Congress.

"REPORTS

"SEC. 134. The Assistant Secretary shall transmit to the President and to the Congress a report on such results from the activities conducted pursuant to this part as may be completed by Jan-

uary 1, 1978, together with such legislative recommendations as he may deem appropriate. The Assistant Secretary shall similarly report annually thereafter."

SEC. 125. Part A of Title IV of the Act is amended by redesignating subpart 5, and all references thereto, as subpart 6, and by inserting immediately after subpart 4 the following new subpart:

"SUBPART 5—EDUCATIONAL INFORMATION

"PROGRAM AUTHORIZATION

"SEC. 418A. (a) The Commissioner shall, in accordance with the provisions of this subpart, make grants to States to pay the Federal share of the cost of planning, establishing, and operating Educational Information Centers to provide educational information, guidance, counseling, and referral services for all individuals, including individuals residing in rural areas.

"(b) (1) For the purpose of enabling the Commissioner to carry out this subpart, there are authorized to be appropriated $20,000,000 for fiscal year 1977, $30,000,000 for fiscal year 1978, and $40,000,000 for fiscal year 1979.

"(2) The Commissioner shall allocate funds appropriated in each year under this subpart to each State submitting a plan approved under section 418B an amount which bears the same ratio to such funds as the population of such State bears to the population of all the States, except that for each fiscal year no State which submitted an approved plan shall receive from such funds less than $50,000 for that year. In making allocations under this paragraph, the Commissioner shall use the latest available actual data, including data on previous participation, which is satisfactory to him.

"(c) The Federal share of the cost of planning, establishing, and operating Educational Information Centers for any fiscal year under this subpart shall be 66⅔ per centum, and the non-Federal share may be in cash or in kind.

"(d) For the purposes of this subpart, the term 'Educational

Information Center' means an institution or agency, or combination of institutions or agencies, organized to provide services to a population in a geographical area no greater than that which will afford all persons within the area reasonable access to the services of the Center. Such services shall include—

"(1) information and talent search services designed to seek out and encourage participation in full-time and part-time postsecondary education or training of persons who could benefit from such education or training if it were not for cultural or financial barriers, physical handicap, deficiencies in secondary education, or lack of information about available programs or financial assistance;

"(2) information and referral services to persons within the area served by the Center, including such services with regard to—

"(A) postsecondary education and training programs in the region and procedures and requirements for applying and gaining acceptance to such programs;

"(B) available Federal, State, and other financial assistance, including information on procedures to be followed in applying for such assistance;

"(C) available assistance for job placement or gaining admission to postsecondary education institutions including, but not limited to, such institutions offering professional, occupational, technical, vocational, work-study, cooperative education, or other education programs designed to prepare persons for careers, or for retraining, continuing education, or upgrading of skills;

"(D) competency-based learning opportunities, including opportunities for testing of existing competencies for the purpose of certification, awarding of credit, or advance placement in postsecondary education programs;

"(E) guidance and counseling services designed to assist persons from the area served by the Center to identify postsecondary education or training opportunities, including part-time opportunities for individuals who are employed, appropriate to their needs and in relationship to each individual's career plans; and

"(F) remedial or tutorial services designed to prepare persons for postsecondary education opportunities or training programs, including such services provided to persons enrolled in postsecondary education institutions within the area served by the Center.

Services may be provided by a Center either directly or by way of contract or other agreement with agencies and institutions within the area to be served by the Center.

"(e) Nothing in this subpart shall be construed to affect funds allocated to the establishment and operation of Educational Opportunity Centers for the disadvantaged pursuant to section 417 (B) (b) (4) of this part.

"ADMINISTRATION OF STATE PROGRAMS

"SEC. 418B. (a) Each State receiving a grant under this part is authorized in accordance with its State plan submitted pursuant to subsection (b) of this section, to make grants to, and contracts with, institutions of higher education, including institutions with vocational and career education programs, and combinations of such institutions, public and private agencies and organizations, and local education agencies in combination with any institution of higher education, for planning, establishing, and operating Educational Information Centers within the State.

"(b) Any State desiring to receive a grant under this subpart shall submit for the approval of the Commissioner a State plan, which shall include—

"(1) a comprehensive strategy for establishment or expansion of Educational Information Centers, designed to achieve the goal, within a reasonable period of time, of making available within reasonable distance to all residents of the State the services of an Educational Information Center;

"(2) assurances concerning the source and availability

of State, local, and private funds to meet the non-Federal
share of the cost of the State plan required by section 418A
(c); and

"TITLE X—ESTABLISHMENT AND EXPANSION OF COMMUNITY COLLEGES."

(2) Such title is amended by striking out

"PART A—ESTABLISHMENT AND EXPANSION OF COMMUNITY COLLEGES

"SUBPART 1—STATEWIDE PLANS"

and inserting in lieu thereof:

"PART A—STATEWIDE PLANS."

(3) Section 1001 (a) of the Act is amended by striking out
"subpart" and inserting in lieu thereof "part."

(4) Section 1001 (b) (1) of the Act is amended to read as
follows:

"(b) (1) There are authorized to be appropriated $15,700,000
for each of the fiscal years ending prior to October 1, 1979, to carry
out the provisions of this section."

(5) Section 1001 of the Act is further amended by striking
the last sentence of subsection (c) and inserting in lieu thereof:
"The Commissioner shall not disapprove any plan unless he determines, after reasonable notice and opportunity for hearing and
comment, that it is inconsistent with the requirements set forth in
this section."

(b) (1) Such title is further amended by striking out "Subpart
2" in the heading following section 1001 and inserting in lieu
thereof "Part B."

(2) (A) Section 1011 (a) of the Act is amended by striking
out "subpart" and inserting in lieu thereof "part."

(B) Section 1011 (b) of the Act is amended to read as follows:

"(b) For the purpose of carrying out this part, there are authorized to be appropriated $150,000,000 for each of the fiscal
years ending prior to October 1, 1979."

(3) Section 1012 (b) of the Act is amended by striking out "subpart" and inserting in lieu thereof "part."

(c) Part B of Title X of the Act as in effect prior to the amendments made by subsection (b) of this section is repealed.

(d) The amendments made by paragraphs (1), (2), (3) of subsection (a), paragraphs (1), 2(A), (3) of subsection (b), and subsection (c) shall take effect on September 30, 1977.

EXPANSION GRANTS

Sec. 177. Section 1014 of the Act is amended to read as follows:

"EXPANSION GRANTS

"Sec. 1014. (a) The Commissioner is authorized to make grants, consistent with the terms of the appropriate State plan approved under section 1001, to existing community colleges to enable them to carry out the provisions of subsections (b) and (c) of this section. Of the funds appropriated for subpart 2 of this part, the Commissioner shall make grants pursuant to subsection (b), before making grants under any other subsection or section of this subpart, until such time as he determines all approved requests relating to subsection (b) have been funded.

"(b) The Commissioner is authorized to make grants to eligible institutions to assist them in modifying their educational programs and instructional delivery systems to provide educational programs especially suited to those persons whose educational needs have been inadequately served, especially those among the handicapped, older persons, persons who can attend only part-time, and persons who otherwise would be unlikely to continue their education beyond the high school. Such programs may include, but are not limited to, methods designed to eliminate such barriers to student access as inflexible course schedules, location of instructional programs, and inadequate transportation.

"(c) The Commissioner is also authorized to make grants to eligible institutions to assist them in expanding their enrollment capacity or in establishing new educational sites as documented in the State plan. Any grants related to facilities may only be made to institutions which have provided the Commissioner with such assurances as he requires that they have first explored the possibilities of using existing facilities on the campus of the applying institution, existing facilities in the community which are suitable and available for educational programs without unreasonable cost to the institution, and explored the willingness of other institutions within a reasonable commuting distance to provide educational programs, or space or other components of an educational delivery system, through contract or other agreement with the institution."

REVISION OF DEFINITION OF COMMUNITY COLLEGE

SEC. 178 Paragraphs (2) and (3) of section 1018 of the Act are amended to read as follows:

"(2) admits as regular students persons who are high school graduates or the equivalent, or beyond the age of compulsory school attendance;

"(3) provides a postsecondary education program leading to an associate degree or acceptable for credit toward a bachelor's degree;".

CHAPTER SIX

Information Resources: Organizations, Publications, and Projects

Judith Bonnett Hirabayashi

This chapter is in the nature of a set of directories. It is intended as a guide to information and other assistance for lifelong learning policy makers and program planners. As will be apparent, there are a great many organizations with interests, programs, and expertise related to lifelong learning. The assumption underlying this chapter is that planners ought not to do their work in a vacuum—their policies and plans are likely to be effective to the extent they are informed by the knowledge and experience of others.

Much, though not all, of the information presented here is contained in other publications. We have attempted to be current—as of late 1978. Other directories are also "current" as of their publication dates—1976, 1977, and early 1978. Rapid advancements are being made in the general fields of adult education and lifelong learning. New organizations and publications come into existence monthly, and planners are urged to consult new directories as they become available, and also older ones.

Basic Sources of Information

Clearinghouse ADELL (Adult Education and Lifelong Learning) is a resource with which users of this volume should be familiar. Funded by the Division of Adult Education of U.S. Office of Education, its goal is to facilitate national coordination, dissemination, and utilization of information for the benefit of the adult education community. In its primary function as a referral source, the Clearinghouse seeks to be an active networking organization with links to numerous organizations in the field. In response to requests, it specifies relevant resources together with explanations of the types of information to be expected. ADELL provides access to information on any aspect of adult education to anyone involved or concerned with the field, free of charge. Its toll-free number is 800-638-6628 (in Maryland, 301-770-3000). Its address is Clearinghouse ADELL, Informatics, Inc., 6011 Executive Blvd., Rockville, MD 20852.

Another key information source is the national Educational Resources Information Center (ERIC)—a nationwide information system that disseminates educational research results, research-related materials, and other resource information. It specializes in noncopyrighted, unpublished material such as project reports, speech texts, research findings, locally produced materials, reviews of literature, bibliographies, conference papers, speeches, and newsletters. ERIC uses a national system of clearinghouses to gather, index, and catalogue these materials. Each of ERIC's sixteen clearinghouses specializes in a particular subject area of education. Addresses and phone numbers of the clearinghouses pertinent to lifelong learning are given at a later point in this chapter.

ERIC provides two major information services. First, it provides readable medium-length abstracts of all materials. These are contained in two monthly catalogs, *Resources in Education (RIE)* and *Current Index to Journals in Education (CIJE)*, which are available at many educational libraries, information centers, and departments of education. *RIE* provides summaries of the usually unpublished education-related reports. *CIJE* is devoted exclusively to periodical literature in the field of education.

Second, ERIC furnishes inexpensive microfiche of the complete text of many noncopyrighted and unpublished materials. Documents cited in *RIE* are available in microfiche from the ERIC Document Reproduction Service. Information on how to order is found in any recent issue of *RIE*. For the articles indexed in *CIJE*, a reprint service is available from University Microfilms International, Article Copy Service—*CIJE*, 300 North Zeeb Road, Ann Arbor, MI 48106.

Three comprehensive information sources have been compiled under the sponsorship of the National Institute of Education (NIE). The first, the *1978 Directory of Resources for the Education of Adults,* was prepared by ERIC Clearinghouse on Adult, Career, and Vocational Education in cooperation with the Adult Education Association of the U.S.A. Its narrative section includes strategies for finding resources in a dozen adult learning "problem situations"; the areas covered range from program management and funding to self-directed learning and the teaching of handicapped learners. The directory contains sections on training programs for educating adults; governmental and private agencies, organizations, and associations; research centers; information systems; publications and publishers; and sources of demographic data. The *Directory* is to be available early in 1979 from National Center Publications at Ohio State University (1960 Kenny Road, Columbus, OH 43210).

The second source, *Resources for Educational Issues, 1978,* is directed to policy makers concerned with education at all levels. Volume I, *Basic Sources of Information in Education,* directs the planner to resources such as yearbooks, statistical sources, associations, and sources of information about federal projects. Volume II focuses on resources relevant to three important educational issues—

accountability, governance, and competency-based education—and is primarily directed to planners of primary and secondary education. Prepared by Southwest Educational Development Laboratory (211 E. 7th Street, Austin, TX 78701), the two reports are available through ERIC.

Third is *Higher Education Planning—A Bibliographic Handbook* (Halstead, 1978), which seeks to alert planners to important recent books in twenty-two topical areas of higher education. Experts in the different areas—ranging from "Admission, Retention, Articulation" to "Work and Education"—each contributed a short overview of the area plus summaries of a small number of selected books in the area. The topic of "Equal Opportunity" is divided into several subtopics; one is "Adult Learners," which includes descriptions of six key books. Numerous other parts of the volume would also be of interest to broad-gauge planners. Individual copies are free from the National Institute of Education.

A final compendium of information warranting mention is the *Yearbook of Adult and Continuing Education.* Published by Marquis Academic Media (200 East Ohio Street, Chicago, IL 60611), it consists almost entirely of previously published articles and reports. The 1977–78 edition is divided into sections on adult education, lifelong learning, education for the elderly, professional continuing education, cooperative education/career education, alternatives and innovation, and organizations. The section entitled "Alternatives and Innovations," for example, contains articles on the University of Mid-America, the University Without Walls, contract learning, free universities, educational brokering, crediting prior learning, library-based education, and courses by newspaper.

Numerous broad-ranging books and monographs contain extensive bibliographies. Particularly useful are Broschart (1977), Cross (1978c), Halstead (1978), Harrington (1977), Hiemstra (1976), Houle (1973), Knox (1977), Lifelong Learning Project (1978), Penland (1977), and Shulman (1978). An exceptionally valuable resource in this regard is a report stemming from the NCES/NCHEMS Handbook Project (described later in this chapter), which contains a comprehensive review and synthesis of recent literature related to adult learning opportunities, together with annotations of close to 400 documents (Segal, 1977). An extensive bibliography on state and local planning for adult education opportunities is available from George Nolfi at University Consultants, Inc. (45 Hancock Street, Cambridge, MA 02139). Finally, annotated bibliographies and other documents on worldwide lifelong learning developments are available from UNESCO (Adult Education Section, 7 Place de Fontenoy, 75700 Paris) and the Organization for Economic Cooperation and Development (OECD, Centre for Educational Research and Innovation, Château de la Muette, Paris).

Nongovernmental Organizations

Of all the nonprofit, nongovernmental organizations advancing adult and lifelong learning concepts or actually providing such services, the following 100 organizations seem to be the most actively interested in extending lifelong learning opportunities in the United States. They are divided into three categories: (1) organizations of educators and other providers of adult learning services, (2) organizations of recipients, or consumers, of adult learning services, and (3) other interested organizations, primarily providers of noninstructional, research, testing, and policy analysis services. These organizations, all of which have their own special interests, provide various kinds of information. Many conduct research and publish special reports; most have directories of member institutions; many publish journals or newsletters. Such materials are generally available to nonmembers as well as members. The list, which gives a reasonably good sense of the many interested parties, could be used to structure advisory panels and communication networks for policy, research, demonstration, and other projects. And it could also be used in fashioning coalitions necessary for *advocating* particular policies to government agencies.

Organizations of Providers of Education

Adult Education Action Council
4201 Cathedral Avenue, NW
Suite 1205 East
Washington, DC 20016
(202) 244-6167

*Adult Education Association of the
USA*
810 18th Street, NW
Washington, DC 20006
(202) 347-9574

*American Association of
  Community and Junior Colleges*
One Dupont Circle, NW
Suite 410
Washington, DC 20036
(202) 293-7050

*American Association for Higher
  Education*
One Dupont Circle, NW
Suite 780
Washington, DC 20036
(202) 293-6440

*American Association of State
  Colleges and Universities*
One Dupont Circle, NW
Suite 700
Washington, DC 20036
(202) 293-7070

American Council on Education
One Dupont Circle, NW
Suite 800
Washington, DC 20036
(202) 833-4700

*American Federation of Teachers,
  AFL-CIO*
11 Dupont Circle, NW
Washington, DC 20036
(202) 797-4400

American Library Association
50 East Huron Street
Chicago, IL 60611
(312) 944-6780

*American Management
  Associations*
135 West 50th Street
New York, NY 10020
(212) 584-8100

American Museum Association
2233 Wisconsin Avenue, NW
Washington, DC 20007
(202) 338-5300

*American Society for Training and
  Development*
P.O. Box 5307
Madison, WI 53705
(608) 274-3440

American Vocational Association
1510 H Street, NW
Washington, DC 20005
(202) 737-3722

Association of American Colleges
1818 R Street, NW
Washington, DC 20009
(202) 387-3760

*Association for Continuing Higher
  Education*
1700 Asp Avenue
Norman, OK 73069
(405) 325-1021

*Association for Continuing
  Professional Education*
402 Graham Hall
Northern Illinois University
DeKalb, IL 60115
(815) 753-1847

*Association for Independent
Colleges and Schools*
1730 M Street, NW
Suite 410
Washington, DC 20036
(202) 659-2460

*Association for Innovation in
Higher Education*
Box 12560
St. Petersburg, FL 33733
(813) 867-1166

Broadcast Education Association
1771 N Street, NW
Washington, DC 20036
(202) 293-3519

*Canadian Association for Adult
Education*
29 Prince Arthur Avenue
Toronto, Ontario, M5R 1B2
Canada
(416) 924-6607

*Coalition of Adult Education
Organizations*
810 18th Street, NW
Washington, DC 20006
(202) 347-9574

*Coalition for Alternatives in
Postsecondary Education*
1211 Connecticut Avenue, NW
Suite 301
Washington, DC 20036
(202) 466-2450

Cooperative Education Association
c/o Drexel University
32nd and Chestnut Streets
Philadelphia, PA 19104
(215) 895-2186

*Corporation for Public
Broadcasting*
1111 16th Street, NW
Washington, DC 20036
(202) 293-6160

*Council of National Organizations
for Adult Education*
1740 Broadway, 17th Floor
New York, NY 10019
(212) 581-0500

*Council for Noncollegiate
Continuing Education*
6 N. 6th Street
Richmond, VA 23219
(804) 648-6742

*Folk College Association of
America*
CPO 287
Berea, KY 40404
(606) 986-9341 Ext. 453

*International Council for Adult
Education*
29 Prince Arthur Avenue
Toronto, Ontario M5R 1B2
Canada

International Reading Association
800 Barksdale Road
Newark, DE 19711
(302) 731-1600

Interversitas
Northeastern Illinois
  University
5500 N. St. Louis Avenue
Chicago, IL 60624
(312) 583-4050 Ext. 421

Literacy Volunteers of America
700 E. Water Street
Room 623, Midtown Plaza
Syracuse, NY 13210
(315) 437-8381

National Association of County
  Agricultural Agents
203 West Nueva
Room 310
San Antonio, TX 78207

National Association of
  Educational Broadcasting
1346 Connecticut Avenue, NW
Washington, DC 20036
(202) 785-1100

National Association of
  Independent Colleges and
  Universities
1717 Massachusetts Avenue,
  NW
Suite 503
Washington, DC 20036
(202) 387-7623

National Association for Public
  Continuing and Adult
  Education
1201 16th Street, NW
Suite 429
Washington, DC 20036
(202) 833-5486

National Association of Trade and
  Technical Schools
2021 K Street, NW
Washington, DC 20006
(202) 296-8892

National Commission on
  Cooperative Education
360 Huntington Avenue
Boston, MA 02115
(617) 437-3778

National Community Education
  Association
1030 15th Street, NW
Suite 536
Washington, DC 20005
(202) 466-3530

National Council on Adult Jewish
  Education
114 Fifth Avenue
New York, NY 10011
(212) 675-5656

National Council of Churches of
  Christ in the USA
475 Riverside Drive
Room 880
New York, NY 10027
(212) 870-2511

*National Council on Community
  Services and Continuing
  Education*
One Dupont Circle, NW
Suite 410
Washington, DC 20036
(202) 293-7050

*National Council for Public
  Service Internship Programs*
1735 I Street, NW
Washington, DC 20006
(202) 331-1516

*National Council of State
  Directors of Adult Education*
1201 16th Street, NW
Suite 429
Washington, DC 20036
(202) 833-5489

*National Council of Urban
  Administrators of Adult
  Education*
1201 16th Street, NW
Suite 429
Washington, DC 20036
(202) 833-5486

National Education Association
1201 16th Street, NW
Washington, DC 20036
(202) 833-4000

National Educational Television
10 Columbus Circle
New York, NY 10019
(212) 262-4200

*National Extension Homemakers
  Council*
Route One, Box 129
Bunker Hill, IN 46914
(317) 689-7118

National Home Study Council
1601 18th Street, NW
Washington, DC 20009
(202) 234-5100

*National Indian Education
  Association*
3036 University Avenue, SE
Minneapolis, MN 55414
(612) 378-0482

*National Manpower Training
  Association*
591 Washington Street
Memphis, TN 38105
(901) 526-6555

National Public Radio
2025 M Street, NW
Washington, DC 20036
(202) 785-5400

*National Recreation and Park
  Association*
1601 North Kent Street
Arlington, VA 22209
(703) 525-0606

*National University Extension
  Association*
One Dupont Circle, NW
Suite 360
Washington, DC 20036
(202) 659-3220

North American Association of
    Summer Sessions
Box 1145
Washington University
St. Louis, MO 63130
(314) 889-5000

Public Broadcasting Service
475 L'Enfant Plaza West, SW
Washington, DC 20024
(202) 488-5000

Public Service Satellite Consortium
4040 Sorrento Valley
    Boulevard
San Diego, CA 92121
(714) 452-1140

Religious Education Association
409 Prospect Street
New Haven, CT 06510
(203) 865-6141

Society for Field Experience
    Education
College of Charleston
Charleston, SC 29401
(803) 722-0181

State Higher Education Executive
    Officers
Education Commission of the
    States
1860 Lincoln Street
Suite 300
Denver, CO 80295
(303) 893-5200

Union for Experimenting Colleges
    and Universities
930 Corry Street
Yellow Springs, OH 45387
(513) 767-7655

Organizations of Education Recipients

American Association of Retired
    Persons
1909 K Street, NW
Washington, DC 20006
(202) 872-4800

American Association of University
    Women
2401 Virginia Avenue, NW
Washington, DC 20037
(202) 785-7700

American Federation of Labor/
    Congress of Industrial
    Organizations
815 17th Street, NW
Washington, DC 20006
(202) 637-5141

Association for Hospital Medical
    Education
1911 Jefferson Davis Highway
Suite 905
Arlington, VA 22202
(703) 521-1133

B'nai B'rith
1640 Rhode Island Avenue,
NW
Washington, DC 20036
(202) 393-5284

Center for Displaced Homemakers
Mills College
Oakland, CA 94613
(415) 632-2700

*Center for the Study of Parent
Involvement*
5240 Boyd Avenue
Oakland, CA 94618
(415) 658-7557

Institute of Lifetime Learning
1909 K Street, NW
Washington, DC 20049
(202) 872-4800

League of Women Voters
1730 M Street, NW
Washington, DC 20036
(202) 296-1770

*National Association for Industry-
Education Cooperation*
235 Hendricks Boulevard
Buffalo, NY 14226
(716) 278-5760

*National Coalition for
Instructional
Telecommunications*
Nova University
3301 College Ave
Fort Lauderdale, FL
(305) 587-6660

National Council on Aging
1828 L Street, NW
Washington, DC 20036
(202) 223-6250

*National Council of Negro
Women*
1346 Connecticut Avenue, NW
Washington, DC 20036
(202) 223-2363

*National Council of Senior
Citizens*
1511 K Street, NW
Washington, DC 20005
(202) 783-6850

*National Retired Teachers
Association*
1909 K Street, NW
Washington, DC
(202) 872-4800

*Rural/Regional Education
Association*
1201 16th Street, NW
Washington, DC 20036
(202) 833-4460

United Auto Workers
1125 15th Street, NW
Washington, DC 20005
(202) 296-7484

United States Association of
  Evening Students
950 North Erie Avenue
Lindenhurst, NY 11757
(516) 957-0158

University and College Labor
  Education Association
580 Spruce Street
Morgantown, WV 26505
(304) 293-3323

Women's Lobby
110 Maryland Avenue, NE
Washington, DC 20002
(202) 547-0044

Other Interested Organizations

Academy for Educational
  Development
680 Fifth Avenue
New York, NY 10019
(212) 397-0040

Adult Education Research
  Conference
160 Gabel Hall
DeKalb, IL 60115
(815) 753-1448

Adult Student Personnel
  Association
Hostos Community College
475 Grand Concourse ,
Bronx, NY 10451
(212) 960-1200

American College Personnel
  Association
1607 New Hampshire Avenue,
  NW
Washington, DC 20009
(202) 483-4633

American College Testing
  Program
2201 North Dodge Street
P.O. Box 168
Iowa City, IA 52240
(319) 356-3711

American Institute of Cooperation
1129 20th Street, NW
Washington, DC 20036
(202) 296-6825

Aspen Institute for Humanistic
  Studies
1000 North Third Street
Aspen, CO 81611
(303) 925-7010

Association of American Publishers
1 Park Avenue
New York, NY 10016
(212) 689-8920

Association of Computer-Based Systems for Career Information
670 American Center Building
150 East Kellogg Boulevard
St. Paul, MN 55101

Association for Gerontology in Higher Education
1835 K Street, NW
Suite 305
Washington, DC 20006
(202) 466-6750

Carnegie Council on Policy Studies in Higher Education
2150 Shattuck Avenue
Berkeley, CA 94704
(415) 849-4474

The College Board
888 7th Avenue
New York, NY 10019
(212) 582-6210

Commission of Professors of Adult Education
Department of Education
Room 276
University of Illinois
Urbana, IL 61801
(217) 333-7368

The Commission on Voluntary Service and Action
475 Riverside Drive
New York, NY 10027
(212) 870-2707

Council for the Advancement of Experiential Learning
American City Building
Suite 208
Columbia, MD 21044
(301) 997-3535

Council for Advancement and Support of Education
One Dupont Circle, NW
Suite 530
Washington, DC 20036
(202) 659-3820

Council on the Continuing Education Unit
Evening College and Summer Session
Shaffer Hall
Johns Hopkins University
Baltimore, MD 21218
(301) 338-7190

Council for Financial Aid to Education
680 Fifth Avenue
New York, NY 10019
(212) 541-4050

Council on Postsecondary Accreditation
One Dupont Circle, NW
Suite 760
Washington, DC 20036
(202) 452-1433

*Education Commission of the
States*
1860 Lincoln Street
Suite 300
Denver, CO 80203
(303) 893-5200

Educational Testing Service
Rosedale Road
Princeton, NJ 08540
(609) 921-9000

*Extension Committee on
Organization Policy*
National Association of State
Universities and Land-Grant
Colleges
One Dupont Circle, NW
Suite 710
Washington, DC 20036
(202) 293-7120

*Institute of International
Education*
809 United Nations Plaza
New York, NY 10017
(212) 883-8200

Institute for Responsive Education
704 Commonwealth Avenue
Boston, MA 02215
(617) 353-3309

Manpower Education Institute
127 East 35th Street
New York, NY 10017
(212) 532-4747

National Academy of Education
11 Dupont Circle, NW
Suite 130
Washington, DC 20036
(202) 232-7600

*National Affiliation for Literacy
Advance*
1011 Harrison Street
Syracuse, NY 13210
(315) 422-9121

*National Association for Human
Development*
1750 Pennsylvania Avenue
Washington, DC 20006
(202) 393-1882

*National Center for Educational
Brokering*
1211 Connecticut Avenue, NW
Suite 400
Washington, DC 20036
(202) 466-5530

*National Commission on Libraries
and Information Science*
1717 K Street, NW
Suite 601
Washington, DC 20037
(202) 653-6252

*National Institute of Labor
Education*
Federal City College
1424 K Street, NW
Washington, DC 20005
(202) 727-1000

National Manpower Institute
1211 Connecticut Avenue, NW
Suite 301
Washington, DC 20036
(202) 466-4420

National School Volunteer
  Program
300 North Washington Street
Alexandria, VA 22314
(703) 836-4880

National Urban League
425 13th Street, NW
Washington, DC 20004
(202) 393-4332

National Vocational Guidance
  Association
1607 New Hampshire Avenue,
  NW
Washington, DC 20009
(202) 483-4633

Work in America Institute
700 White Plains Road
Scarsdale, NY 10583
(914) 472-9600

World Education
1414 Sixth Avenue
New York, NY 10019
(212) 838-5255

Federal Statutory Advisory Councils

These groups, whose members are presidential appointees, have staffs who prepare annual reports, occasionally conduct surveys, prepare policy papers, and engage heavily in lobbying. Published materials from all these activities are usually available to anyone interested.

Community Education Advisory
  Council
Regional Office Building No. 3
Room 5622
7th and D Streets, SW
Washington, DC 20202
(202) 245-0691

National Advisory Council on
  Adult Education
425 13th Street, NW
Suite 323
Washington, DC 20004
(202) 376-8892

National Advisory Council for
  Career Education
Regional Office Building No. 3
Room 3100
7th and D Streets, SW
Washington, DC 20202
(202) 245-2284

*National Advisory Council on
    Extension and Continuing
    Education*
425 13th Street, NW
Suite 529
Washington, DC 20004
(202) 376-8888

*National Adivsory Council on
    Vocational Education*
425 13th Street, NW
Washington, DC 20004
(202) 376-8873

*National Advisory Council on
    Women's Educational Programs*
1832 M Street, NW
Suite 821
Washington, DC 20036
(202) 382-3862

Clearinghouses

The primary function of clearinghouses is to provide information; they should be able to respond helpfully to almost any kind of request, either broadly (within the purview of the particular clearinghouse) or narrowly gauged. Several nongovernmental organizations listed earlier are also listed here as clearinghouses. Presumably, the new Clearinghouse ADELL (Adult Education and Lifelong Learning), owing to its broad charge, will be of particularly great use to persons seeking information about all facets of lifelong learning.

*The Adult Performance Level
    (APL) Project*
Extension Building 202
University of Texas
Austin, TX 78712
(512) 471-4623

*American Society for Training and
    Development*
P.O. Box 5307
Madison, WI 53705
(608) 274-3440

Brookdale Center on Aging
Hunter College
129 E. 79th Street
New York, NY 10021
(212) 744-2386

*Center for Alternatives In/To
    Higher Education*
1118 S. Harrison
East Lansing, MI 48823
(517) 332-0861

Center for Community Education
American Association for
  Community and Junior
  Colleges
One Dupont Circle, NW
Suite 410
Washington, DC 20036
(202) 293-7050

Center for Education and Work
National Manpower Institute
1211 Connecticut Avenue, NW
Suite 301
Washington, DC 20036
(202)466-4420

*Center for Helping Organizations
  Improve Choice in Education
  (CHOICE)*
Department of Higher/
  Postsecondary Education
227 Huntington Hall
Syracuse, NY 13210
(315) 423-3701/4761

Center for Museum Education
George Washington University
Washington, DC 20052
(202) 676-6682

Center for Personalized Instruction
Georgetown University
Washington, DC 20057
(202) 625-3176

Center for Vocational Education
Ohio State University
1960 Kenny Road
Columbus, OH 43210
(614) 486-3655

Clearinghouse ADELL (ADULT
  EDUCATION AND LIFELONG
  LEARNING)
Informatics, Inc.
6000 Executive Blvd.
Rockville, MD 20852
(800) 638-6628 Toll-Free
(301) 770-3000 Maryland
  Residents

*Clearinghouse for Community
  Based Free Standing
  Educational Institutions*
1806 Vernon Street, NW
Washington, DC 20009
(202) 638-7934

*Clearinghouse—Resources for
  Educators of Adults*
224 Huntington Hall
Syracuse University
Syracuse, NY 13210
(315) 423-3034

The College Board
Future Directions for a
  Learning Society Project
888 Seventh Avenue
New York, NY 10019
(212) 582-6210

The Commission on Voluntary Service and Action
475 Riverside Drive
New York, NY 10027
(212) 870-2707

Consortium for Public Library Innovation
300 Nicolet Mall
Minneapolis, MN 55401
(612) 372-6611

Cooperative Education Research Center
408 Churchill Hall
Northeastern University
Boston, MA 02115
(617) 437-3780

Council for the Advancement of Experiential Learning (CAEL)
American City Building
Suite 208
Columbia, MD 21044
(301) 997-3535

Education for Aging Resource Center
Montclair State College
Montclair, NJ 07043
(201) 893-4318

Education Commission of the States
1860 Lincoln Street
Suite 300
Denver, CO 80295
(303) 893-5200

ERIC Clearinghouse on Adult, Career, and Vocational Education
National Center for Research in Vocational Education
Ohio State University
1960 Kenny Road
Columbus, OH 43210
(614) 486-3655

ERIC Clearinghouse on Counseling and Personnel Services
University of Michigan
2108 School of Education Building
Ann Arbor, MI 48104
(313) 764-9492

ERIC Clearinghouse on Higher Education
One Dupont Circle, NW
Suite 630
Washington, DC 20036
(202) 296-2597

ERIC Clearinghouse on Junior Colleges
University of California at Los Angeles
96 Powell Library Building
Los Angeles, CA 90024
(213) 825-3931

ERIC Clearinghouse on Rural Education and Small Schools
New Mexico State University
Box 3AP
Las Cruces, NM 88001
(505) 646-2623

Federal Community Education
  Clearinghouse
Informatics, Inc.
6011 Executive Boulevard
Rockville, MD 20852
(800) 638-6698
(301) 770-3000

Free University Network
1221 Thurston Street
Manhattan, KS 66502
(913) 532-5866

Institute of Lifetime Learning
American Association of
  Retired Persons
1909 K Street, NW
Washington, DC 20049
(202) 872-4800

National Adult Education
  Clearinghouse
Montclair State College
848 Valley Road
Upper Montclair, NJ 07043
(201) 893-4000

National Center for Career Life
  Planning
American Management
  Associations
135 W 50 Street
New York, NY 10020
(212) 586-8100

National Center for Community
  Education
1017 Avon Street
Flint, MI 48503
(313) 238-0463

National Center for Educational
  Brokering
1211 Connecticut Avenue, NW
Suite 400
Washington, DC 20036
(202) 466-5530

National Center for Public Service
  Internships
1735 I Street, NW
Suite 601
Washington, DC 20006
(202) 331-1516

The National Center for Voluntary
  Action
1785 Massachusetts Avenue
Washington, DC 20036
(202) 467-5560

National Clearinghouse on Aging
Administration on Aging
Department of Health,
  Education, and Welfare
HEW North Building
330 Independence Avenue,
  SW
Washington, DC 20201
(202) 245-2158

National Clearinghouse for
  Commuter Programs
1195 Student Union Bldg.
University of Maryland
College Park, MD 20742
(301) 454-2807

*National Commission on
Cooperative Education*
360 Huntington Avenue
Boston, MA 02115
(617) 437-3778

National Home Study Council
1601 18th Street, NW
Washington, DC 20009
(202) 234-5100

*National Information Center on
Volunteerism*
P.O. Box 4179
Boulder, CO 80306
(303) 447-0492

*National Institute of Labor
Education*
Federal City College
1424 K Street, NW
Washington, DC 20005
(202) 727-1000

*National Rural Career Guidance
Network*
National Center for Research
in Vocational Education
Ohio State University
1960 Kenny Road
Columbus, OH 43210
(800) 848-6560

*National Self-Help Resource
Center*
2000 S Street, NW
Washington, DC 20009
(202) 338-5704

*Network of Counseling Centers
Serving Women*
Catalyst
14 East 60th Street
New York, NY 10022
(212) 759-9700

*Non-Formal Education
Information Centre*
Institute for International
Studies in Education
513 Erickson Hall
Michigan State University
East Lansing, MI 48824
(517) 355-5522

Office on Educational Credit
American Council on
Education
One Dupont Circle, NW
Washington, DC 20036
(202) 833-4772

*Resource Center for Planned
Change*
American Association of State
Colleges and Universities
One Dupont Circle, NW
Suite 700
Washington, DC 20036
(202) 293-7070

Service Center for Community College–Labor Union Cooperation
American Association of Community and Junior Colleges
One Dupont Circle, NW
Suite 410
Washington, DC 20036
(202) 293-7050

Service-Learning Resource Center
403 Breckinridge Hall
University of Kentucky
Lexington, KY 40506
(606) 258-4941

Study of Adult Education
New York State Department of Education
Albany, NY 12234
(518) 474-5972

Washington Center for Learning Alternatives
1705 De Sales Street, NW
Washington, DC 20036
(202) 659-8510

Journals

Most of the journals listed here can be found in School of Education libraries at most American universities. Foreign journals, with the exception of several from Canada and Britain, are not included. Because of its broad scope, the new periodical *Lifelong Learning: The Adult Years* will probably be the single most useful journal for broad-perspective planners.

Adult Education
Adult Education Association of the USA
810 Eighteenth Street, NW
Washington, DC 20006
Quarterly   *$7.50*

Adult Education
National Institute of Adult Education
35 Queen Anne Street
London WIM OBL England
Bimonthly   *£3.75*

Adult Education in Public Schools
New York Association of Public School Adult Educators
236 Goundry Street
North Tonawanda, NY 14120
Quarterly   *Membership*

Adult Literacy and Basic Education
203 Petrie Hall
Auburn University
Auburn, AL 36830
Quarterly   *$8.50*

Aging
Superintendent of Documents
U.S. Government Printing
   Office
Washington, DC 20402
Bimonthly $5.05

Alternative Higher Education:
   The Journal of Non-
   Traditional Studies
Human Sciences Press
72 Fifth Avenue
New York, NY 10011
Quarterly $7.95

American Education
U.S. Office of Education
400 Maryland Avenue, SW
Washington, DC 20202
Monthly $3.75

American Vocational Journal
American Vocational
   Association, Inc.
1510 H Street, NW
Washington, DC 20005
Monthly $8.00

Canadian Journal of University
   Continuing Education
Simon Fraser University
Burnaby, British Columbia
Canada V5A 1S6
Semiannually

The College Board Review
College Board Publication
   Orders
Box 2815
Princeton, NJ 08540
Quarterly $5.00

The Community Services Catalyst
Atlantic Community College
Mays Landing, NJ 08330
Biannually $2.50

Continuing Education
Data Bases
Pennsylvania Research
   Associates, Inc.
1428 Ford Road
Cornwell Heights, PA 19020
Quarterly $35.00

Continuum
The National University
   Extension Association
One Dupont Circle, NW
Washington, DC 20036
Quarterly $7.50

Convergence
International Council for
   Adult Education
29 Prince Arthur Avenue
Toronto, Ontario
Canada M5R 1B2
Quarterly $12.00

Educational Gerontology
Adult Education Program
School of Education
Virginia Commonwealth
   University
Richmond, VA 23284
Quarterly $19.50

The Futurist
World Future Society
P.O. Box 30369
Bethesda Branch
Washington, DC 20014
Bimonthly $15.00

Interface Journal
Interface Learning Collective,
  Inc.
P.O. Box 970
Utica, NY 13503
Quarterly $8.00

*International Journal of
  Continuing Education and
  Training*
Baywood Publishing Co.
43 Central Avenue
Framingdale, NY 11735
Quarterly $23.00

*Journal of the Community
  Development Society*
College of Public and
  Community Service
University of Missouri—
  Columbia
7th Floor, Clark Hall
Columbia, MO 65201
Semiannually $15.00

Journal of Extension
North Carolina State
  University
310 Poe Hall
Raleigh, NC 27607
Bimonthly $9.00

*Journal of Developmental and
  Remedial Education*
Center for Developmental
  Education
Appalachian State University
Boone, NC 28608
Three times a year $7.50

Journal of Higher Education
American Association of
  Higher Education
Ohio State University Press
2070 Neil Avenue
Columbus, OH 43210
Monthly $10.00

*Lifelong Learning: The Adult
  Years*
Adult Education Association of
  the USA
810 18th Street, NW
Washington, DC 20006
Ten times a year $18.00

Mass Media/Adult Education
State University of New York
  at Albany
1400 Washington Avenue
Albany, NY 12222
Quarterly Free

*Mountain Plains Journal of Adult
  Education*
Office of Extension Classes
University of Wyoming
P.O. Box 3274
Laramie, WY 82071
Semiannually $5.00

NAPCAE Exchange
National Association for Public
    Continuing and Adult
    Education
1201 16th Street, NW
Washington, DC 20036
Three times a year $7.00

Parks & Recreation
National Recreation and Park
    Association
1700 Pennsylvania Avenue
Washington, DC 20006
Monthly $7.50

Prospects
UNESCO Press
7 Place de Fontenoy
75700 Paris, France
Quarterly $12.50

Public Telecommunications Review
National Association of
    Education Broadcasters
1346 Connecticut Avenue, NW
Washington, DC 20036
Bimonthly $20.00

Reports
World Education
1414 Sixth Avenue
New York, NY 10019
Quarterly $5.00

Teaching Adults
National Institute of Adult
    Education
35 Queen Anne Street
London, WIM OBL England
Quarterly   £0.80

Techniques for Teachers of Adults
National Association for Public
    Continuing and Adult
    Education
1201 16th Street, NW
Washington, DC 20036
Eight times a year $5.00

*Technological Horizons in
    Education (T.H.E.) Journal*
Information Synergy, Inc.
P.O. Box 992
Acton, MA 01720
Bimonthly $15.00

*Training and Development
    Journal*
American Society for Training
    and Development
P.O. Box 5307
Madison, WI 53705
Monthly $20.00

World Education's Reports
World Education
1414 6th Avenue
New York, NY 10019
Nine times a year   *Free*

Newsletters

To an even greater extent than journals, newsletters are specialized—reflecting the interests and activities of their respective organizations or publishers. Obviously, the following list is a small selection; almost every national organization gets out a newsletter of some kind. Because of its breadth of coverage and lively writing, *Adult and Continuing Education Today* is by all odds the most useful and readable newsletter available for people concerned with lifelong learning—particularly federal activities. Within its narrower focus, the (no-cost) *Bulletin* of the National Center for Educational Brokering is also an excellent source of information.

AARP Bulletin
American Association of
  Retired Persons
215 Long Beach Boulevard
Long Beach, CA 90801
Monthly   *$3.00*

ACTivity
The American College Testing
  Program
P.O. Box 168
Iowa City, IA 52240
Quarterly   *Free*

*Administrator's Swap Shop
  Newsletter*
National Association for Public
  Continuing and Adult
  Education
1201 16th Street, NW
Washington, DC 20036
Bimonthly   *$8.00*

*Adult and Continuing Education
  Today*
Today Publications
National Press Building
Washington, DC 20045
Biweekly   *$36.00*

*Adult Education Clearinghouse
  Newsletter*
Montclair State College
Dept. of Adult Continuing
  Education
Upper Montclair, NJ 07043
Monthly   *$5.00*

*Adult Education Information
  Notes*
Adult Education Section
Division of Structures,
  Contents, Methods, and
  Techniques of Education
UNESCO
7 Place de Fontenoy
75700 Paris, France
Quarterly   *Free*

AEA Dateline
Adult Education Association
810 18th Street, NW
Washington, DC 20006
Monthly   *Free*

*American Family National Action
    Overview*
Wakefield Washington
    Associates
1129 20th Street, NW
Washington, DC 20236
Bimonthly $35.00

*Association of University Evening
    Colleges Newsletter*
Bradley University Evening
    College
Peoria, IL 61606
Quarterly $5.00

Bulletin
National Center for
    Educational Brokering
405 Oak Street
Syracuse, NY 13203
Monthly   Free

CAEL Newsletter
Council for the Advancement
    of Experiential Learning
Suite 208
American City Building
Columbia, MD 21044
Three times a year $2.50

CBFSEI Newsletter
Clearinghouse for Community
    Based Free Standing
    Educational Institutions
1239 G Street, NW
Washington, DC 20005
Quarterly   Free

CHOICE Comments
Center for Helping
    Organizations Improve
    Choice in Education
Department of Higher/
    Postsecondary Education
227 Huntington Hall
Syracuse, NY 13210
Periodically   Free

Citizen Action in Education
Institute for Responsive
    Education
704 Commonwealth Avenue
Boston, MA 02215
Quarterly   Free

Citizen Education Bulletin
Alliance for Citizen Education
Room 810
401 N. Broad Street
Philadelphia, PA 19108
Bimonthly $5.00

The College Board News
Office of Public Affairs
The College Board
888 Seventh Avenue
New York, NY 10019
Quarterly   Free

Community Education Calendar
Federal Community Education
    Clearinghouse
Informatics, Inc.
6000 Executive Boulevard
Rockville, MD 20852
Quarterly   Free

Continuing Education Report
University Press
University of Chicago
5835 S. Kimbark
Chicago, IL 60637
Seven times a year *Free*

Cooperation (Work, Education, Labor Unions)
American Association of
Community and Junior
Colleges
One Dupont Circle, NW
Washington, DC 20036
Monthly *Free*

CPB Report
Corporation for Public
Broadcasting
1111 16th Street, NW
Washington, DC 20036
Biweekly *Free*

CREA Newsletter
Clearinghouse—Resources for
Educators of Adults
School of Education
224 Huntington Hall
Syracuse University
Syracuse, NY 13210
Monthly *Free*

Education for Aging News
Brookdale Center on Aging
Hunter College
129 E. 79th Street
New York, NY 10021
Bimonthly *Free*

Education and Work
Capitol Publications
Suite G-12
2430 Pennsylvania Avenue,
NW
Washington, DC 20037
Biweekly *$85.00*

Experiential Education
Society for Field Experience
Education and the National
Center for Public Service
Internship Programs
1735 I St., NW
Suite 601
Washington, DC 20006
Quarterly *Free*

Extension Service Review
Superintendent of Documents
Government Printing Office
Washington, DC 20402
Monthly *$2.25*

Findings
Educational Testing Service
Princeton, NJ 08540
Quarterly *Free*

Free University News
Free University Network
1221 Thurston
Manhattan, KA 66502
Monthly *$8.00*

Growing Without Schooling
Holt Associates, Inc.
308 Boylston Street
Boston, MA 02116
Bimonthly *$10.00*

*Higher Education and National
   Affairs*
American Council on
   Education
One Dupont Circle, NW
Washington, DC 20036
Weekly   Free

Individualized Learning Letter
67 East Shore Road
Huntington, NY 11743
Monthly $40.00

*Interchange: A Newsletter for
   Learning Networks*
The Learning Exchange
P.O. Box 920
Evanston, IL 60204
Bimonthly $12.00

*Intergenerational Education
   Report*
1576 Summit Avenue
St. Paul, MN 55101
Periodically   Free

Interversitas Newsletter
Interversitas
Northeastern Illinois
   University
5500 N. St. Louis Avenue
Chicago, IL 60625
Bimonthly $15.00

JCET News
Joint Council on Educational
   Telecommunications
1126 16th Street, NW
Washington, DC 20036
Monthly   Free

Lifelong Learners Newsletter
The Lila Acheson Wallace
   School of Community
   Service and Public Affairs
University of Oregon
Eugene, OR 97403
Bimonthly   Free

*Manpower and Vocational
   Education Weekly*
Capitol Publications
Suite G-12
2430 Pennsylvania Avenue,
   NW
Washington, DC 20036
Weekly $117.00

NAEB Newsletter
National Association of
   Educational Broadcasters
1346 Connecticut Avenue, NW
Washington, DC 20036
Monthly $15.00

*National Report for Training and
   Development*
American Society for Training
   and Development
Suite 400
One Dupont Circle, NW
Washington, DC 20036
Biweekly $35.00

NATTS News
National Association of Trade
   and Technical Schools
2021 L Street, NW
Washington, DC 20036
Monthly   Free

The NFE Exchance
Non-Formal Education
  Information Centre
513 Erickson Hall
Michigan State University
East Lansing, MI 48824
Bimonthly   Free

NUEA Newsletter
National University Extension
  Association
One Dupont Circle, NW
Washington, DC 20036
Biweekly $27.50

OEC Newsletter
Office on Educational Credit
American Council on
  Education
One Dupont Circle, NW
Washington, DC 20036
Three times a year   Free

*Second Thoughts (on Continuing
  Education)*
Basic Choices
Madison Campus Ministry
1121 University Avenue
Madison, WI 53715
Periodically   Free

The Work-Education Exchange
National Manpower Institute
1211 Connecticut Avenue, NW
Suite 301
Washington, DC 20036
Bimonthly   Free

Research or Development Projects

This section abstracts over 70 recently completed and on-going studies related to lifelong learning, beginning with the three or four that deal most comprehensively with the topic. Many more might have been included. Only a sampling of the scores of projects funded by the Fund for the Improvement of Postsecondary Education, including the 94 initiated in just the past year, are reviewed.[1] The project descriptions are grouped into twelve categories: general and policy-oriented projects; community and regional organization strategies; projects relating education and work; programs for older people; programs for women; programs for other special populations; mid-career change projects; information and counseling projects; television and other media-based projects;

[1]For descriptions of all these projects, one can consult the 1976, 1977, and 1978 editions of the Fund's publication *Resources for Change*. A new (1979) Fund program focuses on dissemination of information about programs that have been particularly effective in responding to adult learning needs.

library and museum projects; external degree studies; and other projects. Planners seeking empirical bases for their plans, as well as researchers, can benefit from contact with relevant in-progress research projects. Research findings often build on each other to lead to fairly firm conclusions, as shown in Chapter Two.

General and Policy-Oriented Projects

AMERICAN ASSOCIATION OF COMMUNITY AND JUNIOR COLLEGES (AACJC) POLICIES FOR LIFELONG EDUCATION PROJECT

In this three-year nationwide effort, the American Association of Community and Junior Colleges is conducting an analysis of local, state, and national policies affecting expansion of community-based community college lifelong education programs. Information and insights gained will be used to stimulate changes in policies, where necessary, to bring about improvement in the climate for development of services for all citizens. The association will conduct forums for policy makers and practitioners of continuing and lifelong education and will create a clearinghouse for persons and agencies seeking information and technical assistance in promoting programs. Consultative services will be provided. New policies and practices to facilitate lifelong learning, especially cooperative efforts among community colleges and other community-based agencies, will be tested. A rationale for lifelong learning will be developed for consideration by persons and agencies involved in policy formation. Funding: Kellogg Foundation. Final Report: Spring 1981.

Jamison Gilder
American Association of Community and Junior Colleges
One Dupont Circle, NW
Suite 410
Washington, DC 20036

DEVELOPMENT OF A HANDBOOK OF TERMINOLOGY FOR CLASSIFYING AND DESCRIBING THE LEARNING ACTIVITIES OF ADULTS

The general purpose of this two-year project was to improve communication about the field of adult and continuing education.

The handbook is intended to serve the information needs of those who provide learning activities for adults, as well as the federal, state, and local agencies that collect and report information about the conditions of adult learning. Its four major sections are (1) an introduction and overview, (2) a general categorization of information about adult learning activities (the major categories are Learners, Providers, Communities, Purposes/Outcomes, Content, Methods, Human Resources, Physical Resources, Financial Resources, Time Resources, and Support Functions), (3) definitions for items of information within each major category, and (4) a glossary of nationally used terms related to the items of information used in the handbook to describe adult learning activities. The handbook underwent five cycles of tryout and revision and was reviewed by over 500 representatives of education, business, community organizations, and other groups. The handbook is available at cost from the Superintendent of Documents, U.S. Government Printing Office, Washington, DC 20402. Funding: National Center for Education Statistics. Publication of handbook: Winter 1978–1979.

G. Roger Sell
National Center for Higher Education Management Systems (NCHEMS)
P.O. Drawer P
Boulder, CO 80302

FUTURE DIRECTIONS FOR A LEARNING SOCIETY

In this broad ranging three-year project (fall 1977–1980), The College Board is undertaking a variety of activities centering on nine goals. These are (1) to examine major assumptions underlying the learning society, (2) to inventory the current extent of participation in adult learning, (3) to analyze conditions that may determine the future extent of participation in adult learning, (4) to facilitate informed public (and professional) opinion regarding adult learning, (5) to assist in examining and formulating public policy options concerning adult learning, (6) to provide for exchange of ideas and information concerning lifelong learning, (7) to design, with other agencies, services to assist adult learners in transition to and from institutions, (8) to disseminate information about effective existing programs, and (9) to conduct demonstrations of needed adult learning services not presently available. Planned activities include preparation of a research and development agenda for adult education; limited survey research; identification of successful programs; design and demonstration of new adult learning services; cooperative work with numerous organizations; futures studies; forums; and publications. Funding: Exxon Education Foundation.

Rex Moon
Future Directions for a Learning Society Project
The College Board
888 7th Avenue
New York, NY 10019

LIFELONG LEARNING PROJECT OF THE DEPARTMENT OF HEALTH, EDUCATION, AND WELFARE

> The Assistant Secretary shall transmit to the president and to the Congress a report on such results from the activities conducted pursuant to this part [Part B, Title I, of the 1976 Amendments to the Higher Education Act of 1965] as may be completed by January 1, 1978, together with such legislative recommendations as he may deem appropriate [Public Law 94-482, Section 134].

This concluding section to what is known as the Mondale Lifelong Learning Act led to creation in January 1977 of the HEW Lifelong Learning Project as a research and planning group under the Assistant Secretary for Education. Its report to the president and Congress, entitled *Lifelong Learning and Public Policy,* drew on advice from a great many individuals and institutions. The report's analyses and recommendations fall into three major categories: Under "The Concept of Lifelong Learning" the key concepts of "lifelong learning" and "learning opportunities" are defined, and a vision of a "learning society"—involving individual learners, collaborating local providers, and facilitating governmental policy— is put forth. The second section discusses "The Lifelong Learning Act: Federal, State, and Local Implications," and offers seventeen recommendations. The third part, "The Learning Problems of Special Groups," contains analyses and recommendations regarding workers, urban youth, women, and older adults. Twenty-six background papers by recognized experts were commissioned by the project; it is expected that they will be published in book form in 1979. Funding: Department of Health, Education, and Welfare. Report: February 1978.

Office of the Assistant Secretary for Education
Department of Health, Education, and Welfare
Washington, DC 20202

NATIONAL CENTER FOR EDUCATION STATISTICS (NCES) SURVEYS OF SPONSORS OF ADULT EDUCATION

NCES has made a number of studies of the adult and continuing education activities offered by various types of sponsors. These include studies of noncredit activities sponsored by colleges and universities (conducted in 1967–68 and 1975–76), community agencies (nonprofit local and national groups, including churches, conducted in 1972), public education agencies (1969–70), and correspondence schools (1975–76). In addition, an annual summary of statistics on the federally funded Adult Basic Education Program is prepared. Funding: National Center for Education Statistics.

Adult and Vocational Education Surveys Branch
National Center for Education Statistics
400 Maryland Avenue, SW
Room 3071B
Washington, DC 20202

NATIONAL CENTER FOR EDUCATION STATISTICS (NCES) TRIENNIAL SURVEYS OF PARTICIPATION IN ADULT EDUCATION

NCES conducts a survey through the Current Population Survey of the U.S. Bureau of the Census to determine the extent to which individuals report participation in adult education. The survey, providing both baseline and trend data, was conducted in 1969, 1972, 1975, and 1978. Data available from the survey include participation rates by age, sex, race, prior education, occupation, employment status, family income, and other variables. The types of activities or courses, their length, and sources of funding also are included. Funding: National Center for Education Statistics. Report of 1978 results: Fall 1979.

Adult and Vocational Education Surveys Branch
National Center for Education Statistics
400 Maryland Avenue, SW
Room 3071B
Washington, DC 20202

STUDY OF ADULT EDUCATION

The purpose of this project is to maintain an ongoing assessment of future learning needs of adults and the public policies and programs required to meet those needs. It includes special attention to the financing of learning opportunities for adults. The project has resulted in a series of working papers, a publication called *Entitlement Studies,* available from the National Institute of Education, and the publication of a series of papers in the May 1978 issue of *The School Review.* Funding: National Institute of Education, Ford Foundation.

Norman D. Kurland
Study of Adult Education
New York State Education Department
Albany, NY 12234

Community and Regional Organization Strategies

ADULT EDUCATION COUNCIL OF METROPOLITAN DENVER

The purpose of this project is to expand the educational information services of the council, which already exists as an independent, neutral educational information and resource center for adults in metropolitan Denver. Project activities include increased publications with diversified distribution, as well as intensified communication with business and industry to evaluate ways in which alternative education practices can be utilized in the business community. Funding: Fund for the Improvement of Postsecondary Education. Final Report: Fall 1980.

Bette J. Overfield
Adult Education Council of Metropolitan Denver
1100 Acoma Street
Denver, CO 80204

BROOKLYN EDUCATIONAL AND CULTURAL ALLIANCE (BECA) EDUCATIONAL-CULTURAL CURRICULUM

Under the umbrella of BECA, seven institutions in the community have organized a comprehensive educational-cultural curriculum that will utilize the special resources of each institution. Cooperating organizations include: Pratt Institute, St. Joseph's College, St. Francis College, the Long Island Historical Society, the Brooklyn Museum, the public library, and the Brooklyn Academy of Music. Learning activities include: degree-oriented courses, informal lectures, walking tours, films, exhibits, and performances. Funding: National Endowment for the Humanities. Report: Fall 1979.

Barbara Kramer
Brooklyn Educational and Cultural Alliance
26 Court Street
Brooklyn, NY 11242

THE COMMUNITY CONGRESS OF SAN DIEGO

The purpose of this project is to create educational opportunities for workers in community-based human service organizations. The project will establish a replicable organizational "self-help model" and build the foundations for a decentralized citywide system of educational counseling. Goals include (1) definition of emerging worker roles and career ladders, (2) identification of education and training needs of these workers, (3) identification of relevant existing educational programs, (4) assisting worker usage of accessible educational programs, (5) removal of barriers to inaccessible programs, and (6) development of new programs where needs are unmet. Funding: Fund for the Improvement of Postsecondary Education. Final Report: Fall 1980.

Jeff Unsicker
The Community Congress of San Diego
1172 Morena Boulevard
San Diego, CA 92110

PENNSYLVANIA REGION I CONTINUING EDUCATION PROJECT

This project is a two-year cooperative effort by more than forty colleges and universities to design and implement a regional postsecondary continuing education program. Its objectives are (1) to assess the continuing education activities and needs of the region, (2) to help colleges and universities evaluate and grant credit for nontraditional learning experiences, (3) to establish counseling centers within reasonable commuting distance of all citizens, and (4) to bring non-degree-granting institutions, such as museums and art institutes, into the continuing education community. Task groups address each of the project's major objectives. Funding: Kellogg Foundation. Final Report: Winter 1979–80.

Sister Patricia Kremins
Widener College
Chester, PA 19013

ROCHESTER URBANARIUM

The purpose of this project is to improve the competence of Rochester citizens to make well-informed policy choices on important community issues. The Urbanarium, which has recently incorporated under the sponsorship of nine institutions (colleges and universities and community organizations), functions as an independent catalyst for change. Its goals include (1) assessment of citizen education needs on a systematic, communitywide scale, (2) facilitation of a wide variety of methods for community education and communication, (3) collection and dissemination of information to interested publics on problems, alternative solutions, and the experience of other areas in solving them, and (4) establishment of cooperative arrangements among diverse educational, research, and communication institutions and community groups and agencies. Funding: Kellogg Foundation, nine sponsoring organizations.

Gene DePrez
Urbanarium Coordinating Offices
50 Main Street West
Rochester, NY 14614

UNIVERSITY FOR MAN (UFM) COMMUNITY EDUCATION
PROJECT (1)

This project's purpose was to assist in revitalization of public life in small towns by helping create educational programs based on local talent. Over two years, programs offering a variety of educational opportunities—all free of grades, credits, costs, or prerequisites—were established in twelve small Kansas communities by UFM coordinators, assisted by two VISTA volunteers in each community. Eleven of the twelve programs are now locally controlled and funded. A film depicting the UFM experience and profiles of each community's education program was prepared. Funding: Fund for the Improvement of Postsecondary Education, United Fund, KSU Division of Continuing Education, Student Government Association. Final report: Summer 1978.

Sue C. Maes
University for Man
1221 Thurston
Manhattan, KS 66502

UNIVERSITY FOR MAN (UFM) COMMUNITY EDUCATION
PROJECT (2)

This project seeks to develop a national model for implementing free university-community educational programs. It currently creates and develops all types of educational opportunities—free of grades, credits, costs, and prerequisites—using the resources of local volunteers and responding to local needs. Training workshops and technical assistance in generating free university-community educational projects are provided, a training manual has been produced, and a monthly newsletter is being published. Funding: Fund for the Improvement of Postsecondary Education. Final report: Fall 1979.

Sue C. Maes
Jim Killacky
University for Man
1221 Thurston
Manhattan, KS 66502

Programs Relating Education and Work

AMERICAN ASSOCIATION OF COMMUNITY AND JUNIOR COLLEGES/AMERICAN VOCATIONAL ASSOCIATION (AACJC/AVA) JOINT STUDY OF COOPERATIVE POSTSECONDARY OCCUPATIONAL EDUCATION

The purpose of this project sponsored by the American Association of Community and Junior Colleges and the American Vocational Association was to document and promote cooperative relationships among postsecondary nonbaccalaureate occupational education programs. Following a nationwide survey of public and private organizations, the study was to (1) identify policies that facilitate or impede cooperation, (2) develop recommendations for consideration at federal, state, and local levels, (3) disseminate findings and recommendations, and (4) establish a mechanism for continued cooperation between AACJC and AVA. Funding: Bureau of Adult and Vocational Education, U.S. Office of Education. Final report: Summer 1978.

David S. Bushnell
AACJC/AVA Joint Study
One Dupont Circle, NW
Suite 410
Washington, DC 20036

COMMUNITY EDUCATION-WORK COUNCILS

The purpose of this two-year project is to demonstrate how education-work councils (as proposed in Willard Wirtz's *The Bound-*

less Resource) may be established with community colleges as initiators and facilitators. Councils are assisting in creation of working partnerships between local education and service agencies, business and industry, labor unions, and government. Activities include career days, special topic community forums and workshops, data collection, and job acquisition skills courses for youths. Six communities are participating; each is planning to generate its own financial resources after the contract expires. Funding: U.S. Department of Labor. Final report: Winter 1978–79.

James Mahoney
American Association of Community and Junior Colleges
One Dupont Circle, NW
Washington, DC 20036

CONTINUING EDUCATION AND EARLY CAREER ATTAINMENTS: DETERMINANTS AND OCCUPATIONAL EFFECTS OF GOING BACK TO SCHOOL

The purpose of this project is to examine occupational effects of continuing education by focusing on three issues: (1) antecedents of stopping schooling, (2) occupational effects, in terms of income, prestige, and career patterns, of resumed educational activities, and (3) relative payoffs of differing educational activities. The analysis uses data covering twenty years of experiences, since age fourteen, of a representative sample of American men. Funding: National Institute of Education. Final report: Fall 1978.

Nancy Karweit
Center for Social Organization of Schools
Johns Hopkins University
Baltimore, MD 21218

FIELD EXPERIENCE EDUCATION EVALUATION PROJECT

The purpose of this project was to evaluate a number of off-campus learning programs to establish a comprehensive theoretical base for accredited field experience as a mode of college education. Program characteristics and student outcomes were investigated for eleven field experience programs at six institutions nationwide.

Funding: National Institute of Social Sciences. Final report: Fall 1978.

John S. Duley
Snyder Hall
Justin S. Morrill College
Michigan State University
East Lansing, MI 48824

LABOR EDUCATION IN THE UNION HALL

This project will explore special teaching materials and pedagogical techniques for union workers. The institute will systematically compare its own courses on political economy, labor history, and union procedures with those of other educators active in the field, with an emphasis on determining the importance of the local labor hall environment for the educational process and educational outcome. Funding: Fund for the Improvement of Postsecondary Education. Final report: Fall 1980.

Franco Freedman
Institute for Labor Education and Research, Inc.
853 Broadway
Room 2007
New York, NY 10003

LIBERAL ARTS AND THE BLUE-COLLAR WORKER

The purpose of this project was to develop a program to bridge the gap between the traditional liberal arts college and the world of the adult blue-collar worker. Research with members of the target population yielded data for designing and implementing individually tailored learning packages. Curriculum goals were to develop competencies in five areas: problem solving, group participation, effective communication, developing personal identity, and understanding the human environment. Emphasis has been placed on subjects and skills readily usable in three environments: home, work, and the social or civic environment. Sponsoring organizations, such as labor unions, social clubs, and companies, have provided incentives for members as well as locations for learning.

Funding: Fund for the Improvement of Postsecondary Education. Final report: Fall 1978.

Brother Leonard Courtney
Saint Mary's College
Winona, MN 55987

NON-COMPLETERS IN PUBLIC AND PROPRIETARY SCHOOLS

The purpose of this project was to measure the ability of proprietary and public schools to retain students long enough to teach them marketable skills. In an earlier study by Wilms, labor market success records of graduates from the two types of schools were compared and correlated with various institutional factors. Since noncompletion rate for public schools is so high—an estimated 50 percent noncompletion in two years—this study also looked at skills acquired by noncompleters. Funding: National Institute of Education. Final report: Summer 1978.

Wellford Wilms
Graduate School of Education
University of California
Los Angeles, CA 90024

PILOT PROJECT TO INTEGRATE LIFE-ROLE AND ACADEMIC LEARNING

The purpose of this project was to provide means for adult learners to better associate the learning gained through various social roles—as citizens, workers, parents—with the knowledge gained through traditional college curriculums. Students enrolled in seminars in which they worked on individual projects and produced portfolios documenting their work. Portfolios described any type of life experience that could be verified as a legitimate learning experience related in some way to academic learning. If the pilot project is judged successful, it will be installed as a part of the regular college program. Credit obtained in this way could constitute up to one fourth the total credits required for a B.A. and would lower the cost of a degree by about 10 percent. Funding:

Fund for the Improvement of Postsecondary Education. Final report: Fall 1978.

Richard L. Hopkins
College of Professional and Continuing Education
Clark University
Worcester, MA 01610

PROJECT INTEGRATING VOCATIONAL-TECHNICAL HIGH SCHOOL AND COMMUNITY COLLEGE WORK

The purpose of this project was to improve local administration of career education by combining the last two years of vocational-technical high school with the first two years of college. The "Middle College," established by the Hudson County Community College Commission and the Hudson County Area Vocational-Technical Schools, is an effort to (1) ensure articulation between secondary and postsecondary levels, (2) provide joint planning for programs in emerging career areas, (3) develop alternative strategies for maximizing use of existing resources, and (4) act as a coordinating agency to improve cooperation with industry, manpower training programs, and other community and educational units. Funding: Fund for the Improvement of Postsecondary Education. Final report: Winter 1977–78.

Ramon Bonachea
Hudson County Community College Commission
26 Journal Square
Jersey City, NJ 07306

PROJECT ON QUALITY OF WORK LIFE

The purpose of this program is to assist labor unions and management to improve the quality of life at work and to enhance organizational effectiveness by expanding opportunities for participation in education at the work site. The project cooperates with the National Center for Educational Brokering in selecting and training workers at action sites to identify learning needs and organize learning activities among coworkers through the use of educational brokering techniques: information gathering, counseling, assessment, and advocacy. Local labor-management committees shape, promote, and approve all phases of the project. Funding: Fund for the Improvement of Postsecondary Education.

Edward Cohen-Rosenthal
The American Center for the Quality of Work Life
3301 New Mexico Avenue, NW
Suite 202
Washington, DC 20016

PROJECT ON TRANSLATING JOB EXPERIENCE TO ACADEMIC CREDIT

The general purpose of this project was to explore problems in utilizing nonschool educational resources by (1) translating job experiences into educational credit, (2) applying performance-based criteria in awarding postsecondary credentials, (3) meeting individual needs in an individual way, and (4) facilitating access to postsecondary education for nontraditional students. The first year, the project focused on the Comprehensive Employment and Training Act (CETA) as a candidate noneducational organization. The second year, representative educational programs in the Illinois Department of Transportation were also included. Funding: Fund for the Improvement of Postsecondary Education. Final report: Fall 1978.

Arden L. Pratt
School of Technical Careers
Southern Illinois University
Carbondale, IL 62901

PROJECT TO IMPROVE EDUCATIONAL OPPORTUNITIES FOR LOW-INCOME WORKERS

This project establishes a collaborative relationship between a private university and a trade union to reduce barriers to postsecondary education for low-income workers. The combined resources of Hofstra University and District 65 of the Distributive Workers of America enable workers to pursue a specially designed degree program at convenient times and places at reduced cost. A field-based social science curriculum has been developed that uses an interdisciplinary approach, involving a wide range of subject areas and the interaction of professional practitioners with academic faculty. Field projects, internships, and team teaching are emphasized. Funding: Fund for the Improvement of Postsecondary Education. Final report: Fall 1979.

Bertram Silverman
Alice Kessler-Harris
Center for the Study of Work and Leisure
Hofstra University
Hempstead, NY 11550

STUDY OF NEGOTIATED TUITION-AID PLANS

The purposes of this project are (1) to describe tuition-aid programs for workers resulting from collective bargaining agreements, (2) to explore the extent of worker participation in such plans, and (3) to identify and analyze factors that affect level of participation. Partial survey results on the prevalence of such plans and the level of participation in them are given in a July 1977 document. A second phase involves monitoring use of tuition-assistance plans at five to eight plants. Funding: National Institute of Education. Report (Phase I): Winter 1977–78.

Archie LaPointe
National Manpower Institute
1211 Connecticut Avenue, NW
Suite 301
Washington, DC 20036

WORK-EDUCATION CONSORTIUM PROJECT

The general purpose of this project is to improve the education-to-work transition for youths. Objectives are (1) to help develop local community education-work councils to serve as models, (2) to generate technical assistance capabilities, (3) to provide leadershjp in education-work policy, (4) to foster community participation, and (5) to create linkages with career education. The project has two components: (1) a consortium of twenty-one communities developing major collaborative efforts to solve education-work transition problems and (2) an Information Exchange Service to facilitate flow of information and technical assistance mainly among consortium communities. The National Manpower Institute and local councils are preparing technical assistance materials for communities interested in initiating local collaborative efforts. Funding: U.S. Department of Labor.

Dennis Gallagher
National Manpower Institute
1211 Connecticut Avenue, NW
Suite 301
Washington, DC 20036

Programs for Older People

CHICAGO OLDER ADULT LIFE OPTIONS PROGRAM

In cooperation with the Chicago Community Trust (a community foundation), this project increases educational opportunities for older persons. It links thirty-eight colleges and universities, twenty-five social agencies, three area agencies on aging, and forty-five individual associate members in the common goal of promoting a full range of educational experiences for the postretirement population. Services include a Resource Bank containing information about current educational opportunities for older adults; educational brokering and counseling services; seminars for registrars, financial aid officers, and faculty; and programs to increase public understanding of the relevance of education to the elderly. Funding: Fund for the Improvement of Postsecondary Education. Final report: Fall 1979.

Norma J. Wisor
Older Adult Life Options Program
The Chicago Community Trust
208 So. LaSalle Street, Suite 805
Chicago, IL 60604

DEVELOPMENT OF AN INSTITUTIONAL MODEL FOR COMMUNITY SERVICE AND CONTINUING EDUCATION FOR THE ELDERLY

The purpose of this project was to develop and test ways to increase higher education access for the elderly. The project was conducted by a consortium of four institutions in Tennessee

(Dyersburg State Community College, East Tennessee State University, Tennessee Technical University, University of Tennessee). Funding: Title I of the Higher Education Act of 1965. Final report: Summer 1978.

C. Brent Poulton
Center for Community Education
University of Tennessee at Nashville
Tenth and Charlotte
Nashville, TN 37203

INTERGENERATIONAL EDUCATION PROJECT

The general purpose of this program is to extend effective educational opportunity to older persons, particularly in intergenerational settings, thereby also enriching the traditional educational process for youth. Specific goals of the project are (1) to train staff who can conduct training sessions on approximately thirty-six college campuses in Minnesota, (2) to use these training sessions to educate the representatives of institutions and systems to the advantages of integrating retired persons as a new clientele, (3) to make the state a model of intergenerational education for other states to follow, and (4) to implement intergenerational living and learning in order to influence federal policy in the direction of a national learning society. A nationwide listing of schools involved in intergenerational education, compiled by state and type of school, is available from the project. Funding: Fund for the Improvement of Postsecondary Education. Final report: Spring 1979.

Dorothy Ferber
Macalester College
1576 Summit Avenue
St. Paul, MN 55101

NEW ENGLAND COLLEGE PIONEERS PROGRAM

This project encourages intergenerational learning while supplying postsecondary educational opportunities to a population of older adults. It provides a modular format for courses so that older adults can participate in short, coherent blocks of instruction while full-time students receive a complete academic course. The education of each group is enhanced by the presence of the other. Room and board on campus is available as well as nonresidential participation. Funding: Fund for the Improvement of Postsecondary Education. Final report: Fall 1979.

James Verschueren
Pioneers
New England College
Henniker, NH 03242

SENIORS AS VOLUNTEERS IN POSTSECONDARY EDUCATION

This is a three-year project to demonstrate how older persons can be used in all phases of college services. It has created a network of community colleges providing paid and volunteer employment for retired people. Funding: Edna McConnell Clark Foundation. Final report: Winter 1979–80.

Jeanne B. Aronson
American Association of Community and Junior Colleges
One Dupont Circle, NW
Suite 410
Washington, DC 20036

Programs for Women

ENCHANTED PLACES

This project establishes an outreach postsecondary system that teaches literacy, communication and self-help skills, parenting, life strategies, and marketable careperson skills to rural women. It provides a climate of support for rural women to overcome barriers to postsecondary education and encourages a network of communication in isolated areas by way of a newsletter, group demonstrations, a handbook, and a toy lending library. Funding: Fund for the Improvement of Postsecondary Education. Final report: Fall 1980.

Mary Ann Cravens, President
Enchanted Places
504 Porter Street
Taylor, TX 76574

MODEL STAFF TRAINING PROGRAM TO SENSITIZE
COLLEGE PERSONNEL TO WOMEN'S CAREER NEEDS

Catalyst, a national organization concerned with the expansion of career opportunities for women, has developed a model training program through which teams of college personnel may acquire (1) awareness of career development problems of women, (2) information about the needs and demands of the work sector, and (3) resources for professional staff development related to issues of women's career needs. Five postsecondary institutions in the New York metropolitan area are participating. Trained college teams are expected to be able to instruct and train colleagues and to effect constructive change in college policies, counseling, and curriculums at their respective institutions. Funding: Fund for the Improvement of Postsecondary Education. Final report: Fall 1978.

Charlene Newburg
Catalyst
14 East 60 Street
New York, NY 10022

NATIONAL COMMISSION ON WORKING WOMEN

The purposes of this project are (1) to identify and study needs of working women, (2) to draft model legislation to improve womens' working conditions and to end occupational segregation by sex, (3) to support innovative projects that deal with working womens' problems, and (4) to create a forum for discussion of relevant issues. The primary focus will be on women in traditionally "female" occupations. Planned activities include pilot projects, publicity, and education. Funding: National Institute of Education, Ford Foundation, Rockefeller Foundation. Final report: Fall 1979.

Joan Goodin
Center for Women and Work
1211 Connecticut Avenue, NW
Suite 400
Washington, DC 20036

THE NATIONAL CONGRESS OF NEIGHBORHOOD
WOMEN'S "BIG SISTER" PROJECT

This project provides technical assistance for two urban neighborhood groups as they develop a cosponsored college program for neighborhood women. NCNW will assist in making contact with an educational institution in addition to developing a special curriculum, holding workshops for faculty, administrators, and students, and establishing the Sister Schools Consortium Committee, a network for dissemination. The two model Sister Schools that result will utilize the neighborhood as a learning laboratory, in which 100 neighborhood women can increase their leadership skills, raise their self-esteem, and improve both their academic skills and basic knowledge. Funding: Fund for the Improvement of Postsecondary Education. Final report: Fall 1981.

Laura Polla Scanlon
11-29 Catherine Street
Brooklyn, NY 11211

PROJECT CHANCE

This project addresses the special needs of women entering postsecondary education, with a particular emphasis on providing access to education for poor and working-class women, traditionally bypassed by liberal arts colleges and even by the mainstream of the women's movement. The project provides comprehensive reentry assistance as well as support services including math and writing workshops; survival skills workshops; assertiveness training; tutoring; and academic, personal, and vocational counseling. Funding: Fund for the Improvement of Postsecondary Education. Final report: Fall 1979.

Sandra E. Adickes
Project Chance
Brooklyn College
Brooklyn, NY 11210

Programs for Other Special Populations

CAREER AWARENESS PROJECT FOR EX-OFFENDERS

The purposes of this project are to assist ex-offenders in choosing appropriate career goals and to develop training, education, and job placements to break the recidivism cycle and reduce costs of incarceration. The individualized four- to six-week curriculum taken by eighty parolees and probationers includes components in survival and communication skills, consumer education, aptitude and interest testing, self-esteem, and job-seeking and retraining skills. The project places participants in academic or vocational education programs and on-the-job training. Funding: Fund for the Improvement of Postsecondary Education. Final report: Fall 1980.

Merritt D. Long
Corrections Clearinghouse
Employment Security Department
Airdustrial Park, Building 17
Olympia, WN 98504

COLLEGE CENTER ON A SIOUX RESERVATION

This program assesses, designs, develops, delivers, and evaluates opportunities for postsecondary education for the Dakota Sioux living on the Lake Traverse Reservation in Northeastern South Dakota. The program serves as a model for institutional cooperation and coordination in assisting American Indians to achieve their goal of self-determined educational attainment as well as in providing individual educational opportunities for participants. Faculty from cooperating institutions and the local community teach at selected sites on the reservation; counseling and advising services are provided when and where students desire. Ultimately, the program will test the feasibility of establishing a free-standing community college on the reservation. Funding: Fund for the Improvement of Postsecondary Education. Final report: Fall 1979.

Roger S. McCannon
Continuing Education and Regional Programs
226 Community Services
University of Minnesota, Morris
Morris, MN 56267

MILES COLLEGE—EUTAW CAMPUS

This project represents a cooperative effort between college and community to develop a program tailored to the needs of a working adult student body in a small, rural, predominantly black community. The project seeks to increase the percentage of course completions for students whose job requirements prevent regular attendance of classes. The project has two basic components: (1) a series of workshops that involve faculty members in rewriting the curriculum based on the modular curriculum design, and (2) a writing and speech laboratory, which works intensively with students to develop individualized learning strategies. Funding: Fund for the Improvement of Postsecondary Education. Final report: Fall 1981.

Carol Prejean Zippert
Miles College—Eutaw
P.O. Box 31
Eutaw, AL 35462

NEW LEARNERS PROJECT AT SUNY

This project offers individualized degree programs to adults whose family or work responsibilities prohibit the traditional curricular patterns. It has developed collaborative programs between Empire State College, four other State University of New York (SUNY) Colleges, and several private institutions to combine individualized learning strategies with more formal academic and continuing education programs. A faculty member trained in the individualized, contract mode of learning developed by Empire State is on location at each campus to help students develop programs responsive to their needs. The project serves as a model for designing programs for a diverse student population. Funding: Fund for the Improvement of Postsecondary Education. Final report: Fall 1980

Peter J. Ristuben
Empire State College
1300 Elmwood Avenue
Buffalo, NY 14222

AN OPEN UNIVERSITY FOR FIRE SERVICE PERSONNEL

The purpose of this project is to develop an "open university delivery system" for providing a program of courses in fire science and related subjects, culminating in a B.A. degree. The use of techniques such as programmed texts and correspondence courses is envisioned as a solution to education needs of fire fighters. The four-year project consists of four phases: (1) an educational needs analysis, (2) identification of target groups, (3) development and evaluation of an open university system, and (4) provision of systems and model courses to participating academic institutions. Funding: National Fire Prevention and Control Administration, Department of Commerce. Report (Phase I): Spring 1978.

W. H. McClennan
International Association of Fire Fighters
1750 New York Avenue, NW
Washington, DC 20006

PIKEVILLE COLLEGE RURAL OUTREACH PROGRAM

The purpose of this project is to remove some of the social barriers to education in secluded sections of eastern Kentucky. The program will develop a number of satellite centers offering non-credit courses for isolated and economically depressed individuals, who tend to fear and distrust traditional education. Initial courses will be taught and coordinated by local personnel and will emphasize recreational and self-improvement subjects with high appeal in the community. Funding: Fund for the Improvement of Postsecondary Education. Final report: Fall 1981.

John K. Sohn
Center for Continuing Education
Pikeville College
Pikeville, KY 41501

PROJECT TO INCREASE EDUCATIONAL
OPPORTUNITIES FOR ADULT HISPANIC LEARNERS

The purpose of this project is to expand availability of adult education to the Hispanic community now underserved by the Boston postsecondary education system. The Boston Community School, in collaboration with Casa del Sol, a Hispanic community education agency, has developed a one-year program that will serve as an information and referral service for both the adult Hispanic learner and personnel of the postsecondary institutions.

It entails a course on cable TV, several workshops, and the development of a Hispanic community advisory board. Funding: Fund for the Improvement of Postsecondary Education. Final report: Fall 1979.

Henry Allen
Boston Community School
107 South Street
Boston, MA 02111

Mid-Career Change Projects

ADULT CAREER ADVOCATES TRAINING PROGRAM

The purpose of this project was to identify, describe, and evaluate existing career guidance and counseling programs for adults. Surveys and case studies were employed to discover what knowledge and skills facilitate efficient delivery of services in each of three administrative arrangements: (1) centers operated within a single institution, (2) centers operated through consortia of vocational and postsecondary institutions, and (3) community-based centers planned around the needs of individual clients. The study produced designs for operating centers under each of the three administrative models. Funding: Title I of the Higher Education Act of 1965. Report: Fall 1978.

Marilyn D. Jacobson
School of Education
Northwestern University
Evanston, IL 60201

CAREER CHANGE PROJECT

This project is designed to provide educators and employers with an overview of existing career change education in the United States, as well as in-depth looks at successful and less successful career change programs. Fifteen hundred postsecondary educational institutions and the 800 largest manufacturing and service firms in the United States were surveyed to identify programs. Case histories are available for eleven programs selected for in-depth study. An illustrated career change handbook describes exemplary programs in business and industry, postsecondary educational institutions, government agencies, and professional associations. Funding: Bureau of Adult and Vocational Education, U.S. Office of Education. Final report: Winter 1978–79.

Paul Ferrini
Technical Education Research Centers
44 Brattle Street
Cambridge, MA 02138

LEARNING PROCESSES IN ADULT DEVELOPMENT: A STUDY OF COGNITIVE AND SOCIAL FACTORS IN MID-LIFE TRANSITION

This project has five objectives: (1) to develop the experiential learning theory of adult development, (2) to develop valid instruments to assess the progress of adult development and the stages of adult life, (3) to begin a longitudinal study of adult lives centering on the learning styles, social patterns, and phenomenology of adult development, (4) to examine relations between structural dimensions of adult development and phenomenological and social changes over time, and (5) to identify causes and consequences of midlife crises. Funding: Spencer Foundation. Final report: Winter 1980–81.

Donald M. Wolfe
David A. Kolb
Department of Organizational Behavior
School of Management
Case Western Reserve University
Cleveland, OH 44106

MID-CAREER CHANGE: AN EVALUATIVE STUDY OF DIVERSE MODELS OF CONTINUING EDUCATION FOR PERSONS SEEKING MID-CAREER EMPLOYMENT CHANGE

This project is assessing six exemplary postsecondary programs aimed at problems of job mobility or reentry. In each case, the impact of state-level planning for continuing education and the impact of community-level organizations formed to coordinate and promote delivery of such programs will also be evaluated. The last six months is being devoted to dissemination—explaining the adaptability of the programs and, if warranted, encouraging their adoption. Funding: Title I of the Higher Education Act of 1965. Final report: Winter 1978–79.

Gilbert Paltridge
Department of Education
University of California, Berkeley
Berkeley, CA 94720

Information and Counseling Projects

ADULT EDUCATION INFORMATION CENTER

This project provides a comprehensive counseling and referral service to working adults interested in pursuing postsecondary educational opportunities. Counseling services include interest testing and assistance in development of individual education plans tailored to the scheduling and situational requirements of employed adults. Funding: Fund for the Improvement of Postsecondary Education. Final report: Fall 1979.

Noel C. Baker
Consortium for Urban Education/Adult Education
155 East Market Street
Room 809
Indianapolis, IN 46204

CAREER AND EDUCATIONAL COUNSELING PROGRAM OF THE REGIONAL LEARNING SERVICE (RLS) OF CENTRAL NEW YORK

Through a network of learning consultants, RLS has provided information and counseling to more than 9,000 adults since 1974. A recent (three-year) Kellogg grant will enable (1) developing new programs in life/work planning, (2) testing a variety of group counseling formats, (3) establishing procedures to enlarge career/educational opportunities for rural women and urban clerical workers, and (4) building supportive relationships between RLS and other institutions throughout the United States to find ways to better accommodate needs of adult learners. Funding: Kellogg Foundation. Final report: 1980.

Jean Kordalewski, Director
Regional Learning Service of Central New York
405 Oak Street
Syracuse, NY 13203

OUTREACH ADULT COUNSELING AND INFORMATION SERVICES (OACIS)

This project serves a very diverse group of Colorado mountain communities as an educational information and referral service, assisting individuals in establishing goals, evaluating options and alternatives, making decisions, and contacting the necessary resources. It utilizes a staff of part-time educational advisers to provide individual counseling and coordinate a comprehensive referral service. It will publish a complete community resource directory to furnish career and educational information on local, state, and national levels. Funding: Fund for the Improvement of Postsecondary Education. Final report: Fall 1980.

David Beyer
Colorado Mountain College
526 Pine
Glenwood Springs, CO 81601

UNIVERSITY OF OREGON CAREER INFORMATION CENTER

Cosponsored by the National Occupational Information Coordinating Council, this project provides technical assistance to states in establishing a cooperative career information system along the lines of the Oregon model. Activities include conducting introductory workshops in selected areas, developing support materials for state committees that are implementing systems of career information, and writing training materials to improve and extend staff training. Funding: Fund for the Improvement of Postsecondary Education. Final report: Fall 1981.

Bruce McKinlay
Career Information System
247 Hendricks Hall
University of Oregon
Eugene, OR 97403

Television and Other Media-Based Projects

AMERICAN ASSOCIATION OF COMMUNITY AND JUNIOR COLLEGES (AACJC) "TELECOURSE" PROJECT

This project will facilitate cooperative relationships among community colleges, public broadcasters, and community organizations in the use of television in postsecondary education. It will include (1) research into both the current and the potential use of the "telecourse," a teaching approach that combines entertaining and instructive video programs with printed study materials, and (2) formation of a National Advisory Council on Postsecondary Uses of Television. Funding: Fund for the Improvement of Postsecondary Education. Final report: Fall 1979.

Marilyn Kressel
American Association of Community and Junior Colleges
One Dupont Circle, NW
Suite 410
Washington, DC 20036

CARNEGIE COMMISSION ON THE FUTURE OF PUBLIC BROADCASTING

The purpose of this project is a long-range look at public broadcasting with respect to creative programming, public participation, impact of new technologies, funding levels and sources, and structure of the broadcasting system. This is the second commission of its kind funded by the Carnegie Corporation; the first one issued a report in 1967. Final report: February 1979.

William McGill (Chairman)
Office of the President
Columbia University
New York, NY 10027

DEVELOPMENT OF TELEVISION-BASED ASSOCIATE DEGREE PROGRAMS

Public television station WNET/13 of New York has designed a new educational system to serve needs of adult learners, with particular emphasis on needs of working adults, minorities, and other categories of people often excluded from educational opportunities by physical or psychological barriers. The system involves (1) development of programs of study enabling students to earn A.A. or A.S. degree from participating colleges, with approximately one third of the courses offered via WNET courses, and (2) concurrent establishment of a linkage system composed of fifteen colleges and selected business and community organizations working together to formulate program content and participating in delivery of television courses. Funding: Fund for the Improvement of Postsecondary Education. Final report: Fall 1978.

Shirley B. Gillette
WNET/Channel Thirteen
356 West 58th Street
New York, NY 10019

UNIVERSITY OF MID-AMERICA (UMA)

UMA is a major regional experiment in open learning and teaching at a distance. Governed by a consortium of eleven midwestern state universities, it has as its broad mission to foster development of a new approach to learning that permits learners to achieve personal and career goals through accessible and affordable opportunities for quality educational experiences. More specifically, its goals are (1) to develop multi-media courses of sufficient quality to ensure widespread use in the UMA region and elsewhere, (2) to assist consortium members in developing statewide delivery systems in partnership with other postsecondary institutions, (3) to distribute course materials to institutions nationwide, and (4) to improve the ability of higher education to serve new audiences through research and dissemination activities. Students enroll through the delivery systems of member institutions; thus, the curriculum available to any student is that provided by the participating university. The long-range curriculum plan specifies four areas of undergraduate course development—business, energy and environment, the humanities, and agriculture—as well as continuing education for professionals. Eleven courses have been developed, which are available for lease or purchase. Funding: National Institute of Education.

University of Mid-America
1600 North 33rd Street
Box 82006
Lincoln, NB 68501

VIDEO OUTREACH PROGRAM

The purpose of this program is to develop an effective state-wide delivery system to meet continuing education needs. Public libraries will house thirteen video tape centers, which will allow students to view classes either individually or in small groups. Classes will be conducted on a degree or nondegree basis and will concentrate on (but not be restricted to) engineering, agriculture, forestry, business, and mining. The University of Idaho, recipient of the grant, anticipates that centers and equipment will be used by other colleges and universities, government agencies, businesses, and citizens for educational and civic purposes outside the project. Funding: Kellogg Foundation. Final report: Fall 1980.

Susan Burcaw
Office of Continuing Education
University of Idaho
Moscow, ID 83843

WNET ADULT OPEN LEARNING PROJECT

WNET, the New York Educational Broadcasting Corporation's television station, is working with seven degree-granting institutions in the metropolitan New York area in a pilot project to develop new approaches for bringing education to the general adult population. Students will have access to three main learning sources: (1) a printed curriculum, (2) visual materials that are televised at pre-established times, and (3) easily accessible off-campus centers. When the project is fully operational, a liberal arts curriculum equivalent to the first year of college will be offered. Funding: Fund for the Improvement of Postsecondary Education. Final report: Fall 1979.

Barbara Caress
WNET/Channel Thirteen
356 West 58th Street
New York, NY 10019

Library and Museum Projects

CULTURAL VOUCHER PROGRAM

The purposes of this program are (1) to bring a broader range of people into contact with the educational programs of cultural institutions such as museums and galleries and (2) to provide these institutions with incentives to develop services for new audiences. The program awards money—in the form of vouchers—to ten community organizations (which together reach some 75,000 people) to enable their members to "purchase" services such as lessons in the arts and special tours of their choice at eight participating cultural institutions. These institutions redeem the vouchers for cash from Museums Collaborative, Inc., a consortium of city-affiliated cultural institutions in New York and sponsor of the program. More than 200 projects—from workshops on fund raising to weekly lessons in poetry—were implemented within one year. The voucher plan will ultimately be proposed as an alternative funding system for part of the state's annual budget allocation for the arts. Funding: Fund for the Improvement of Postsecondary Education. Final report: Summer 1980.

Holly Sidford
Museums Collaborative, Inc.
830 Fifth Avenue
New York, NY 10021

HIGHER EDUCATION LIBRARY ADVISORY SERVICE (HELAS)

The purposes of this two-year demonstration project were to improve library advisement of individuals regarding postsecondary education opportunities and financial aid sources, and to demonstrate that the public library can play an active role in linking potential adult learners with the educational community. Full-time librarian-advisers in three representative library systems provided information and referral services using regularly updated directories of local educational resources and the libraries' established collections and resources. Funding: Fund for the Improvement of Postsecondary Education. Final report: Fall 1978.

Patricia S. Dyer
Twin Towers, Room 1919
99 Washington Avenue
Albany, NY 12230

OPEN ACCESS SATELLITE EDUCATION SERVICES (OASES) PROJECT

This project was a joint effort of the Oklahoma County Libraries System and South Oklahoma Junior College. Its general purpose was to offer improved continuing education opportunities through a cost-effective partnership that would take advantage of previously successful programs, combined administration, and existing physical facilities. In the first year, a branch library was outfitted as a satellite adult education center. Academic and nonacademic programs were designed for the immediate target populations—primarily Mexican Americans, Native Americans, and older people. Studies of cost effectiveness focusing on both consumers and providers were conducted, and a preliminary model of cooperation was created that identified the most effective programs (those that could be economically replicated). Funding: Fund for the Improvement of Postsecondary Education. Final report: Fall 1978.

Sandy Ingraham
OASES Center
334 S. M. 26
Oklahoma City, OK 73159

PROJECT TO EXPAND THE FUNCTIONS OF A RURAL LIBRARY SYSTEM

Northeast Regional Library serves a population having a median of 9.8 years of schooling. Its project goals were (1) to create library learning situations, either formally or informally structured, so that the library could offer programs of interest and value to patrons with varied educational backgrounds, (2) to function as an information clearinghouse for learners, and (3) to act as a referral service to link learners with educational opportunities outside the library. Funding: Fund for the Improvement of Postsecondary Education. Final report: Fall 1977.

William McMullin
Northeast Regional Library
1023 Fillmore Street
Corinth, MS 38834

External Degree Studies

THE BERKELEY PROJECT ON EVALUATION OF NONTRADITIONAL DEGREE PROGRAMS

A nine-month project was undertaken by the Center for Research and Development in Higher Education at Berkeley to plan an evaluation of nontraditional degree programs. This project consists of three mini-projects with the following purposes, respectively: (1) to provide a conceptual framework consisting of typologies of learner needs and program responses to learner needs (K. Patricia Cross and Ami Zusman), (2) to identify policy questions of concern to decision makers (Frank Bowen, Stewart Edelstein, Leland Medsker), and (3) to produce specifications for instruments to gather information of concern to decision makers (Janet Ruyle and Richard Watkins). Funding: National Institute of Education. Reports available (from NIE): Winter 1978–79.

Charles Stalford
National Institute of Education
1200 19th Street, NW
Washington, DC 20208

BUREAU OF SOCIAL SCIENCE RESEARCH/AMERICAN COUNCIL ON EDUCATION (BSSR/ACE) EXTERNAL DEGREE PROJECT

This project, conducted in 1977 by the Bureau of Social Science Research in cooperation with the American Council on Education, has three aspects: (1) preparation of a descriptive guide to external degree programs, (2) analysis of external degree programs and student characteristics, and (3) analysis of external degrees as credentials useful for further study or employment purposes. The study was based on survey data from 134 institutions (which sponsored 244 external degree programs in 1977) and 3,000 external degree recipients. Funding: National Institute of Education. Reports from NIE: December 1977; Spring 1978.

Carol P. Sosdian
Laure M. Sharp
Bureau of Social Science Research
1990 M Street, NW
Washington, DC 20036

THE RELATIONSHIP OF STUDENT CONSUMER PROTECTION STRATEGIES TO EXTERNAL DEGREE PROGRAMS

The purposes of this project were (1) to determine why students are enrolled in an external, nontraditional program as opposed to a traditional educational program, (2) to determine whether students are enrolled in nontraditional programs to meet occupational or personal goals, and (3) to examine the issue of consumer protection by asking whether students are receiving the educational services expected by them or promised to them by institutions. Data gathered from a sample of California B.A., M.A., and Ph.D. candidates were used to develop a profile of the nontraditional student and to serve as a basis for suggested consumer protection strategies. Funding: American Institutes for Research. Final report: Winter 1978–79.

Jeanette Wheeler
American Institutes for Research
P.O. Box 1113
Palo Alto, CA 94302

Other Projects

ADULT COMPETENCY-BASED DIPLOMA PROJECT

This project, which addresses the needs of adults who lack skills and knowledge to function effectively in contemporary society, has two primary goals: (1) to develop and validate Competency Achievement Packets (CAPs) for teaching and assessing some forty functional competencies—grouped into five content areas—judged crucial to success in everyday life and (2) to develop and validate a plan for implementing competency-based instruction and assessment. Funding: Division of Adult and Community Education, California State Department of Education. Reports: Summer 1978; Summer 1979.

Rosemary Dawson
Division of Career and Continuing Education
Los Angeles Unified School District
Marengo Center, Room 101
1200 N. Cornwall Street
Los Angeles, CA 90033

CIVIC LITERACY PROJECT

The purpose of this project is to provide a model for (1) enabling citizen participation in governmental processes and (2) defining a new role for a school of education—direct involvement in the continuing learning of adults in the community served by the institution. Syracuse University, in cooperation with citizens and state officials, will conduct a series of participatory workshops, with subsequent supportive services and training designed to reduce alienation of citizens from government. Funding: Title I of the Higher Education Act of 1965. Final report: Summer 1979.

Grace Healy
The Civic Literacy Project
Huntington Hall
University of Syracuse
Syracuse, NY 13210

COUNCIL ON POSTSECONDARY ACCREDITATION (COPA) PROJECT TO DEVELOP EVALUATIVE CRITERIA AND PROCEDURES FOR THE ACCREDITATION OF NONTRADITIONAL EDUCATIONAL PROGRAMS

The purpose of this project was to study nontraditional education and emerging learning forms in postsecondary education institutions, as well as accreditation procedures, in order to

(1) identify "essential elements" in accrediting nontraditional institutions, (2) develop a classification of the types of nontraditional study programs, and (3) develop appropriate evaluative criteria for accreditation purposes. The study is expected to produce new national policy recommendations to guide the Council on Postsecondary Accreditation (COPA) and regional accrediting commissions in developing uniform approaches to accrediting nontraditional programs, institutions, and delivery systems. Funding: Kellogg Foundation. Final report (Guidelines): Fall 1978.

Grover J. Andrews, Associate Executive Secretary
Southern Association of Colleges and Schools
795 Peachtree Street, NE
Atlanta, GA 30308

DIFFERENTIAL TUITION PROJECT

This project establishes a differential pricing system for tuition equitable to part-time and evening students, who are generally charged for services appropriate only to the full-time day student. It assigns separate prices to the services included in tuition, then recombines them into a package tailored to the needs of each part-time student. Market forces are allowed to come into play so that the college can shift resources into areas most clearly responsive to student needs. Funding: Fund for the Improvement of Postsecondary Education. Final report: Fall 1979.

Joseph P. O'Neill, Executive Director
Conference of Small Private Colleges
145 Witherspoon Street
Princeton, NJ 08540

EDUCATIONAL PASSPORT

The purpose of this project is to enable individuals to assemble a comprehensive record of educational and vocational credentials in a single, easily carried document with readily available copies. The educational passport should facilitate movement, for example, from one educational institution to another, from military service to college, from college to job, from job to job. The individual gathers and organizes materials; Educational Testing

Service produces a wallet-sized microfiche and returns the original documents to the sender. A pocket viewer is sent with copies. Developmental phase through 1977. Funding: Lilly Endowment.

John R. Valley, Project Director
Educational Passport
Educational Testing Service
Princeton, NJ 08540

FACTORS INFLUENCING ADULTS' QUALITY OF LIFE

The purpose of this program was to analyze major components of "quality of life." Data are based on "critical incidents" (specific events or situations that people find important or satisfying) and detailed interviews with samples of 1,000 persons in their early thirties (Project TALENT participants), fifty-year-olds, and seventy-year-olds. A November 1977 paper by Steel and Russ-Eft (of American Institutes for Research) explored the extent of learning in the three age groups and the relations between continued learning and quality of life. Funding: National Institute of Education, Administration on Aging (HEW). Final report: Summer 1978.

John C. Flanagan
American Institutes for Research
P.O. Box 1113
Palo Alto, CA 94302

GUILD EDUCATION PROJECT

This project was an effort to "fulfill the promise of the community as educator" through implementation of "guild education" at Windsor Mill, a former textile mill. Since 1972 Hoosuck Community Resources Corporation (HCRC) has used the mill for a variety of programs and services concerned with economic development, urban planning, and the environmental arts. Faculty of the Windsor Mill Guild School, educational arm of HCRC, were master professionals resident in or associated with the mill; students included community members seeking avocational (or vocational) skills, students enrolled in area postsecondary institutions, teachers seeking retraining in the arts, and committed artisans desiring professional training. The grant enabled HCRC and the Guild School to refine, expand, and formally implement its "guild education" concepts over a two-year period. The program is ultimately expected to provide an educational alternative for students throughout the state college system. Funding: Fund for the Improvement of Postsecondary Education. Final report: Fall 1978.

Mary Ann Beinecke
Hoosuck Community Resources Corporation
121 Union Street
North Adams, MA 01247

IMPROVING LEARNING EXCHANGES

The Learning Exchange (TLE) in Evanston, like those in other localities, was established as a service for linking individual learners with instructors. With its current grant, TLE is (1) designing, testing, and implementing a number of new arrangements with area institutions to encourage broader participation in the TLE program, (2) conducting technical assistance and networking programs to reduce the failure rate of learning exchanges in other cities, and (3) assisting five new learning exchanges (listing and referral services) throughout the United States. Funding: Fund for the Improvement of Postsecondary Education. Final report: Spring 1979.

Diane R. Kinishi
The Learning Exchange
P.O. Box 920
Evanston, IL 60204

THE LEARNERS' COOPERATIVE

The general purpose of this project is to create a learners' cooperative—a self-advocacy educational consumer group, open to all, by means of which individuals can organize to obtain desired educational services. The cooperative will negotiate with area colleges and universities for (1) tuition rates lower than those charged to regular students and (2) curriculum, delivery system, and other

modifications consistent with member educational goals. The cooperative will also facilitate peer support and interaction. Funding:
Fund for the Improvement of Postsecondary Education. Final report: Fall 1979.

Stephen B. Plumer
The Learners' Cooperative
Center for Human Services
5530 Wisconsin Avenue, NW
Suite 1600
Washington, DC 20015

STUDY OF THE DETERMINATION OF FINANCIAL NEED FOR CAREER-RELATED ADULT EDUCATION

The purposes of this project were (1) to review the rationale,
assumptions, and procedures of existing public and private systems
of financial need analysis for their applicability (or inapplicability)
to adult part-time learners, (2) to suggest alternative strategies for
equitable assessment of the need for public subsidy of alternative
procedures of evaluating ability to pay for postsecondary education, and (3) to estimate the numbers of needy adult part-time
learners and their aggregate need for public subsidy given alternative methods of need analysis. Funding: National Institute of
Education. Final report: Spring 1978.

James L. Bowman
Financial Aid Studies and Programs
College Board Programs Division
Educational Testing Service
Princeton, NJ 08540

Services for Adult Learning Programs

This section describes what may be regarded as services, as
distinguished from research or development projects. Each makes
available one or more types of assistance to organizations operating
adult learning programs—information, consulting services, guidelines for practice, for example—sometimes for a fee. A number of

the services described have to do basically with assessment—either of individuals or of courses.

ADULT BASIC LEARNING EXAMINATION (ABLE)

ABLE is a battery of tests designed to measure the level of educational achievement of adults. Although designed for use with adults and consisting of items with adult content, this examination may be used to assess achievement as low as primary-grade level. ABLE was developed to determine the general educational level of adults who have not completed formal twelfth-grade education and to evaluate efforts to raise the educational level of such adults. Three batteries are available: grades one to four, five to eight, and nine to twelve. Tests can be scored locally or sent to the publisher for machine scoring.

Test Department
Harcourt Brace Jovanovich, Inc.
757 Third Avenue
New York, NY 10017

ADULT PERFORMANCE LEVEL (APL) PROGRAM

The purpose of this program is to assess functional competency of adults. The program is based on a USOE/University of Texas cross-classification of five content/knowledge areas (community resources, occupational knowledge, consumer economics, health, government, and law) and five skill areas (identifying facts and terms, reading, writing, computation, and problem solving). The program comprises six measures: in-depth tests of each of the five content areas, and the forty-item APL Survey, which provides a "total competency rating," five content ratings, and five skill ratings. Tests are given by group administration; various individual and group score reports are provided.

APL Department
The American College Testing Program
P.O. Box 168
Iowa City, IA 52240

AMERICAN ASSOCIATION OF COMMUNITY AND
JUNIOR COLLEGES (AACJC) CENTER FOR COMMUNITY
EDUCATION

The general purpose of the AACJC Center is to advance
cooperation among community colleges, public schools, and other
community-based organizations (for example, park and recreation
departments) in providing educational and other human services.
The center uses interns and regional representatives. Funding:
Charles Stewart Mott Foundation. Annual reports: December.

Suzanne M. Fletcher
American Association of Community and Junior Colleges
One Dupont Circle, NW
Suite 410
Washington, DC 20036

AMERICAN COLLEGE TESTING PROGRAM (ACT)
NATIONAL REGISTRY

This is a computer-based registry designed to help associations and organizations maintain records and provide transcripts
of their members' continuing education accomplishments. It provides the same recordkeeping and transcript service for the broad
range of continuing education students that colleges and universities routinely provide for their more traditional students. The
American Council on Education's Project on Noncollegiate Sponsored Instruction is the first national organization to use the registry.

Michael Ham
ACT Continuing Education Services
American College Testing Program
P.O. Box 168
Iowa City, IA 52240

THE BRITISH OPEN UNIVERSITY FOUNDATION, INC.

This nonprofit organization was activated in 1977, super-
seding the North American Office of The Open University. Its
general purposes are (1) to foster cooperation among institutions
concerned or involved with distance-learning techniques,
(2) to bring students a greater variety of learning materials, and

(3) to reduce the cost and improve the quality of instruction offered to students using distance-learning techniques. The foundation's activities include (1) promotion of co-production and exchange of course material between the United States and England, (2) acting as an agency for the exchange of information and academic personnel between the two countries, (3) initiating and assisting in research in the field, and (4) acting as a liaison with national and international coordinating and policy-making bodies toward the ends of optimizing allocation and use of educational resources.

Gordon Lammie
The British Open University Foundation, Inc.
110 East 59th Street
New York, NY 10022

CENTER FOR EDUCATION AND WORK

The activities of this newly established center focus on ways to develop better relations between institutions of work and education and to improve people's access to and movement between these organizations. Center staff work with representatives from business, labor, education, community-based organizations, government, and the Comprehensive Employment and Training Act (CETA) prime sponsors, particularly at the local level, to form policies and approaches to improve linkages between education and work institutions, to identify existing programs and projects, and to bring them to the attention of other concerned individuals and organizations. The Center also seeks to work with governmental officials toward greater community participation in such programs as CETA, the Youth Employment and Demonstration Projects Act (YEDPA), the Private Sector Initiative Program (PSIP), vocational and occupational education, career education, adult education, and community education.

Dennis Gallagher
Center for Education and Work
National Manpower Institute
1211 Connecticut Avenue, NW
Suite 301
Washington, DC 20036

CLEARINGHOUSE FOR COMMUNITY-BASED FREE STANDING EDUCATIONAL INSTITUTIONS

CBFSEI is a national membership organization of thirty educational institutions that are community based and controlled, and independent of state support. The national office has the following functions: (1) communication and information exchange among member institutions, (2) resource development and dissemination, (3) technical assistance to member and emerging institutions, and (4) articulation and projection of community-based concepts and approaches. Funding: Fund for the Improvement of Postsecondary Education.

Christofer P. Zachariadis
CBFSEI
1806 Vernon Street, NW
Washington, DC 20005

COLLEGE-LEVEL EXAMINATION PROGRAM (CLEP)

This program enables both traditional and nontraditional students to earn college credit by examination. Two types of tests are offered: General Examinations, which measure achievement in five basic areas of liberal arts usually covered in the first two years of college, and forty-seven Subject Examinations, which are used to grant exemption from and credit for specific college courses. Institutions determine how much credit will be given for scores sent to them. Tests are offered monthly at 900 locations nationwide. Each examination costs $20.

Charles Bedford
College-Level Examination Program
The College Board
888 Seventh Avenue
New York, NY 10019

COUNCIL FOR THE ADVANCEMENT OF EXPERIENTIAL LEARNING (CAEL)

CAEL is an educational association established to foster experiential learning and valid and reliable assessment of its outcomes. Originally known as the Cooperative Assessment of Experiential Learning, the new CAEL, chartered by the Regents of the

State of New York, is a consortium of approximately 300 institutions of higher education and other educational organizations. It has two major programs. Broad goals of the Institutional Development Program are improvements in quality assurance and greater sophistication in judgments about cost effectiveness in two areas of practice: (1) use of experiential elements in the design and conduct of educational programs and (2) assessment of the learning outcomes of these programs. The Professional Development Program offers regional workshops for faculty and administrators in (1) assessing prior experiential learning and (2) planning, implementing, and administering experiential learning programs on campus. In addition, CAEL has a broad publications program, issues a newsletter three times a year, holds twice-yearly meetings for all members (The Assembly), and sponsors one-day regional drive-in meetings on issues of interest to area institutions. Funding: Carnegie Corporation of New York (initially), Ford Foundation, Fund for the Improvement of Postsecondary Education, Lilly Endowment, Kellogg Foundation.

Morris T. Keeton, Executive Director
Council for the Advancement of Experiential Learning
American City Building
Suite 208
Columbia, MD 21044

COUNCIL ON THE CONTINUING EDUCATION UNIT

This council is a nonprofit postsecondary association of education and training organizations and individuals devoted to constructive and consistent use of the Continuing Education Unit (CEU) and to improvement in the quality and effectiveness of continuing education. The council, in 1977, was formed by and succeeded the National Task Force on the Continuing Education Unit. The CEU, defined as ten contact hours of participation in an organized continuing education experience under responsible sponsorship, capable direction, and qualified instruction, is used to measure and to provide recognition for noncredit continuing education. The council's purposes are (1) to promote development, interpretation, and dissemination of the best methods, standards, and ideals for the use of the CEU, (2) to ensure continuity in the development of the CEU and to seek consistency in the application of the CEU, (3) to promote strengthening of standards in continuing education, (4) to work cooperatively with educational organizations, professional societies, associations, units of government, and other organizations engaged in noncredit continuing education and training, (5) to serve as a forum and publish information relative to the CEU and continuing education, and (6) to conduct research and provide better information about the CEU and continuing education to enhance their effectiveness and quality.

Keith Glancy
Council on the CEU
Evening College and Summer Session
Shaffer Hall
The Johns Hopkins University
Baltimore, MD 21218

NATIONAL ASSESSMENT OF EDUCATIONAL PROGRESS (NAEP)

This project of the Education Commission of the States surveys the educational attainments of nine-, thirteen-, and seventeen-year-olds and adults (ages twenty-six to thirty-five) in ten learning areas: art, career and occupational development, citizenship, literature, mathematics, music, reading, science, social studies, and writing. Different learning areas are periodically reassessed in order to measure change in educational achievement. In 1977 adult skills and attitudes were assessed in science, reading, energy, and health. Recent "probes" of adults have been carried out in life/survival skills, basic skills, and adult work skills and knowledge. All NAEP items, or "exercises," are made available to local jurisdictions at no cost. A monthly newsletter is published. Funding: National Institute of Education.

National Assessment of Educational Progress
1860 Lincoln Street
Suite 700
Denver, CO 80295

NATIONAL CENTER FOR EDUCATIONAL BROKERING

The basic purposes of educational brokering services are to assist adults to make career and educational decisions and then to help them act upon them. Brokering services include information about educational and career opportunities, counseling, individual assessment, and advocacy (active aid to clients in securing services from institutions). Brokering units exist in a variety of organizational settings, such as libraries and other community organizations, businesses, labor unions, military units, and women's centers. Educational brokers are neutral; their services are performed in the interests of individual learners, not in the interests of (provider) organizations. Activities of the National Center for Educational Brokering include (1) organizational development for brokering programs—experienced practitioners assist program staffs with development of services, selection and training of staff, outreach and delivery, finance, management, counseling and assessment techniques, and evaluation, (2) dissemination of information on educational brokering and adult learning—NCEB publishes a newsletter (the *Bulletin*) as well as monographs and articles, and it operates a clearinghouse of relevant documents, and (3) assistance to policy makers—state and federal officials are provided with special studies, draft legislation, and guidance on the use of brokering services to meet policy objectives by means of workshops, consultations, publications, and special mailings. Funding: Carnegie Corporation of New York, Fund for the Improvement of Postsecondary Education.

Francis U. Macy
National Center for Educational Brokering
1211 Connecticut Avenue, NW
Suite 400
Washington, DC 20036

NEW YORK PROGRAM ON NONCOLLEGIATE
SPONSORED INSTRUCTION

The purpose of this program is to review formal educational courses sponsored by noncollegiate organizations and to make appropriate college credit recommendations for the courses evaluated. The program has evaluated nearly 1,000 courses offered by seventy organizations (for example, businesses) since its inception in 1974. The program is conducted in cooperation with other agencies in other parts of the country, all cooperating agencies following jointly established policies and procedures. Cooperating agencies are the American Council on Education, the Consortium of the California State University and Colleges, and the Commonwealth of Pennsylvania Education Department.

John J. McGarraghy
The Office on Noncollegiate Sponsored Instruction
New York State Education Department
99 Washington Avenue, Room 1845
Albany, NY 12230

OFFICE OF EDUCATIONAL CREDIT (OEC), AMERICAN COUNCIL ON EDUCATION

OEC is a division of the American Council on Education (ACE). It was formerly the Commission on Accreditation of Service Experiences (CASE)—before its expansion of functions and name change in 1974. The roles of the Office and its policy-making and advisory arm, the Commission on Educational Credit, are:

- To analyze educational credit and credentialing policies for post-secondary education.
- To foster and operate programs to establish credit equivalencies among educational alternatives.
- To assist agencies and institutions in providing persons with due recognition for competency, knowledge, and skills, wherever and however obtained.
- To provide individuals with an alternative means of demonstrating high school–equivalent competencies.

OEC currently conducts the following programs:

Task Force on Educational Credit and Credentials. The purposes of this program are (1) to formulate a philosophical framework and basic definitions for educational credit and credentials and (2) to devise a unified credit system applicable to all types of learning and instructional modes at the postsecondary level. The Task Force's *Recommendations on Credentialing Educational Accomplishments* (1978), suggests changes in credit and credentialing systems to improve the quality of information conveyed. Funding: Carnegie Corporation of New York.

General Educational Development (GED) Testing Service. All fifty states, the District of Columbia, seven U.S. territories and possessions, and most Canadian provinces and territories participate in the GED Testing Program. GED tests of high school equivalency are available in English, Spanish, French, and in special editions for the blind. Funding is currently being sought for a special edition for the deaf and hearing impaired. Testing volume in 1976 was about 700,000 administrations to 550,000 persons; over 350,000 high school credentials are issued by states each year. New editions of the GED tests were scheduled for release in 1978.

Formal Military Course Evaluations. OEC regularly publishes its *Guide to the Evaluation of Educational Experiences in the Armed Services,* which contains credit recommendations for more than 6,000 formal military courses and more than 275 Army enlisted military occupational specialties (MOSs). A new edition was scheduled for Summer 1978. This program also operates an advisory service responding to inquiries concerning use of credit recommendations.

Occupational Assessment Programs. The general purpose of these programs is to devise means of using occupational classification systems as bases for making recommendations for educational credit and advanced standing in apprenticeship programs. Studies of Army and Navy enlisted occupations, of Army officer and warrant officer occupations, and of apprenticeship programs registered with the Bureau of Apprenticeship and Training (Department of Labor) are currently underway. Exploration of possible applications to additional job classification systems (certification, licensure, registration) is planned.

Program on Noncollegiate Sponsored Instruction. This program evaluates courses offered by organizations whose primary purpose is not education. More than 1,600 courses sponsored by over eighty organizations have been evaluated to date. Credit recommendations are available in the *Guide to Educational Programs in Noncollegiate Organizations* and *The National Guide to Credit Recommendations For Noncollegiate Courses* (1978 edition). Funding: Carnegie Corporation, Fund for the Improvement of Postsecondary Education, Kellogg Foundation.

Home Study Project. This project evaluates courses offered by schools accredited by the National Home Study Council; recommendations are made regarding the number of college-level semester credits, level in a degree program, and appropriate subject areas in which credit might be awarded. Courses to be reviewed are selected by each school. Recommendations are announced in the OEC newsletter and annual catalog. Evaluation costs and costs associated with the continuation of the project are borne by participating schools.

Apprenticeship Evaluation Program. This is a recently initiated project to evaluate apprenticeship training programs and develop credit recommendations for use by colleges and other postsecondary institutions. During a feasibility study for the Department of Labor, OCE evaluated eight apprenticeship programs, for which credit recommendations have been published.

Credit By Examination. This program's general purpose is to promote high standards and constructive use of credit-by-examination tests. OEC has developed criteria and evaluation procedures for appraising any and all such tests submitted for review by test publishers. Results of evaluations were published in 1978 in a form useful to institutions in establishing policies for awarding credit by examination. Regular updating of recommendations is planned.

Registry of Credit Recommendations. This program provides students with a record of educational accomplishments outside of colleges and universities. Established in September 1977, it will initially be used by students taking courses offered by organizations that participate in the ACE Program on Noncollegiate Sponsored Instruction. Rapid expansion to other ACE evaluation programs is planned. The purpose is to provide an effective link between the ACE evaluation process and the credit award process in academic institutions.

Henry Spille, Director
Office on Educational Credit
American Council on Education
One Dupont Circle
Washington, DC 20036

PROFICIENCY EXAMINATION PROGRAM (PEP)

PEP offers forty-seven proficiency examinations based on college-level course requirements. Tests cover a broad range of subject and career areas, with the greatest emphasis on nursing and business. They are administered four times a year in approximately 100 locations throughout the United States. The program is in its third year as a nationwide service.

O. W. Hascall
Proficiency Examination Program
The American College Testing Program
P.O. Box 168
Iowa City, IA 52240

SERVICE CENTER FOR COMMUNITY COLLEGE–LABOR UNION COOPERATION

This three-year program was started August 1976 to promote community college–labor union cooperation in six areas: apprenticeship training, journeyman retraining, preretirement education, labor studies, credit for work experience, and increasing utilization of tuition benefits in labor contracts. Funding: U.S. Department of Labor.

William Abbott
American Association of Community and Junior Colleges
One Dupont Circle, NW
Suite 410
Washington, DC 20036

TESTS OF ADULT BASIC EDUCATION (TABE)

These are tests measuring adult proficiency in reading, mathematics, and language at three competence levels. Content emphasizes general understanding and applications, not specific knowledge or recall of facts. Tests analyze and evaluate needs of adults wishing to undertake vocational-technical training or general literacy and self-improvement study. They are adapted from the 1970 edition of the California Achievement Tests.

Marketing Services Department
CTB/McGraw-Hill
Del Monte Research Park
Monterey, CA 93940

CHAPTER SEVEN

Implications and Consequences for the Future

Richard E. Peterson

The preceding chapters have enabled us to comprehend in some detail the existing dimensions of adult education and learning in the United States. In Chapter One we surveyed the many "providers" of education—the sources from which people may learn—and we reviewed the evidence that more people are learning from nonschool than from school-based sources. We saw in Chapter Two that participation of adults in the so-called learning force has been increasing steadily for the past decade, that much is known about adult learners' needs and problems, but that, significantly, poorly educated adults have tended to shy away from educational programs. We saw in Chapter Three that a great variety of new adult learning programs and services have been initiated at the local level, but that usually there is little coordination among the various "providers." In Chapter Four we saw evidence of much discussion and many proposals at the state level, particularly regarding new programs at established four-year colleges and universities, but little indication in most states of actual implementation of innovative strategies. In Chapter Five we were reminded of the many long-standing federal programs for adults, of the flurry of interest surrounding the Mondale Lifelong Learning Act and the HEW Lifelong Learning Project, and then of the disappointing rejection by Congress of appropriations pursuant to the act. Finally, in Chapter Six, we were shown, in directory form, the myriad sources of information and expertise—including interested organizations, periodicals, projects, and services—available to planners and directors of adult learning programs.

This concluding chapter builds on the factual material of these earlier chapters to make the case for increased lifelong learning opportunities. It develops a typology of benefits that are likely to flow from these opportunities and then draws a number of implications and consequences for policy makers and planners if these benefits are to be realized.

The Case for Lifelong Learning

While lifelong education and learning policies are gaining favor in numerous foreign countries, notably in Scandinavia, there are at the moment signs of slackening progress in this country. This present retrenchment, which affects numerous public services besides education, can in large part be attributed to the general mood of fiscal conservatism presently spreading in America (reflected, most dramatically, in the tax-reduction movements in many states).

It is a critical time for the education community. Public esteem for public education has been declining for more than a decade. Now public revenues are being reduced. Conceivably, in the near future we may be forced to rethink entirely our conceptions of how, and to what ends, education and learning in this country are to take place. After this reassessment, there may be new understandings regarding education as a national priority, and possibly also the basic outlines of educational policy and practice in this country. If this eventual reformulation is to be guided by life-long learning principles, educators and others concerned about human development must join the political fray. We would be remiss to stand aside, leaving it to politicians and tax cutters to establish the new priorities for public policy.

The case for the importance of expanded learning opportunities—for all individuals—to the well-being of the nation must be forcefully presented. A convincing analysis of the educational needs, relevant social trends, and likely benefits to individuals and society can be a key part of feasibility studies, planning proposals, and testimony before school boards, college boards of trustees, city councils, statewide commissions, and legislative committees.

Outlined below are ten main lines of reasoning that may be used to advocate expanded adult learning services. They range in order from the most incontrovertible to the most conjectural. Together, on the face of it, they constitute a highly convincing case.

Increasing Numbers of Older People. The case for lifelong learning usually begins with the observation that, owing to past birthrates and modern medical advances, the population is aging. New studies and projections consistently make clear that the average age of Americans will continue to rise in the decades ahead. This means that there will be substantially larger numbers of older people, who will comprise an increasingly larger proportion of the total population. Their political power will grow. Their learning needs will have to be met.

The Education–More Education "Law." The American population is increasingly better educated; recent generations have had higher secondary school and college completion rates than earlier ones. As Cross noted in Chapter Two, the more education people have, the more they want. Education is addictive.

Women Seeking Employment. Recent statistics on the enrollment of part-time students (summarized by Eddy, 1978) indicate that these students are predominantly women and that they are enrolling disproportionately in vocationally oriented programs. We know, also, that women are joining the work force in unprecedented numbers. Unquestionably, many women part-time students are preparing for gainful employment, and this is a trend that will not soon subside.

Societal Demands for Professional Competency. We spoke in Chapter One of the rise of consumer insistence on quality of professional services. In response, more and more states are requiring professionals of all kinds to be periodically relicensed on the basis of evidence of continued competency. Continuing learning for professionals will be necessary and proper.

Technological Change. The argument here, in barest form, is that technological change, by modifying or eliminating numerous types of jobs, renders many workers obsolete. Training and retraining opportunities are clearly needed by the individuals affected. For the society, such labor force retraining may be viewed as a national investment (see Striner, 1972). Job upgrading, which usually means higher pay for the individual, also means larger tax revenues for government.

Careers in Transition. According to a survey recently released by The College Board's Future Directions for a Learning Society project (Arbeiter and others, 1978a), roughly one out of three adult Americans reports being "in transition" (either undergoing or anticipating a job or career change). Financial considerations were most often cited as the motivating reason. Many such people, in order to make the transition successfully, are seeking further education, and many more (according to the Arbeiter study) would like counseling and other brokerage services.

The Quest for Self-Fulfillment. Many individuals, particularly people with some amount of higher education, are seeking sources of personal meaning and fulfillment outside the traditional domains of work and family. Development of talents, cultural interests, and recreational pursuits can be both an antidote to an otherwise unsatisfying existence and a stimulus to fuller development. Mohrman (1978) uses the term *consumption benefits* to refer to the satisfaction or enjoyment derived while participating in ("consuming") a learning activity. If modern life is as dull and alienating as some observers assert it to be, the mere fact of pleasant involvement in some "outside" learning activity may be a benefit of no small consequence.

Individual Competency Needs. The conception of lifelong learning in America set forth in the Introduction emphasized that reduction of illiteracy among people of all ages must be a high-priority goal. Without literacy, existence in modern society is dif-

ficult at best, and lifelong learning is pretty much out of the
question.

Two other types of competency can be advanced by lifelong
learning. Many parents need to become more competent as parents. There is evidence (from successful programs) that this competency can indeed be learned. Many adults also need to become
more competent as citizens. They need to understand political institutions and processes and the skills necessary for participation
in them. Political competency, in the sense of intelligent participation, most certainly can be learned.

Social Equity. Lifelong learning opportunities can be instrumental in bringing about economic equity—a more equal distribution of the nation's wealth. Widely available and effective job
training programs have the potential for enabling employment and
breaking cycles of near-poverty and welfare dependence. Interestingly, in many foreign countries economic equity considerations
are explicitly the chief goals of adult education and lifelong learning policies.

Lifelong learning opportunities also have the potential for
reducing racial, educational, and, as implied earlier, sexual barriers
to career advancement. They can mean a second chance for people
who for any reason have dropped out of school or college.

Indirect Benefits to Society. Numerous analysts, the present one
included (Peterson and Hefferlin, 1975), have pointed to the prob-
ability of indirect benefits to the broader society from extensive
involvement of people of all ages in learning activities. Such indirect or "avoidance benefits" (Mohrman, 1978) might include reduced welfare dependency, reduced crime and incarceration rates,
and improved mental and general health.

Counter-arguments to these benefits would include the contention that America is saddled with an overeducated, underemployed, disaffected, even revolt-prone intelligentsia—personified
by the embittered taxi driver with a Ph.D. in medieval history. But
the contention that Americans are already overeducated (see, for
example, Freeman, 1976) warrants rebuttal. First, the economic
benefits from higher education are by no means the only benefits,
either for individuals or society. Second, lifelong learning deals
only peripherally with production of highly trained specialists

(Ph.D.s, for example). And third, assuming little or no expansion in the job market for well-educated people, there should be efforts to create incentives for employers to take on more employees by, for example, granting leaves for education and other reasons (teacher "burn-out," for example) and by providing for job sharing, as between two half-time employees, as proposed by Best (1978) and implemented by the Oregon state government.

A Typology of Benefits of Lifelong Learning

As a guide to classifying and conveniently comprehending the potential benefits of lifelong learning, a typology of likely benefits may be useful. First, however, a glance at relevant literature.

The benefits or outcomes of higher education—college, as opposed to adult education—have been topics for fairly extensive conceptual work in recent years. For example, in their important book *Investment in Learning,* Bowen and his colleagues (1977) organized "Consequences for Individuals" into four subdivisions (each with a number of further divisions): cognitive learning; emotional and moral development; practical competence for citizenship and economic productivity; and practical competence for family life, consumer behavior, leisure, and health. In an earlier analysis, Lenning (1974) grouped (nonmonetary) benefits into seven categories of student development: academic; intellectual; personality; motivational/aspirational; social; esthetic/cultural; and moral.

With regard to benefits from adult or lifelong learning, while much has been written recently that is interesting and even inspiring (for example, Barnes, 1978; Bennis, 1978; DeMott, 1975; Leagans, 1978; McCan, 1978; Nolfi, 1976b, 1977a; Striner, 1972; Wirtz, 1978), these commentaries were generally not intended to be comprehensive. Mohrman's (1978) paper is a useful review of the major types of benefits. Perhaps the single document most pertinent to this topic is the *Handbook for Classifying and Describing the Learning Activities of Adults* prepared by the National Center for Higher Education Management Systems for NCES (Sell, 1978; described in Chapter Six). In its final draft, "Learner Purposes/ Outcomes" are divided into seven categories: basic education, occupational (including entry level, advancement, and change), family, civic, leisure and recreation, self-development, and social development.

In the typology proposed here, the four key categories are (1) individual benefits, as distinct from (2) societal benefits, and (3) personal or noneconomic benefits, as distinct from (4) economic benefits. The categorization is developed in Table 1.

This typology should be helpful to officials in building the case for lifelong learning. It should be taken as a beginning framework, to be modified in view of local circumstances and sentiments. Researchers interested in the general topic of educational effects may also find the typology useful. As an attempt to summarize the range of likely benefits of adult and lifelong learning described in the literature, it is meant to help answer the question: What results might we reasonably expect if people, en masse, were to become lifelong learners?

Table 1. Benefits of Lifelong Learning

To Individuals	*To Society*
Personal (Noneconomic) Development	*Societal Development*
1. Intellectual benefits	1. Direct benefits
a. Literacy	a. Literate population
b. Skills/knowledge for effective living	b. Informed, skilled citizens
. . . as a consumer	. . . in the marketplace
. . . as a parent	. . . in the family
. . . as a participant in politics	. . . in political life
c. General/academic education	c. Generally educated/ knowledgeable people
d. Capacity for continuous learning	d. Many lifelong learners
2. Personality benefits	
a. Sense of self-reliance, personal autonomy, empowerment	e. Citizenry not dependent on institutions
b. Self-esteem, self-worth, meaning, fulfillment	f. Social morale/lack of anomie
c. Social attitudes: tolerance, mutual respect	g. Harmonious, trustful social relations
d. Values, ethics	h. Humane culture

Table 1. Benefits of Lifelong Learning (Continued)

To Individuals *Personal (Noneconomic) Development*	*To Society* *Societal Development*

3. Avocational/cultural benefits
  a. Avocational/recreational skills/interests
  b. Artistic/esthetic skills/ appreciations
4. Consumption benefits (experienced during participation in learning activities)
	i. Population actively pursuing diverse interests
	j. Culturally sophisticated/vital society
	2. Indirect benefits
	  a. Reduced welfare dependency
	  b. Reduced crime, incarceration rates
	  c. Improved general health
	  d. More equitable distribution of wealth
	  e. More equitable distribution of other life amenities

Individual Economic Advancement	*Development of the Economy*

1. Entry-level training
 	
2. On-the-job advancement
  a. Increased responsibility/ status
  b. Increased earnings
3. Vocational renewal
  a. Job-upgrading/retraining
 	
  b. Training for a new/different vocation
4. Occupational flexibility
	1. Availability of trained manpower
	2. Increased job satisfaction
	3. Increased general standard of living
	4. Increased tax revenues
	5. High employee productivity
	6. Relatively low unemployment rate despite rapid technological change
	
	7. Employees capable of readily moving among related jobs

Implications for Planners and Program Directors

We have now reviewed some of the arguments in the case for lifelong learning, including certain needs created by current societal trends, and we have noted some of the likely benefits of lifelong learning to individuals and society. In the remaining pages we will set forth, on the basis of all the information presented thus far in this volume, fifteen sets of implications for planners and others seeking to make lifelong learning in America a reality.

Financing of Lifelong Learning

Planners ought not, in the near future, count on large new influxes of government money for lifelong learning activities— either for direct support of programs or, indirectly, for aid to students. This was the judgment of Powell and of Hartle and Kutner in their reviews of state and federal activities, respectively. Passage of Proposition 13 and similar measures reinforces their conclusion. As areas for new public policy initiatives, adult and lifelong learning simply do not have high priority in the late 1970s. The various provocative ideas for lifelong learning entitlements and other financing schemes put forth by Kurland (1977), Nolfi (1977a), Striner (1972), and contributors to the Windham, Kurland, and Levinsohn (1978) book are apparently not politically feasible in the immediate future, as Hartle and Kutner point out; they are ideas whose time, unfortunately, has yet to come.

This is not to say that the numerous categorical programs will not be continued—Adult Basic Education, Right to Read, CETA programs, Career Education, the Educational Information Centers—or even expanded, such as federal and state programs for the aging. State and local planners should be well informed and act aggressively to obtain funds from these sources. Promising innovative programs can often be launched through grants from private foundations (such as the Kellogg Foundation), the National Institute of Education (NIE), or especially the Fund for the Improvement of Postsecondary Education (FIPSE). For colleges and universities, Title IA of the Higher Education Act of 1965 (Community Services and Continuing Education), which is administered through the states, is a source of funds for innovation.

But for basic operating costs for new programs (or for adult student aid), support is not likely to be forthcoming in appreciable amounts from government sources, particularly as Proposition 13 attitudes take hold in the early 1980s. The challenge to local and state planners in a fiscally conservative environment will be no small one. More of the offerings from public schools and colleges will need to be self-supporting—that is, supported by student fees.

Cooperating organizations in the community will need to contribute all sorts of "in kind" services—material (for example, space) as well as human. Other sources of funding will need to be explored. Volunteers will need to be recruited. Perhaps the biggest challenge will be to accommodate low-income people, who will not be able to afford the going fees. They must be accommodated, however, and it *is* likely that federal funds will increasingly be available for this purpose, though still in categories for "targeted" groups such as the unemployed, the unskilled, the elderly, and the handicapped.

Limited Federal and State Roles

We saw that the Congress eliminated the small—$5 million—allocation for Lifelong Learning (pursuant to the Mondale Act) from President Carter's 1979 budget. Possibly the only new federal program reflecting lifelong learning ideas is the Educational Information Centers (EIC) program (described in Chapter Four); $3 million was appropriated for FY 1979, to be divided among the forty-four states that submitted suitable plans.

We saw in Chapter Five that the federal government sponsors a great range of programs that channel money into the education and training of adults. The Lifelong Learning Project of HEW (1978) recommended better coordination of all these programs, which would be no small task, as Baldwin (1978) points out. Improved coordination would, of course, be a very great help to local and state planners. The Lifelong Learning Project also recommended federal support for coordination of state and local adult learning activities, for research, and for demonstration and dissemination efforts. Other observers have made similar recommendations. Jonsen (1978b), for example, sees the need for federal funds for coordination of state and local lifelong learning activities; programmatic support, in the form of new subsidies to individuals or institutions; and research. Almost all experts emphasize the federal government's role in promoting social equity by making learning opportunities accessible to disadvantaged populations—usually through categorical programs. Indeed, if the federal government can be said to have a policy on lifelong learning, it seems to consist of providing opportunities for further education to certain groups on behalf of certain national goals (for example, equity).

While policies vary widely from one state to another, it

seems clear from Powell's review that new lifelong learning opportunities initiated at the state level have been limited largely to
new programs at state four-year colleges and universities. With a
few notable exceptions—for example, New York's Empire State
College and Regents External Degree—these new programs have
been rather restricted in size and inventiveness. Judging from the
state documents cited at the end of Chapter Four, there is indeed
active interest in major new forms of adult learning services in
numerous states. Yet few major programs have been implemented,
both because of legislative priorities and fiscal constraints, as Powell
points out, and also, we suspect, because of opposition from entrenched higher education interests (see Nolfi, 1978b).

Despite the considerable interest in new adult learning services, it is noteworthy that there are almost no indications of state-
level interest in programs that combine the services of diverse
providers—school and nonschool—which we regard as a key lifelong learning concept. New York may again be an exception
(Ambach, 1977). In Kansas, a statewide Kansas Association for
Lifelong Learning (KALL), to focus chiefly on clearinghouse work,
is presently being formed—not by a state agency (though state
agencies are participants) but by individuals in local organizations,
school and nonschool (address: 1221 Thurston, Manhattan, KS
66502).

This is not to say that the state role in underwriting lifelong
learning has not been substantial. Almost all of public education—
kindergarten through graduate school—is heavily supported by
state revenues. Yet many types of educational programs in which
the enrollees are predominately adults are *not* state supported, and
there is no discernible movement toward such support. Furthermore, since passage of the numerous Proposition 13-like measures,
many programs that have been in part state supported—school
district and community college evening programs in California, for
example—have been cut back and fees have been increased.

In sum, while we may hope that federal and state agencies
and officials will exercise leadership in promoting lifelong learning
ideals, and even provide funds for students or programs, we do
not expect general programmatic funds to be forthcoming in the
near future. We do, however, expect expanding federal funding

of categorical programs designed to increase lifelong learning opportunities for low-income and other disadvantaged groups. And
we do expect expanding federal sponsorship of (1) research and
demonstration projects and (2) clearinghouse and dissemination
activities, all of which should substantially benefit state and local
planners.

Local Organizing—The Key

Since federal and state governments are unlikely to assume
more than support roles in developing adult learning programs,
it will be primarily up to local individuals and organizations to create and maintain lifelong learning opportunities. Many, this writer
included, would contend that this is as it should be. As with other
human services, learning services should be maximally responsive
to the interests and needs of the people to be served; and this can
best be ensured when programs are planned and conducted in
close cooperation with the recipients of the services. This *local organizing principle* (a phrase used by Russell Garth of FIPSE) may
be put into effect in a community such as a neighborhood or small
town, citywide, or throughout metropolitan areas or regions. Local initiatives seem not only the politically most feasible strategy but
also the best strategy for effectively meeting people's learning
needs (see Rosenthal, 1978).

As we saw in Chapter Three, and as we see all around us
in communities of any size, there is already a wide range of school
and nonschool providers—the kinds of "sources" of education and
learning described in Chapter One. A city may have a two-year
community college close by, which, with its greater resources, may
well have progressed further than any of the other local providers
toward systematically meeting community education needs. There
are also likely to be programs of the city recreation department,
a branch library, churches, possibly a museum, and a variety of
other community organizations. In most localities, however, each
of the many providers tends to operate in isolation from the
others—and often in competition with the others (as noted in
Chapter One). Exaggerated advertising is not uncommon as organizations serve their own interests at the expense of those of the

student consumer; the latter—especially relatively uninformed, unsophisticated potential students—are the losers.

Some kind of local planning and coordinating body is typically needed. For our discussion purposes here, such a unit will be referred to as a Community Lifelong Learning Council (CLLC). (Rosenthal [1978] has proposed a somewhat similar device: the CLOC, Community Learning Opportunities Council.) Since so many resources already exist, an important function of this hypothetical council is simply to build communication links among diverse providers, so that all can begin to be informed about the capabilities of each. Leadership for the CLLC can come forward from the various participating organizations. The ultimate purpose of the council would be to orchestrate learning resources in the area in order to maximize participation of community people in learning activities that effectively meet their needs.

There are seemingly very few such cooperative community-wide organizations in existence. One of the most successful is The Adult Education Council of Metropolitan Denver. Another is the Rochester Urbanarium. A number of community learning councils have recently been established (or identified) through projects conducted by the National Manpower Institute and the American Association of Community and Junior Colleges. The Pennsylvania Region I Continuing Education Project is an extremely significant attempt at cooperation and coordination throughout a large metropolitan area (greater Philadelphia). The Council for the Advancement of Lifelong Learning (CALL, Box 489, 849 New Loudon Road, Latham, NY 12110) is a similar undertaking in an even larger though more sparsely populated region (Northeastern New York). All of these projects are described in Chapter Six or in earlier chapters. Planners working on the basis of the "local organizing principle" would do well to obtain information about as many such organizations as possible.

Planning Techniques

A step-by-step guide to planning will not be offered here. Too many unique circumstances in each locality, including the personalities of key actors, usually render such "cookbooks" of little value. For varying perspectives on establishing adult learning programs, planners at the local and state levels could consult, among others, Cross, Valley, and Associates (1974), Dwyer and others (1978), Florida Postsecondary Education Commission (1977), Hamilton (1976), Houle (1972), Karwin (1973), Knox (1977), Medsker and others (1975), Nolfi (1975), Peat, Marwick, Mitchell and Co. (1978), Peterson and Hefferlin (1975), Tough (1971), Wilson (1976), and the documents recommended in Halstead (1978).

We will comment briefly on four general activities of a substantive nature and one set of "process" considerations important in community-based planning for lifelong learning.

A fundamental planning tool, we would assert first, is the needs assessment. Ideally, it should take the form of a comprehensive analysis of the total range of learning interests and needs of all area residents. It may be supplemented by a survey of employer needs. Survey design and interpretation can be complicated; use of professional consultants would usually be advantageous. General familiarity with the literature, some of which is cited in the Cross and Valley chapters, would likewise be advantageous. A useful conceptual review has been provided by Monette (1977). An appreciation of the limitations of surveys of adult educational needs is also important, as pointed out by Cross (and also by Griffith, 1978; O'Keefe, 1977; Peat, Marwick, Mitchell and Co., 1978; and Pilsworth and Ruddock, 1975). Depending on available resources, multiple approaches to assessing needs—as used, for example, by Hefferlin, Peterson, and Roelfs (1975) and Peterson, Roelfs, and others (1975)—could lead to relatively firm conclusions about priority needs. Assessment of community educational needs is a logical early planning activity for a newly formed Community Lifelong Learning Council (CLLC). It provides a focus for interest and involvement of council members, and it has the potential for sensitizing members to the broader needs of the community.

A second important planning technique is an inventory of all available resources for education and learning in the locality. It serves some of the same organizational, attitudinal, and political purposes as the needs survey. The typology of sources of education and learning given in Chapter One could serve as the framework for the inventory, which should cover, among other data, access

requirements for each program—cost, previous education required, limitation to certain clientele groups, and the like. Examples of the use of inventories of community educational resources
are found in Coles (1976) and Peterson, Roelfs, and others (1975).
Examples of statewide inventories are Hamilton (1976), Nolfi and
Nelson (1973), and Salner (1975).

A logical third activity is analysis of gaps between assessed
needs and existing resources. This is typically a less objective, less
formal procedure than the first two. Planners try to see how resources stack up against needs, to determine what needs are not
being met, or not being met effectively. For an illustration of this
procedure, see Peterson and Hefferlin, 1975.

The fourth general planning activity is to agree on how to,
or who will, fill the gaps—meet the unmet needs. This may call for
negotiation. Particular organizations may wish to expand their programs to meet certain of the needs. In instances where it is judged
that available resources cannot meet a particular priority need, the
council itself may wish to seek the necessary funds and create its
own programs.

The critical "process" considerations in community-based
planning for lifelong learning are, first, that it be broadly participatory and, second, that it be essentially open. Participation of
education-providers should be, in Dave's (1976) terms, both "horizontal" and "vertical": "horizontal" in the sense of including all
organizations that serve people in a given general age bracket,
whether their primary function is education or some other service,
such as transportation or housing; and "vertical" in the sense of
including all levels in a large bureaucracy—for example, elementary, secondary, and collegiate units of a public education system.
Equally important in participatory planning is to involve potential
students—the consumers—either directly or through devices such
as advisory boards. All these actors should have the opportunity
to participate in all four of the general planning activities just described—from designing needs and resources surveys, to interpreting results and identifying gaps in services, to determining
which organizations will assume responsibility for providing which
services.

Finally, all aspects of the planning process need to be entirely open to public scrutiny. Needless to say, such a broadly participative and open planning process will call for large measures of sensitivity, patience, and capacity for cooperation and compromise on the part of leaders, and indeed from all parties involved.

Design of Learning Services

Comments here will again be brief and general. The ten programming principles outlined in this section apply to the total configuration of a community's or region's lifelong learning programs, as cooperatively planned and coordinated by, let us say, a hypothetical CLLC. Many of the suggestions flow rather directly from Cross' survey-based conclusions in Chapter Two about adult learners and potential learners.

Diversified Learning Opportunities. In terms of subject matter, level of difficulty, and learning methods, the range of lifelong learning opportunities in a given locality should correspond as closely as possible to the learning interests, levels of sophistication, and preferred learning modes (for example, lectures, workshops, or independent work) of the population of learners in the locality.

Program Openness. Services should be essentially open, in the sense that there should be no age or sex restrictions anywhere in the program and minimum use of aptitude, ability, or previous-education requirements.

Credit and Noncredit Options. Students should be able to take courses for high school or college degree credit (with standards the same as on campus) or, if they choose, noncredit courses. It should also be possible for students to obtain degree credit for learning acquired in noncollegiate settings, by means of assessment procedures such as those developed by the Council for the Advancement of Experiential Learning (described in Chapter Six).

Aids to Independent Learners. A comprehensive lifelong learning program should provide assistance to the large numbers of independent learners. The libraries may be particularly suited for this service. Numerous ideas for such a service are contained in Cross (1978c), Gross (1977a), Knowles (1975), and Tough (1971).

Financial Accessibility. Fees should be as low as possible—consistent with instructional quality. Special fee schedules may be advisable for certain groups, such as low-income or older people.

Geographical Accessibility. Program components should be deployed throughout the locality in a way such that transportation (and parking) problems are minimized and convenience and safety are maximized.

Temporal Accessibility. Program components should be scheduled at various times during the day and evening, and throughout the week (and, indeed, the year), to fit as well as possible the various schedules of the potential student population.

Simplified Bureaucratic Routines. Most adults are put off by cumbersome, time-consuming, inefficient administrative procedures: many older people are intimidated by them. Various application, registration, and other recordkeeping processes should be held to a minimum and then operated in as simple and efficient a manner as possible.

Effective Public Information. Potential learners in the community need to know about the range of opportunities available to them. Designers of advertising campaigns can learn much from the experience of other programs throughout the country. Conducted ideally by the proposed CLLC, the advertising should not aim to promote particular institutions, and altogether (and in its specifics) it should not promise more than can be delivered, as DeMott (1978) and Sawhill (1978) have sharply warned us.

Avoidance of Paternalism. The experience of most educators has been with young people. Paternal and patronizing attitudes, however, must be resisted in conducting lifelong learning programs. It would be well, as Green and his colleagues (1978) have said, to view adult learners "as partners in learning . . . the last thing (they) need is to be treated like children."

Planning groups should know about and draw upon the experience of other programs, as we have said. At the same time, planners should strive to be visionary and creative as well. Indeed, innovation—invention of entirely new types of services or methods of delivery—may not only better meet learners' needs, it is the lifeblood by which the lifelong learning movement will progress.

Accommodation of Low-Income People

Programs must be designed, and financing somehow secured, so that economically disadvantaged people will be attracted. The total adult education outlay nationally has been widely criticized for serving primarily the privileged classes (see Fiske, 1977; Rosenthal, 1977); the criticism is fully justified, as can be seen in the data in Chapter Two. Future, more comprehensive lifelong learning programs will be equally vulnerable, so much so that public funding for such programs can hardly be expected unless low-income people are represented in at least their proportions in the general population. This is an absolute imperative for comprehensive planners. Inasmuch as social equity is a general federal policy objective, all avenues for possible funds from federal sources should be explored.

Educational Brokering Services

A relatively new concept, educational brokering was described from several perspectives in earlier chapters (see also Heffernan, Macy, and Vickers, 1976). Combining several distinct but related services—counseling and individual assessment, information about area learning opportunities, referral, and advocacy (as active assistance to the potential learner in pursuing his goals)—the brokering agency can function as a means to link the individual learner to the *set* of learning opportunities that best meets his particular needs. Properly conducted, a brokering service is a natural adjunct to a pluralistic, cooperative network of learning programs.

Such brokering services must be *neutral* in relation to the specific colleges and other providers in the locality. That is, they cannot operate as recruiting agencies for particular institutions: they must operate first and foremost in the interests of individual learners. They should charge minimal fees and be open to everyone in the community. A Community Lifelong Learning Council could ensure that a well-run brokering service (or network of services dispersed for maximum convenience of users) is in operation in the area. The hypothetical council could conceivably design and conduct the brokering program itself, as a service to participating organizations. However organized, effective counseling and information services can provide the keys to new learning experiences, especially for people who have been away from school for some time.

Involvement of Volunteers

In Chapter One we noted the important role of volunteers in various educational activities, such as programs of Cooperative Extension, the churches, the Red Cross, and other community agencies. According to recent polls, as many as one fourth of the adults in the United States do some sort of volunteer work. While there was probably a decline in the level of volunteerism in the late 1960s and the early 1970s, owing to the women's movement, women's desire for paid work to help support households, and other factors (Manser and Cass, 1976),[1] more recently there have been indications that new populations, such as retired people and people changing careers, are being attracted to volunteer work. In the aftermath of Proposition 13 there may conceivably be new incentives and perhaps new satisfactions (from providing essential public services), and with these, new public attitudes about volunteerism in the United States (see Morrow, 1978).

Lifelong learning programs should seek to engage volunteers in a variety of roles: classroom teaching, consulting (academic or administrative), brokering work (after suitable training), advising independent learners, and clerking and recordkeeping, for example. Retired people are an obvious pool from which to recruit lifelong learning facilitators (see Murphy and Florio, 1978). Not only will involvement of volunteers contribute to cost-effective programs, such a policy will provide opportunities for educationally rewarding activities as well as an outlet for a generous motive that arguably deserves to be abetted.

[1]A Census Bureau poll completed for ACTION, the agency that coordinates federally supported volunteer programs (including the Peace Corps and Vista), however, found an increase in volunteerism among Americans aged fourteen and older: from 18 percent in 1965 to 24 percent in 1974 (ACTION, 1975).

Continuing Education of Professionals

A number of difficult and controversial issues have grown up around the problem of maintaining competence among professionals. We noted in Chapter One the burgeoning public consumer concern for professional competence (among, for example, doctors) and the resulting trend in many states toward mandatory continuing education for certain professional groups.

Continuing education for professionals is commonly, though by no means always, carried out through universities or the appropriate professional associations. Thus, Community Lifelong Learning Councils of the sort envisioned here may or may not become involved, depending on perhaps the proximity of university professional schools or the extent to which various state associations (for example, bar or medical) conduct continuing education programs.

This said, there are at least two questions that a CLLC needs to answer with regard to providing continuing education courses for professionals: First, can completion of one or more courses be said to *guarantee* competence in some sense? Second, should the CLLC in some way *certify* competence? The answer to both questions, in our judgment, must be no. What the CLLC can do is to work with professional groups to set up learning experiences in any of a number of formats (whichever make most sense to the participants), with the expectation that the certification of continued competency will be accomplished separately—for example, through an examination administered by a state licensing board.

Finally, mandatory continuing education raises for some observers the spectre of mandatory lifelong education or schooling—a notion quite at odds with the concept of lifelong learning proposed here and by most other writers. Nevertheless, there is a substantial literature (for example, Gueulette, 1976; Lisman and Ohliger, 1978; Williams, 1974; the newsletter *Second Thoughts*) that upbraids the continuing education establishment for seeking to coerce people into continued schooling, in part to preserve jobs for academics. While this criticism is valuable, so long as lifelong learning programs are based primarily on learner interests (and professionals have substantial freedom to upgrade their skills in any of a variety of ways), there would be little prospect that lifelong learning will become compulsory.

Accountability to the Student-Consumer

Since student fees will probably be the largest single source of operating funds for lifelong learning programs in the near future, it is logical that accountability be primarily to the student-consumer. Even under other—predominantly public—funding arrangements, the case can be made that human service agencies ought in justice to be accountable to the recipients of their services.

Program leaders cannot simply give lip service to the principle of accountability to the student and patronizingly assume that adult students, like most younger students, lack the sophistication and assertiveness to make it known when they believe they are receiving poor treatment. A Community Lifelong Learning Council should have a general policy of keeping all its operations—planning, deliberating, deciding—open to public view. It should also have more or less formal mechanisms by which accountability to consumers can be realized, and here the distinction between implementing accountability and participating in governance becomes somewhat blurred. Perhaps ideally the two activities should be combined; that is, the constituents to whom the program is accountable ought to be involved meaningfully in governing the program.

A CLLC could conceivably be set up so that all or most members of the council are lay citizens and potential students (rather than representatives of providing institutions); under this model the council would function as a school board or college board of trustees—hiring the director, setting policies, approving programs, and so forth, and receiving evaluation reports and making judgments about program effectiveness.

Beyond, or instead of, this board of trustees model, the CLLC should utilize a range of citizen-student consultant panels. These groups could advise the council on such matters as evaluating community education needs, setting goals, planning, evaluating instructional programs generally, evaluating faculty specifically, evaluating the brokering service, and selecting sites for services. Panels of this sort would both contribute significantly to decisions and also be the chief recipients and evaluators of evaluation reports, all in an environment of public openness.

These comments are admittedly conjectural. Surprisingly, we have seen no descriptions of methods by which adult education programs have implemented accountability. Yet, no matter how it is carried out, systematic accounting to the student-consumer will be a must for lifelong learning programs of the future.

Program Quality

As Sawhill (1978), among others, admonishes, quality will be an absolutely essential attribute of lifelong learning programs of the future. Very practically, under the model of a CLLC as essentially a consortium of institutions (providers), it is likely that a good many higher education institutions would refuse to join without assurance of quality (by a definition that may have to be negotiated); nor would they care to continue their association with the CLLC if there were signs of inattention to quality. And without a continuing reputation for quality in all its operations, a lifelong learning program can hardly be expected to thrive in the community; to gain the respect of the general public or individual cultural arbiters; to be held in esteem in other academic circles in the region and state; or to attract funds from government, foundations, or other sources.

The word *quality* is as elusive as it is widely used in American education; indeed, it seems to have as many meanings as there are users of the term. In the context of adult or lifelong learning, we think it best to define quality primarily in terms of the *satisfaction* of the student. Operationally, quality would be evidenced by comments on evaluation forms like "It was a great course (or seminar, or whatever)," or "The program really prepared me well to _____," or "The advisers at _____ Center were extremely helpful when I was trying to decide _____."

In order to maximize student satisfaction, many of the traditional indexes of quality may indeed often be necessary: well-trained (even degreed), knowledgeable, experienced instructors; sizable, accessible libraries; skilled, sensitive brokering workers;

efficient administrative procedures; pleasant physical facilities; a general climate of congenial yet productive relations between staff and students; and so forth.

The matter of accreditation frequently enters discussions of quality in education. No doubt if a new type of educational institution, an organization that orchestrates community-based lifelong learning, should evolve, yet another new accrediting agency—following one of the seemingly immutable laws of postsecondary education in the United States—would need to be created. One must trust that it will be staffed by people of vision, free of fixed ideas about education.

Whether or not there will be external accreditors, it will be critical that leaders of lifelong learning programs constantly attend to the matter of quality. Too many lifelong learning programs have come under attack for alleged fraud. Relatively unsophisticated students, especially, who may say they are satisfied with inferior courses, must be protected from being cheated—perhaps by some reliable mechanism for screening proposed offerings. Continued attention to quality, of course, is important to survival of programs in a totally voluntary education and learning system. It is important also for the success of the lifelong learning movement nationwide.

New Roles for Schools and Colleges

Assuming the desirability, even the reality, of a burgeoning population of lifelong learners, what are the implications for the nation's thousands of schools and colleges—the country's educational backbone? Can this gigantic establishment, or at least major parts of it, be turned in important ways to better serve learners of all ages?

First, we commented in Chapter One on the severely fragmented nature of public education in America. In order for this "system" to serve lifelong learners effectively, it must somehow begin to pull together. The various segments need to begin talking with each other—about, for example, how to facilitate transition of students from one level to another and movement in and out of formal education throughout the lifespan. Conceivably, this communication could take place under the auspices of local CLLC-like agencies.

Second, the schools, as enrollments continue to decline over the next decade, should adopt *community education* concepts, notably to make school facilities available during the day and evening for all manner of community-responsive learning activities (as suggested by the Community Schools Act of 1974 and Charles Stewart Mott Foundation [1978b] initiatives). These new directions could also be carried out within a framework set by the multi-institutional CLLC.

Third, school districts' adult education programs should become active partners in comprehensive community lifelong learning enterprises, such as a CLLC. Public school adult education has occasionally been a whipping boy, and one does sense that it tends to be isolated from the main currents of educational discourse and that its instructional methods have changed relatively little over the years. Possibly, association with a CLLC-like organization could contribute to its revitalization.

The greatest reform, however, is needed in the colleges and universities, since they are the institutions to which most adults will turn as they pursue further learning. The need for change is less among the two-year community colleges, many of which, as Valley points out in Chapter Three, have been extremely resourceful in devising programs for older adults. In the eyes of some (perhaps envious) observers, however, they have been too active—too aggressive, entrepreneurial, and uncooperative compared with other providers in a given locality. The point, though, is that most community colleges have come to accept providing a range of educational services for adults of all ages as a fundamental institutional goal.

Not so for most four-year institutions. While many, to be sure, have taken steps on behalf of older students—external degrees, special programs for returning women, fee reductions for senior citizens, and other measures as described in Chapters Three and Four (and by Atelsek and Gomberg, 1977)—by and large they are small steps, often taken mostly because of declining enrollments of "regular" students. Comprehensive institutional commitment to lifelong learning concepts, as described by Bennis (1978), is extremely rare.

It would be easy to make a general appeal about how all of

the nation's colleges and universities should open their doors to people of all ages. From a broad perspective, however, this would probably not be good advice. Much can be (and has been) said for a truly diversified higher education system in a pluralistic society. The private colleges in the country should be able to set their own missions. The nationally renowned research universities, not in danger of losing appreciable numbers of (traditional-aged) applicants, should probably continue to pursue their present goals.

But what about all the middle-level public four-year institutions? Supported as they are by taxes from all the citizens, ought they not to be committed to serving all people, regardless of age, who are desirous of continuing their learning? Here we think the answer is clearly yes. What we are seeing, however—the modest "add-on" programs for particular populations of adults—will not be sufficient. What will be required, instead, is a fundamental reorientation of the institution—embracing the attitudes and values of staff as well as all manner of campus policies and practices—if older adults are to receive educational services of a quality similar to those received by younger adults.

In the spirit of the times, reform should probably be undertaken incrementally. Colleges that have not done so could first consider the kinds of innovations described by Valley and Powell; and then, perhaps, the "institutional initiatives" recommended by Hesburgh, Miller, and Wharton (1973); and then the more fundamental reforms proposed by Bennis (1978). Eventually, the broad goal should be complete equality of opportunities and services for qualified adults of all ages. It is hard to know, in planning major institutional reform, where to break into the cycle of institutional functioning. There would first need to be wide deliberation and consultation, to include state legislators. Campus leaders and governing board members would then articulate the new institutional philosophy and the new incentive-reward system for faculty. Academic leaders—department chairmen, for example, bent on enhancing the prestige of their respective units in the usual sense of research and publications—will need to be persuaded. Such persuasion of the faculty may be more difficult; most are products of research universities and have their own career agendas, which usually do not include teaching older adults.

At the same time, a host of new policies will need to be implemented. New curriculums will need to be developed. For example, many new programs would be career oriented—intended mainly for employed persons seeking job advancement or older persons preparing for initial entry into the work force. For that matter, many commentators have suggested the need for teaching lifelong learning skills to "regular age" college students. Hesburgh, Miller, and Wharton (1973), for example, recommend that "A substantial part of the university's undergraduate curriculum in every subject matter area should be redesigned to help students learn how to carry out a program of self-education and lifelong learning." This writer has come across no accounts of such curriculums. They would offer a substantial challenge to an instructional design specialist, it would seem (see Smith and Haverkamp, 1977; and Thomas and Harri-Augstein, 1977).

Courses will need to be offered in the evening, late afternoon, on Fridays, perhaps on weekends. Student services will need to be available during all those hours. Various administrative procedures affecting students will need to be simplified and otherwise made more humane. Courses and other educational activities should be conducted in numerous locations away from the campuses. Four-year colleges and universities should help set up and then support and participate in community lifelong learning organizations of the sort described. The broad goal, in sum, is to achieve a genuine and pervasive commitment to age-neutralism at the college or university, thus enabling it to become a key instrument for lifelong learning throughout the region.

Expanded Roles for Nonschool Organizations

Chapter One went to considerable length to portray the extensive involvement of nonschool organizations in the education and learning of Americans. If, again, we assume the desirability of something akin to a learning society—a society in which learning pervades the entire fabric of the community—what are some of the implications for nonschool organizations and institutions interested in the growth and well-being of the community and its citizens?

Such an analysis could be immense. The following suggestions are illustrative of the many possibilities. They spring for the most part from the Chapter One overview and are ordered roughly as that chapter is ordered. Further implications for nonschool organizations can be found in, among other sources, Commission on Non-Traditional Study (1973), Cremin (1976), Knox (1977), and the papers from the HEW Lifelong Learning Project. The kinds of activities indicated here could for the most part be carried out in cooperation with a Community Lifelong Learning Council or similar agency.

- Private businesses should further expand educational benefits and opportunities for their employees. They should attempt to make work environments as interesting as possible. Pursuant to the federal Cooperative Education Act, they should participate in *cooperative education* programs in which students have part-time jobs related to their studies at local businesses and industries. Large installations should operate educational brokering services. Company experts should teach courses in the community and otherwise aid in the work of CLLC-like organizations.
- Professional associations should expand continuing education activities for their members and experiment with a variety of learning formats as alternatives to familiar classroom courses. For purposes of licensure and relicensure, their policy should be that members periodically demonstrate competency rather than merely complete courses.
- Trade unions should press in negotiations for even broader educational benefits. They should find ways to encourage more members to make use of educational benefits. Along with management, they should seek to make work situations more varied and less routine, as by rotating positions, work schedules, and the like. They should experiment with union-conceived and operated educational programs in a variety of subject areas, as well as establishing educational brokering services for members and their families. Their apprentice programs should be entirely open and nondiscriminating.
- Government agencies at all levels should further expand educational benefits and opportunities and urge employees to use them. They should expand internship programs for people of all ages. Government agency-based experts should be encour-

aged to participate as instructors in community learning activities.
- Federal manpower programs should be further expanded to provide training and retraining opportunities for people of all ages in all geographical areas. They should be responsive to local training needs, and agency—for example, CETA—officials should participate in CLLC-like organizations to help assure appropriate diversity and coordination of programs.
- The military services should also participate in coordinated community lifelong learning enterprises. Military base facilities and expertise may be shared. Numerous educational programs in the community could enroll military personnel of all ages and ranks.
- Agriculture extension has an enviable record. To its wide-ranging programs it could usefully add educational brokering services—to aid members of farm families to clarify personal goals and understand how various educational routes may be used to reach them. Cooperative Extension should also have an active role in rural area CLLCs.
- City recreation departments will need to develop political expertise, including developing constituencies, in order to make their case and protect their budgets in a spreading Proposition 13 environment. They should expand use of volunteers. They should be active participants in CLLC-like bodies.
- Community organizations of all kinds need to become more fully aware of their potentials as instruments for learning. Member learning interests should be canvassed and educational programs initiated. New roles for volunteers should be tried out. Libraries, in particular, should experiment with new types of services to independent lifelong learners. Libraries, museums, Y's, and other community agencies should be key participants in community-wide lifelong learning organizations.
- Churches and synagogues likewise have great potential as places for learning for people of all ages. They are the principle center of social activity for many people, especially older adults. They should conduct diversified programs, covering nonreligious as well as religious topics, for members—and nonmembers—of all ages.
- Free universities need to develop ways to attract a broader spectrum of students—mainly people with relatively little previous education and also those (often with extensive schooling) who

desire that substantial "respectability" or "legitimacy" be associated with their learning activities.

- Parks and forests, as they increase in numbers and attract greater throngs, have great potential for communicating facts and attitudes about nature and conservation of natural resources. Larger portions of park budgets should be allocated to educational activities.

Continuous Evaluation

Plans for lifelong learning programs should not be static. Planners should design in an evaluation component, which would provide the basis for constant program modification and improvement, as well as for program accountability. Evaluation should be a continuing activity, and entirely open; it should be accepted as a normal aspect of organizational functioning.

It is necessary to continuously review broad policies and goals as well as the effectiveness of the various instructional elements and administrative procedures. Thus, program leaders need to continuously question, for example, whether the total community is being served, rather than primarily the educated classes. Are individuals, or institutions, being served first and foremost? More important, are students learning in—do they report they have benefitted from—program X, course Y, or workshop Z? Is the library being used? Are the enrollment procedures efficient? And so forth.

Evaluation can be performed in a great many ways. A forthcoming (fall 1979) issue in the newly inaugurated Jossey-Bass series, *New Directions for Continuing Education,* will deal with assessing the impact of continuing education. Useful general treatments of evaluation strategies in schools and colleges are provided by, among many others, Anderson, Ball, and Murphy (1975), Dressel (1976), and the *New Directions* series on *Program Evaluation* and on *Institutional Research,* also from Jossey-Bass.

Continuous—institutionalized—evaluation serves the twin goals of (1) improving plans and programs and (2) implementing accountability. As we suggested earlier, students should be involved in designing and carrying out evaluation activities, and, in a spirit of genuine accountability, they should be the chief recipients of evaluation results. Probably even more important, institutionalized evaluation serves as an antidote to a kind of mindless satisfiedness that stagnates programs and organizations and inhibits the advance of the broader lifelong learning movement.

Informed Planning and Decision Making

Finally, as we have sifted through the literature of adult education and learning over the last several years, we have found it to be extensive indeed. Add to it the material, often technical or theoretical, that deals with education or learning regardless of age or grade level, or that concerns how to arrange for learning *lifelong* (for example, Cremin, 1976; Dave, 1976; and Faure and others, 1972), and the result is a wealth of ideas, reports of research, and accounts of experiences that can inform the work of planners and administrators. Much is dated, of course, and of marginal value. New material, however, seems to be becoming available at an exponential rate.

Planners can ill afford false starts. Reinvention of wheels can also be wasteful of resources. One cannot know everything, to be sure, but there is much that can be learned by planning groups. They can use the leads provided in Chapter Six and in the References at the end of this book to build a basic library, including, for example, Cremin (1976); Cross, Valley, and Associates (1974); Faure and others (1972); Houle (1976); Knox (1977); *New Directions for Continuing Education* (Jossey-Bass series); Penland (1977); Rockhill (1978); Scanlon (1978); Smith (1976); Tough (1971); Commission on Non-Traditional Study (1973); and the papers from the HEW Lifelong Learning Project. If they work at the state level, they can build a more specialized collection by adding some of the reports cited in Chapters Two and Four. If their base is a college or university, they will need, among others, Houle (1973); Harrington (1977); reports from the Council for the Advancement of Experiential Learning (CAEL), such as Keeton and Tate (1978); and papers from The College Board's Future Directions for a Learning Society project. There are many more sources of information, as is clear from the listings in Chapter Six. They should join one or two national organizations (for example, the Adult Education Association of the United States of America, the American

Association for Higher Education, or the National Association for Public Continuing and Adult Education), attend their meetings, and go to other meetings and workshops. They should use as many clearinghouses as are needed to get hold of what they want, insist that materials be delivered, and get to know their staffs personally. They should have access to the basic ERIC documents, subscribe to journals and newsletters, get on the mailing lists for free publications, contact people running programs similar to theirs, and ask them for leads to other relevant projects. They should make contact with the numerous advanced thinkers in the foundations, in government (for example, at NIE and FIPSE), and at the universities. There is much, needless to say, that can be known. Planning in isolation seems inexcusable.

Much in these last pages may seem utopian. We make no apologies; there must be visions—many more and keener than those in this volume—to provide long-range goals for planners and to help keep the larger lifelong learning movement vital. Novel theories about how best to facilitate learning and bold visions about where we ought to be heading are continuously needed.

In the meantime, however, there are pressing concerns. And it is perhaps necessary that this book, rather than ending in flights of imagination, conclude on a note of responsibility. The flurry of enthusiasm that accompanied the Mondale Act during 1976 and 1977 has passed. In mid 1978, as Hartle and Kutner indicated, both houses of Congress disapproved spending under the act for FY 1979. Add to this the sobering realities of Proposition 13 attitudes as they spread across the land, with adult education programs often being among the first to be cut.

Increased political savvy will be needed to maintain budgets and keep programs going. Offerings of mediocre quality must not be tolerated. No more must be promised than can be delivered. Vested interests should be laid aside in order to serve students rather than organizations. Cooperative communitywide planning and coordinating bodies should be created and supported. Experiments should be launched locally with wholly new approaches to facilitating learning among people of all ages (using, we optimistically assume, government research and development grants).

Lifelong learning advocates should participate actively in forging the new synthesis that will surely emerge as Proposition 13 fulminations recede; new theories and visions should be generated; and then these conceptions can be further refined. Through all of these efforts, the lifelong learning movement will advance. Above all, by planning wisely and resourcefully now, we can help guarantee that we ourselves will soon be able to share in the fruits of the forthcoming learning society.

References

Abbott, W. "College-Labor Union Cooperation." *Community and Junior College Journal,* 1977, *47,* 48–71.

A. C. Nielsen Company. *Adult Educational Interest Survey.* Northbrook, Ill.: A. C. Nielsen, 1973.

ACTION. *Americans Volunteer—1974.* Washington, D.C.: ACTION, 1975.

Adult and Continuing Education Today, August 16, 1976, *6* (17).

Advisory Panel on Research Needs in Lifelong Learning During Adulthood. *Lifelong Learning During Adulthood: An Agenda for Research.* New York: Future Directions for a Learning Society, The College Board, 1978.

Alford, A. "The Education Amendments of 1976." *American Education,* 1977, *13* (1), 6–11.

Alford, H. J. *Continuing Education in Action.* New York: Wiley, 1968.

Ambach, G. M. *Changing Stages of Learning.* Inaugural Address of the President of the University of the State of New York and Commissioner of Education. Albany, N.Y.: Office of the Commissioner of Education, 1977.

American Association of Community and Junior Colleges. *Policies for Lifelong Education.* Washington, D.C.: American Association of Community and Junior Colleges, 1979.

455

American Council on Education. "House Votes for Tax Credit Bill for School and College Tuitions." *Higher Education and National Affairs,* June 2, 1978, *27,* 4.

American Federation of Teachers' Commission on Higher Education. *Financing Higher Education.* Report No. 2. Washington, D.C.: American Federation of Teachers, 1977.

Anderson, S. B., Ball, S., Murphy, R. T., and Associates. *Encyclopedia of Educational Evaluation: Concepts and Techniques for Evaluating Education and Training Programs.* San Francisco: Jossey-Bass, 1975.

Andringa, R. C. "Twenty-One Political Factors Standing in the Way of Federal Education Entitlements for All American Adults." Washington, D.C.: R. C. Andringa, 1977 (Xerox).

Appalachian Adult Education Center. *Different Strokes for Different Folks.* Morehead, Ky.: Morehead State University, n.d.

Arbeiter, S. "Profile of the Adult Learner." *The College Board Review,* Winter 1976–77, *102,* 20–27.

Arbeiter, S., and others. *40 Million Americans in Career Transition.* New York: Future Directions for a Learning Society, The College Board, 1978a.

Arbeiter, S., and others. *Telephone Counseling for Home-Based Adults.* New York: Future Directions for a Learning Society, The College Board, 1978b.

Arizona Board of Regents. *University Development in the Mid-Seventies: A Long Range Plan.* Phoenix: Arizona Board of Regents, 1974.

Atelsek, F. J., and Gomberg, I. L. *College and University Services for Older Adults.* Washington, D.C.: American Council on Education, 1977.

Averill, L. *Summary of Results of the National Consortium Compensation Survey.* Kansas City, Kans.: Kansas City Regional Council for Higher Education, 1976.

Baillie, D., Eignor, D., and Averill, D. *Nontraditional Student Needs Assessment Project.* Amherst: University of Massachusetts, 1977.

Baldwin, F. "Lifelong Learning and Public Policy." Paper prepared for the HEW Lifelong Learning Project, Washington, D.C., 1978.

Bane, M. J. *Here to Stay: American Families in the Twentieth Century.* New York: Basic Books, 1976.

Barlow, B. M., and Timiraos, C. R. *Colorado Adult Needs Assessment. Final Technical Report.* Denver: Colorado Department of Education and State Board for Community Colleges and Occupational Education, 1975.

Barnes, R. E. "An Educator Looks Back from 1996." *The Futurist,* April 1978, *12,* 123–126.

Barton, P. E. "Lifelong Learning: Getting Started." *School Review,* May 1978a, *86* (3), 311–326.

Barton, P. E. "Lifelong Learning: Starting Young." Paper prepared for the HEW Lifelong Learning Project, Washington, D.C., 1978b.

Bashaw, W. L. "The Effect of Community Junior Colleges on the Proportion of Local Population Who Seek Higher Education." *Journal of Educational Research,* 1965, *58* (7), 327–329.

Bennis, W. "Toward a Learning Society: A Basic Challenge to Higher Education." Paper prepared for the HEW Lifelong Learning Project, Washington, D.C., 1978.

Berry, M. F. "Lifelong Learning: Assistant Secretary for Education Speaks." *Lifelong Learning: The Adult Years,* 1977, *1* (1), 6–7.

Bertelsen, P. H., and Cohn, G. (Eds.). *Ways and Means of Strengthening Information and Counselling Services for Adult Learners.* Los Angeles: College of Continuing Eduation, University of Southern California, 1978.

Best, F. "Recycling People: Work-Sharing Through Flexible Life Scheduling." *The Futurist,* February 1978, *12,* 5–16.

Best, F., and Stern, B. *Lifetime Distribution of Education, Work, and Leisure: Research, Speculations, and Policy Implications of Changing Life Patterns.* Washington, D.C.: Postsecondary Education Convening Authority, 1976.

Best, F., and Stern, B. "Education, Work, and Leisure: Must They Come in That Order?" *Monthly Labor Review,* July 1977, *100,* 3–10.

Biedenbach, J. M. "Currently Used Mechanisms and Delivery Modes for Non-Academic Personnel." In Directorate for Science Education, *Continuing Education in Science and Engineering.* Washington, D.C.: National Science Foundation, 1977.

Bigham, D. "Community Leadership." *Center for Creative Leadership* (Greenboro, N.C.), 1977, *4* (3), 8–9.

Bishop, J., and Van Dyk, K. "Can Adults Be Hooked on College?" *Journal of Higher Education,* 1977, *48,* 39–62.

Blaugh, M., and Mace, J. "Recurrent Education—The New Jerusalem." *Higher Education,* 1977, *6,* 277–299.

Board of Higher Education. *Summary of Data: Study of Illinois Adult Learners.* Springfield: Illinois Office of Education, 1978.

Board of Regents, University of the State of New York. *The Regents Statewide Plan for the Development of Postsecondary Education, 1976.* Albany: Board of Regents, University of the State of New York, 1976.

Boaz, R. L. *Participation in Adult Education, Final Report 1975.* Washington, D.C.: National Center for Education Statistics, 1978.

Bonham, G. W. "The Open University: Lessons for the Future." *Change,* November 1978, *10,* 14–15.

Botsman, P. B. *An Analysis of the Continuing Education Interests and Needs of Blue-Collar Factory Workers.* Ithaca, N.Y.: Institute for Research and Development in Occupational Education, Cornell University, 1975a.

Botsman, P. B. *The Learning Needs and Interests of Adult Blue-Collar Factory Workers.* Ithaca: New York State College of Human Ecology, Cornell University, 1975b.

Bowen, H. R. *Investment in Learning: The Individual and Social Value of American Higher Education.* San Francisco: Jossey-Bass, 1977.

Boyer, E. L. "The Federal Stake in a Learning Society." *Change,* May 1978, *10,* 21–25.

Branscomb, L. M., and Gilmore, P. C. "Education in Private Industry." *Daedalus,* Winter 1975, *104,* 229–250.

Braybrooke, D., and Lindblom, C. E. *A Strategy of Decision.* New York: Free Press, 1963.

Breneman, D. "Education." In J. A. Pechman (Ed.), *Setting National Priorities: The 1979 Budget.* Washington, D.C.: Brookings Institution, 1978.

Brickman, L. "Being a Participant." *Lifelong Learning: The Adult Years,* June 1978, *1,* 14 and 34.

Bridge, G. "Information Imperfections: The Achilles' Heel of Entitlement Plans." *School Review,* May 1978, *86* (3), 504–529.

Brightman, S. C. (Ed.). *Adult and Continuing Education Today,* August 1977, *7* (16), 81.

Broschart, J. G. *Lifelong Learning in the Nation's Third Century.* Washington, D.C.: U.S. Government Printing Office, 1977.

Brown, C. A. "Municipal Training Programs: 1975." In *Urban Data*

Service Reports #8. Washington, D.C.: International City Management Association, 1976.

Brown, L. "Six Ohio Cities Turn Cable TV to Community Use." *New York Times,* April 19, 1978, p. C25.

Bryan, D., and Forman, D. C. *Characteristics of SUN Learners (First Five Offerings): Statistical Summary No. 4.* Lincoln, Nebr.: University of Mid-America, 1977.

Budget of the United States Government: Special Analysis FY 1978. Washington, D.C.: U.S. Office of Management and Budget, 1977.

Budget of the United States Government: Special Analysis FY 1979. Washington, D.C.: U.S. Office of Management and Budget, 1978.

Bunnell, E. M. "Special Degree Programs for Adults in Smaller Private Colleges." Unpublished doctoral dissertation, University of Michigan, 1974.

Bunting, C. I., Moon, R., and Peterson, R. E. "Next Steps Toward Lifelong Learning: Views from Three National Projects." In *Current Issues in Higher Education.* Washington, D.C.: American Assocation for Higher Education, 1978.

Burgess, P. "Reasons for Adult Participation in Group Educational Activities." *Adult Education,* 1971, *22,* 3–29.

Burkett, J. E. "Higher Education's Growing Edge." *Educational Record,* Summer 1977, *58,* 259–269.

Bushnell, D. S. *Education and Training: A Guide to Interinstitutional Cooperation.* Arlington, Va.: American Vocational Association, 1979.

California Postsecondary Education Commission. *Educational Brokering in California, I: An Introductory Report.* Sacramento: California Postsecondary Education Commission, 1977.

Calvert, R. *Adult Education in the United States: Its Programs, Participants, Sponsors, and Financing.* Washington, D.C.: National Center for Education Statistics, 1974.

Campbell, M., and others. *New Students: New Markets for the University of Arkansas? Educational Needs and Interests in the Northwest Arkansas Area.* Fayetteville: University of Arkansas, 1974.

Carl, J. *Legislative Update.* Washington, D.C.: Postsecondary Education Convening Authority, 1977.

Carlisle, R. D. B. *Media and the Adult Student: One Man's Journal.*

Lincoln, Nebr.: Great Plains National Instructional Television Library, 1976.

Carlivati, P. A. *Toward Developing a Coordinated System of Postsecondary Continuing Education in the Genessee Valley Region: A Summary Report.* Rochester, N.Y.: Rochester Area Colleges, 1975.

Carlson, R. B. *Summary Data, Vocational Education, Fiscal Year 1975.* Washington, D.C.: Division of Vocational and Technical Education, U.S. Office of Education, 1976.

Carnegie Commission on Higher Education. *Toward a Learning Society.* New York: McGraw-Hill, 1973.

Carnegie Task Force on Public Broadcasting. *Summary Report.* New York: Carnegie Corporation of New York, 1977.

Carp, A., Peterson, R. E. and Roelfs, P. J. "Adult Learning Interests and Experiences." In K. P. Cross, J. R. Valley, and Associates, *Planning Non-Traditional Programs: An Analysis of the Issues for Postsecondary Education.* San Francisco: Jossey-Bass, 1974.

Carr, T. W. "All-Volunteer Armed Forces and Career Education." Speech to the Commissioner's National Conference on Career Education, Houston, Tex., November 1976.

Cartter, A. *The Need for a New Approach to Financing Recurrent Education.* Berkeley, Calif.: Carnegie Commission on Higher Education, 1973.

CBFSEI Newsletter. Winter-Spring, *1* (1 and 2), 1978.

Center for Continuing Education, University of Notre Dame. *The Learning Society.* Notre Dame, Ind.: Center for Continuing Education, University of Notre Dame, n.d.

Center for Museum Education. *Lifelong Learning/Adult Audiences, Sourcebook #1.* Washington, D.C.: George Washington University, 1978.

Centra, J. A. *College Enrollment in the 1980s: Projections and Possibilities.* New York: The College Board, 1978.

Charland, W. A. "A New Look at Lifelong Learning." *Union Press Monographs.* Yellow Springs, Ohio: Union for Experimenting Colleges and Universities, March 1976.

Charles Stewart Mott Foundation. *Letter.* April 1978a, *4* (3), 1–7.

Charles Stewart Mott Foundation. *Surplus School Space—The Problem and the Possibilities.* Flint, Mich.: Mott Foundation, 1978b.

Charner, I., and others. *An Untapped Resource: Negotiated Tuition-*

Aid in the Private Sector. Washington, D.C.: National Manpower Institute, 1978.

Charters, A. N. (Ed.). *International Handbook of Resources for Educators of Adults.* Syracuse, N.Y.: University of Syracuse, 1977.

Christoffel, P. H. "Current Federal Programs for Lifelong Learning: A $14 Billion Effort." *School Review,* 1978a, *86* (3), 348–359.

Christoffel, P. H. "Future Federal Funding of Lifelong Learning." *Lifelong Learning: The Adult Years,* June 1978b, *1,* 17–24.

Christoffel, P. H. "The Older Adult and Federal Programs for Lifelong Learning." Paper prepared for the HEW Lifelong Learning Project, Washington, D.C., 1978c.

Christoffel, P. H. *Toward a Learning Society: Future Federal Funding for Lifelong Learning.* New York: Future Directions for a Learning Society, The College Board, 1978d.

Clark, R. E. "An Approach to Research on Learning Opportunities for Adults." Paper prepared for the HEW Lifelong Learning Project, Washington, D.C., 1978.

Clearinghouse ADELL. *Catalog of Adult Education Projects.* Rockville, Md.: Clearinghouse ADELL (Adult Education and Lifelong Learning), 1978.

Coles, W., and others. *A Method of Inventory for the Lifelong Education Activities in a Community.* East Lansing, Mich.: Institute for Community Development, Michigan State University, 1976.

College Board, The. *College Placement and Credit by Examination: Guide to Institutional Policies: 1978.* New York: College Board, 1978.

College Board News, 1976, *4* (4), 1–2.

"College Today, Part IV: Lifelong Learning." Options in Education Transcript. Washington, D.C.: National Public Radio and the Institute for Educational Leadership, March 1978.

Commission on Non-Traditional Study (S. B. Gould, Chairman). *Diversity by Design.* San Francisco: Jossey-Bass, 1973.

Committee on the Financing of Higher Education for Adult Students. *Financing Part-Time Students: The New Majority in Postsecondary Education.* Washington, D.C.: American Council on Education, 1974.

Community Service and Continuing Education Program. "Quasi-Annual Report—FY 1976." Report to the National Advisory Council on Extension and Continuing Education, 1977a (Xerox).

Community Service and Continuing Education Program. *State Supported Projects in Community Service and Continuing Education (Title I, Higher Education Act of 1965): Fiscal Year 1976.* Washington, D.C.: Community Service and Continuing Education Program, U.S. Office of Education, Department of Health, Education, and Welfare, 1977b.

Comptroller General of the U.S. *The Adult Basic Education Program: Progress in Reducing Illiteracy and Improvements Needed.* Washington, D.C.: U.S. Government Printing Office, 1975.

Comstock, C. "Lifelong Learning for Blue-Collar Workers." Paper prepared for HEW Lifelong Learning Project, Washington, D.C., 1978.

Congressional Budget Office. *Postsecondary Education: The Current Federal Role and Alternative Approaches.* Washington, D.C.: U.S. Government Printing Office, 1977.

Connecticut Commission for Higher Education. *Connecticut Master Plan Update: Biennial Supplement.* Hartford: Connecticut Commission for Higher Education, 1976.

Continuing Education/Community Service Task Force for Lifelong Learning. *Master Planning for Postsecondary Education in Utah.* Salt Lake City, Utah: State Board of Regents, 1976 (Draft).

The Continuum, Report of Programs and Progress, 1976–77. Staten Island, N.Y.: Cooperative Continuum of Education, 1977 (Mimeo).

Coolican, P. M. "Self-Planned Learning: Implications for the Future of Adult Education." An addendum to the 1974 paper. Prepared for the Division of Adult Education, U.S. Office of Education, Washington, D.C., 1975 (Xerox).

Coordinating Committee on Research in Vocational Education. *Guide to Federal Funding in Career Education, Education and Work, and Vocational Education.* Washington, D.C.: Bureau of Occupational and Adult Education, U.S. Office of Education, Department of Health, Education, and Welfare, 1978.

Correa, J. M. *Regional Needs and Resources for Postsecondary Education: A Report of the Northern Region Postsecondary Education Group.* Potsdam, N.Y.: Associated Colleges of the St. Lawrence Valley, 1976.

Council on Public Higher Education. *Kentucky and Comprehensive*

Planning for Higher Education. Frankfort, Ky.: Council on Public Higher Education, 1976.

Cowen, P. "Book Reviews." *Harvard Educational Review,* May 1977, *47,* 232–236. (See also "Correspondence" in November 1977 issue.)

Craig, R. L. (Ed.). *Training and Development Handbook.* (2nd ed.), New York: McGraw-Hill, 1977.

Cremin, L. A. *Public Education.* New York: Basic Books, 1976.

Cross, K. P. "For All and For Each." In *The Third Century.* New Rochelle, N.Y.: Change Magazine Press, 1977.

Cross, K. P. "The Adult Learner." In *Current Issues in Higher Education.* Washington, D.C.: American Association for Higher Education, 1978a.

Cross, K. P. "A Critical Review of State and National Studies of the Needs and Interests of Adult Learners." In C. B. Stalford (Ed.), *Adult Learning Needs and the Demand for Lifelong Learning.* Washington, D.C.: National Institute of Education, 1978b.

Cross, K. P. *The Missing Link: Connecting Adult Learners to Learning Resources.* New York: Future Directions for a Learning Society, The College Board, 1978c.

Cross, K. P., Valley, J. R., and Associates. *Planning Non-Traditional Programs: An Analysis of the Issues for Postsecondary Education.* San Francisco: Jossey-Bass, 1974.

Cross, K. P., and Zusman, A. "The Needs of Non-Traditional Learners and the Responses of Non-Traditional Programs." In C. B. Stalford (Ed.), *An Evaluative Look at Non-Traditional Education.* Washington, D.C.: National Institute of Education, 1979.

Cross, W. *The Weekend Education Sourcebook.* New York: Harper's Magazine Press, 1976.

Cross, W., and Florio, C. *You Are Never Too Old to Learn.* New York: McGraw-Hill, 1978.

Daloz, L. A. "Giving Education Back to the Learner." *International Journal of Career and Continuing Education,* Fall 1975, *1,* 97–102.

Dauksza, W. *Adult Literacy Education in the United States.* Newark, Del.: International Reading Association, 1977.

Dave, R. H. (Ed.). *Reflections on Lifelong Education and the School.* Hamburg, West Germany: UNESCO Institute for Education, 1975.

Dave, R. H. (Ed.). *Foundations of Lifelong Education.* Oxford, England: UNESCO Institute for Education and Pergamon Press, 1976.

Dave, R. H., and Lengrand, P. (Eds.). "Lifelong Education and Learning Strategies." *International Review of Education* (special issue), 1974, *20* (4).

DeMott, B. "Adult Ed'—The Ultimate Goal." *Saturday Review,* September 20, 1975, *2*, 27–29.

DeMott, B. "The Thrills and Shills of Lifelong Learning." *Change,* April 1978, *10,* 53–55.

Denver Regional Training Center. *Training Catalog.* Denver, Colo.: U.S. Civil Service Commission, 1977.

Dickenson, G., and Clark, K. M. "Learning Orientations and Participation in Self-Education and Continuing Education." *Adult Education,* 1975, *26* (1), 3–15.

Dressel, P. L. *Handbook of Academic Evaluation: Assessing Institutional Effectiveness, Student Progress, and Professional Performance for Decision Making in Higher Education.* San Francisco: Jossey-Bass, 1976.

Dwyer, M. C., and others. *The Kansas Community Education Manual.* Manhattan: Kansas State University, 1978.

Dwyer, R. "Workers' Education, Labor Education, Labor Studies: An Historical Delineation." *Review of Educational Research,* 1977, *47* (1), 179–207.

Eddy, M. S. "Part-Time Students." *AAHE-ERIC/Higher Education Research Currents,* June 1978.

Education Coalition, The. *Fundamentals for Equity in Federal Education Policy: Lessons, Principles, Recommendations.* Washington, D.C.: The Education Coalition, 1977.

Education Commission of the States. *Final Report and Recommendations: Task Force on State, Institutional, and Federal Responsibilities in Providing Postsecondary Educational Opportunity to Service Personnel.* Denver, Colo.: Education Commission of the States, 1977a.

Education Commission of the States. *Higher Education in the States.* Denver, Colo.: Education Commission of the States, 1977b.

Education Commission of the States, and others. *State Postsecondary Education Profiles Handbook.* Denver, Colo.: Education Commission of the States, 1977.

Education Training and Market Report. September 2, 1974.

Education-Work Council. (1) *Final Report,* October 1977; (2) *Progress Report,* February-March 1978; (3) *Progress Report,* March-May 1978; Enfield, Conn.

Eggert, J. D. *An Examination of Goals of Potential and Actual Learners: University of Mid-America/State University of Nebraska* (Working Paper No. 1). Lincoln: Office of Research and Evaluation, University of Mid-America/State University of Nebraska, 1974.

Eisley, J. G., and Coppard, L. C. *Extending Opportunities for Graduate Studies in Michigan: A Preliminary Report on the Feasibility of External Graduate Programs.* Ann Arbor: Horace H. Rackham School of Graduate Studies, University of Michigan, 1977.

Elazar, D. J. *American Federalism: A View from the States.* New York: Crowell, 1972.

Employment and Training Report of the President. Washington, D.C.: U.S. Department of Labor Employment and Training Administration, and Office of Human Development, Department of Health, Education, and Welfare, 1977.

Entine, A. "Lifelong Learning in the Transitional Years." Paper prepared for the HEW Lifelong Learning Project, Washington, D.C., 1978.

Extension Service, U.S. Department of Agriculture. *Cooperative Extension Service Programs: A Unique Partnership Between Public and Private Interests.* Washington, D.C.: Extension Service, U.S. Department of Agriculture, 1976.

Fantini, M. D. "Toward a Redefinition of American Education." *Educational Leadership,* 1977, *35,* 167–172.

Farmer, J. A., Jr., and Knox, A. B. *Alternative Patterns for Strengthening Community Service Programs in Institutions of Higher Education.* Urbana: Office for the Study of Professional Continuing Education, University of Illinois, 1977.

Faure, E., and others. *Learning To Be: The World of Education Today and Tomorrow.* New York: Unipub, 1972.

Federal Community Education Clearinghouse. *Catalog of Resource Material on Community Education.* Washington, D.C.: U.S. Government Printing Office, 1978a.

Federal Community Education Clearinghouse. *Directory of Community Education Projects: Fiscal Year 1977.* Washington, D.C.: U.S. Government Printing Office, 1978b.

Federal Interagency Committee on Education. *Toward a Comprehensive Federal Education Policy.* Washington, D.C.: U.S. Department of Health, Education, and Welfare, April 1978.

Federal Trade Commission, Staff of the Bureau of Consumer Protection. *Proprietary Vocational and Home-Study Schools: Final Report to the Federal Trade Commission and Proposed Trade Regulation Rule.* Washington, D.C.: U.S. Government Printing Office, 1976.

Fehnel, R. A., and McIntyre, V. L. *Nontraditional Learners and Postsecondary Education Policy.* Report to the Oregon Educational Coordinating Commission. Eugene: University of Oregon, 1977.

Ferrin, R. E., and Arbeiter, S. *Bridging the Gap: A Selection of Education-to-Work Linkages.* New York: The College Board, 1975.

Fey, P. A. "Family College: A Future Form for Lifelong Learning." *Community and Junior College Journal,* 1977, *48,* 18–20.

Fiske, E. B. "Programs Bypass Neediest." *New York Times,* September 11, 1977, Section 12, pp. 1 and 11.

Fletcher, S. M., Rue, R. W., and Young, R. "Community Education." *Community and Junior College Journal,* May 1977, *47,* 24–26.

Florida Commission on Educational Outreach and Service. *Access to Knowledge.* Vol. 1. Tallahassee: State University System of Florida, 1976a.

Florida Commission on Educational Outreach and Service. *Access to Knowledge.* Vol. 2: *Supporting Data.* Tallahassee: State University System of Florida, 1976b.

Florida Postsecondary Education Commission, and others. *State Planning for Lifelong Learning: Improving Access for All Citizens.* Tallahassee: Florida Department of Education, 1977.

Florio, C. "Education and Work Training Programs for Older Persons." Paper prepared for the HEW Lifelong Learning Project, Washington, D.C., 1978.

Francke, C., and Frederick, R. *Presentation to the PECA Monthly Dialogue on Lifelong Learning.* Washington, D.C.: Postsecondary Education Convening Authority, 1977.

Franklin, P. L. *Stages in Implementing a Career Information System.* Eugene: Oregon Career Information System, University of Oregon, 1978a.

Franklin, P. L. *Summary of Existing Career Information Systems.* Eugene: Oregon Career Information System, University of Oregon, 1978b.

Free University Network. *1979 National Directory of Free Universities and Learning Networks*. Manhattan, Kans.: Free University Network, 1979.

Freeman, R. B. *The Overeducated American*. New York: Academic Press, 1976.

Froomkin, J., and Wolfson, R. J. *Adult Education 1972, A Re-Analysis*. Washington, D.C.: Froomkin, 1977.

Fund for the Improvement of Postsecondary Education. *Resources for Change: A Guide To Projects 1977–1978*. Washington, D.C.: U.S. Department of Health, Education, and Welfare, 1977.

Fund for the Improvement of Postsecondary Education. *Resources for Change: A Guide to Projects 1978–1979*. Washington, D.C.: U.S. Department of Health, Education, and Welfare, 1978.

Furter, P. *The Planner and Lifelong Education*. Paris: UNESCO, 1977.

Gardner, D. P., and Zelan, J. *A Strategy for Change in Higher Education. The Extended University of the University of California*. Paris: Organization for Economic Cooperation and Development, 1972.

Getzels, J. W. "The Communities of Education," *Teachers College Record*, May 1978, *79*, 659–682.

Gladieux, L. E., and Wolanin, T. R. *Congress and the Colleges: The National Politics of Higher Education*. Lexington, Mass.: Heath, 1976.

Gleazer, E. J., Jr. "Beyond the Open Door, The Open College." *Community and Junior College Journal*, August-September 1974, *45* (1), 6–12.

Glen, H. G. "Financing of Higher Education for Adult Students." *The Spectator*, December 1974, *37*, 24–28.

Golden, J. *The Best Years, 1945–50*. New York: Atheneum, 1976.

Gollattscheck, J. F., and others. *College Leadership for Community Renewal: Beyond Community-Based Education*. San Francisco: Jossey-Bass, 1976.

Gould, S. B., and Cross, K. P. (Eds.). *Explorations in Non-Traditional Study*. San Francisco: Jossey-Bass, 1972.

Grant, G. "The Politics of the Coleman Report." Unpublished doctoral dissertation, Harvard University, 1972.

Grant, W. V., and Lind, C. G. *Digest of Education Statistics: 1975 Edition*. Washington, D.C.: National Center for Education Statistics, 1976.

Gray, E. E., and Greben, S. "Future Perspectives." *Parks and Recreation,* July 1974, *9,* 7–24.

Green, T. F., Erickson, D., and Seidman, R. H. "Lifelong Learning and the Educational System: Expansion or Reform?" Paper prepared for the HEW Lifelong Learning Project, Washington, D.C., 1978.

Greenwald, S. M. *Survey of Professional Society Continuing Education Programs.* New York: American Society of Mechanical Engineers, 1977.

Griffith, W. S. "Adult Educators and Politics." *Adult Education,* 1976, *26* (4), 270–297.

Griffith, W. S. "Educational Needs: Definition, Assessment, and Utilization." *School Review,* May 1978, *86* (3), 382–394.

Griffith, W. S., and Cervero, R. M. "The Adult Performance Level Program: A Serious and Deliberate Examination." *Adult Education,* Summer 1977, *27* (4), 209–224.

Gross, R. *Higher/Wider/Education: A Report on Open Learning.* New York: Ford Foundation, 1976.

Gross, R. *The Lifelong Learner: A Guide to Self-Development.* New York: Simon & Schuster, 1977a.

Gross, R. *New Paths to Learning: College Education for Adults.* Public Affairs Pamphlet No. 546. New York: Public Affairs Committee, 1977b.

Gross, R. "The Other Open University. Parts I and II." *Planning for Higher Education,* August 1978, *7,* 9–19 and 25–36.

Gross, R., Hebert, T., and Tough, A. *Independent, Self-Directed Learners in American Life: The Other Eighty Percent of Learning.* Washington, D.C.: Postsecondary Education Convening Authority, 1977.

Gueulette, D. G. "Exorcising the Spectre of Permanent Schooling." *Adult Education,* Fall 1976, *27,* 48–53.

Halstead, D. K. (Ed.). *Higher Education Planning—A Bibliographic Handbook.* Washington, D.C.: National Institute of Education, 1978.

Hamilton, I. B. *The Third Century: Postsecondary Planning for the Nontraditional Learner.* Princeton, N.J.: Educational Testing Service, 1976.

Hanley, R. "County Colleges Merging Studies with Those of Vocational Schools." *New York Times,* June 2, 1978, p. B3.

Harmon, D. (Ed.). *New Directions for Higher Education: Expanding Recurrent and Nonformal Education,* no. 14. San Francisco: Jossey-Bass, 1976.

Harrington, F. H. *The Future of Adult Education: New Responsibilities of Colleges and Universities.* San Francisco: Jossey-Bass, 1977.

Hebert, T., and Coyne, J. *Getting Skilled: A Guide to Private Trade and Technical Schools.* New York: Dutton, 1976.

Hefferlin, J. L., Peterson, R. E., and Roelfs, P. J. *California's Need for Postsecondary Alternatives.* First Technical Report, Part One. Sacramento: California Legislature, 1975.

Heffernan, J. M. *A Synthesis of the Clearwater Conference for Directors of State Studies of Adult Education.* Washington, D.C.: Postsecondary Education Convening Authority, 1976.

Heffernan, J. M., Macy, F. U., and Vickers, D. F. *Educational Brokering: A New Service for Adult Learners.* Washington, D.C.: National Center for Educational Brokering, 1976.

Henderson, C. *Changes in Enrollment by 1985.* Policy Analysis Service Reports, No. 3. Washington, D.C.: American Council on Education, 1977.

Hersrud, M. M. "From Where I Sit: My Thoughts on Lifelong Learning." *Educational Record,* Spring 1978, *59,* 134–141.

Hesburgh, T. M., Miller, P. A., and Wharton, C. R., Jr. *Patterns for Lifelong Learning.* San Francisco: Jossey-Bass, 1973.

Heston, W. M., and Fantz, J. C. *Toward a Comprehensive Coordinated System of Postsecondary Continuing Education for Long Island.* New York: Long Island Regional Advisory Council on Higher Education, 1976.

Hiemstra, R. *Lifelong Learning: An Exploration of Adult and Continuing Education Within a Setting of Lifelong Learning Needs.* Lincoln, Nebr.: Professional Educators Publications, 1976.

Hiemstra, R. "Future: Friend or Foe?" *Lifelong Learning: The Adult Years,* October 1977, *1,* 10–12.

Hobbs, D. S. *A State Plan for the 1970s: Revision and Supplement.* Oklahoma City: Oklahoma State Regents for Higher Education, 1976.

Hodgkinson, H. "Look Who's Coming to College: New Learners, New Tasks." *NASPA Journal,* Summer 1976, *14,* 2–14.

Holmberg, B. *Distance Education: A Survey and Bibliography.* New York: Nichols, 1977.

Honey, J. C. "The Politics of Entitlement." In N. D. Kurland (Ed.), *Entitlement Studies.* Washington, D.C.: National Institute of Education, 1977.

Honey, J. C., and Hartle, T. W. "Beyond the Bicentennial—Postsecondary Education in the 1990s." Paper prepared for the U.S. Assistant Secretary of Education, August 1974 (Xerox).

Honey, J. C., and Hartle, T. W. *A Career Education Entitlement Plan: Administrative and Political Issues.* Syracuse, N.Y.: Syracuse University Research Center, 1975a.

Honey, J. C., and Hartle, T. W. *Federal-State-Institutional Relations in Postsecondary Education.* Princeton, N.J.: Educational Testing Service, 1975b.

Houle, C. O. *The Inquiring Mind.* Madison: University of Wisconsin Press, 1961.

Houle, C. O. *The Design of Education.* San Francisco: Jossey-Bass, 1972.

Houle, C. O. *The External Degree.* San Francisco: Jossey-Bass, 1973.

Houle, C. O. "The Nature of Continuing Professional Education." In R. M. Smith (Ed.), *Adult Learning: Issues and Innovations.* DeKalb: Program in Career Information, Northern Illinois University, 1976.

Howe, M. J. A. (Ed.). *Adult Learning: Psychological Research and Applications.* New York: Wiley, 1977.

Hoyt, D. P. *Appraisal of Interest in Continuing Education Opportunities Among Kansas Adults.* Manhattan: Kansas State University, 1975.

Hoyt, K. *Refining the Career Education Concept.* Washington, D.C.: Office of Career Education, U.S. Office of Education, Department of Health, Education, and Welfare, 1976.

Huffman, J. L., and Trauth, D. M. "Cable Television: Diversity or Duplication?" *Intellect,* October 1977, *106,* 157–158.

Hunter, W. J. *The Non-Traditional Community College Project—Survey of Postsecondary Youth and Adult Learning.* St. Louis, Mo.: Junior College District of St. Louis, 1974.

Hyde, W. D., Jr. *Metropolitan Vocational Proprietary Schools.* Lexington, Mass.: Lexington Books, 1976.

Illich, I. *Deschooling Society.* New York: Harper & Row, 1971.

Ilsley, P., and Feeney, J. M. "Voluntarism: An Action Proposal for Adult Educators." *Lifelong Learning: The Adult Years,* September 1978, *2,* 8–11 and 30–31.

Ironside, D. J. *Counselling and Information Services for Adult Learners in North America.* Paris: UNESCO International Bureau of Education, 1976.

Jacquet, C. H., Jr. (Ed.). *Yearbook of American and Canadian Churches.* Nashville, Tenn.: Abingdon, 1976.

Jensen, C. R. *Outdoor Recreation in America: Trends, Problems, and Opportunities.* Minneapolis, Minn.: Burgess, 1973.

Jensen, G. S. "Will Adult Education Come of Age?" *The College Board Review,* Winter 1977–1978, *106,* 8–12.

Jepson, P. *Assessment of Training Needs of Adults in Mohave County.* Kingman, Ariz.: Mohave Community College, 1974.

Jessup, F. (Ed.). *Lifelong Learning.* Oxford, England: Pergamon Press, 1969.

Johnson, P., and Ross, N. (Eds.). *On Your Own—But Not Alone, Lifelabs Approach To Learning.* Miami, Fla.: Miami-Dade Community College, n.d.

Johnson, S. "Subcontracted Courses Stir Controversy." *New York Times,* September 11, 1977, Section 12, p. 5.

Johnstone, J. W. C., and Rivera, R. J. *Volunteers for Learning.* Chicago: Aldine, 1965.

Joint Committee on the Master Plan for Higher Education. *Report of the Joint Committee on the Master Plan for Higher Education.* Sacramento: California Legislature, 1973.

Jonsen, R. W. "Lifelong Learning: State Policies." *School Review,* May 1978a, *86,* 360–381.

Jonsen, R. W. *State Policies and State/Federal Relationships: Priorities, Issues, and Alternatives.* Prepared for the HEW Lifelong Learning Project. Denver, Colo.: Education Commission of the States, 1978b.

Kansas Board of Regents. *Guidelines for Increasing Efficiency at State Colleges and Universities.* Topeka: Kansas Board of Regents, 1972.

Kanter, R. M. "Work in a New America." *Daedalus,* Winter 1978, *107,* 47–78.

Kanun, C., and Swanson, R. H. (Eds.). *Programs and Registrations: 1975–1976.* Washington, D.C.: Association for Continuing Higher Education and National University Extension Association, 1977.

Karwin, T. A. *Flying a Learning Center.* New York: McGraw-Hill, 1973.

Katz, L. "University-Union Partnerships, Prospects, and Problems."

Lifelong Learning: The Adult Years, October 1978, *2,* 18–19.

Kay, E. R. *Adult Education in Community Organizations, 1972.* Washington, D.C.: National Center for Education Statistics, 1974.

Kay, E. R. *Programs and Enrollments in Non-Collegiate Postsecondary School: 1973–74.* Washington, D.C.: National Center for Education Statistics, 1976.

Keeton, M. T., and Associates. *Experiential Learning: Rationale, Characteristics, and Assessment.* San Francisco: Jossey-Bass, 1976.

Keeton, M..T., and Tate, P. J. (Eds.). *New Directions for Experiential Learning: Learning by Experience—What, Why, How,* no. 1. San Francisco: Jossey-Bass, 1978.

Kemp, F. B. *Noncredit Activities in Institutions of Higher Education for the Year Ending June 30, 1976.* Washington, D.C.: National Center for Education Statistics, 1978.

Keniston, K., and the Carnegie Council on Children. *All Our Children: The American Family Under Pressure.* New York: Harcourt Brace Jovanovich, 1977.

Kent, W. P. *A Longitudinal Study of Adult Basic Education Programs.* Falls Church, Va.: Systems Development Corp., 1973.

Keppel, F. *Educational Policy in the Next Decade.* Aspen, Colo.: Aspen Institute for Humanistic Studies, 1976.

Kidd, J. R. "Adult Learning in the 1970s." In R. M. Smith (Ed.), *Adult Learning: Issues and Innovations.* DeKalb: Program in Career Information, Northern Illinois University, 1976.

Klinger, K., and Marienau, C. "Barriers to Adult Learning." *Delivery,* 1978, *1* (2), 3–4.

Knight, D. *Alternatives for Lifelong Learning in Minnesota: The Nonformal Educational Sector, Summary Report.* St. Paul: Minnesota State Planning Agency, 1976.

Knight, D. *Lifelong Learning in Minnesota: The Nonformal Educational Sector, Final Report.* St. Paul: Minnesota State Planning Agency, 1977.

Knowles, M. S. *The Adult Learner.* Houston, Tex.: Gulf Publishing, 1973.

Knowles, M. S. *Self-Directed Learning: A Guide for Learners and Teachers.* New York: Association Press, 1975.

Knox, A. B. "Helping Adults to Learn." In R. M. Smith (Ed.), *Adult Learning: Issues and Innovations.* DeKalb: Program in Career Information, Northern Illinois University, 1976.

Knox, A. B. *Adult Development and Learning: A Handbook on Individual Growth and Competence in the Adult Years for Education and the Helping Professions.* San Francisco: Jossey-Bass, 1977.

Knox, A., and Grotelueschen, A. "Adult Roles in Non-Occupational Lifelong Learning." Paper prepared for the HEW Lifelong Learning Project, Washington, D.C., 1978.

Koos, L. V. "Local Versus Regional Junior Colleges," *School Review,* November 1944, *52* (9), 525–531.

Kovenock, D. *The Demand for Adult Education in Maine.* Orono: Social Science Research Institute, University of Maine, 1978.

Kreitlow, B. W. "Innovation in Organizing Learning for Adults— The New Technology." In R. M. Smith (Ed.), *Adult Learning: Issues and Innovations.* DeKalb: Program in Career Information, Northern Illinois University, 1976.

Kurland, N. D. (Ed.). *Entitlement Studies.* Washington, D.C.: National Institute of Education, 1977.

Kurland, N. D. "Financing Learning Opportunities for Adults: Policy Implications." *School Review,* May 1978a, *86* (3), 530–543.

Kurland, N. D. *Financing Lifelong Education, Parts I and II.* Albany: New York State Department of Education, 1978b.

Kurland, N. D. "A National Strategy for Lifelong Learning." *Phi Delta Kappan,* February 1978c, *59,* 385–389.

Kurland, N. D. *The Scandinavian Study Circle—An Idea for the U.S.?* Albany: New York State Department of Education, 1978d.

Kurland, N. D., and Comly, L. T. "Financing Lifelong Education: Next Steps in Exploring the Entitlement Approach." Albany: Study of Adult Education, New York State Department of Education, 1975.

Kurland, N. D., and others. *Postsecondary Continuing Education and Lifelong Learning.* Albany: New York State Department of Education, 1976.

Leagans, J. P. "Education Beyond Youth: An Emerging Social Imperative." *Lifelong Learning: The Adult Years,* February 1978, *1,* 12–15.

Learning Exchange. *Catalog.* Evanston, Ill.: Learning Exchange, 1976.

The Learning Exchange News. 1977, *3,* (1).

Lee, A. M. *Learning a Living Across the Nation: Volume V.* Project Baseline: Fifth National Report. Flagstaff: Northern Arizona University, 1976.

Leichter, H. J. *The Family as Educator.* New York: Teachers College Press, Columbia University, 1975.

Leichter, H. J. "Families and Communities as Educators: Some Concepts of Relationship." *Teachers College Record,* May 1978, *79,* 567–658.

Lengrand, P. *An Introduction to Lifelong Education.* London: Croom Helm, 1975.

Lenning, O. T. *The Benefits Crisis in Higher Education.* Washington, D.C.: American Association for Higher Education, 1974.

Lenning, O. T. *The Outcomes Structure: An Overview and Procedures for Applying It in Postsecondary Education Institutions.* Boulder, Colo.: National Center for Higher Education Management Systems, 1978.

Leubsdorf, D. P. "Carter Changes the Picture for Public TV." *Change,* October 1977, *9,* 46–57.

Levin, H. M. "Voucher and Social Equity." *Change,* October 1973, *5,* 29–34.

Levin, H. M. "Financing Higher Education and Social Equity: Implications for Lifelong Learning." *School Review,* May 1978, *86* (3), 327–347.

Levine, H. A. *Strategies for the Application of Foreign Legislation on Paid Educational Leave to the United States Scene.* New Brunswick, N.J.: Rutgers University Labor Education Center, 1975.

Levine, H. A. *Paid Educational Leave.* Washington, D.C.: National Institute of Education, 1977.

Levine, H. A., and Fried, M. L. "Labor's Role in Lifelong Learning." Paper prepared for the HEW Lifelong Learning Project, Washington, D.C., 1978.

Lewis, R. G. "A Comparative Study of Learning Networks in the United States." Unpublished doctoral dissertation, Northwestern University, 1978a.

Lewis, R. G. "Linking Lifelong Learners with Educational Resources." Paper prepared for the HEW Lifelong Learning Project, Washington, D.C., 1978b.

"Libraries To Take Over Adult Learning Program." *College Board News,* June 1976, pp. 1 and 3.

Lifelong Learning Project, U.S. Department of Health, Education, and Welfare. "Tentative Outline for Report to Congress." Washington, D.C.: Lifelong Learning Project, U.S. Department of Health, Education, and Welfare, 1977.

Lifelong Learning Project, U.S. Department of Health, Education, and Welfare. *Lifelong Learning and Public Policy.* Washington, D.C.: U.S. Government Printing Office, 1978.

Lisman, D., and Ohliger, J. "Must We All Go Back to School?" *Progressive,* October 1978, *42* (10), 35–37.

Liveright, A. A. *A Study of Adult Education in the United States.* Brookline, Mass.: Center for the Study of Liberal Education for Adults, Boston University, 1968.

Long, H. B. (Ed.). "Lifelong Learning." *Journal of Research and Development in Education* (special issue), Summer 1974, 7.

Long, H. B., and Rossing, B. E. "Tuition Waivers for Older Americans." *Lifelong Learning: The Adult Years,* June 1978, *1*, 10–13.

Lord, J. E. *Toward Lifelong Learning: Changes and Innovations in Postsecondary Education in the United States, 1966–76.* Washington, D.C.: National Institute of Education, 1976.

Loring, R. K., LeGates, C., Josephs, M. J., and O'Neill, J. "Adapting Institutions to the Adult Learner: Experiments in Progress." In *Current Issues in Higher Education.* Washington, D.C.: American Association for Higher Education, 1978.

Lowe, J. *The Education of Adults: A World Perspective.* Toronto: UNESCO and Ontario Institute for Studies in Education, 1975.

Luskin, B., and Zigerell, H. "Community Colleges in Forefront of Telecourse Development." *Community and Junior College Journal,* 1978, *48*, 8–9, 44–45.

Lusterman, S. *Education in Industry.* New York: The Conference Board, 1977.

McCabe, G. E., and Straton, R. A. *University Courses via Cable TV: A Survey of Households Within the Service Area of One Cable Company and Projections for a Statewide Program.* Long Beach: Consortium, California State University and Colleges, 1976.

McCan, R. L. "The Importance of Community for Lifelong Learning." Paper prepared for the HEW Lifelong Learning Project, Washington, D.C., 1978.

McClusky, H. "What Research Says About Adult Learning Potential and About Teaching Older Adults." In R. M. Smith (Ed.),

Adult Learning: Issues and Innovations. DeKalb: Program in Career Information, Northern Illinois University, 1976.

McIntosh, N. E. *A Degree of Difference: The Open University of the United Kingdom.* New York: Praeger, 1977.

Macken, E., and others. *Home-Based Education: Needs and Technological Opportunities.* Washington, D.C.: National Institute of Education, 1976.

MacKenzie, N., Postgate, R., and Scupham, J. *Open Learning: Systems and Problems in Postsecondary Education.* Paris: UNESCO, 1975.

MacKenzie, J. R. "The Supply of Learning Opportunities for Workers." Paper prepared for the HEW Lifelong Learning Project, Washington, D.C., 1978.

McLure, G. T. *Recommendations for Lifelong Learning in Iowa in the Third Century, the Final Report.* Des Moines: Higher Education Facilities Commission of the State of Iowa, 1977b.

McMahon, E. E. "The Needs of People and the Needs of Their Communities." In D. B. Raugh (Ed.), *Priorities in Adult Education.* New York: Macmillan, 1972.

Manser, G., and Cass, R. H. *Voluntarism at the Crossroads.* New York: Family Service Association of America, 1976.

Marcec, A. H. "EDUCARE: A New Model for Prepaid Continuing Professional Education." Presentation at the School Health Section, American Public Health Association, Washington, D.C., November 2, 1977.

Marchase, T. J. "The Orlando Conference: A Synthesis." Lake Forest, Ill.: Barat College, 1977 (Xerox).

Marland, S. P. *Career Education: A Proposal for Reform.* New York: McGraw-Hill, 1974.

Martin, J. H., and Harrison, C. H. *Free to Learn: Unlocking and Ungrading American Education.* Englewood Cliffs, N.J.: Prentice-Hall, 1972.

Mathews, E., and others. *The Changing Agenda for American Higher Education.* Washington, D.C.: U.S. Government Printing Office, 1977.

Mavor, A. S., Toro, J. O., and DeProspo, E. R. *The Role of the Public Libraries in Adult Independent Learning (Parts I and II).* New York: The College Board, 1976.

Medsker, L. L., and Edelstein, S. T. *Policymaking Guidelines for Ex-*

tended Degree Programs: A Revision. Washington, D.C.: American Council on Education, 1977.

Medsker, L., and others. *Extending Opportunities for a College Degree: Practices, Problems, and Potentials.* Berkeley: Center for Research and Development In Higher Education, University of California, 1975.

Meeth, L. R. *Government Funding Policies and Nontraditional Programs.* Washington, D.C.: Postsecondary Education Convening Authority, 1975.

Merriam, S. "Philosophical Perspectives on Adult Education: A Critical Review of the Literature." *Adult Education,* Summer 1977, *27* (4), 195–208.

Michaelsen, J. B. "Financing Lifelong Learning: The Case Against Institutional Grants." *School Review,* May 1978, *86* (3), 475–498.

Mohrman, K. "The Federal Role in Lifelong Learning." Paper prepared for the HEW Lifelong Learning Project, Washington, D.C., 1978.

Mondale, W. F. "The Next Step: Lifelong Learning." *Change,* October 1976a, *8* (9), 42–45.

Mondale, W. F. Text of Lifelong Learning speech before the 1976 annual convention of American Association of Community and Junior Colleges, 1976b.

Mondale, W. F. "Lifelong Learning." *The Community Services Catalyst,* Spring 1977, *1,* 1–3.

Monette, M. L. "The Concept of Educational Need: An Analysis of Selected Literature." *Adult Education,* Winter 1977, *27* (2), 116–127.

Moody, H. R. "Perspectives on the Later Years." Paper prepared for the HEW Lifelong Learning Project, Washington, D.C., 1978.

Moore, A. B., Granger, J. C., and Winkfield, P. C. *Case Studies of Selected Cooperative Adult Education Programs.* Columbus: Center for Vocational Education, Ohio State University, 1974.

Morrow, L. "Time Essay: After Proposition 13, Volunteers Needed." *Time,* August 7, 1978, *112,* 34–35.

Morstain, B., and Smart, J. C. "A Motivational Typology of Adult Learners." *Journal of Higher Education,* November/December 1977, *48* (6), 665–679.

Morton, W. N. "A Profile of Weekend Colleges Programming By

Members of the American Association of State Colleges and Universities." Unpublished doctoral dissertation, University of Arkansas, 1977.

Moses, S. *The Learning Force: An Approach to the Politics of Education.* Syracuse, N.Y.: Educational Policy Research Center, Syracuse University, 1970.

Moses, S. *The Learning Force: A More Comprehensive Framework for Educational Policy.* Syracuse, N.Y.: Educational Policy Research Center, Syracuse University, 1971.

Moses, S. *The Learning Force 1975.* Washington, D.C.: Division of Adult Education, U.S. Office of Education, 1975.

Murphy, J., and Florio, C. *Never Too Old To Teach.* New York: Academy for Educational Development, 1978.

Museums Collaborative, Inc. *Cultural Voucher Program.* New York: Museums Collaborative, 1977.

Mushkin, S. J. (Ed.). *Recurrent Education.* Washington, D.C.: National Institute of Education, 1974.

National Advisory Council on Adult Education. *Federal Activities in Support of Adult Education.* Washington, D.C.: U.S. Government Printing Office, 1972.

National Advisory Council on Adult Education. *1975 Annual Report: A Target Population in Adult Education.* Washington, D.C.: U.S. Government Printing Office, 1974.

National Advisory Council on Adult Education. *An Historical Perspective, The Adult Education Act 1964–1974.* Washington, D.C.: U.S. Government Printing Office, 1976a.

National Advisory Council on Adult Education. *1976 Annual Report.* Washington, D.C.: U.S. Government Printing Office, 1976b.

National Advisory Council on Adult Education. *1977 Annual Report: Beyond the Verge.* Washington, D.C.: U.S. Government Printing Office, 1977a.

National Advisory Council on Adult Education. *Adult Education; Futures and Amendments; Survey of State Support. Section II.* Washington, D.C.: U.S. Government Printing Office, 1977b.

National Advisory Council on Extension and Continuing Education. *7th Annual Report: A Measure of Success, Federal Support for Continuing Education.* Washington, D.C.: U.S. Government Printing Office, 1973.

National Advisory Council on Extension and Continuing Education. *9th Annual Report: Equity of Access.* Washington, D.C.: U.S. Government Printing Office, 1975.

National Advisory Council on Extension and Continuing Education. *10th Annual Report: A Decade of Community Service and Continuing Education.* Washington, D.C.: U.S. Government Printing Office, 1976.

National Advisory Council on Extension and Continuing Education. Letter to members of Congress justifying NACECE budget results for Title I, February 22, 1977a.

National Advisory Council on Extension and Continuing Education. *Proceedings of the Invitational Conference on Continuing Education: Manpower Policy and Lifelong Learning.* Washington, D.C.: National Advisory Council on Extension and Continuing Education, 1977b.

National Association for Public Continuing and Adult Education. *Public Continuing and Adult Education 1976 Almanac.* Washington, D.C.: National Association for Public Continuing and Adult Education, 1976.

National Center for Education Statistics. *Participation in Adult Education, Final Report, 1969.* Washington, D.C.: National Center for Education Statistics and U.S. Department of Health, Education, and Welfare, 1974.

National Center for Education Statistics. *Participation in Adult Education, Final Report, 1972.* Washington, D.C.: National Center for Education Statistics and U.S. Department of Health, Education, and Welfare, 1976.

National Center for Education Statistics. *The Condition of Education: 1977 Edition.* Washington, D.C.: U.S. Department of Health, Education, and Welfare, 1977.

National Center for Education Statistics. *Participation in Adult Education, Final Report, 1975.* Washington, D.C.: National Center for Education Statistics and U.S. Department of Health, Education, and Welfare, 1978.

National Center for Educational Brokering. *Bulletin, 1:* a. January 1976; b. Summer 1976; c. September 1976.

National Center for Educational Brokering. *Bulletin, 2:* a. Spring 1977; b. Summer 1977; c. September 1977.

National Center for Educational Brokering. *Directory: Educational and Career Information Services for Adults.* Washington, D.C.: National Center for Educational Brokering, January 1978.

National Commission on the Financing of Postsecondary Education. *Financing Postsecondary Education in the United States.* Washington, D.C.: U.S. Government Printing Office, 1973.

National Manpower Institute. *Negotiated Education: Tuition Assistance in Collective Bargaining Agreements.* Washington, D.C.: National Manpower Institute, 1977.

National Occupational Information Service. *Occupational Information Systems Grants Program: State Project Summaries.* Washington, D.C.: U.S. Department of Labor, 1976.

National Recreation and Parks Association. "Local Parks and Recreation." *Parks and Recreation,* August 1971, *6,* 17–31.

National University Extension Association. *Public Policy Proposals.* Washington, D.C.: National University Extension Association, 1977.

National University Extension Association and the American College Testing Program. *Innovations in Continuing Education.* Iowa City, Iowa: ACT Publications, 1977.

National University Extension Association and the American College Testing Program. *Innovations in Continuing Education.* Iowa City, Iowa: ACT Publications, 1978.

Neidhart, A. C. (Ed.). *Continuing Education for Texas: Special Studies of Non-Traditional Approaches to Education.* San Marcos: Southwest Texas State University, 1974.

Nelson, V. I., Nolfi, G. J., and Bush, J. W., Jr. *Adult Career Education as an Intervention Strategy in Mid-Career Changes.* Boston: University Consultants, 1978.

New Jersey Board of Higher Education. *A Development Plan for Higher Education in New Jersey—Phase II of the Master Plan.* Trenton: New Jersey Board of Higher Education, 1974.

New York State Consumer Protection Board. *The Profits of Failure: The Proprietary Vocational School Industry in New York State.* New York: New York State Consumer Protection Board, 1978.

New York State Education Department. *New Opportunities for New Learners.* Albany: New York State Department of Education, 1976.

New York State Education Department (University of the State of New York), Division of Continuing Education. *New York State Continuing Education Needs Assessment* (Report No. 1: Statewide Analysis). Albany: New York State Department of Education, 1974.

New York Times. Editorial, "How Not to Ease the Tuition Squeeze." October 3, 1977.

Newsom, B. Y. "The Museum as Educator and the Education of Teachers." *Teachers College Record,* February 1978, *69,* 485–497.

Newsom, B. Y., and Silver, A. Z. *The Art Museum as Educator.* Berkeley: University of California Press, 1978.

Nickse, R. S. *Development of a Performance Assessment System for the Central New York External High School Diploma Program: An Educational Alternative for Adults.* Syracuse: Regional Learning Service of Central New York, April 1975.

Nolfi, G. J. *Proposal for a National Recurrent Education Entitlement Program: Financing Open Learning and Continuing Education Through Selective Entitlements.* Cambridge, Mass.: University Consultants, 1974.

Nolfi, G. J. *Design for Open Learning: Implementing a Network of Existing Educational Resources.* Cambridge, Mass.: University Consultants, 1975.

Nolfi, G. J. "Implementing Voucher Financing and Community-Based Counseling at the State Level." In *Proceedings of the Third National Conference on Open Learning and Nontraditional Study.* Lincoln, Nebr.: University of Mid-America, 1976a.

Nolfi, G. J. "Social Needs and Social Benefits of Recurrent Education: The Case for State Action and Recommendations for Policy." *Adult Leadership,* 1976b, *25* (1), 2–4 and 26–28.

Nolfi, G. J. "Why States Should Enact an Adult Recurrent Education Entitlement Voucher Program." *Alternative Higher Education,* 1977a, *1,* 151–164.

Nolfi, G. J. *Factors Influencing the Implementation of Recommendations Made in State Level Studies for Planning Lifelong Learning and an Analysis of Recommendations Made.* Cambridge, Mass.: University Consultants, 1977b.

Nolfi, G. J. *Bibliography: State and Local Planning and Evaluation of Expanded Educational Opportunities for Adults Through Continuing*

Education Community Services and Related Activities. Cambridge, Mass.: University Consultants, 1978a.

Nolfi, G. J. "Factors Influencing the Implementation of Recommendations Made in State Level Studies for Planning Lifelong Learning and an Analysis of Recommendations Made." Paper prepared for the HEW Lifelong Learning Project, Washington, D.C., 1978b.

Nolfi, G. J. "The Lifelong Learning Marketplace." Paper prepared for the HEW Lifelong Learning Project, Washington, D.C., 1978c.

Nolfi, G. J., and Jonsen, R. W. "Lifelong Learning—A New Perspective on Education." *Compact,* 1977, *11* (4), 24–28.

Nolfi, G. J., and Nelson, V. I. *Strengthening the Alternative Postsecondary Education System: Continuing and Part-Time Study in Massachusetts.* Cambridge, Mass.: University Consultants, 1973.

Nolfi, G. J., and Nelson, V. I. *Proprietary Institutions at the Post-Secondary Level.* Cambridge, Mass.: University Consultants, 1976.

Northcutt, N. *Adult Functional Competency: A Summary.* Austin: University of Texas, 1975.

NUEA Newsletter, October 27, 1976.

Nurnberger, R. G. *A Profile of Need: A Study of Postsecondary Education Needs in Northeastern New York State.* Albany: College of General Studies, State University of New York, 1974.

Nyquist, E. B., Arbolino, J. N., and Hawes, G. R. *College Learning, Anytime, Anywhere.* New York: Harcourt Brace Jovanovich, 1977.

Office of Library Independent Study and Guidance Projects. *The Role of Public Libraries in Supporting Adult Independent Learning: An Interim Assessment.* New York: The College Board, June 1974b.

Office of Library Independent Study and Guidance Projects. *The Role of Public Libraries in Supporting Adult Independent Learning: An Interim Assessment.* New York: The College Board, June 1974b.

Ohliger, J. "Prospects for a Learning Society." *Adult Leadership,* September 1974, *24,* 37–39.

O'Keefe, M. *The Adult, Education, and Public Policy.* Aspen, Colo.: Aspen Institute for Humanistic Studies, 1977.

O'Keefe, M., and others. *Conference Report: Educational and Occupational Counseling and Information Systems for Adults.* Washington, D.C.: National Center for Educational Brokering, 1976.

Okes, I. E. *Participation in Adult Education, 1969.* Washington, D.C.:

National Center for Education Statistics, 1974.

Okes, I. E. *Participation in Adult Education, 1972.* Washington, D.C.: National Center for Education Statistics, 1976.

Oklahoma State Regents for Higher Education. *Postsecondary Education in the Ardmore Area: A Study of Needs and Priorities.* Oklahoma City: Oklahoma State Regents for Higher Education, February 1974.

Oregon Educational Coordinating Commission. *Oregon Inventory of Postsecondary Educational Programs for Lifelong Learners, 1976–77.* Salem: Oregon Educational Coordinating Commission, 1977a.

Organization for Economic Cooperation and Development. *Developments in Educational Leave of Absences.* Washington, D.C.: OECD Publications Center, 1976.

Organization for Economic Cooperation and Development. *Learning Opportunities for Adults, Volume I: General Report.* Washington, D.C.: OECD Publications Center, 1978.

Owen, H. J., Jr., and Fletcher, S. *Five Community-Based Programs That Work.* Jacksonville: Florida Junior College, 1977.

Parke, K. *The Folk College in America.* Rochester, N.Y.: Cricket Press, 1977.

Parker, G. T., and Hawes, G. R. *College on Your Own.* New York: Bantam Books, 1978.

Parker, J. T. *Adult Competency Education Resources.* Washington, D.C.: Division of Adult Education, U.S. Office of Education, Department of Health, Education, and Welfare, 1977a.

Parker, J. T. *Competency-Based Adult Education Profile.* Washington, D.C.: Division of Adult Education, U.S. Office of Education, Department of Health, Education, and Welfare, 1977b.

Patton, C. B. "Extended Education in an Elite Institution: Are There Sufficient Incentives to Encourage Faculty Participation?" *Journal of Higher Education,* August 1975, *46,* 427–444.

Peat, Marwick, Mitchell, and Co. *A Study of the Supply of Adult Learning Opportunities.* Washington, D.C.: Peat, Marwick, Mitchell, and Co., 1978.

Penland, P. R. *Individual Self-Planned Learning in America.* Washington, D.C.: Office of Libraries and Learning Resources, U.S. Office of Education, Department of Health, Education, and Welfare, 1977.

PER Editors. "The American Management Associations: The Emerging International Business-Grant School." *The PER Special Reports on Continuing Education Institutions and Programs*, August 1977a, *1*.

PER Editors. "Self-Directed Learning." *The PER Special Reports on Continuing Education Institutions and Programs*, October 1977b, *1*.

PER Editors. "The Peaking of Continuing Education?" *The PER Special Reports on Continuing Education Institutions and Programs*, April 1978, *1*.

Peterfreund, S. "Education in Industry—Today and in the Future." *Training and Development Journal*, May 1976, *30*, 30–40.

Peters, J. M., and Gordon, R. S. *Adult Learning Projects: A Study of Adult Learning in Urban and Rural Tennessee*. Knoxville: University of Tennessee, 1974.

Peterson, R. E., and Hefferlin, J. L. *Postsecondary Alternatives to Meet the Educational Needs of California's Adults*. Sacramento: California Legislature, 1975.

Peterson, R. E., Roelfs, P. J., and others. *Community Needs for Postsecondary Alternatives*. Sacramento: California Legislature, 1975.

Phillips, L. E. *The Status of Mandatory Continuing Education for the Professions*. Washington, D.C.: National University Extension Association, 1977.

Pifer, A. *Women Working: Toward a New Society*. New York: Carnegie Corporation of New York, 1976.

Pilsworth, M., and Ruddock, R. "Some Criticisms of Survey Research Methods in Adult Education." *Convergence*, 1975, *8* (2), 33–43.

Pitchell, R. J. *Financing Part-Time Students: The New Majority in Postsecondary Education*. Washington, D.C.: American Council on Education, 1974.

Polsby, N. "Policy Analysis and Congress." *Public Policy*, Fall 1969, *18* (1), 61–74.

Postsecondary Education Convening Authority. "Interview with Philip Austin and Virginia Smith: Implementation of Title I, Part B of the Education Amendment of 1976." Washington, D.C.: Institute for Educational Leadership, 1976.

Postsecondary Education Convening Authority. *Nontraditional Education: State Level Issues and Concerns*. Conference held at Harvard University Graduate School of Education, May 16–18,

1976. Washington, D.C.: Institute for Educational Leadership, 1977a.

Postsecondary Education Convening Authority. *Report of the PECA Task Force on Lifelong Learning.* Washington, D.C.: Institute for Educational Leadership, 1977b.

Postsecondary Education Convening Authority. *Annotated Directory: PECA Monthly Dialogue on Lifelong Learning.* Washington, D.C.: Institute for Educational Leadership, 1977c.

Powell, S. A. "State Policy and Lifelong Learning: A Critical Re-Assessment." Paper prepared for the HEW Lifelong Learning Project, Washington, D.C., 1977.

Project Communi-Link. *Terminal Report.* Fort Collins: Colorado State University, June 30, 1973.

Psychology Today. February 1975, *8* (9), 34–36.

Public Law 78-346. "The Servicemen's Readjustment Act of 1944."

Public Law 89-329. "Higher Education Act of 1965."

Public Law 89-750. "The Adult Education Act, 1966 Amendments to the Elementary and Secondary Education Act of 1965."

Public Law 90-576. "The Vocational Education Act of 1963."

Public Law 93-380. "Special Projects Act of 1974."

Public Law 94-482. 94th Congress, October 12, 1976, Title I, Part A—Community Services and Continuing Education.

Public Law 94-482. 94th Congress, October 12, 1976, Title I, Part B—Lifelong Learning.

Public Law 94-482. 94th Congress, October 12, 1976, Title IV, Subpart 5—Educational Information.

Public Law 94-482. 94th Congress, October 12, 1976, Title X, Part A—Statewide Plans.

Public Law 94-482. "1976 Amendments to the Higher Education Act of 1965."

Randall, M. E., Pailthorp, K., and Bigelow, M. L. *Postsecondary Education in the Tri-Cities.* Olympia: Washington Council for Postsecondary Education, 1976.

Recurrent Education Policy Group. *Recurrent Education: An Approach to Work and Education.* Cambridge, Mass.: Recurrent Education Policy Group, 1974.

Richards, R. K. *Continuing Medical Education: Perspectives, Problems, Prognosis.* New Haven, Conn.: Yale University Press, 1978.

Robbins, J. N., and others. *1978–1979 Directory of Resources for the*

Education of Adults. Columbus, Ohio: ERIC Clearinghouse on Adult, Career, and Vocational Education, 1979.

Robinson, K., and Herdendorf, P. S. *Final Report on the Survey of Public Demand/Need for Postsecondary Continuing Education for Adults (Lifelong Learning Programs) in Western New York.* Buffalo: Project Impact, Western New York Postsecondary Continuing Education Study, 1976.

Rochester Institute of Technology. *Urbanarium Prospectus.* Rochester, N.Y.: Rochester Institute of Technology, 1977.

Rockhill, K. *From Diplomas to Alternatives: Education and Learning Among Adults with Less Than Twelve Years of Schooling.* Los Angeles: Department of Education, University of California, 1978.

Rosenthal, E. L. "Lifelong Learning—For Some of the People." *Change,* August 1977, *9* (8), 44–45.

Rosenthal, E. L. "Politics and Lifelong Learning: An Exploration of Citizen Strategies." Paper prepared for the HEW Lifelong Learning Project, Washington, D.C., 1978.

Ross, G. R., Brown, R. D., and Hassel, M. *Clientele Study for the Proposed State University of Nebraska (SUN)—A Multi-Media Off-Campus Collegiate Program.* Lincoln: University of Nebraska, 1972.

Roth, E. B. "APL: A Ferment in Education." *American Education,* May 1976, *12* (4), 6–9.

Roth, E. B. "Education's Gray Boom." *American Education,* July 1978, *14* (14), 6–11.

Rutgers Labor Education Center. *A Selected Bibliography on Paid Education Leave, Tuition-Assistance, and Union-Company Educational Opportunity Programs.* New Brunswick, N.J.: Rutgers Labor Education Center, Rutgers University, 1977.

Ruyle, J., and Geiselman, L. A. "Non-Traditional Opportunities and Programs." In K. P. Cross, J. R. Valley, and Associates, *Planning Non-Traditional Programs: An Analysis of the Issues for Postsecondary Education.* San Francisco: Jossey-Bass, 1974.

Salner, M. B. *Inventory of Existing Postsecondary Alternatives.* Sacramento: California Legislature, 1975.

Sarason, S. B. *Work, Aging, and Social Change: Professionals and the One Life–One Career Imperative.* New York: Free Press, 1977.

Sawhill, J. C. "Lifelong Learning: Scandal of the Next Decade?" *Change,* December–January 1978–1979, *10*, 7 and 80.

Scanlon, J. *How to Plan a College Program for Older People.* New York: Academy for Educational Development, 1978.

Schlossberg, N. K., and Entine, A. D. (Eds.). "Counseling Adults." *The Counseling Psychologist* (special issue), 1976, *6* (1).

Schmieder, A. *Adult Education at Chautauqua: A Report of the Adult and Continuing Education Institute at Education Week.* Washington, D.C.: Division of Adult Education, U.S. Office of Education, Department of Health, Education, and Welfare, 1976.

Schuller, T. "Lifelong Learning: Foreign Experience." Paper prepared for the HEW Lifelong Learning Project, Washington, D.C., 1978.

Seashore, M., and others. *Prisoner Education Project New Gate and Other College Programs.* New York: Praeger, 1976.

Seaton, C. *Report on Formal Instructional Programs by Business, Industry, Government, and Military in California.* Sacramento: California Postsecondary Education Commission, 1977.

Segal, J. S. *Learning Opportunities for Adults: A Literature Review.* Boulder, Colo.: National Center for Higher Education Management Systems, 1977.

Sell, G. R. *A Handbook of Terminology for Classifying and Describing The Learning Activities of Adults.* Boulder, Colo.: National Center for Higher Education Management Systems, 1978 (Draft B).

Semas, P. W. " 'Free' Universities: Many Still Thriving." *The Chronicle of Higher Education,* November 22, 1976, *13* (12), 4.

Shay, R. M., and Engdahl, L. E. *Extended Degree Programs in the West: Report of a Survey.* Boulder, Colo.: Western Interstate Commission for Higher Education, 1976.

Shipman, C. C. *The Right to Read: Annual Report.* Washington, D.C.: U.S. Office of Education, Department of Health, Education, and Welfare, 1976.

Shulman, C. H. *Premises and Programs for a Learning Society.* Washington, D.C.: American Association for Higher Education, 1975.

Shulman, C. H. "Implementing Experimental Learning for Adult Students." *AAHE-ERIC/Higher Education Research Currents.* May 1978.

Smilansky, M. *The Family and Lifelong Learning.* Washington, D.C.: National Institute of Education, 1978.

Smith, G. "Lifelong Learning and Urban Disadvantaged Youth."

Paper prepared for the HEW Lifelong Learning Project, Washington, D.C., 1978.

Smith, R. F. "A Funny Thing Is Happening to the Library on Its Way to the Future." *The Futurist*, April 1978, *12*, 85–91.

Smith, R. M. (Ed.). *Adult Learning: Issues and Innovations*. DeKalb: Program in Career Information, Northern Illinois University, 1976.

Smith, R. M., Aker, G. F., and Kidd, J. R. *Handbook of Adult Education*. New York: Macmillan, 1970.

Smith, R. M., and Haverkamp, K. K. "Toward a Theory of Learning How to Learn." *Adult Education*, Fall 1977, *28*, 3–21.

Snow, W. A. "A Management Perspective on Lifelong Learning." Paper prepared for the HEW Lifelong Learning Project, Washington, D.C., 1978.

Solinger, J. W., and Alin, M. C. "Cultural Resources as Part of the Community Lifelong Learning System." Paper prepared for the HEW Lifelong Learning Project, Washington, D.C., 1978.

Sosdian, C. P. *External Degrees: Program and Student Characteristics*. Washington, D.C.: National Institute of Education, 1978.

Sosdian, C. P., and Sharp, L. M. *Guide to Undergraduate External Degree Programs in the United States—Spring 1977*. Washington, D.C.: National Institute of Education, 1977.

Sosdian, C. P., and Sharp, L. M. *The External Degree as a Credential: Graduates' Experiences in Employment and Further Study*. Washington, D.C.: National Institute of Education, 1978.

Spaulding, S. "Lifelong Education: A Modest Model for Planning and Research." *Comparative Education*, June 1974, *10*, 101–113.

Srinivasan, L. *Perspectives on Nonformal Adult Learning*. New York: World Education, 1977.

Stalford, C. B. (Ed.). *An Evaluative Look at Non-Traditional Education*. Washington, D.C.: National Institute of Education, 1979a.

Stalford, C. B. (Ed.). *Adult Learning Needs and Future Demand for Lifelong Learning*. Washington, D.C.: National Institute of Education, 1979b.

Stanford Research Institute. "Anticipating Educational Issues over the Next Two Decades." Cited in J. C. Honey and T. W. Hartle, "Beyond the Bicentennial—Postsecondary Education in the 1990s." Unpublished paper prepared for the U.S. Assistant Secretary of Education, August 1974 (Xerox).

Steiger, J. M., and Kimball, B. "Financial Aid for Lifelong Learning: The Special Case of Women." *School Review,* May 1978, *86* (3), 395–409.

Stelzer, L., and Banthin, J. *A Study of Postsecondary Education Needs in Northeastern New York State: Secondary Analysis.* Latham, N.Y.: Capital Associates, 1975.

Stern, B. E. *Toward a Federal Policy on Education and Work.* Washington, D.C.: U.S. Department of Health, Education, and Welfare, 1977.

Stern, B. E., and Best, F. "Cyclic Life Patterns." In D. W. Vermilye (Ed.), *Relating Work and Education: Current Issues in Higher Education, 1977.* San Francisco: Jossey-Bass, 1977.

Stewart, D. W. "Interest Group Role in Development and Passage of the Mondale Lifelong Learning Legislation." *Adult Education,* Summer 1978, *28* (4), 264–275.

Striner, H. *Continuing Education as a National Capital Investment.* Kalamazoo, Mich.: W. E. Upjohn Institute for Employment Research, 1972.

Syracuse University, University College. *Newsletter,* February 1974.

Task Force on Education and Employment, National Academy of Education. *Education and Employment: Knowledge for Action.* Washington, D.C.: Acropolis Press, 1979.

Task Force on Educational Credit and Credentials. *Recommendations on Credentialing Educational Accomplishments.* Washington, D.C.: American Council on Education, 1978.

The Third Century. New Rochelle, N.Y.: Change Magazine Press, 1977.

Thomas, L., and Harri-Augstein, S. "Learning to Learn: the Personal Construction and Exchange of Meaning." In M. J. A. Howe (Ed.), *Adult Learning: Psychological Research and Applications.* New York: Wiley, 1977.

Tiedeman, D. W., and others. *Key Resources in Career Education: An Annotated Guide.* Washington, D.C.: National Institute of Education, 1976.

Tough, A. *The Adult's Learning Projects: A Fresh Approach to Theory and Practice in Adult Learning.* Toronto: Ontario Institute for Studies in Education, 1971.

Tough, A. "Self-Planned Learning and Major Personal Change."

In R. M. Smith (Ed.), *Adult Learning: Issues and Innovations*. DeKalb: Program in Career Information, Northern Illinois University, 1976.

Tough, A. "Major Learning Efforts: Recent Research and Future Directions." *Adult Education*, Summer 1978, *28* (4), 250–263.

Trent, J. W., and Medsker, L. L. *The Influence of Different Types of Public Higher Education Institutions on College Attendance from Varying Socioeconomic and Ability Levels*. Berkeley: Center for Research and Development in Higher Education, University of California, 1965.

Treseder, C. *A Survey of Attitudes Toward Higher and Continuing Education in Northeastern California*. San Jose, Calif.: Diridon Research Corporation, 1972.

Trivett, D. A. *Academic Credit for Prior Off-Campus Learning*. ERIC/Higher Education Research Report No. 2. Washington, D.C.: American Association for Higher Education, 1975a.

Trivett, D. A. *Competency Programs in Higher Education*. ERIC/Higher Education Research Report No. 7. Washington, D.C.: American Association for Higher Education, 1975b.

Tsang, H. "Jerry and Jimmy." *Adult Leadership*, September 1976, *25* (1), 24–25.

Turner, J. C. "Labor and Continuing Education." In *Proceedings of the Invitational Conference on Continuing Education, Manpower Policy, and Lifelong Learning*. Washington, D.C.: National Advisory Council on Extension and Continuing Education, 1977.

United Nations Educational, Scientific, and Cultural Organization. *Recommendation on the Development of Adult Education*. Paris: UNESCO, 1976.

U.S. Bureau of the Census. *Statistical Abstract of the United States*. Washington, D.C.: U.S. Department of Commerce, 1976.

U.S. Bureau of the Census. *Geographical Mobility: March 1975 to March 1976*. Washington, D.C.: U.S. Department of Commerce, January 1977.

U.S. Civil Service Commission, Bureau of Training. *Employee Training in the Federal Service, Fiscal Year 1973*. Washington, D.C.: U.S. Government Printing Office, 1974.

U.S. Civil Service Commission. *Training Effort Government-Wide*. Washington, D.C.: U.S. Government Printing Office, 1977.

U.S. Congress. House. Testimony of Dr. Paul Hadley, Academic Vice-President of the University of Southern California, for the National University Extension Association. Subcommittee on Postsecondary Education, Committee on Education and Labor, Washington, D.C., 1976.

U.S. Congress. House. "Educational Expenses Deferral Act of 1977." HR 3268. Washington, D.C., 1977.

U.S. Congress. Senate. "The Lifetime Learning Act of 1975." S. 2497. 94th Congress, 1st Session. Washington, D.C., October 1975a.

U.S. Congress. Senate. Committee on Labor and Public Welfare. *Lifetime Learning Act of 1975*. Hearings Before a Subcommittee of the Committee on Labor and Public Welfare. S. 2457. 94th Congress, 2nd Session. Washington, D.C.: U.S. Government Printing Office, 1975b.

U.S. Congress. Senate. *1976 Amendments to the Higher Education Act of 1965*. Senate Report 94-882. 94th Congress, 2nd Session. Washington, D.C.: U.S. Government Printing Office, 1976a.

U.S. Congress. Senate. *Congressional Record,* No. 151—Part III, October 1, 1976b.

U.S. Department of Labor. *Employment and Training Report of the President*. Washington, D.C.: U.S. Department of Labor, 1977.

U.S. House of Representatives. Committee on Education and Labor. Subcommittee on Postsecondary Education. *Hearings on H.R. 3470 and Related Proposals to Amend the Higher Education Act of 1965, as Amended*. Washington, D.C.: U.S. Government Printing Office, 1976.

U.S. Office of Education. *Annual Evaluation Report on Program Administered by the U.S. Office of Education, FY 1977*. Washington, D.C.: Capitol Publications, 1978.

U.S. Office of Education. *Report of the USOE. Invitational Workshop on Adult Competency Education*. Washington, D.C.: U.S. Office of Education, Department of Health, Education, and Welfare, 1978.

U.S. Office of Human Development, Rehabilitiation Services Administration. *Caseload Statistics: State Vocational Rehabilitation Agencies, 1976*. Washington, D.C.: U.S. Government Printing Office, 1977.

University College. *Directory of Residential and Non-Residential Con-*

tinuing Education Centers in the United States. Syracuse, N.Y.: Syracuse University, 1978.

Urbanarium Coordinating Office. Urbanarium *Prospectus.* Rochester, N.Y.: Rochester Institute of Technology, 1977.

Utah State University. *A Proposal to Build Lifespan Learning Facilities at Utah State University.* Logan: Utah State University, n.d.

Valley, J. R. "Lifelong Learning: What Has Been the Real Response." In *Proceedings of the Second National Conference on Open Learning and Nontraditional Study.* Lincoln, Nebr.: University of Mid-America, 1975.

Valley, J. R. "External Degree Programs." In S. E. Goodman (Ed.), *Handbook on Contemporary Education.* New York: Bowker, 1976.

Valley, J. R. "Nontraditional Study in the 1960s." *The College Board Review,* Winter 1977–1978, *106,* 3–7 and 37.

Vermilye, D. W. (Ed.). *Lifelong Learners—A New Clientele for Higher Education: Current Issues in Higher Education 1974.* San Francisco: Jossey-Bass, 1974.

Vivona, R., Miringoff, M., and Watsky, C. *Adult Post-Secondary Continuing Education in the Mid-Hudson Region: Increased Access to Improve the Quality of Life.* Poughkeepsie, N.Y.: Associated Colleges of the Mid-Hudson Area; and New Paltz, N.Y.: Mid-Hudson Region Continuing Education Project, 1975.

von Moltke, K., and Schneevoigt, N. *Educational Leaves for Employees: European Experience for American Consideration.* San Francisco: Jossey-Bass, 1977.

Wager, W. "Academic Significance of the 'Free School.'" *Educational Record,* Spring 1976, *57,* 125–128.

Waniewicz, I. *Demand for Part-Time Learning in Ontario.* Ontario, Canada: Ontario Educational Communications Authority, 1976.

Wann, M. D., and Woodward, M. V. *Participation in Adult Education.* Washington, D.C.: U.S. Government Printing Office, 1959.

Watkins, B. T. "I'll Start Studying after I Read Peanuts." *The Chronicle of Higher Education,* November 28, 1977, *15* (13), 7.

Weathersby, R. "Life Stages and Learning Interests." In *Current Issues in Higher Education.* Washington, D.C.: American Association for Higher Education, 1978.

Weinstock, R. *The Graying of the Campus.* New York: Educational Facilities Laboratories, 1978.

"What Is the Next Thing I Want to Do with My Life?" *Carnegie Quarterly,* Spring 1977, *25* (2), 3–5.

Wilcox, J., Saltford, R. A., and Veres, H. C. *Continuing Education: Bridging the Information Gap.* Ithaca, N.Y.: Institute for Research and Development in Occupational Education, Cornell University, 1975.

Williams, D. C. "The Spectre of Permanent Schooling." *Teachers College Record,* September 1974, *76,* 47–62.

Willingham W. *Free-Access Higher Education.* New York: College Entrance Examination Board, 1970.

Wilms, W. W. *Public and Proprietary Vocational Training: A Study of Effectiveness.* Lexington, Mass.: Heath, 1975.

Wilson, M. *The Effective Management of Volunteer Programs.* Boulder, Colo.: Volunteer Management Associates, 1976.

Wilson, P. *Public Knowledge, Private Ignorance: Toward a Library and Information Policy.* Westport, Conn.: Greenwood Press, 1978.

Windham, D. M. "On Theory and Policy in Financing Lifelong Learning." *School Review,* May 1978, *86* (3), 535–544.

Windham, D. M., Kurland, N. D., and Levinsohn, F. H. "Financing the Learning Society." *School Review* (special issue), May 1978, *86.*

Wingspread Conference on Lifelong Learning in the Public Interest. *Imperatives for Policy and Action in Lifelong Learning.* Washington, D.C.: Coalition of Adult Education Organizations, 1976.

Winkfield, P. A., Granger, J., and Moore, A. B. *A Partial Listing of Cooperative Adult Education Programs.* Columbus: Center for Vocational Education, Ohio State University, June 1975.

Winnick, P. "Serving the Seniors." *American Education,* July 1978, *14,* 18–20.

Wirtz, W. *The Boundless Resource.* Washington, D.C.: New Republic Book Co., 1975.

Wirtz, W. "Lifelong Learning and Living." Paper prepared for the HEW Lifelong Learning Project, Washington, D.C., 1978.

Witherspoon, J. P. *State of the Art, A Study of Current Practices and Trends in Educational Uses of Public Radio and Television.* Washington, D.C.: Advisory Council of National Organizations, August 1974.

Woods, J. A. "Evaluating Life Experiences: Current Practices at the Collegiate Level." *Alternative Higher Education*, Winter 1977, *2*, 105–118.

Yearbook of Adult and Continuing Education, 1978–1979. Chicago: Marquis Academic Media, 1978.

Young, A. M. *Going Back to School at Thirty-Five and Over*. Special Labor Force Report 204. Washington, D.C.: Bureau of Labor Statistics, U.S. Department of Labor, 1977.

Ziegler, J. "From the Commissioner's Desk." *Higher Education Planning*, July/August 1976, *3* (3), 1–3.

Ziegler, W. L. *The Future of Adult Education and Learning in the United States*. Syracuse, N.Y.: Educational Policy Research Center, Syracuse University, 1977.

Name Index

Subject Index